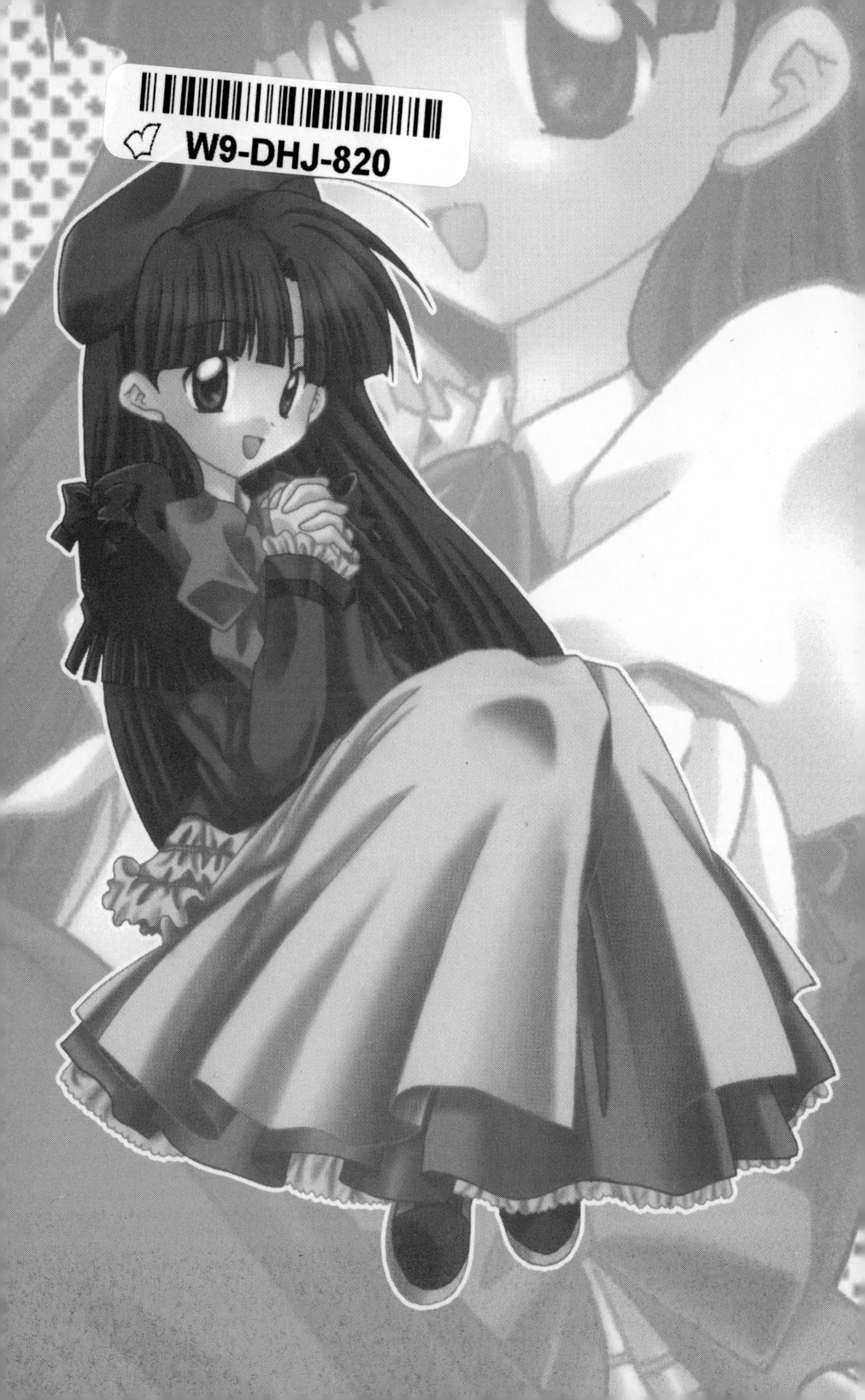

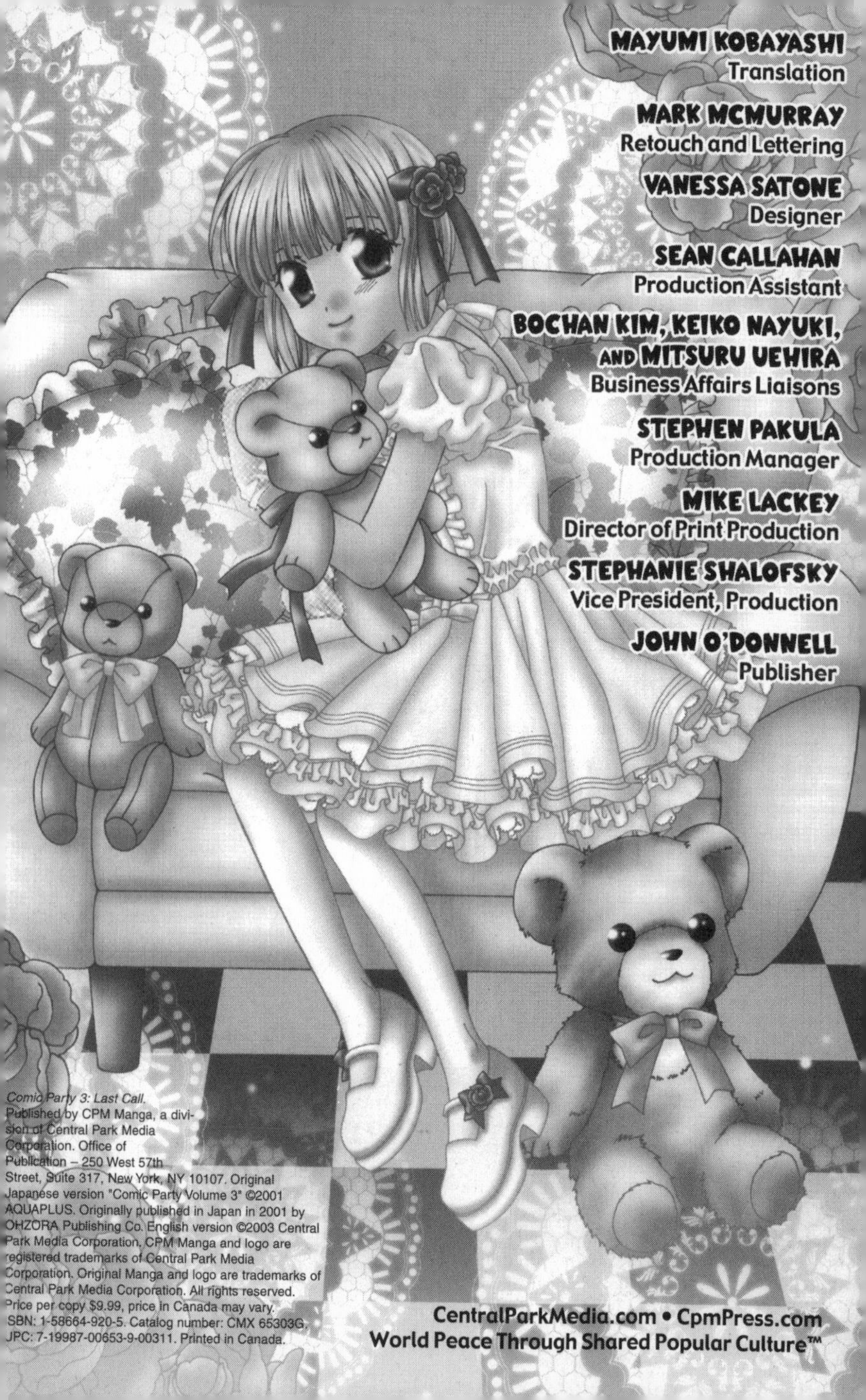

MAYUMI KOBAYASHI
Translation

MARK MCMURRAY
Retouch and Lettering

VANESSA SATONE
Designer

SEAN CALLAHAN
Production Assistant

BOCHAN KIM, KEIKO NAYUKI, AND MITSURU UEHIRA
Business Affairs Liaisons

STEPHEN PAKULA
Production Manager

MIKE LACKEY
Director of Print Production

STEPHANIE SHALOFSKY
Vice President, Production

JOHN O'DONNELL
Publisher

Comic Party 3: Last Call. Published by CPM Manga, a division of Central Park Media Corporation. Office of Publication – 250 West 57th Street, Suite 317, New York, NY 10107. Original Japanese version "Comic Party Volume 3" ©2001 AQUAPLUS. Originally published in Japan in 2001 by OHZORA Publishing Co. English version ©2003 Central Park Media Corporation. CPM Manga and logo are registered trademarks of Central Park Media Corporation. Original Manga and logo are trademarks of Central Park Media Corporation. All rights reserved. Price per copy $9.99, price in Canada may vary. ISBN: 1-58664-920-5. Catalog number: CMX 65303G. UPC: 7-19987-00653-9-00311. Printed in Canada.

CentralParkMedia.com • CpmPress.com
World Peace Through Shared Popular Culture™

COMIC PARTY
LAST CALL

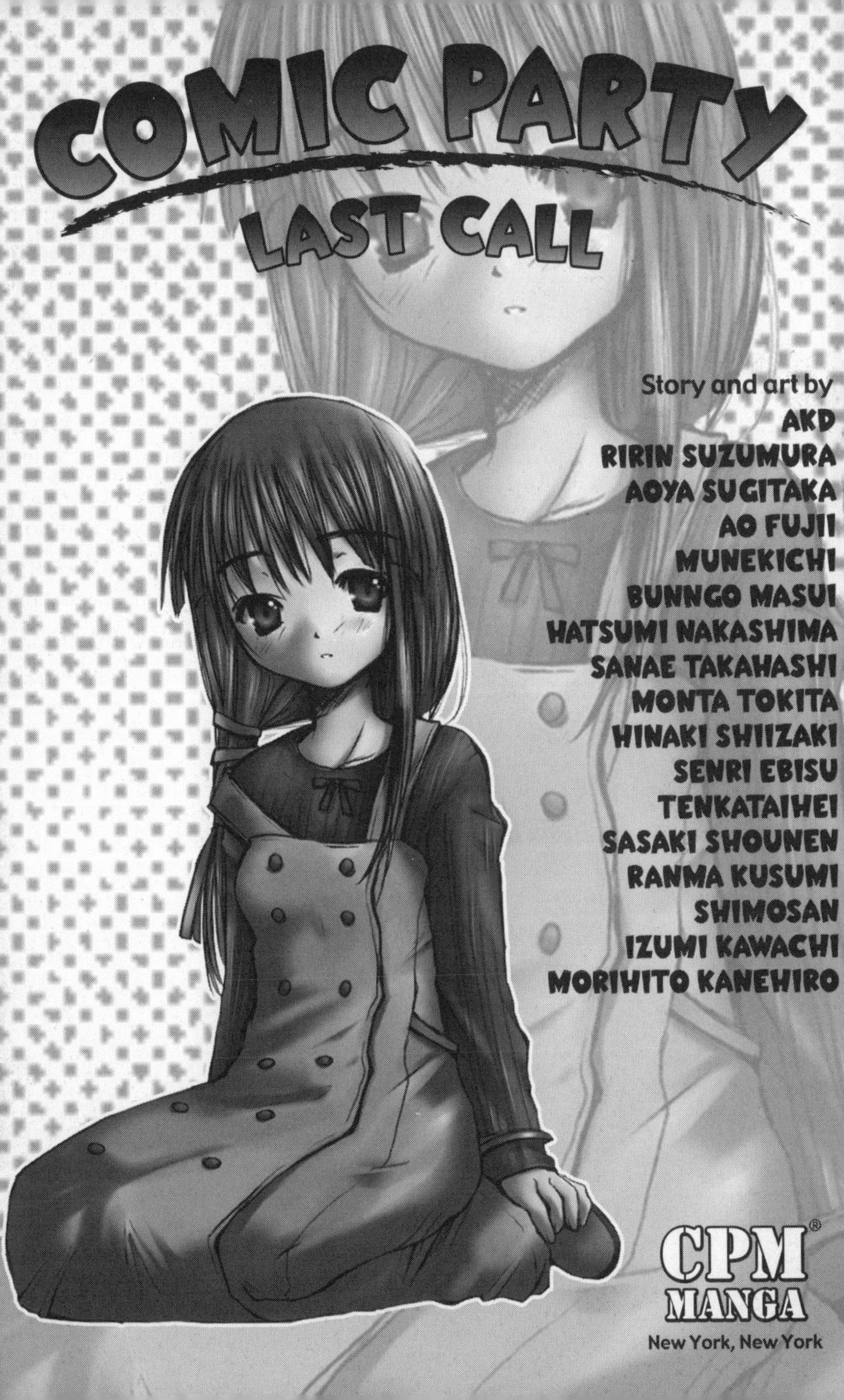

Story and art by
AKD
RIRIN SUZUMURA
AOYA SUGITAKA
AO FUJII
MUNEKICHI
BUNNGO MASUI
HATSUMI NAKASHIMA
SANAE TAKAHASHI
MONTA TOKITA
HINAKI SHIIZAKI
SENRI EBISU
TENKATAIHEI
SASAKI SHOUNEN
RANMA KUSUMI
SHIMOSAN
IZUMI KAWACHI
MORIHITO KANEHIRO

CPM® MANGA
New York, New York

CONTENTS

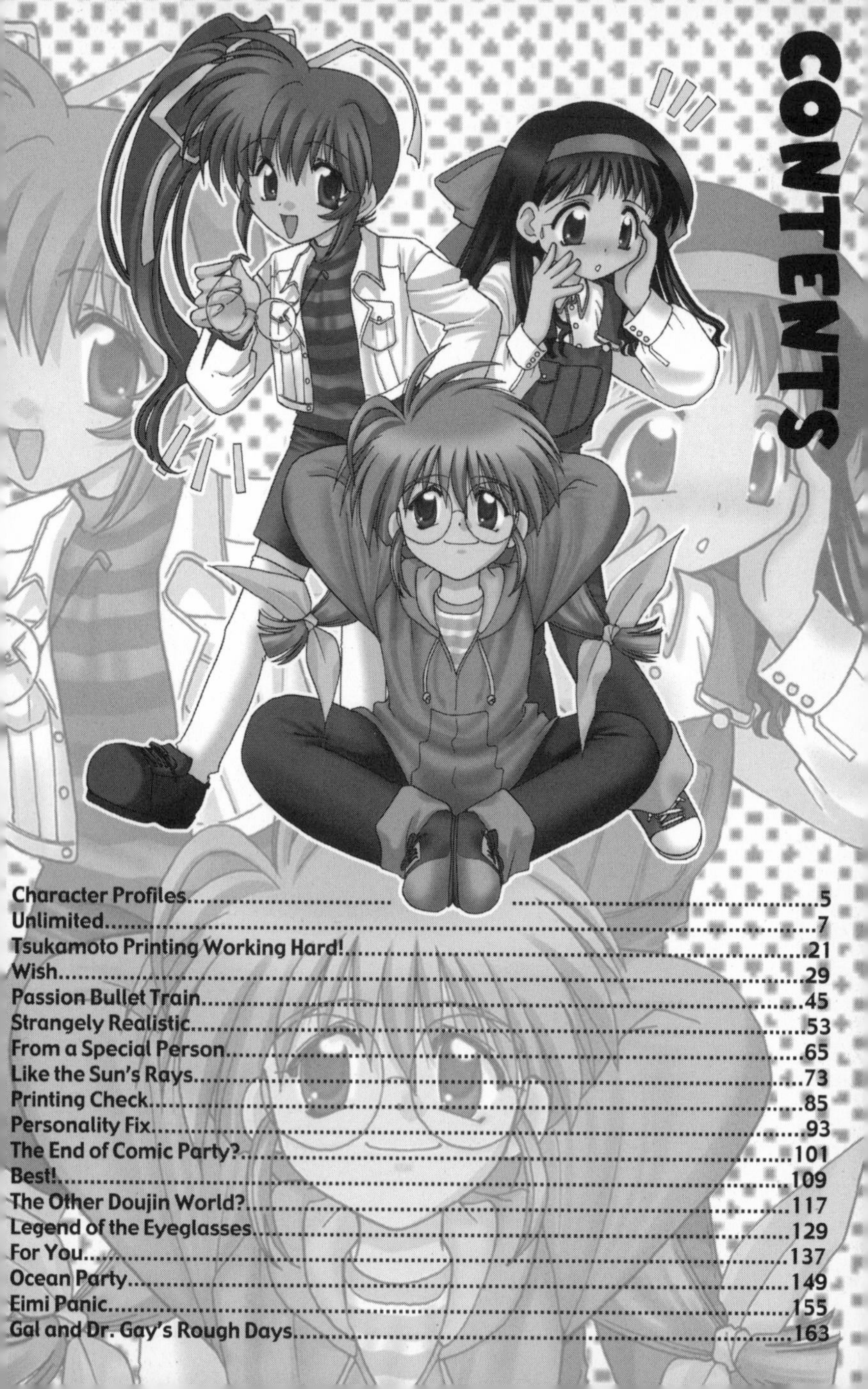

CHARACTER PROFILES

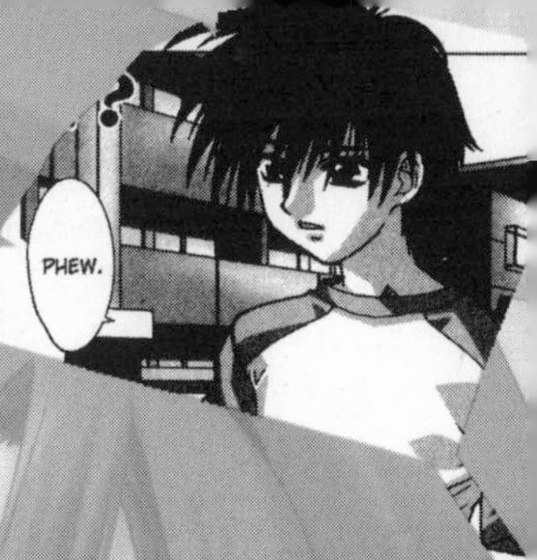
PHEW.

KAZUKI

The "everyman" of Comic Party. Hard working, dedicated, and loyal to his craft. Often unthinking and forgetful about everything else in his life.

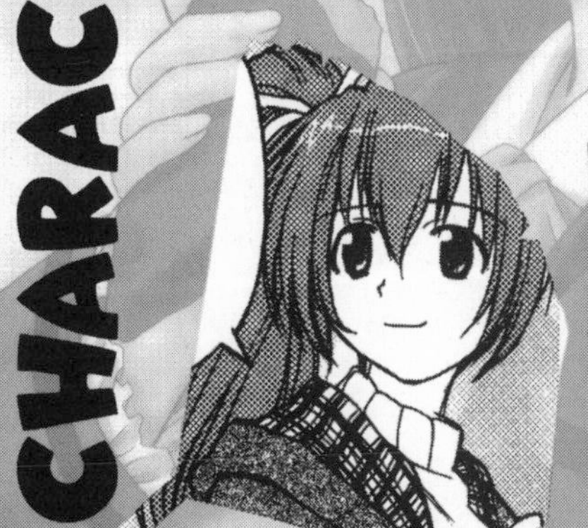

MIZUKI

Kazuki's girlfriend is a sweet, caring person who's willing to overlook Kazuki's shortcomings. Sometimes this can be more difficult than it seems.

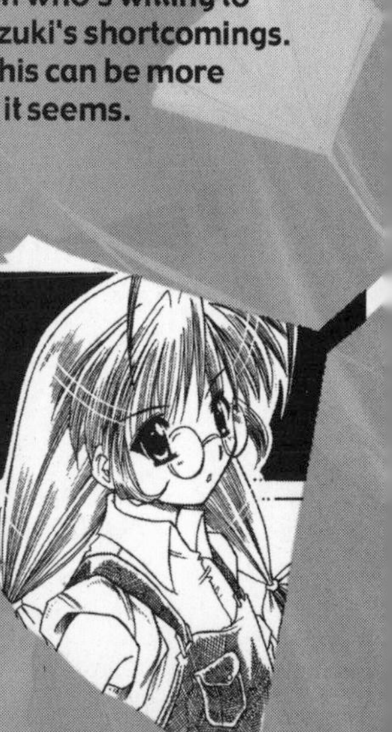

YUU

Frequently manipulates those around her to get what she wants.

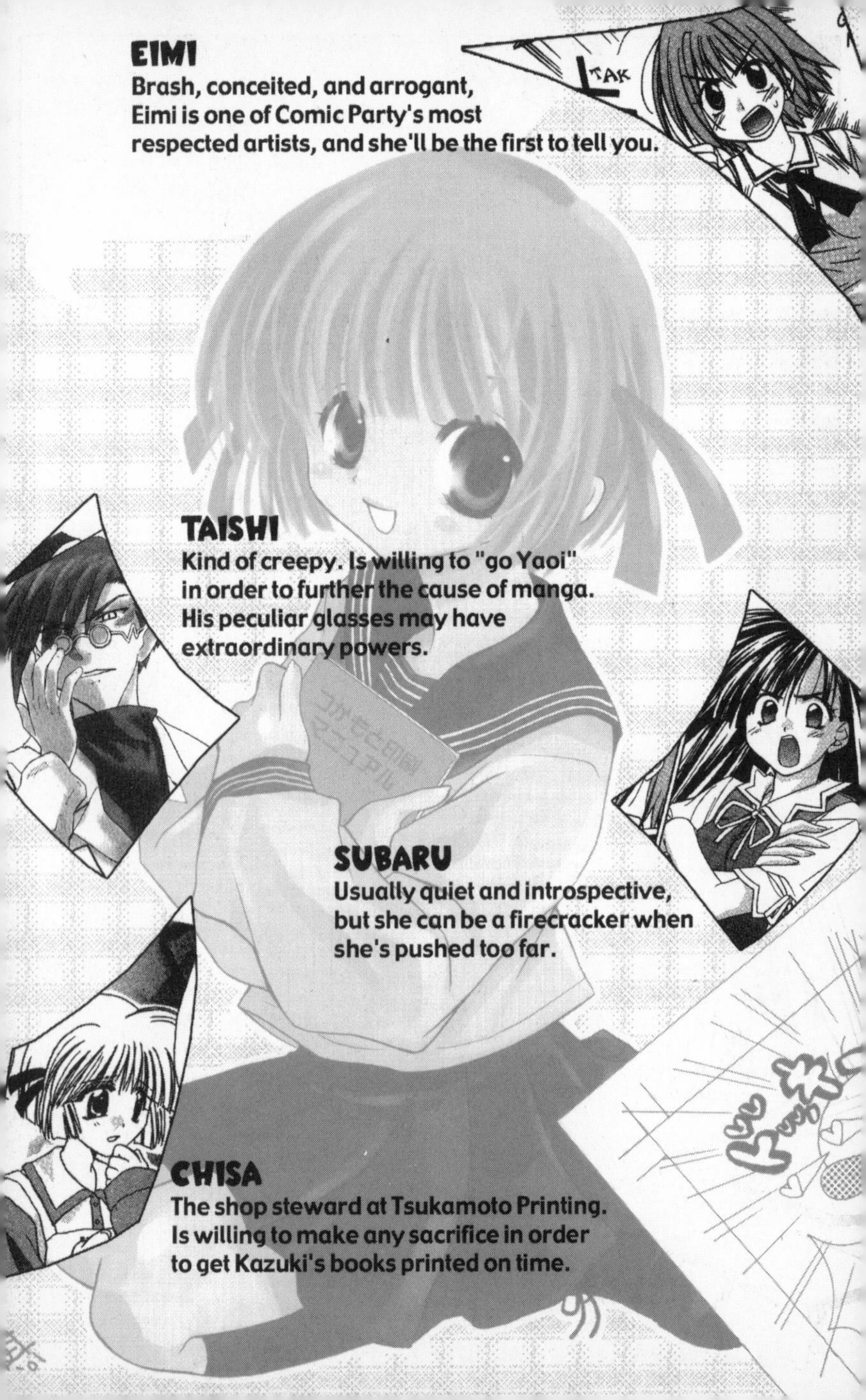
TAK

EIMI

Brash, conceited, and arrogant, Eimi is one of Comic Party's most respected artists, and she'll be the first to tell you.

TAISHI

Kind of creepy. Is willing to "go Yaoi" in order to further the cause of manga. His peculiar glasses may have extraordinary powers.

SUBARU

Usually quiet and introspective, but she can be a firecracker when she's pushed too far.

CHISA

The shop steward at Tsukamoto Printing. Is willing to make any sacrifice in order to get Kazuki's books printed on time.

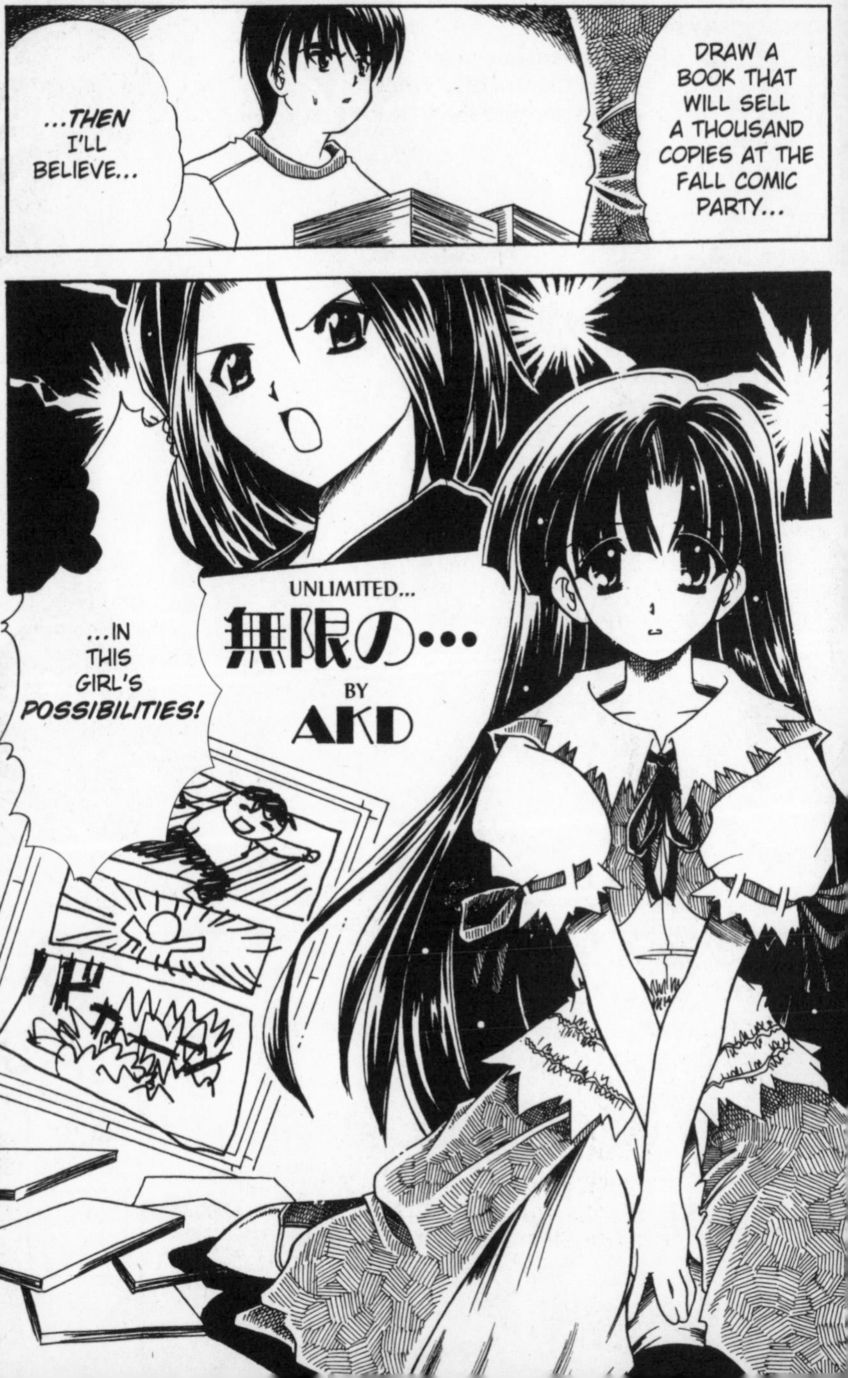
DRAW A BOOK THAT WILL SELL A THOUSAND COPIES AT THE FALL COMIC PARTY...
...THEN I'LL BELIEVE...
UNLIMITED...
無限の・・・
BY
AKD
...IN THIS GIRL'S POSSIBILITIES!

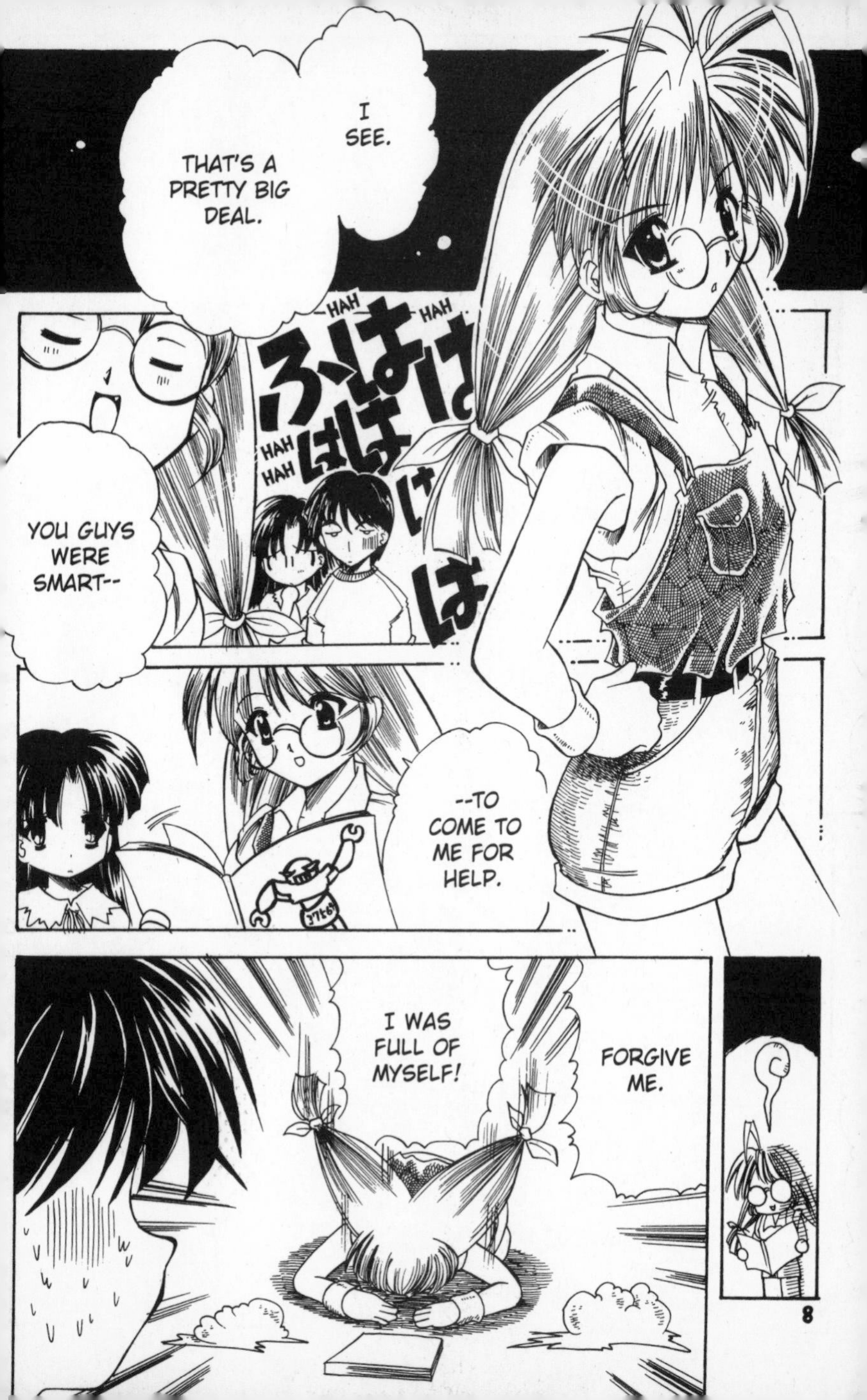
I SEE.
THAT'S A PRETTY BIG DEAL.
HAH HAH
HAH HAH
YOU GUYS WERE SMART--
--TO COME TO ME FOR HELP.
FORGIVE ME.
I WAS FULL OF MYSELF!

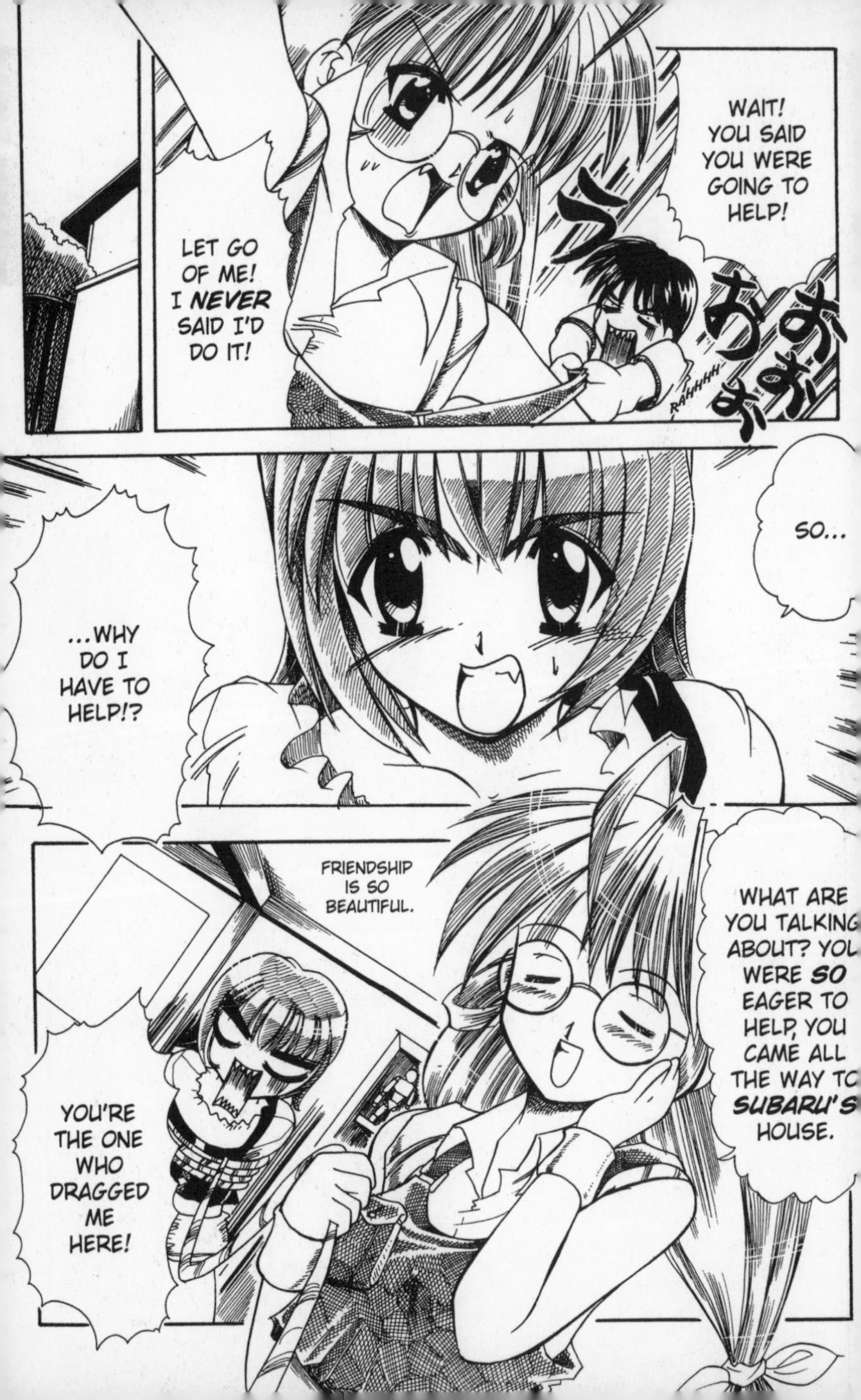
WAIT! YOU SAID YOU WERE GOING TO HELP!
RAHHHHH
LET GO OF ME! I NEVER SAID I'D DO IT!
SO...
...WHY DO I HAVE TO HELP!?
WHAT ARE YOU TALKING ABOUT? YOU WERE SO EAGER TO HELP, YOU CAME ALL THE WAY TO SUBARU'S HOUSE.
FRIENDSHIP IS SO BEAUTIFUL.
YOU'RE THE ONE WHO DRAGGED ME HERE!

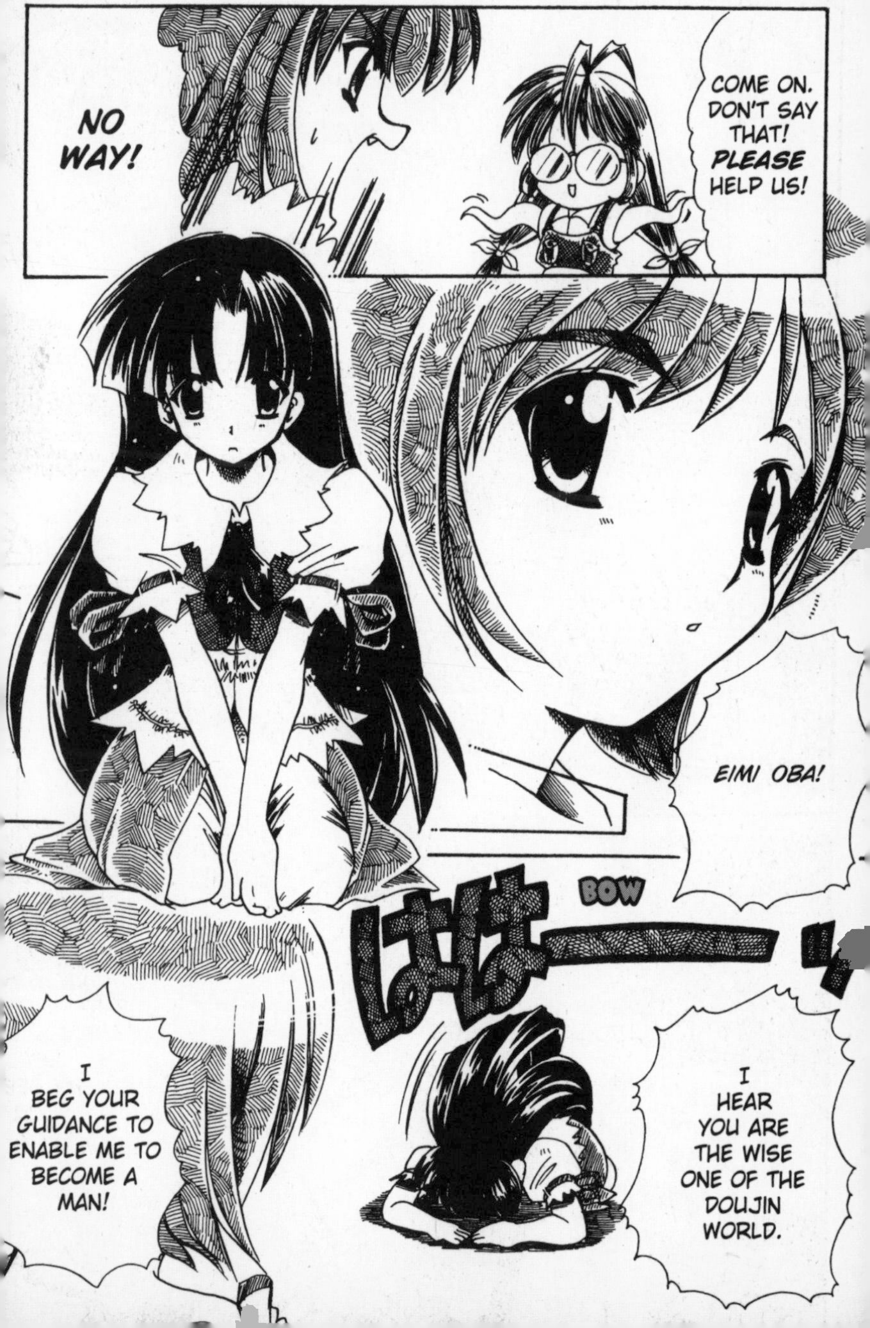
COME ON. DON'T SAY THAT! PLEASE HELP US!
NO WAY!
EIMI OBA!
BOW
ははーっ
I HEAR YOU ARE THE WISE ONE OF THE DOUJIN WORLD.
I BEG YOUR GUIDANCE TO ENABLE ME TO BECOME A MAN!

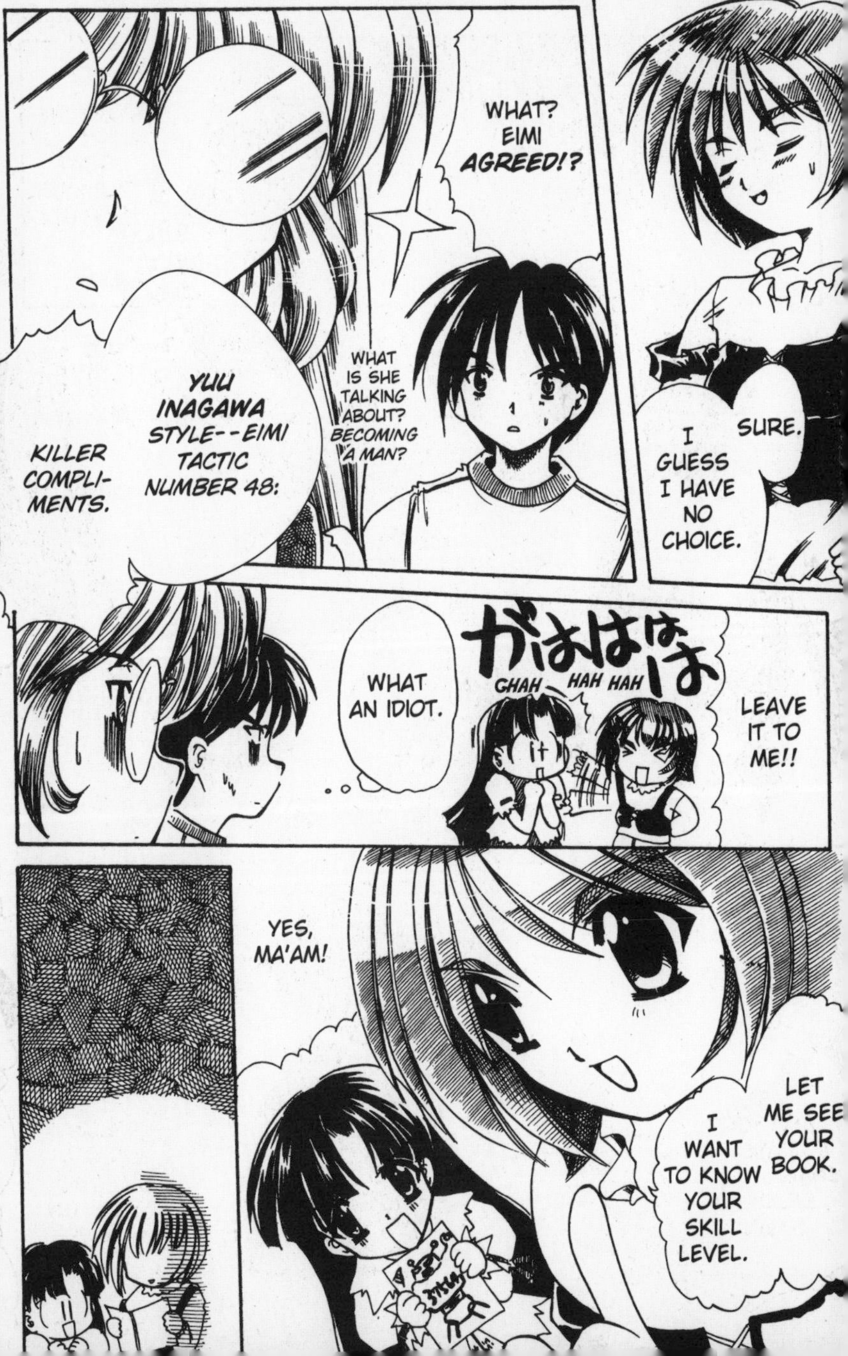
SURE.
I GUESS I HAVE NO CHOICE.
WHAT? EIMI AGREED!?
WHAT IS SHE TALKING ABOUT? BECOMING A MAN?
YUU INAGAWA STYLE--EIMI TACTIC NUMBER 48:
KILLER COMPLI-MENTS.
LEAVE IT TO ME!!
がはははは
GHAH HAH HAH
WHAT AN IDIOT.
LET ME SEE YOUR BOOK.
I WANT TO KNOW YOUR SKILL LEVEL.
YES, MA'AM!

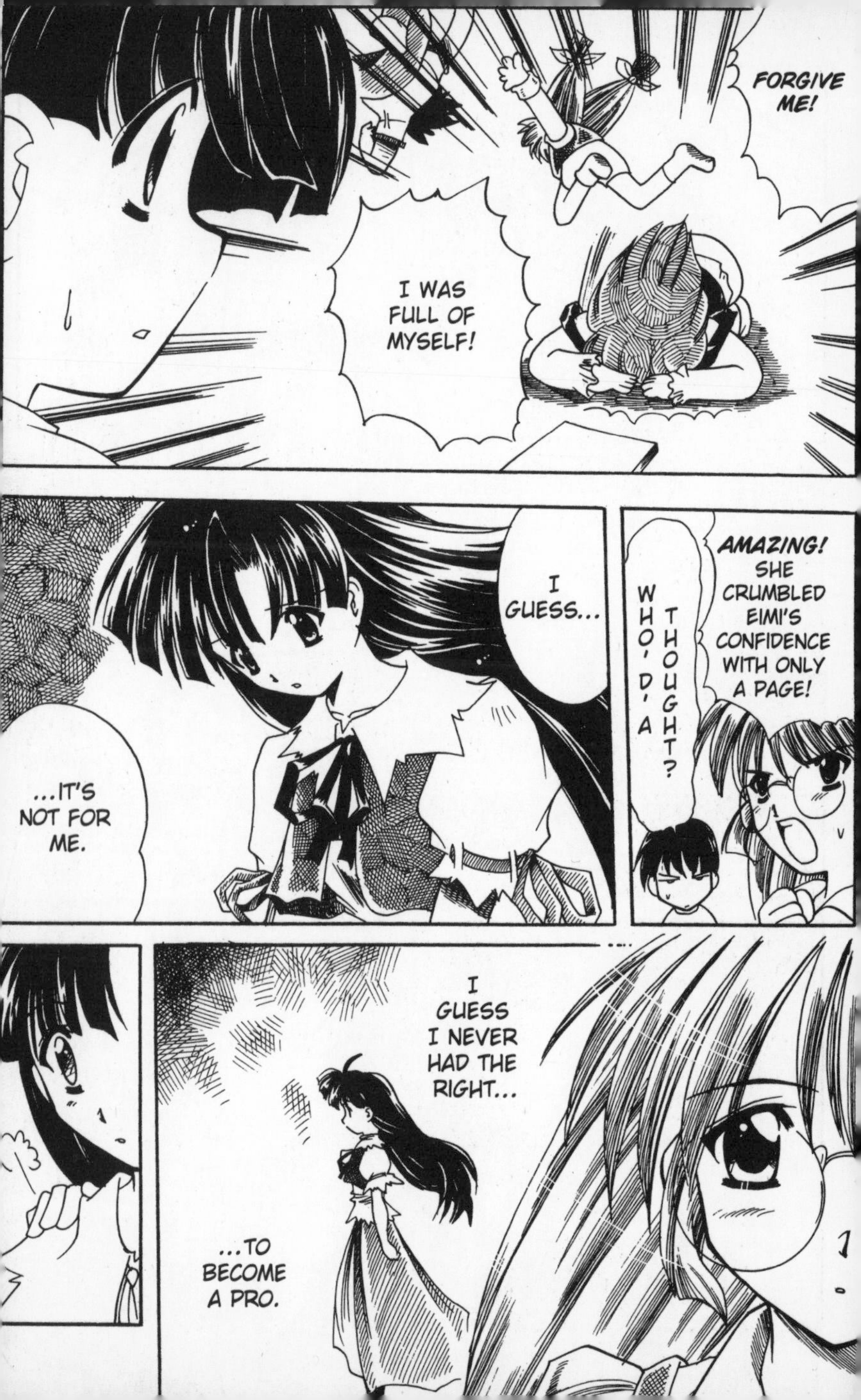
FORGIVE ME!
I WAS FULL OF MYSELF!
AMAZING! SHE CRUMBLED EIMI'S CONFIDENCE WITH ONLY A PAGE!
WHO'D A THOUGHT?
I GUESS...
...IT'S NOT FOR ME.
I GUESS I NEVER HAD THE RIGHT...
...TO BECOME A PRO.

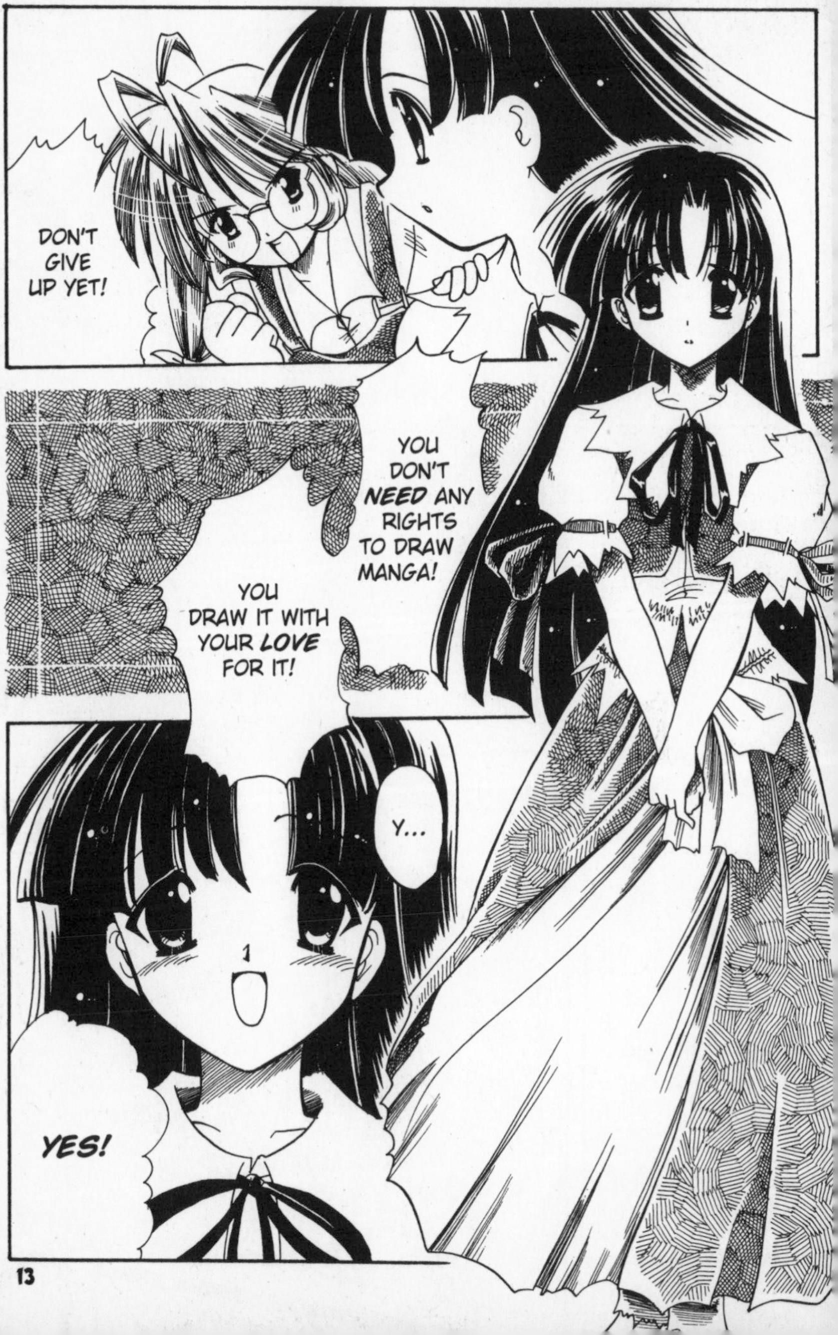
DON'T GIVE UP YET!
YOU DON'T **NEED** ANY RIGHTS TO DRAW MANGA!
YOU DRAW IT WITH YOUR **LOVE** FOR IT!
Y...
YES!

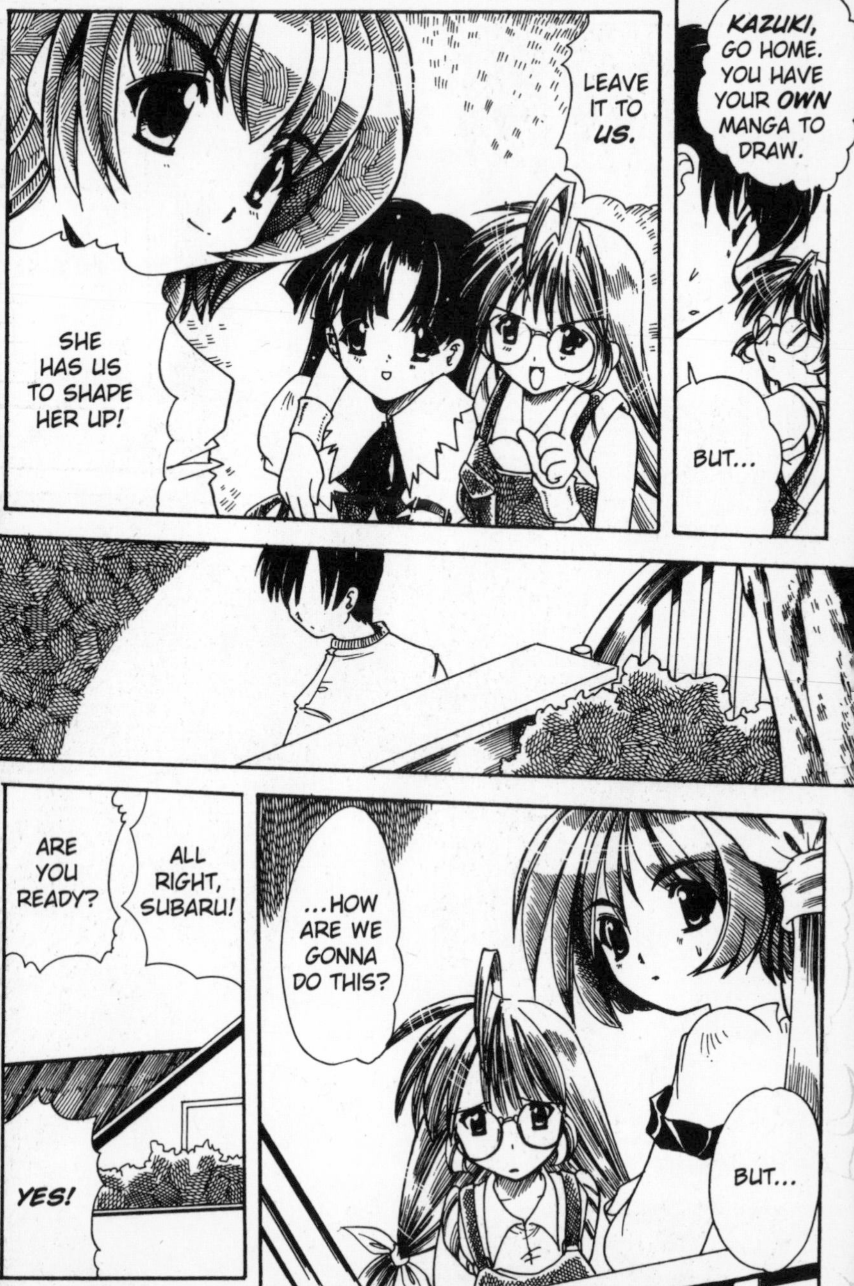
KAZUKI, GO HOME. YOU HAVE YOUR OWN MANGA TO DRAW.
BUT...
LEAVE IT TO US.
SHE HAS US TO SHAPE HER UP!
...HOW ARE WE GONNA DO THIS?
BUT...
ALL RIGHT, SUBARU!
ARE YOU READY?
YES!

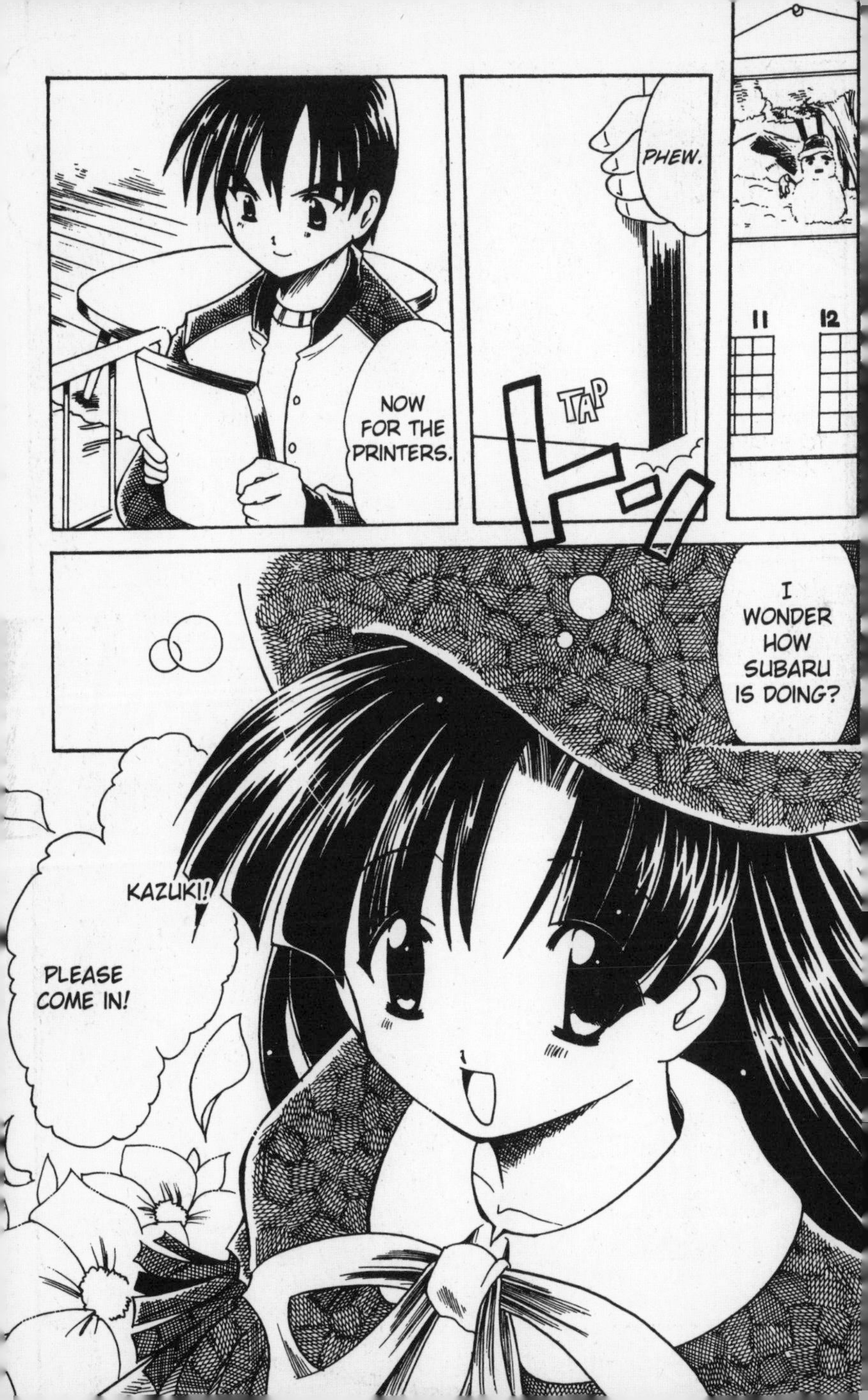
11
12
PHEW.
TAP
NOW FOR THE PRINTERS.
I WONDER HOW SUBARU IS DOING?
KAZUKI!
PLEASE COME IN!

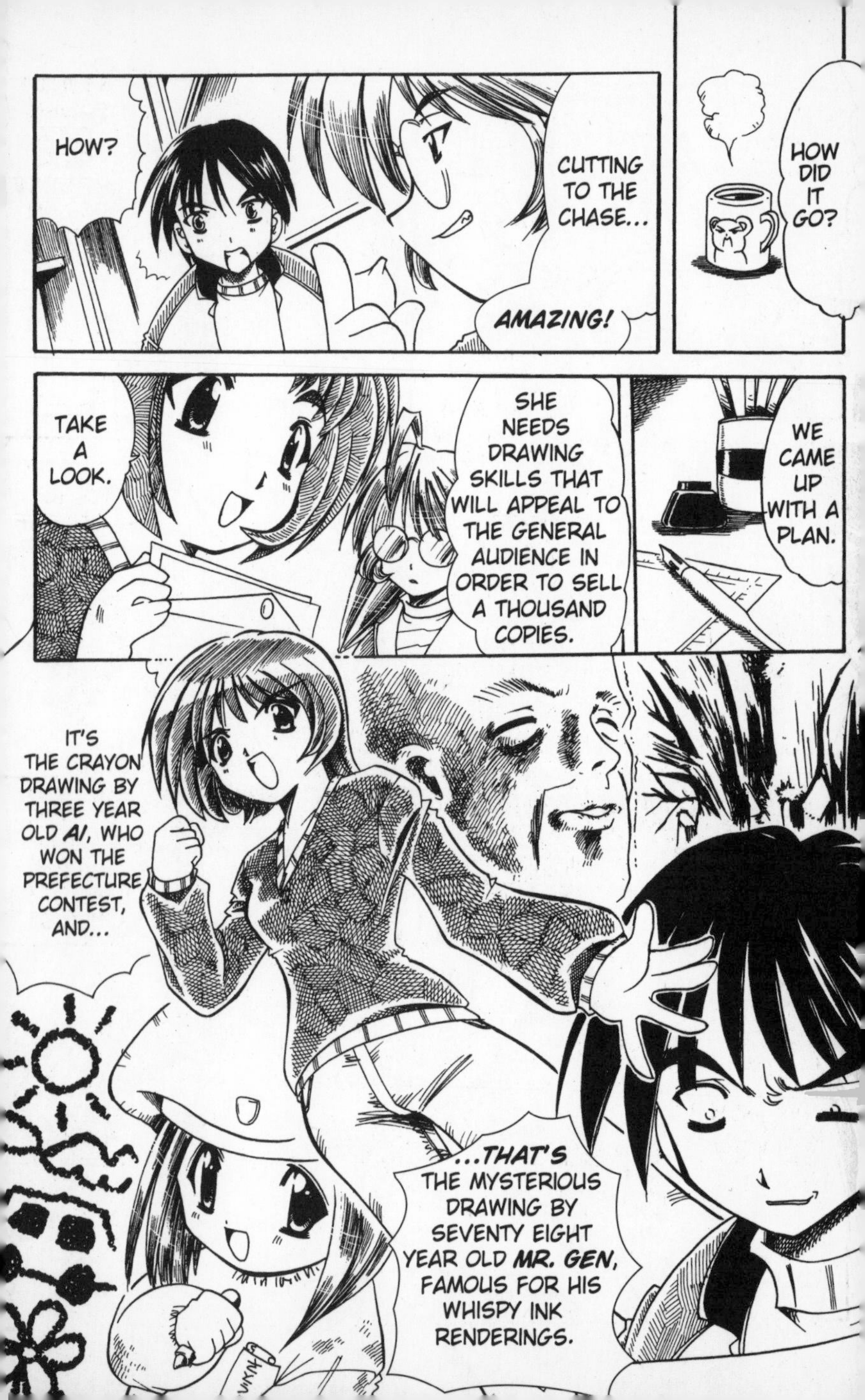
HOW DID IT GO?
CUTTING TO THE CHASE...
AMAZING!
HOW?
WE CAME UP WITH A PLAN.
SHE NEEDS DRAWING SKILLS THAT WILL APPEAL TO THE GENERAL AUDIENCE IN ORDER TO SELL A THOUSAND COPIES.
TAKE A LOOK.
IT'S THE CRAYON DRAWING BY THREE YEAR OLD AI, WHO WON THE PREFECTURE CONTEST, AND...
...THAT'S THE MYSTERIOUS DRAWING BY SEVENTY EIGHT YEAR OLD MR. GEN, FAMOUS FOR HIS WHISPY INK RENDERINGS.

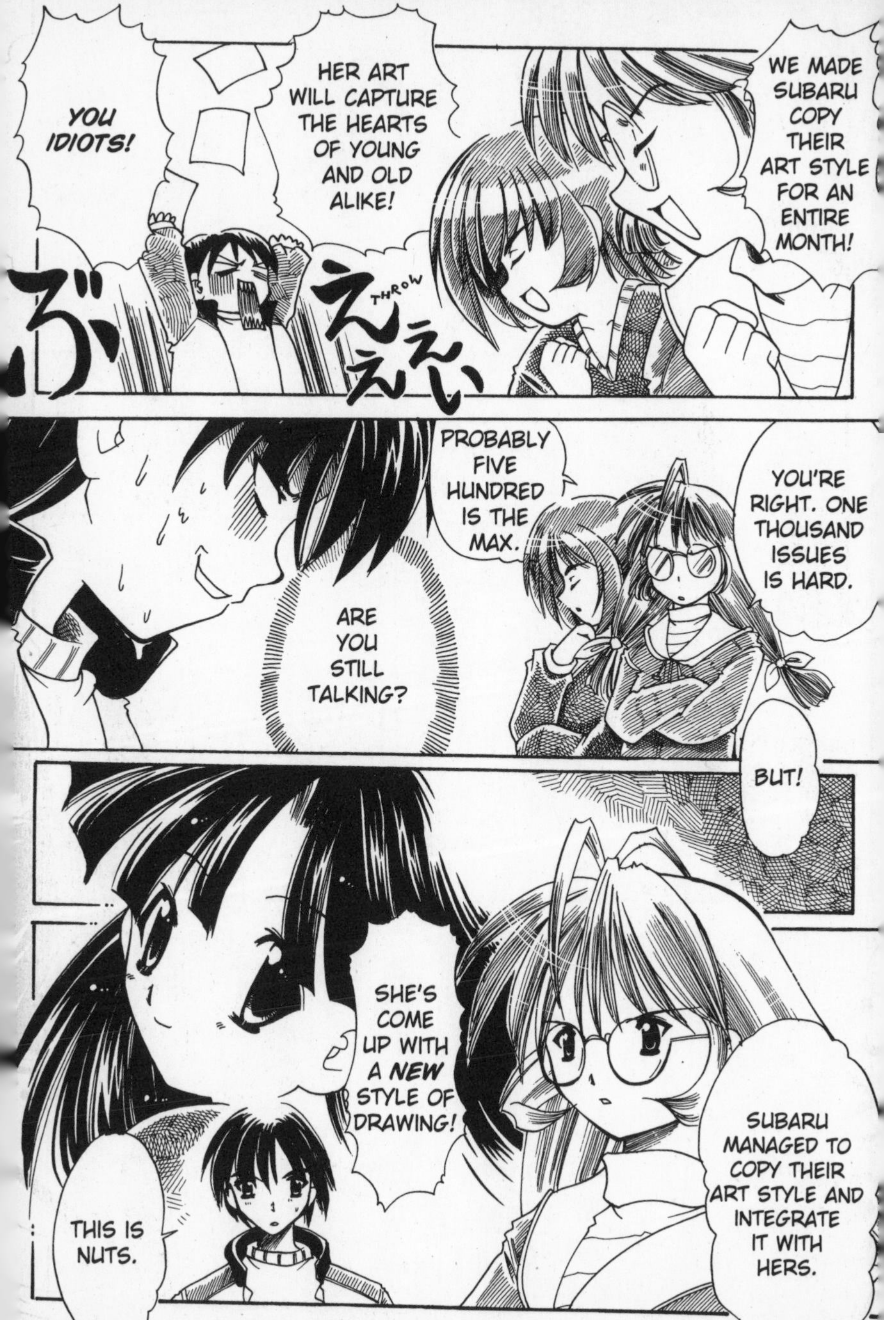
WE MADE SUBARU COPY THEIR ART STYLE FOR AN ENTIRE MONTH!
HER ART WILL CAPTURE THE HEARTS OF YOUNG AND OLD ALIKE!
YOU IDIOTS!
ぶえええい
THROW
YOU'RE RIGHT. ONE THOUSAND ISSUES IS HARD.
PROBABLY FIVE HUNDRED IS THE MAX.
ARE YOU STILL TALKING?
BUT!
SUBARU MANAGED TO COPY THEIR ART STYLE AND INTEGRATE IT WITH HERS.
SHE'S COME UP WITH A *NEW* STYLE OF DRAWING!
THIS IS NUTS.

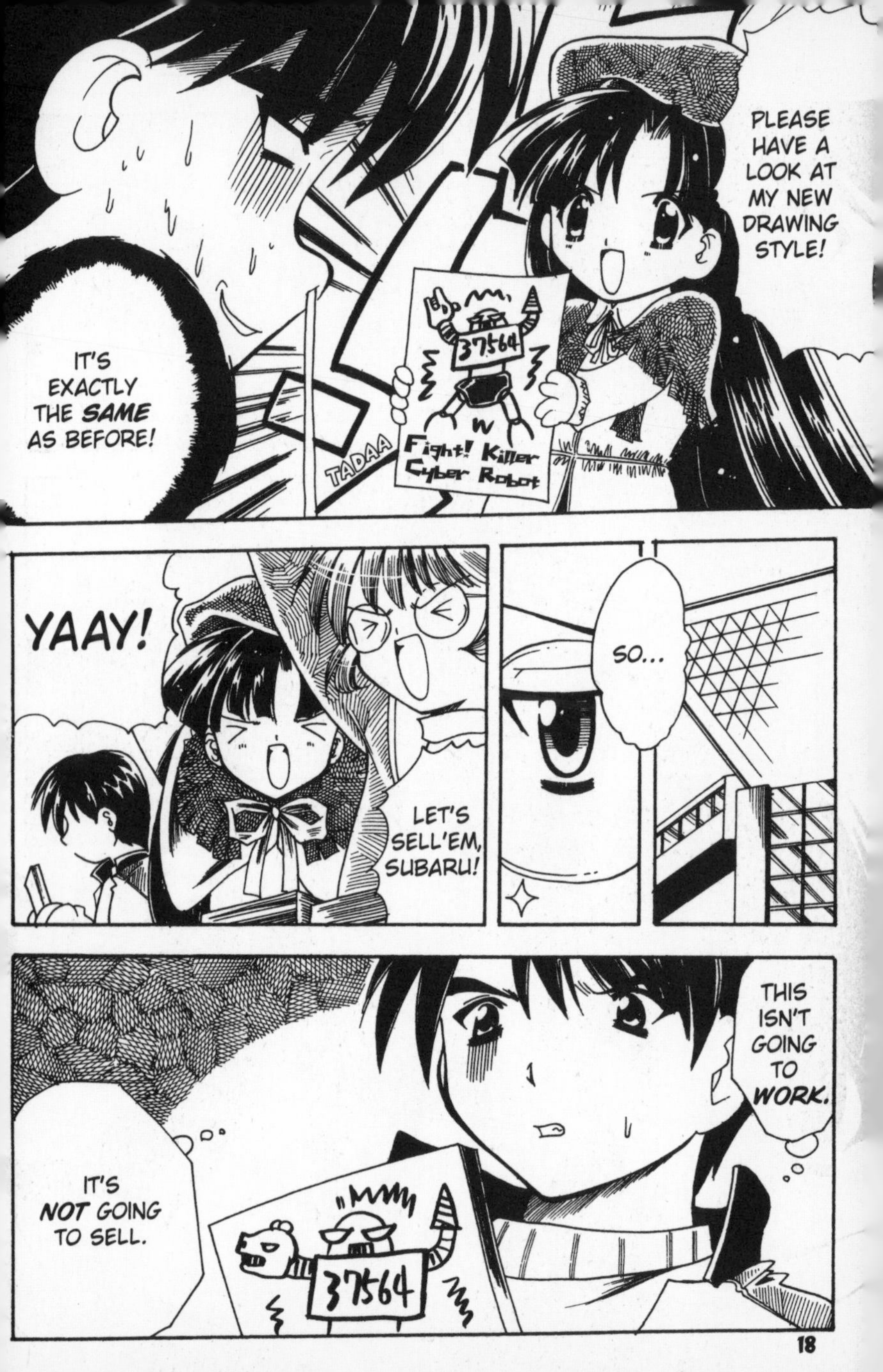
PLEASE HAVE A LOOK AT MY NEW DRAWING STYLE!
37564
Fight! Killer Cyber Robot
TADAA
IT'S EXACTLY THE SAME AS BEFORE!
SO...
LET'S SELL'EM, SUBARU!
YAAY!
THIS ISN'T GOING TO WORK.
IT'S NOT GOING TO SELL.
37564

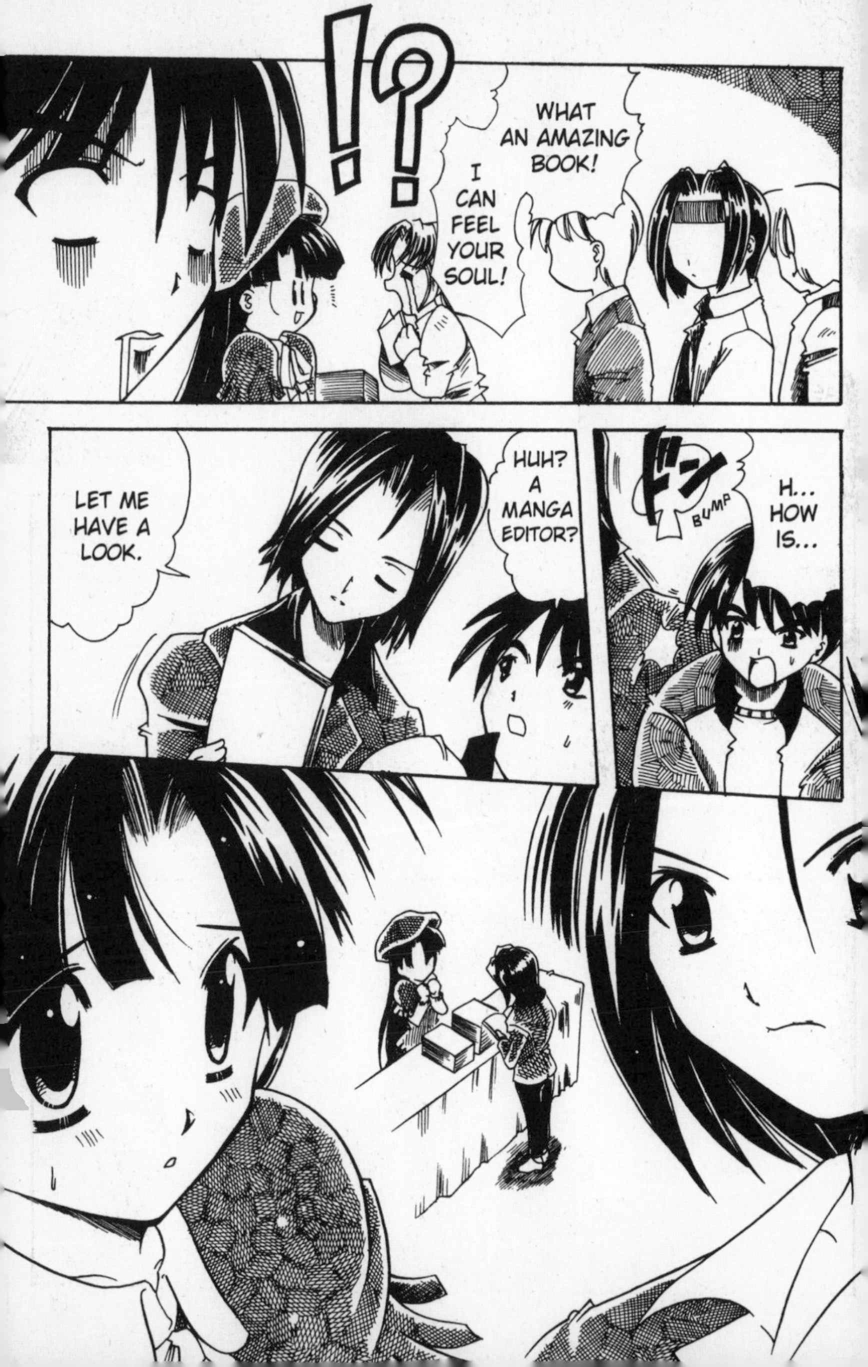
WHAT AN AMAZING BOOK!
I CAN FEEL YOUR SOUL!
!?
ドン
BUMP
H... HOW IS...
HUH? A MANGA EDITOR?
LET ME HAVE A LOOK.

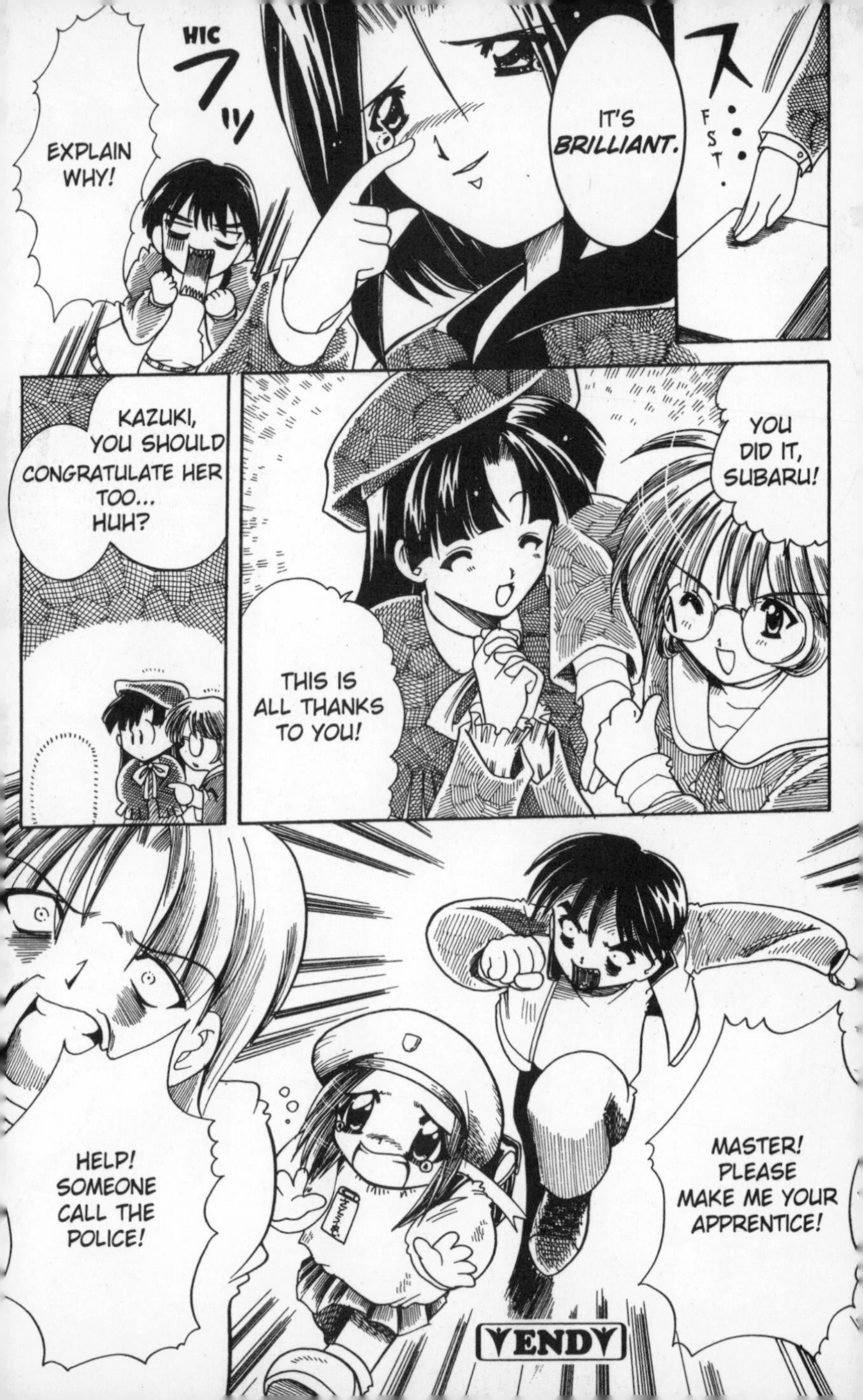
ス
FST
IT'S BRILLIANT.
HIC
フッ
EXPLAIN WHY!
YOU DID IT, SUBARU!
THIS IS ALL THANKS TO YOU!
KAZUKI, YOU SHOULD CONGRATULATE HER TOO... HUH?
MASTER! PLEASE MAKE ME YOUR APPRENTICE!
HELP! SOMEONE CALL THE POLICE!
END

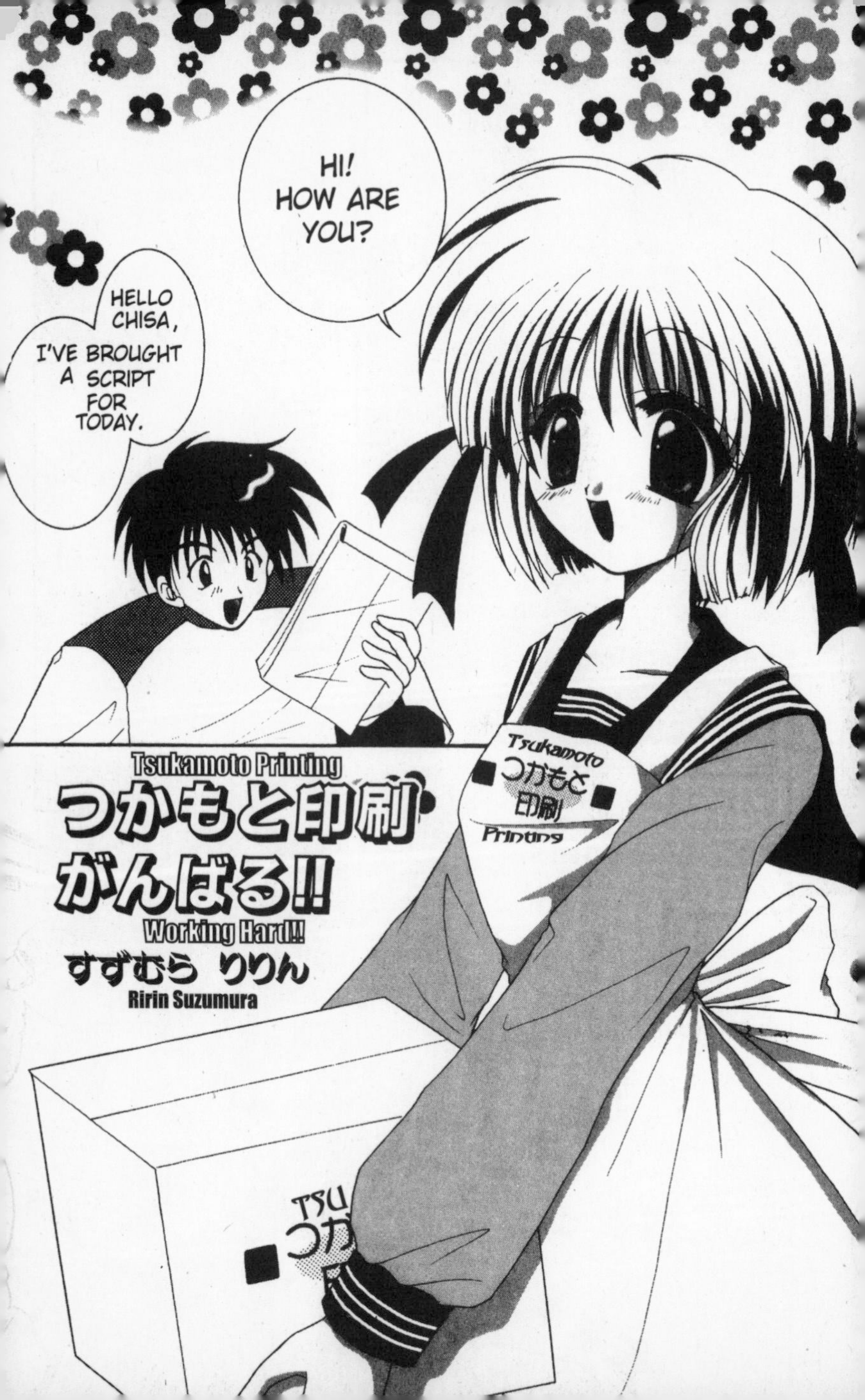
HI! HOW ARE YOU?
HELLO CHISA, I'VE BROUGHT A SCRIPT FOR TODAY.
Tsukamoto Printing
つかもと印刷がんばる!!
Working Hard!!
すずむら りりん
Ririn Suzumura
Tsukamoto つかもと 印刷 Printing

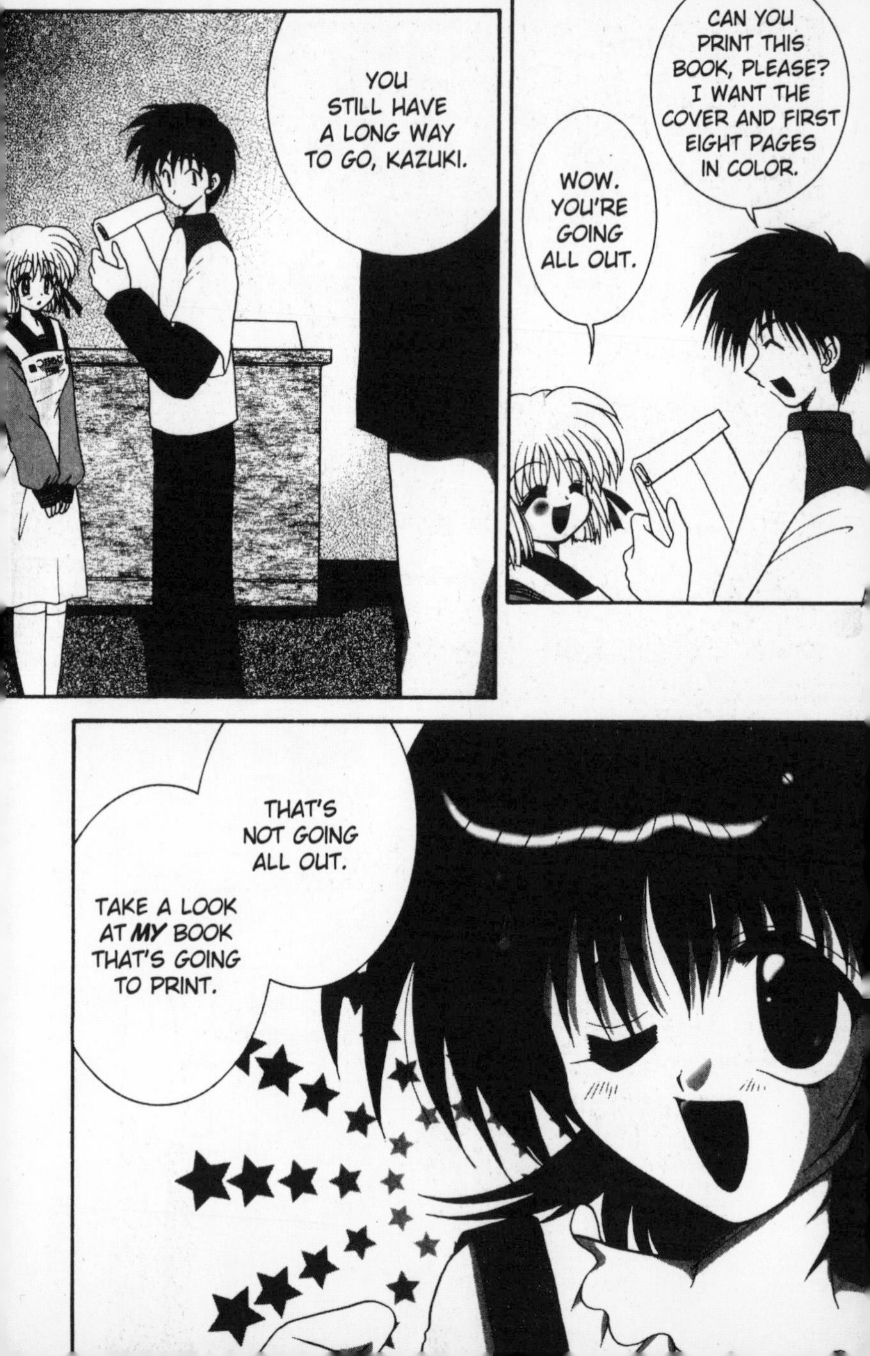
CAN YOU PRINT THIS BOOK, PLEASE? I WANT THE COVER AND FIRST EIGHT PAGES IN COLOR.
WOW. YOU'RE GOING ALL OUT.
YOU STILL HAVE A LONG WAY TO GO, KAZUKI.
THAT'S NOT GOING ALL OUT.
TAKE A LOOK AT *MY* BOOK THAT'S GOING TO PRINT.

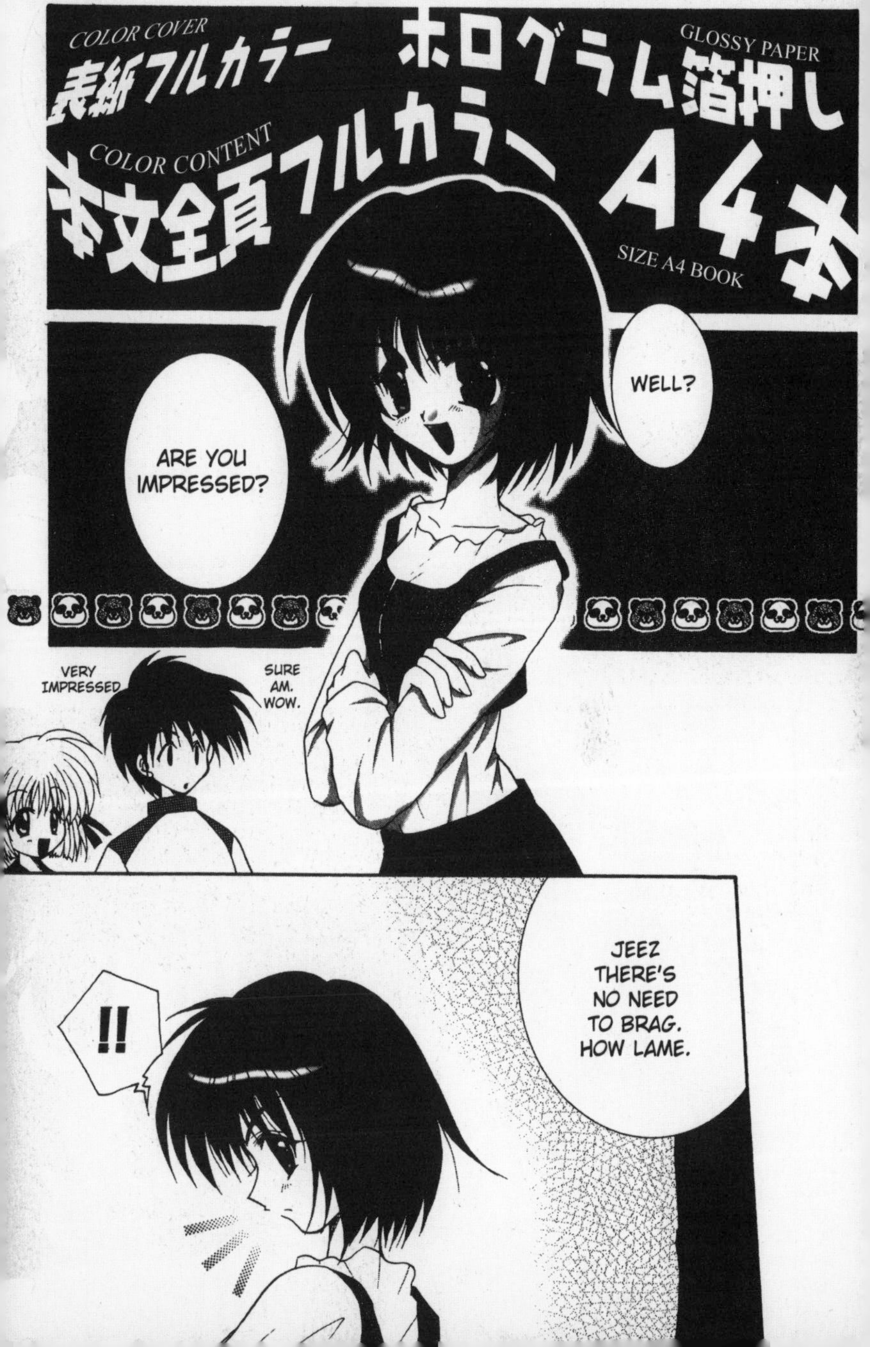
COLOR COVER
表紙フルカラー
GLOSSY PAPER
ホログラム箔押し
COLOR CONTENT
本文全頁フルカラー
A4本
SIZE A4 BOOK
WELL?
ARE YOU IMPRESSED?
SURE AM. WOW.
VERY IMPRESSED
JEEZ THERE'S NO NEED TO BRAG. HOW LAME.
!!

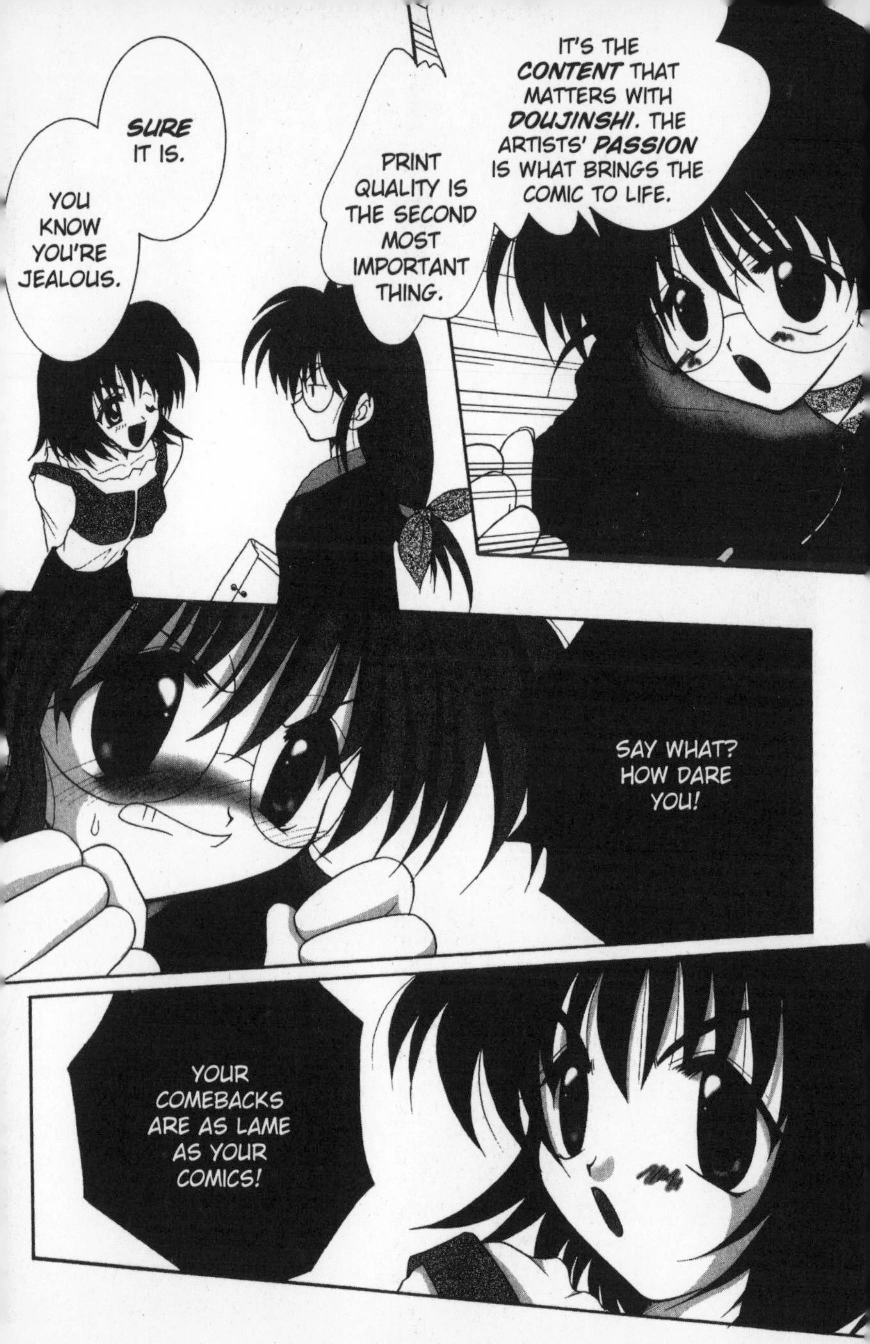
IT'S THE CONTENT THAT MATTERS WITH DOUJINSHI. THE ARTISTS' PASSION IS WHAT BRINGS THE COMIC TO LIFE.
PRINT QUALITY IS THE SECOND MOST IMPORTANT THING.
SURE IT IS.
YOU KNOW YOU'RE JEALOUS.
SAY WHAT? HOW DARE YOU!
YOUR COMEBACKS ARE AS LAME AS YOUR COMICS!

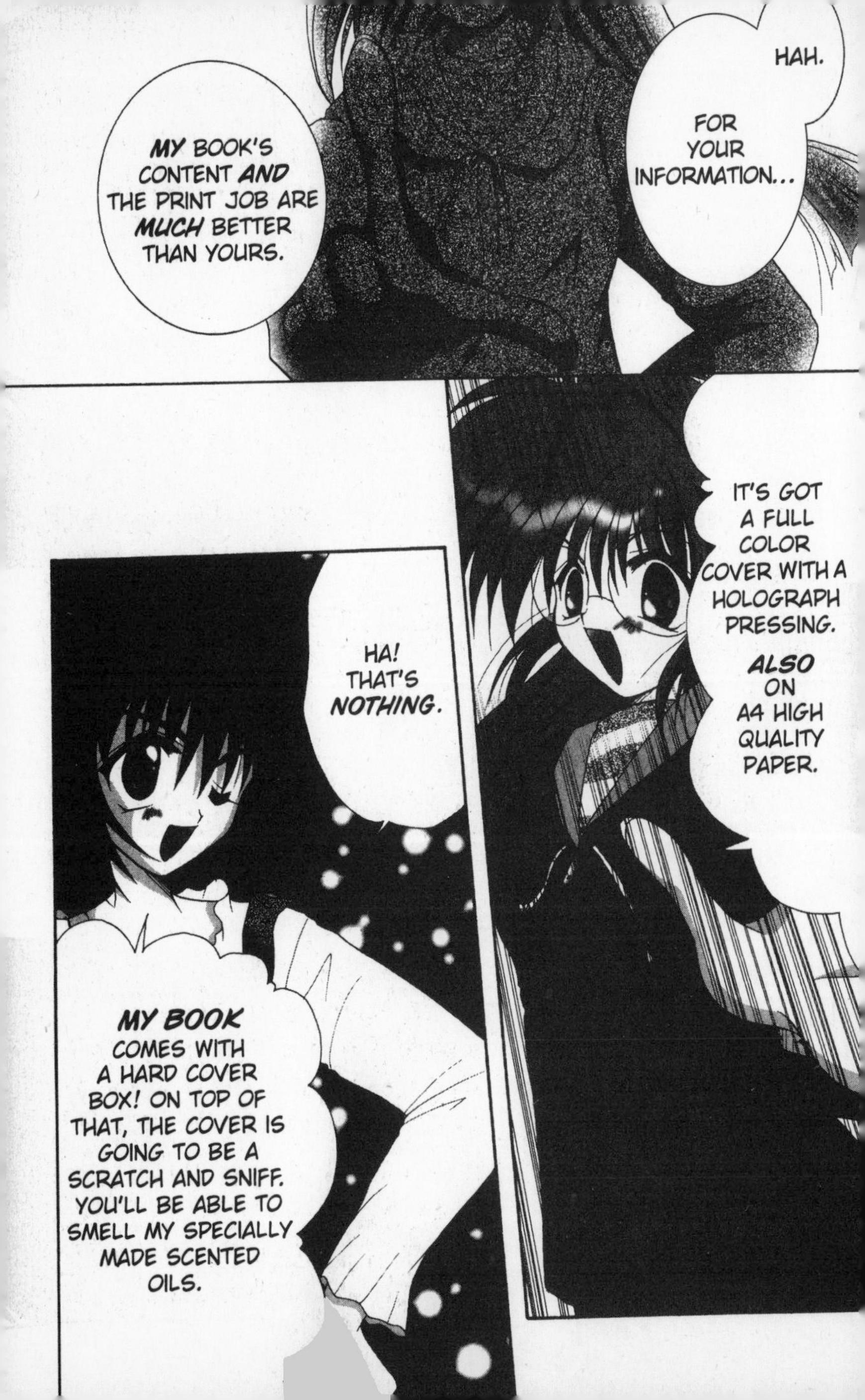
HAH.
FOR YOUR INFORMATION...
MY BOOK'S CONTENT AND THE PRINT JOB ARE MUCH BETTER THAN YOURS.
IT'S GOT A FULL COLOR COVER WITH A HOLOGRAPH PRESSING.
ALSO ON A4 HIGH QUALITY PAPER.
HA! THAT'S NOTHING.
MY BOOK COMES WITH A HARD COVER BOX! ON TOP OF THAT, THE COVER IS GOING TO BE A SCRATCH AND SNIFF. YOU'LL BE ABLE TO SMELL MY SPECIALLY MADE SCENTED OILS.

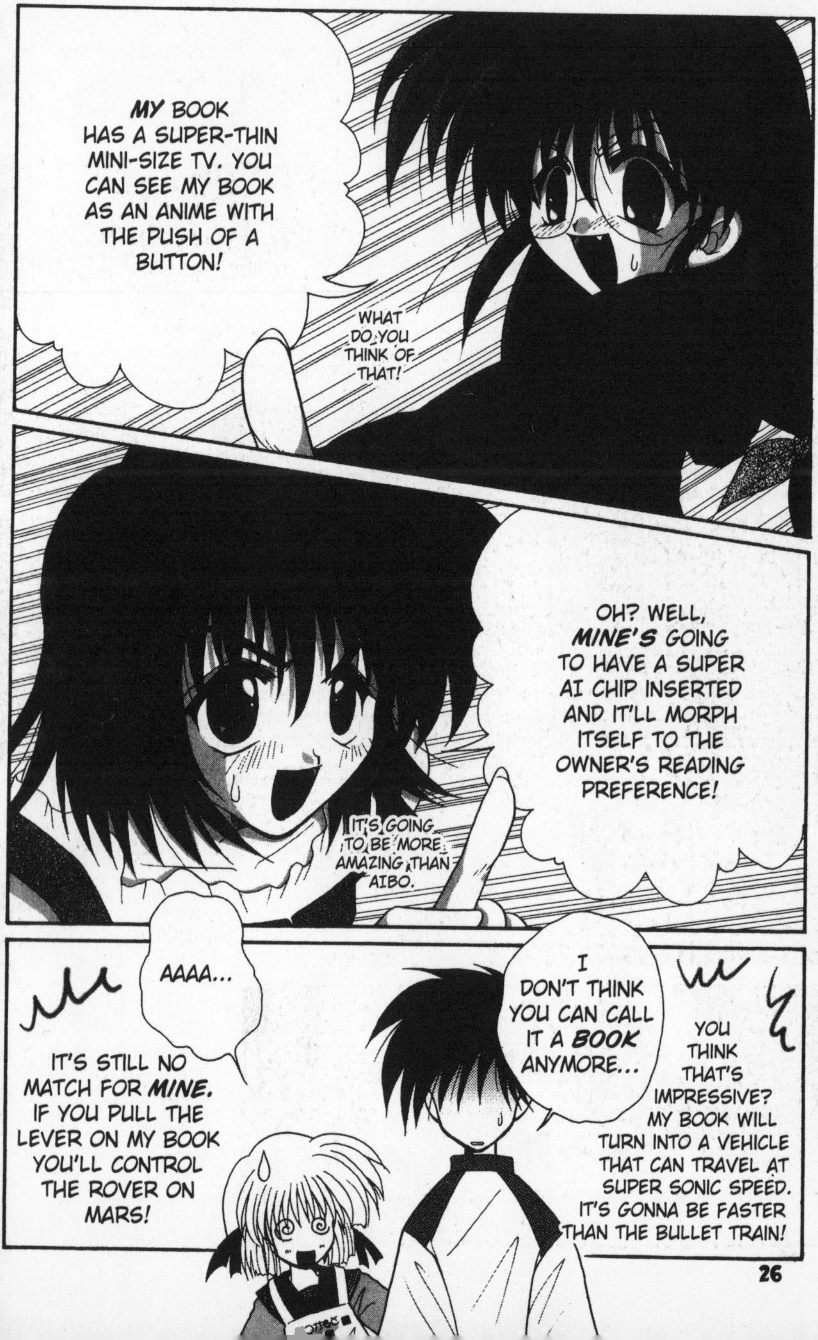
MY BOOK HAS A SUPER-THIN MINI-SIZE TV. YOU CAN SEE MY BOOK AS AN ANIME WITH THE PUSH OF A BUTTON!
WHAT DO YOU THINK OF THAT!
OH? WELL, MINE'S GOING TO HAVE A SUPER AI CHIP INSERTED AND IT'LL MORPH ITSELF TO THE OWNER'S READING PREFERENCE!
IT'S GOING TO BE MORE AMAZING THAN AIBO.
I DON'T THINK YOU CAN CALL IT A BOOK ANYMORE...
YOU THINK THAT'S IMPRESSIVE? MY BOOK WILL TURN INTO A VEHICLE THAT CAN TRAVEL AT SUPER SONIC SPEED. IT'S GONNA BE FASTER THAN THE BULLET TRAIN!
AAAA...
IT'S STILL NO MATCH FOR MINE. IF YOU PULL THE LEVER ON MY BOOK YOU'LL CONTROL THE ROVER ON MARS!

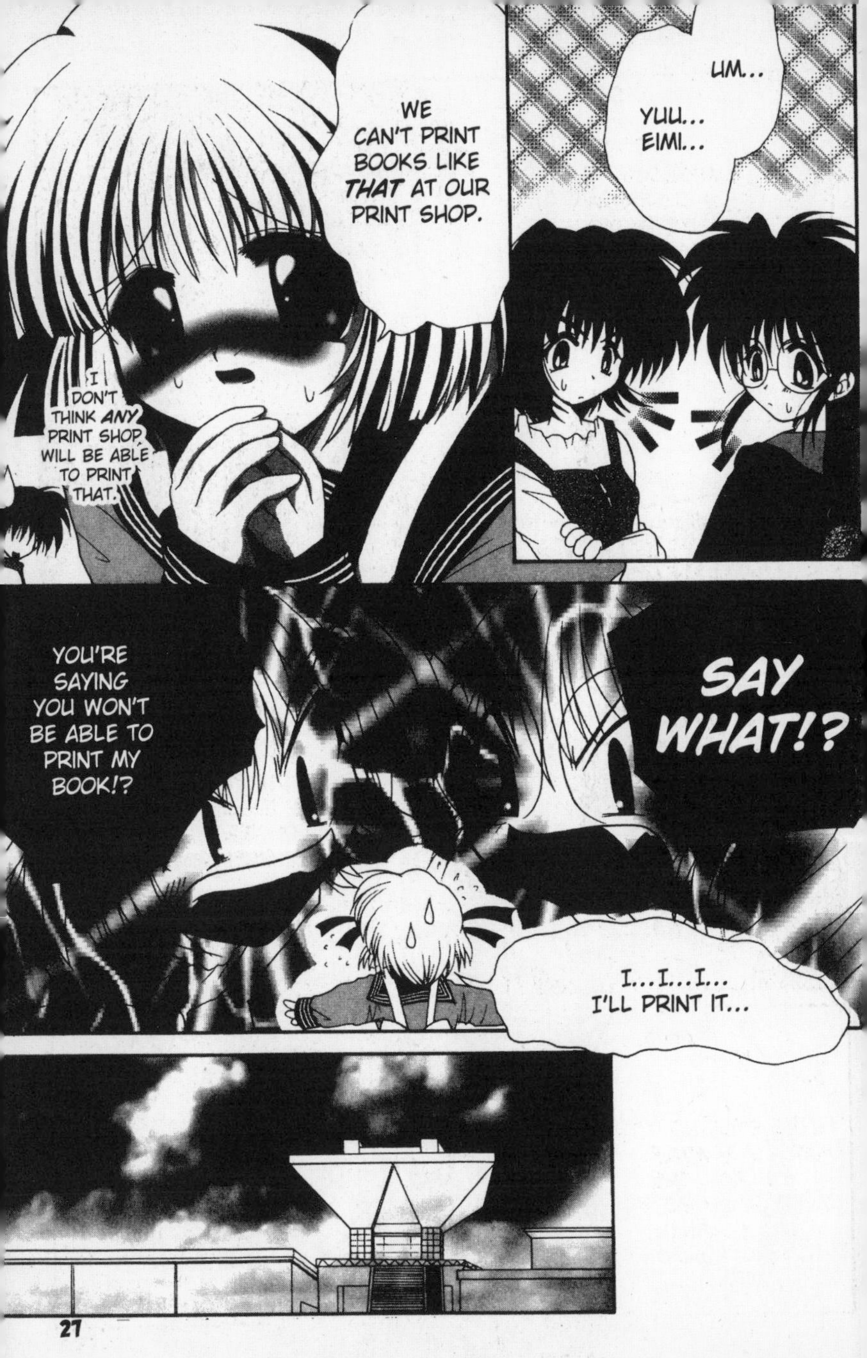
UM...
YUU... EIMI...
WE CAN'T PRINT BOOKS LIKE *THAT* AT OUR PRINT SHOP.
I DON'T THINK *ANY* PRINT SHOP WILL BE ABLE TO PRINT THAT.
SAY WHAT!?
YOU'RE SAYING YOU WON'T BE ABLE TO PRINT MY BOOK!?
I...I...I... I'LL PRINT IT...

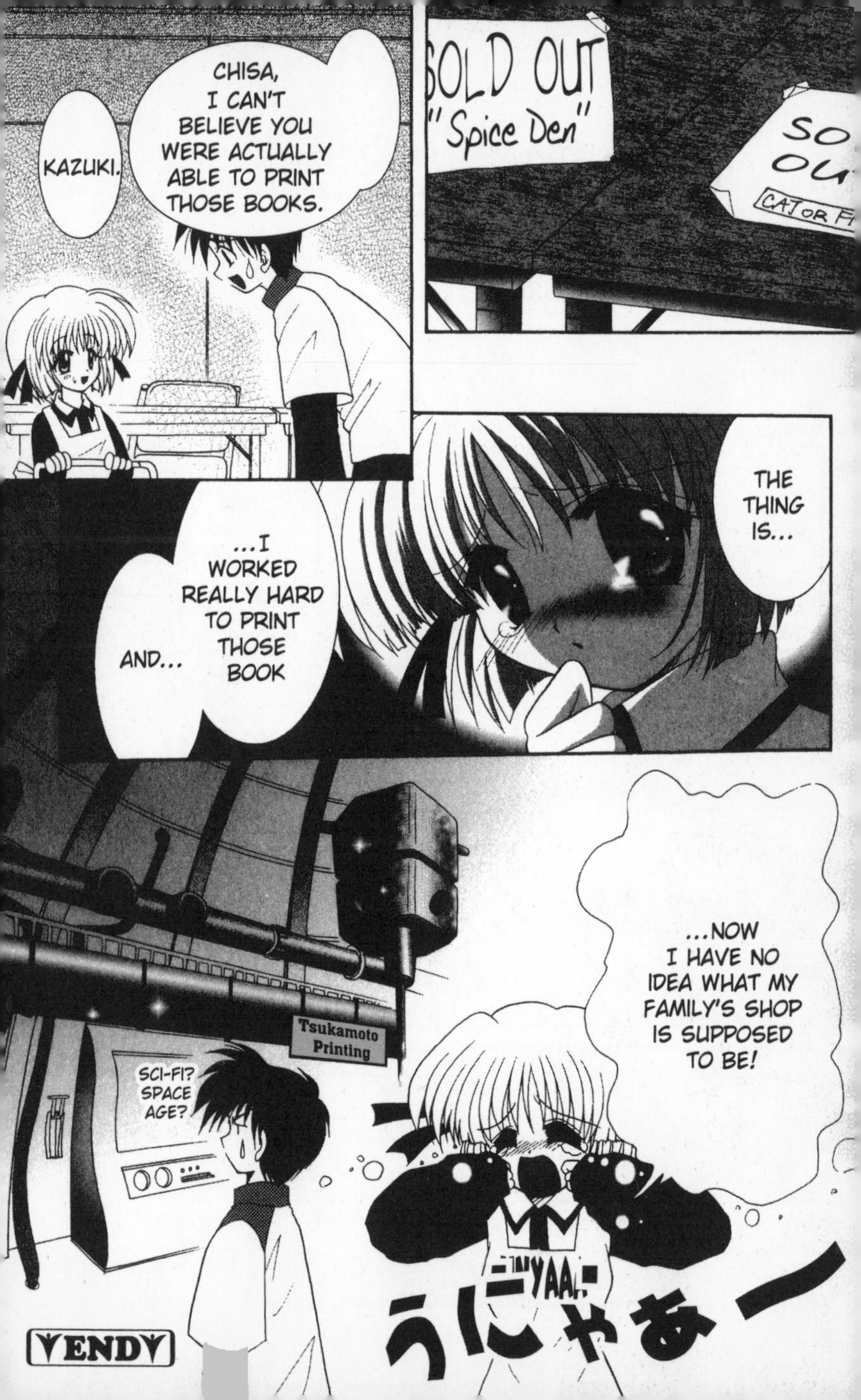
SOLD OUT
"Spice Den"
CHISA, I CAN'T BELIEVE YOU WERE ACTUALLY ABLE TO PRINT THOSE BOOKS.
KAZUKI.
THE THING IS...
...I WORKED REALLY HARD TO PRINT THOSE BOOK
AND...
...NOW I HAVE NO IDEA WHAT MY FAMILY'S SHOP IS SUPPOSED TO BE!
Tsukamoto Printing
SCI-FI? SPACE AGE?
YAA!
うにゃあー
END

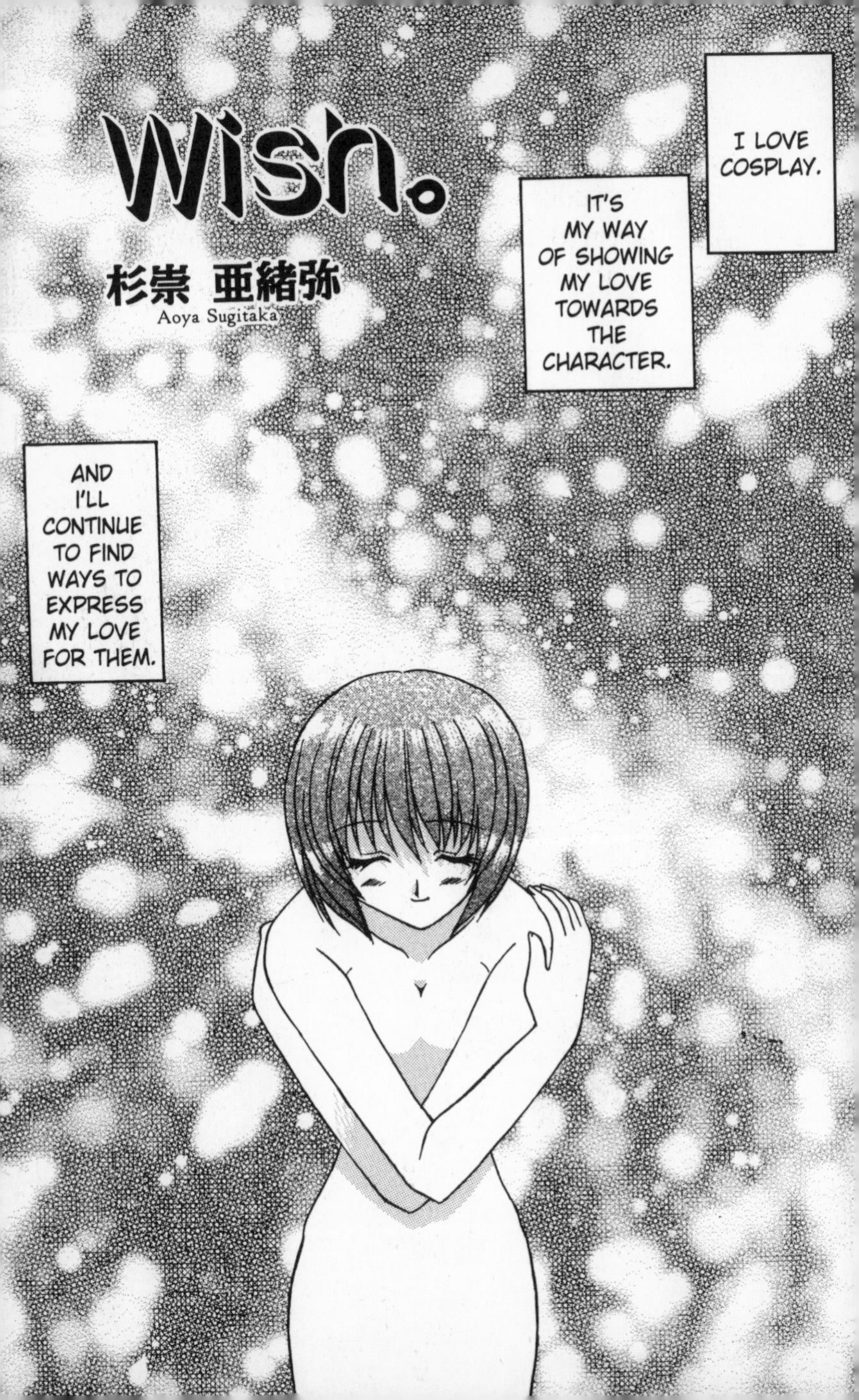
Wish.
杉崇 亜緒弥
Aoya Sugitaka
I LOVE COSPLAY.
IT'S MY WAY OF SHOWING MY LOVE TOWARDS THE CHARACTER.
AND I'LL CONTINUE TO FIND WAYS TO EXPRESS MY LOVE FOR THEM.

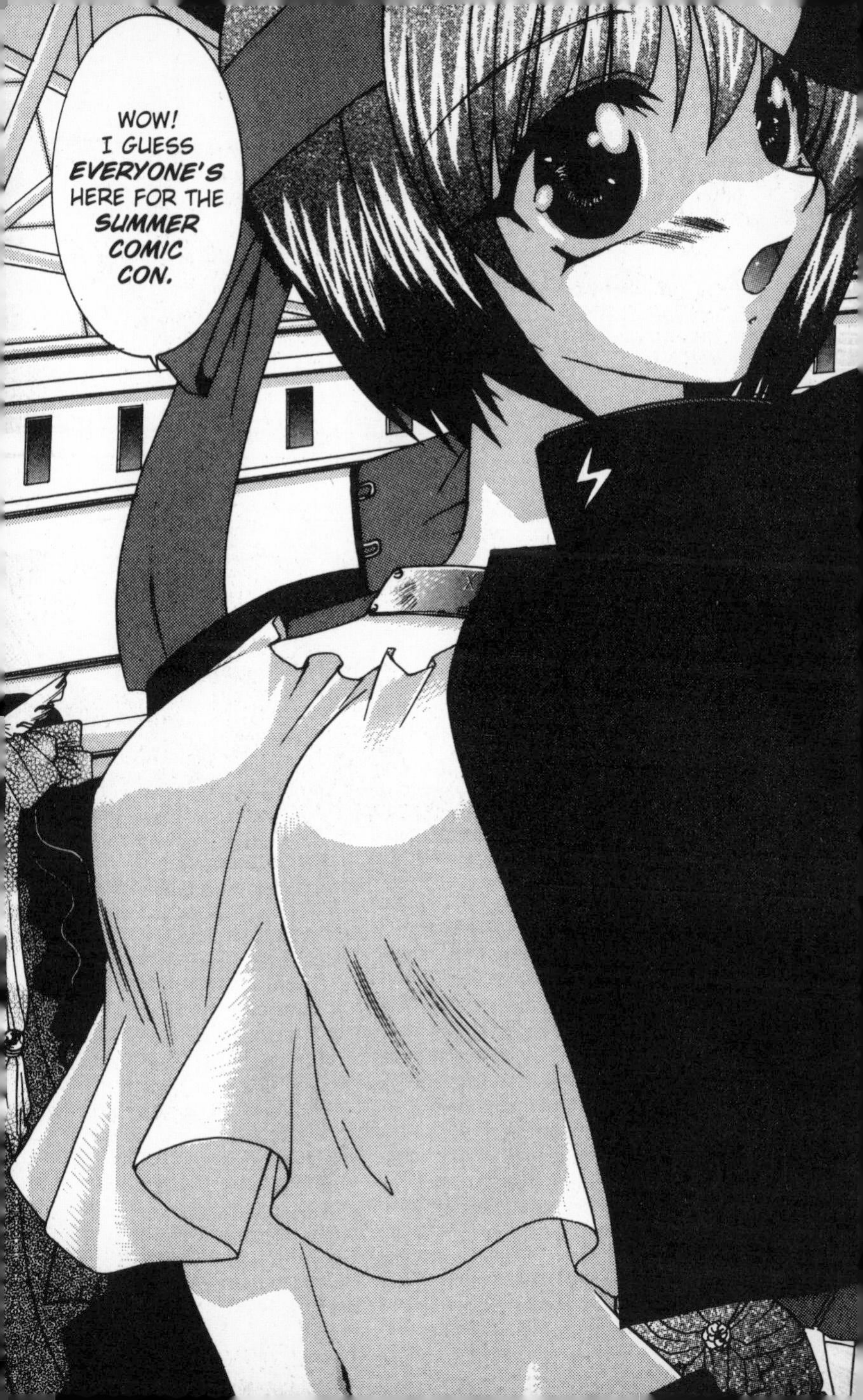
WOW! I GUESS EVERYONE'S HERE FOR THE SUMMER COMIC CON.

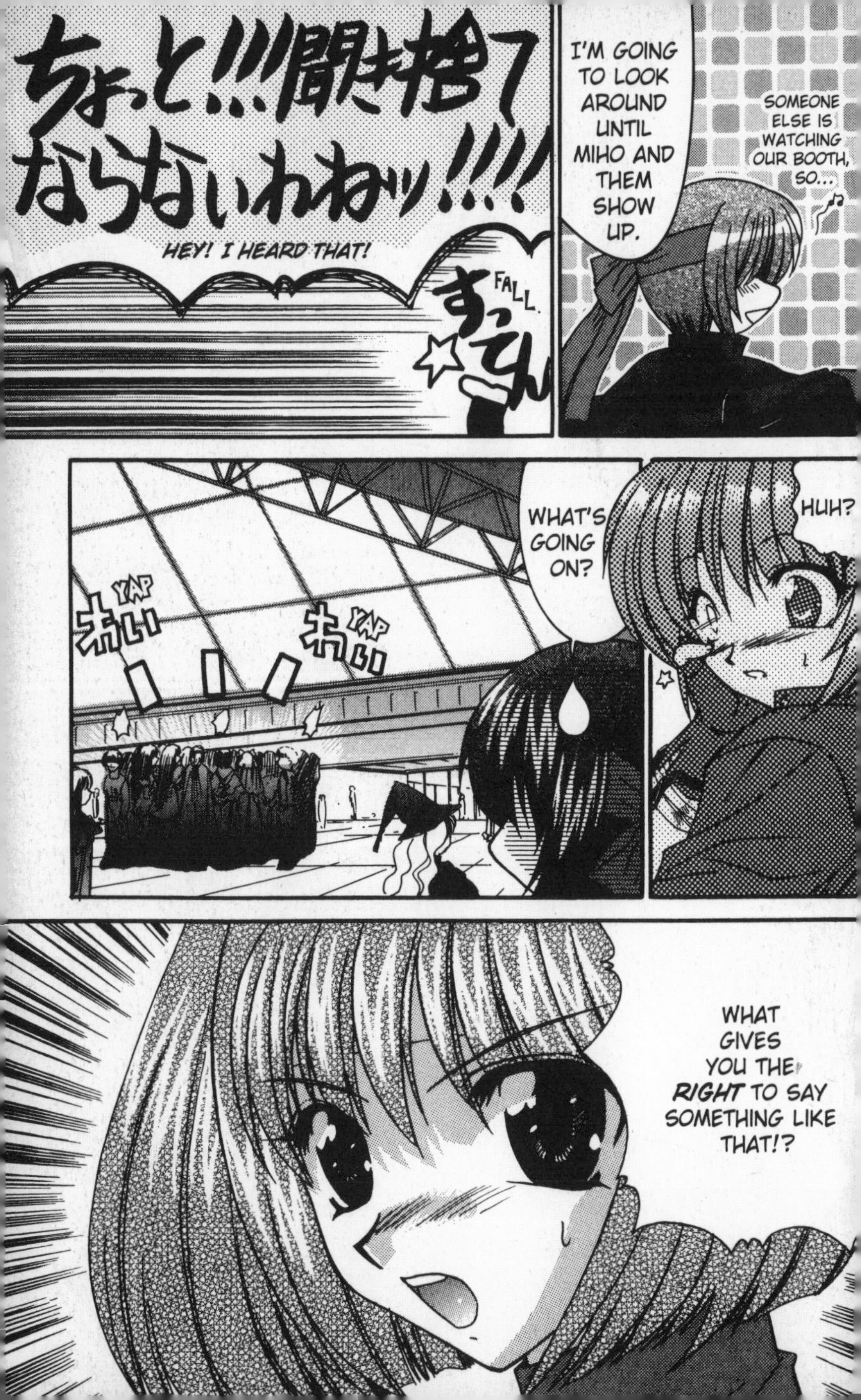

SOMEONE ELSE IS WATCHING OUR BOOTH, SO...
I'M GOING TO LOOK AROUND UNTIL MIHO AND THEM SHOW UP.
ちょっと!!!聞き捨てならないわねッ!!!!
HEY! I HEARD THAT!
すってん
FALL.
HUH?
WHAT'S GOING ON?
わい
YAP
わい
YAP
WHAT GIVES YOU THE RIGHT TO SAY SOMETHING LIKE THAT!?

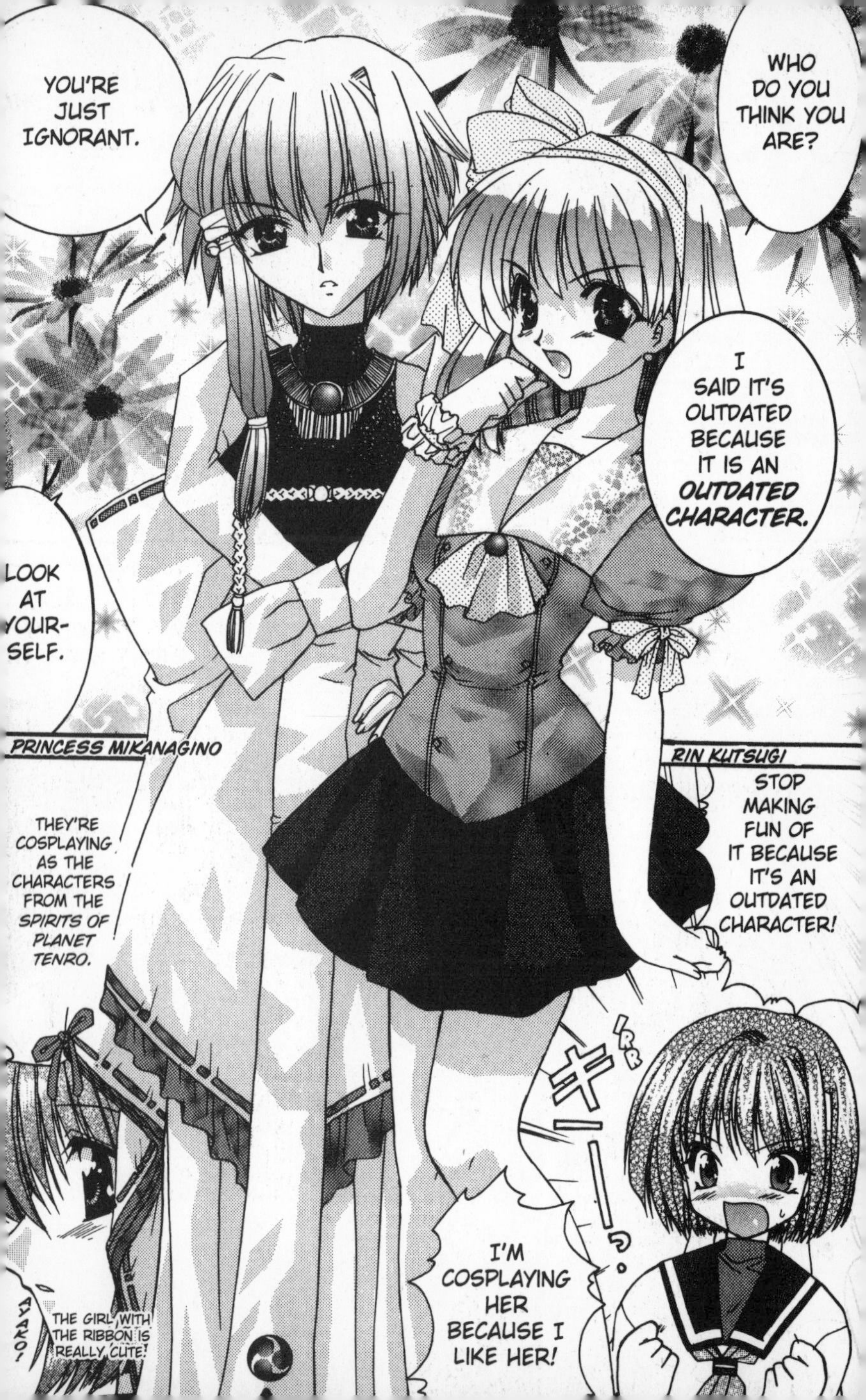
WHO DO YOU THINK YOU ARE?
YOU'RE JUST IGNORANT.
I SAID IT'S OUTDATED BECAUSE IT IS AN *OUTDATED CHARACTER.*
LOOK AT YOURSELF.
RIN KUTSUGI
PRINCESS MIKANAGINO
STOP MAKING FUN OF IT BECAUSE IT'S AN OUTDATED CHARACTER!
THEY'RE COSPLAYING AS THE CHARACTERS FROM THE *SPIRITS OF PLANET TENRO.*
IRR
I'M COSPLAYING HER BECAUSE I LIKE HER!
THE GIRL WITH THE RIBBON IS REALLY CUTE!
AYAKO!

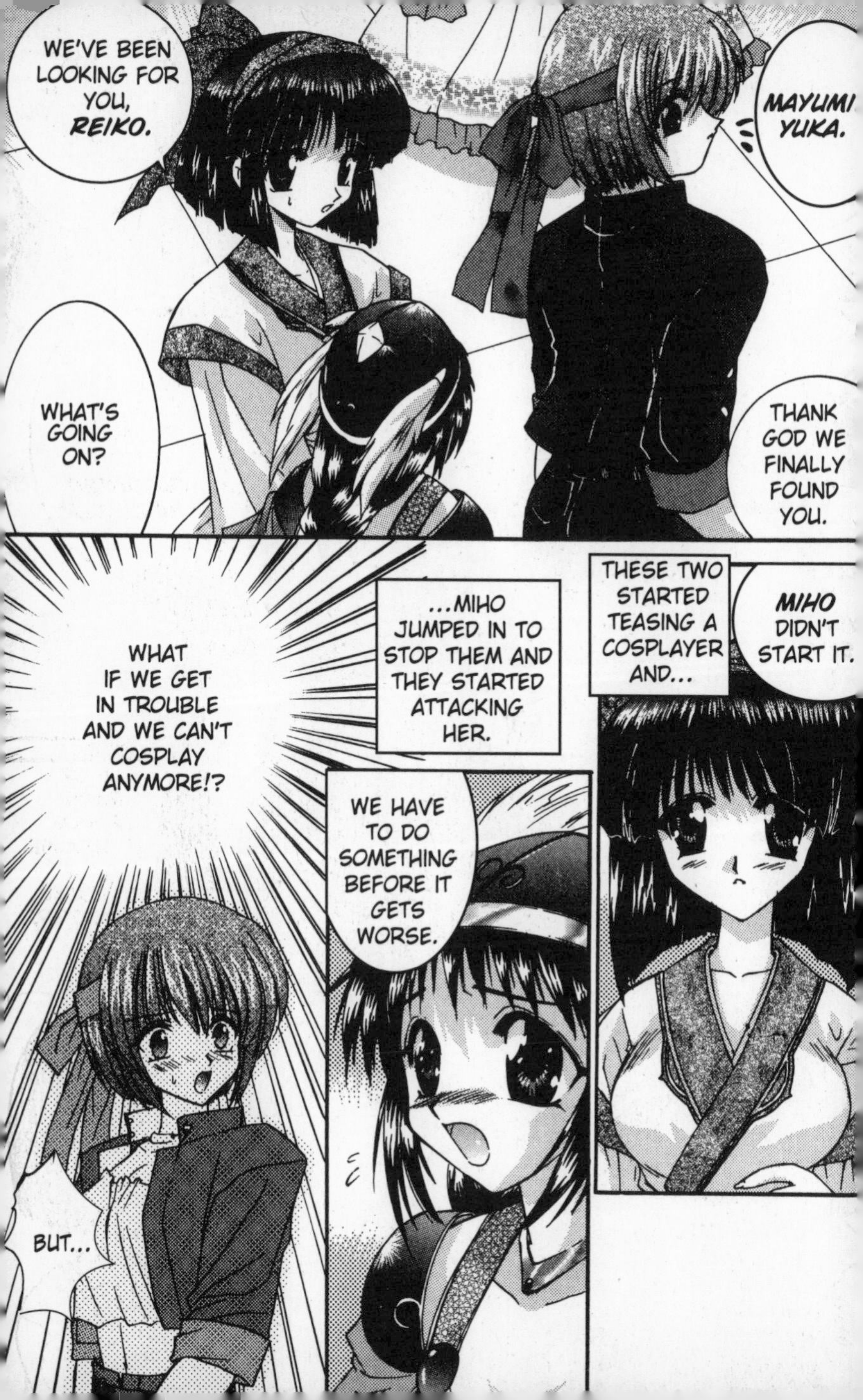

MAYUMI YUKA.
WE'VE BEEN LOOKING FOR YOU, REIKO.
THANK GOD WE FINALLY FOUND YOU.
WHAT'S GOING ON?
MIHO DIDN'T START IT.
THESE TWO STARTED TEASING A COSPLAYER AND...
...MIHO JUMPED IN TO STOP THEM AND THEY STARTED ATTACKING HER.
WE HAVE TO DO SOMETHING BEFORE IT GETS WORSE.
WHAT IF WE GET IN TROUBLE AND WE CAN'T COSPLAY ANYMORE!?
BUT...

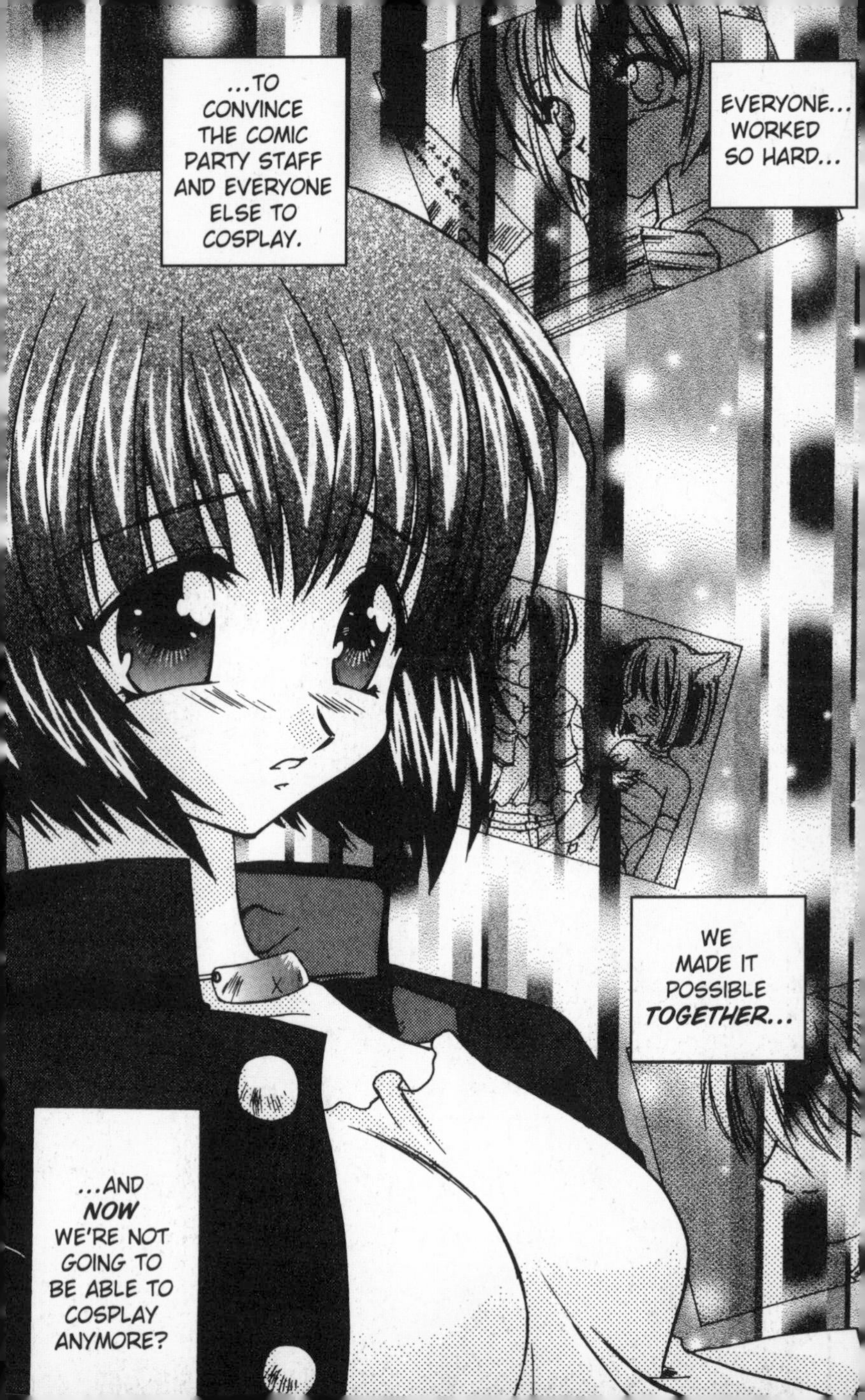
EVERYONE... WORKED SO HARD...
...TO CONVINCE THE COMIC PARTY STAFF AND EVERYONE ELSE TO COSPLAY.
WE MADE IT POSSIBLE *TOGETHER*...
...AND *NOW* WE'RE NOT GOING TO BE ABLE TO COSPLAY ANYMORE?

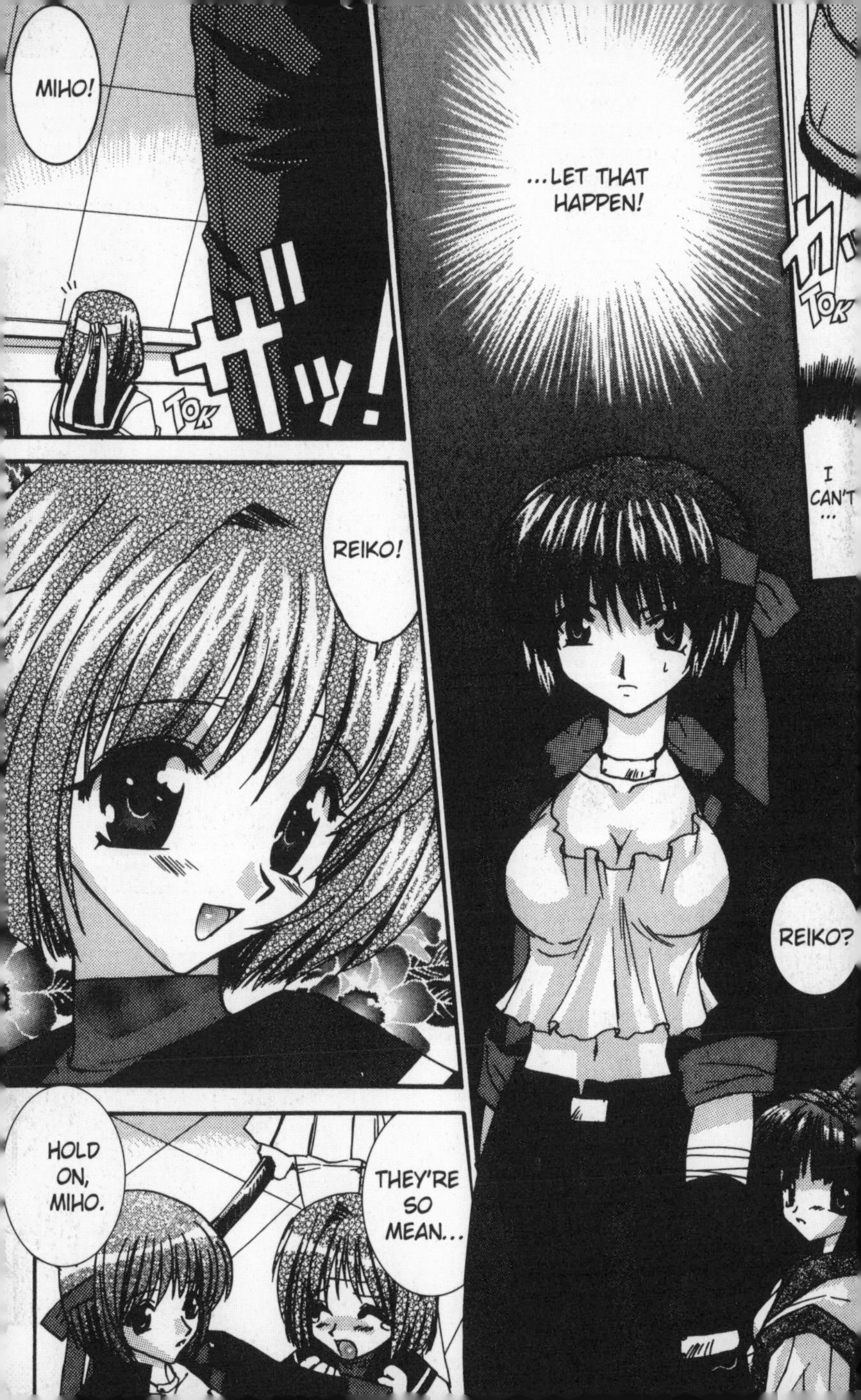
TOK
I CAN'T ...
...LET THAT HAPPEN!
REIKO?
MIHO!
TOK
REIKO!
THEY'RE SO MEAN...
HOLD ON, MIHO.

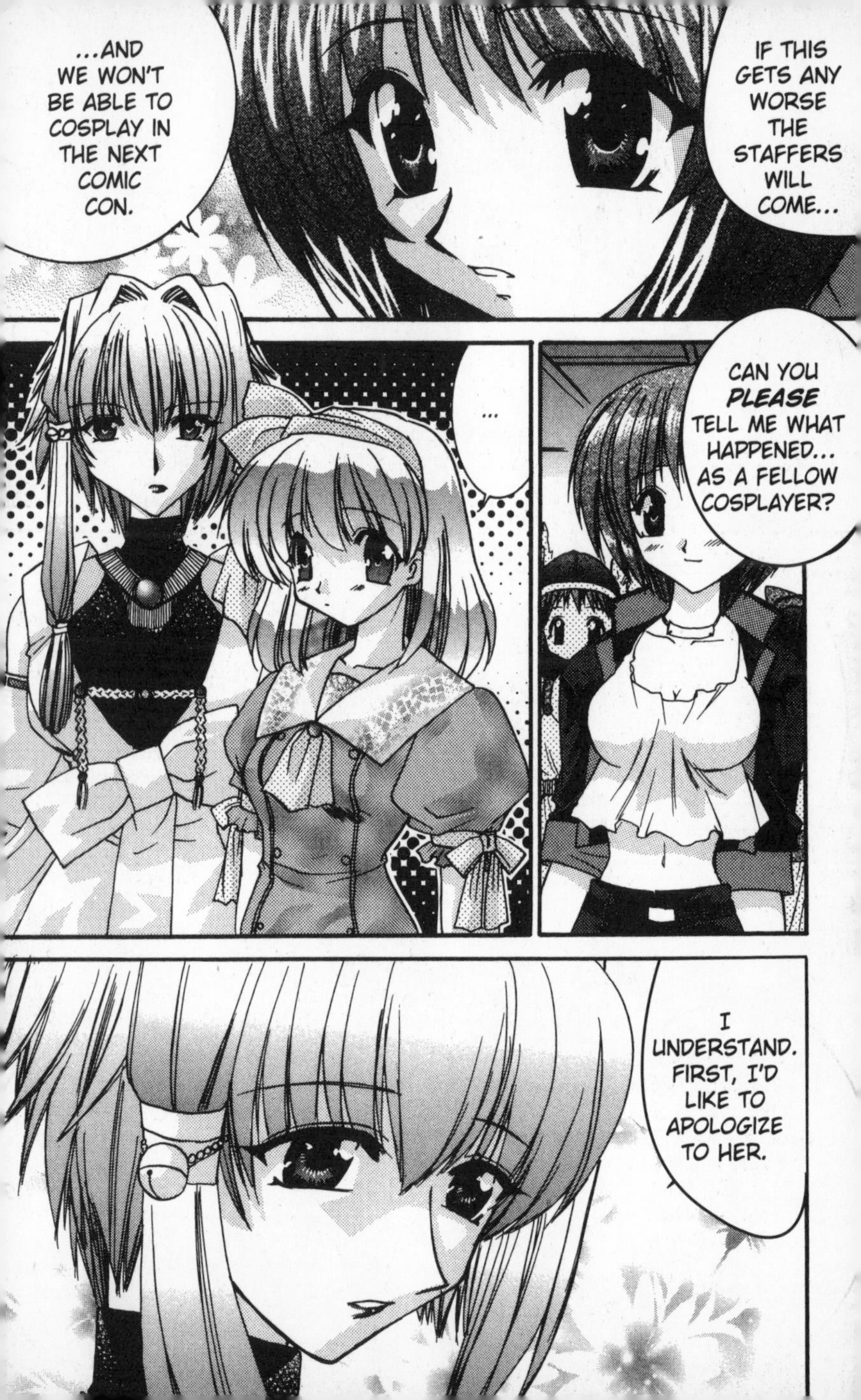
IF THIS GETS ANY WORSE THE STAFFERS WILL COME...
...AND WE WON'T BE ABLE TO COSPLAY IN THE NEXT COMIC CON.
CAN YOU *PLEASE* TELL ME WHAT HAPPENED... AS A FELLOW COSPLAYER?
...
I UNDERSTAND. FIRST, I'D LIKE TO APOLOGIZE TO HER.

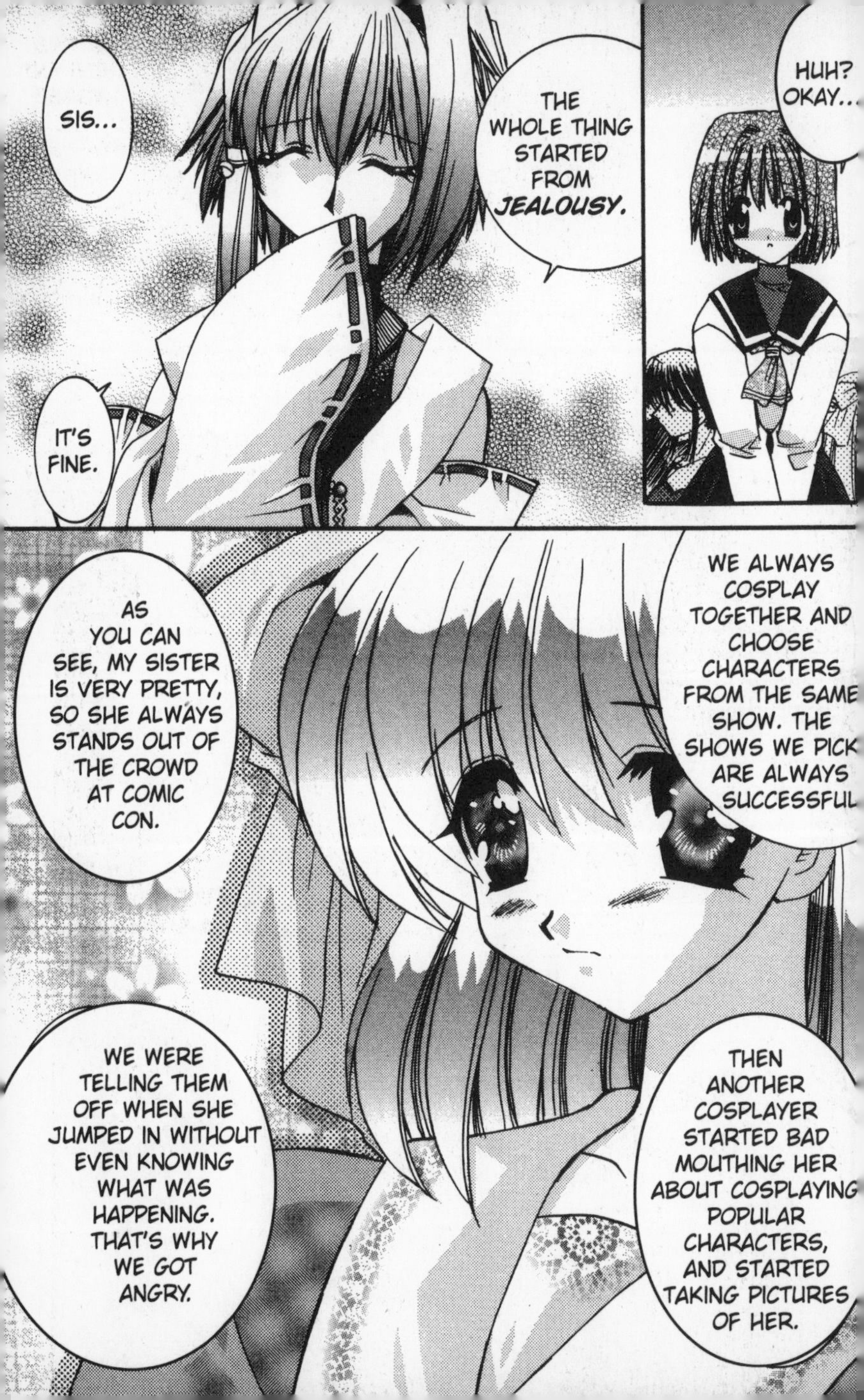
SIS...
IT'S FINE.
THE WHOLE THING STARTED FROM *JEALOUSY.*
HUH? OKAY...
AS YOU CAN SEE, MY SISTER IS VERY PRETTY, SO SHE ALWAYS STANDS OUT OF THE CROWD AT COMIC CON.
WE ALWAYS COSPLAY TOGETHER AND CHOOSE CHARACTERS FROM THE SAME SHOW. THE SHOWS WE PICK ARE ALWAYS SUCCESSFUL
WE WERE TELLING THEM OFF WHEN SHE JUMPED IN WITHOUT EVEN KNOWING WHAT WAS HAPPENING. THAT'S WHY WE GOT ANGRY.
THEN ANOTHER COSPLAYER STARTED BAD MOUTHING HER ABOUT COSPLAYING POPULAR CHARACTERS, AND STARTED TAKING PICTURES OF HER.

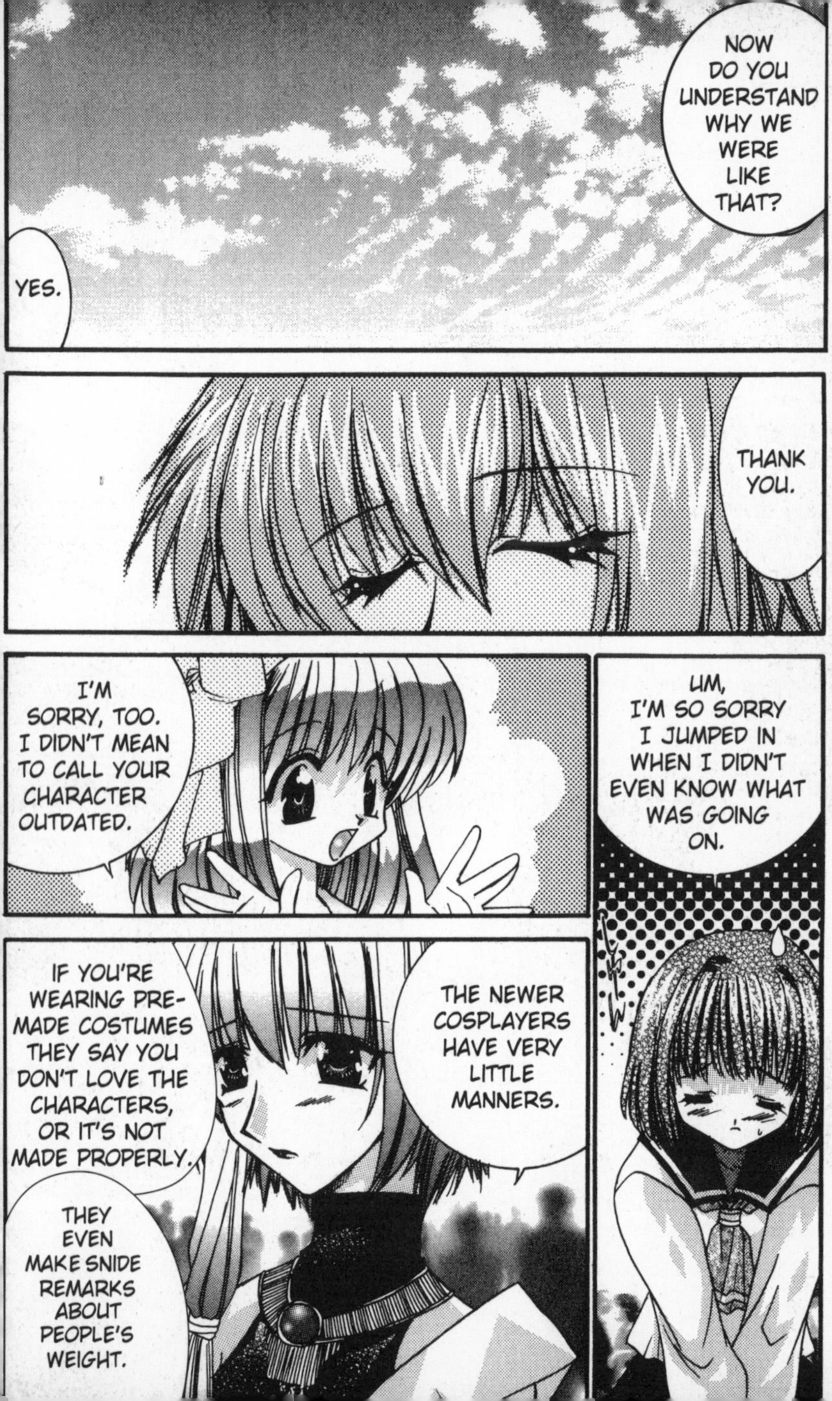
NOW DO YOU UNDERSTAND WHY WE WERE LIKE THAT?
YES.
THANK YOU.
UM, I'M SO SORRY I JUMPED IN WHEN I DIDN'T EVEN KNOW WHAT WAS GOING ON.
I'M SORRY, TOO. I DIDN'T MEAN TO CALL YOUR CHARACTER OUTDATED.
THE NEWER COSPLAYERS HAVE VERY LITTLE MANNERS.
IF YOU'RE WEARING PRE-MADE COSTUMES THEY SAY YOU DON'T LOVE THE CHARACTERS, OR IT'S NOT MADE PROPERLY.
THEY EVEN MAKE SNIDE REMARKS ABOUT PEOPLE'S WEIGHT.

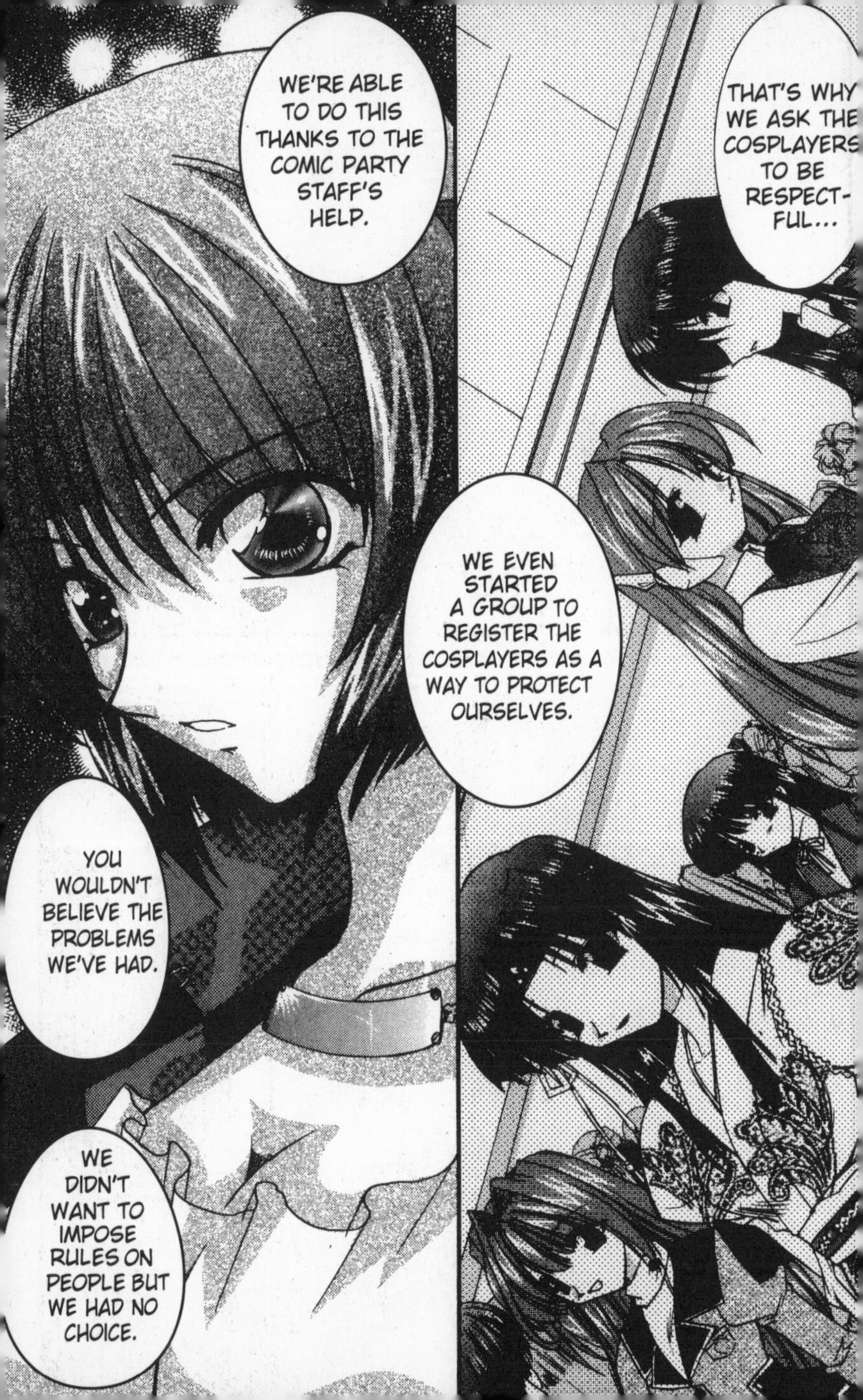
THAT'S WHY WE ASK THE COSPLAYERS TO BE RESPECT-FUL...
WE EVEN STARTED A GROUP TO REGISTER THE COSPLAYERS AS A WAY TO PROTECT OURSELVES.
WE'RE ABLE TO DO THIS THANKS TO THE COMIC PARTY STAFF'S HELP.
YOU WOULDN'T BELIEVE THE PROBLEMS WE'VE HAD.
WE DIDN'T WANT TO IMPOSE RULES ON PEOPLE BUT WE HAD NO CHOICE.

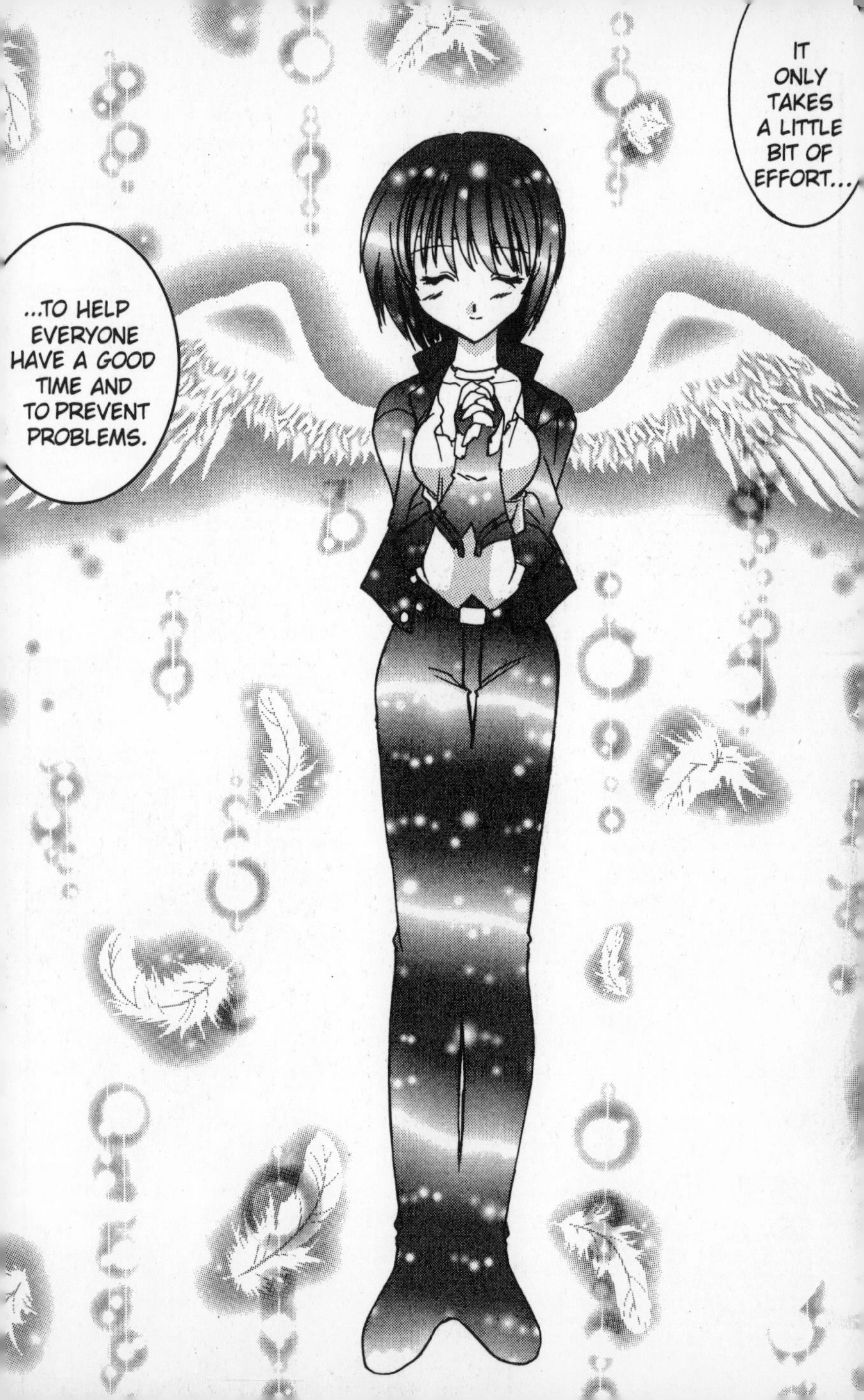
IT ONLY TAKES A LITTLE BIT OF EFFORT...
...TO HELP EVERYONE HAVE A GOOD TIME AND TO PREVENT PROBLEMS.

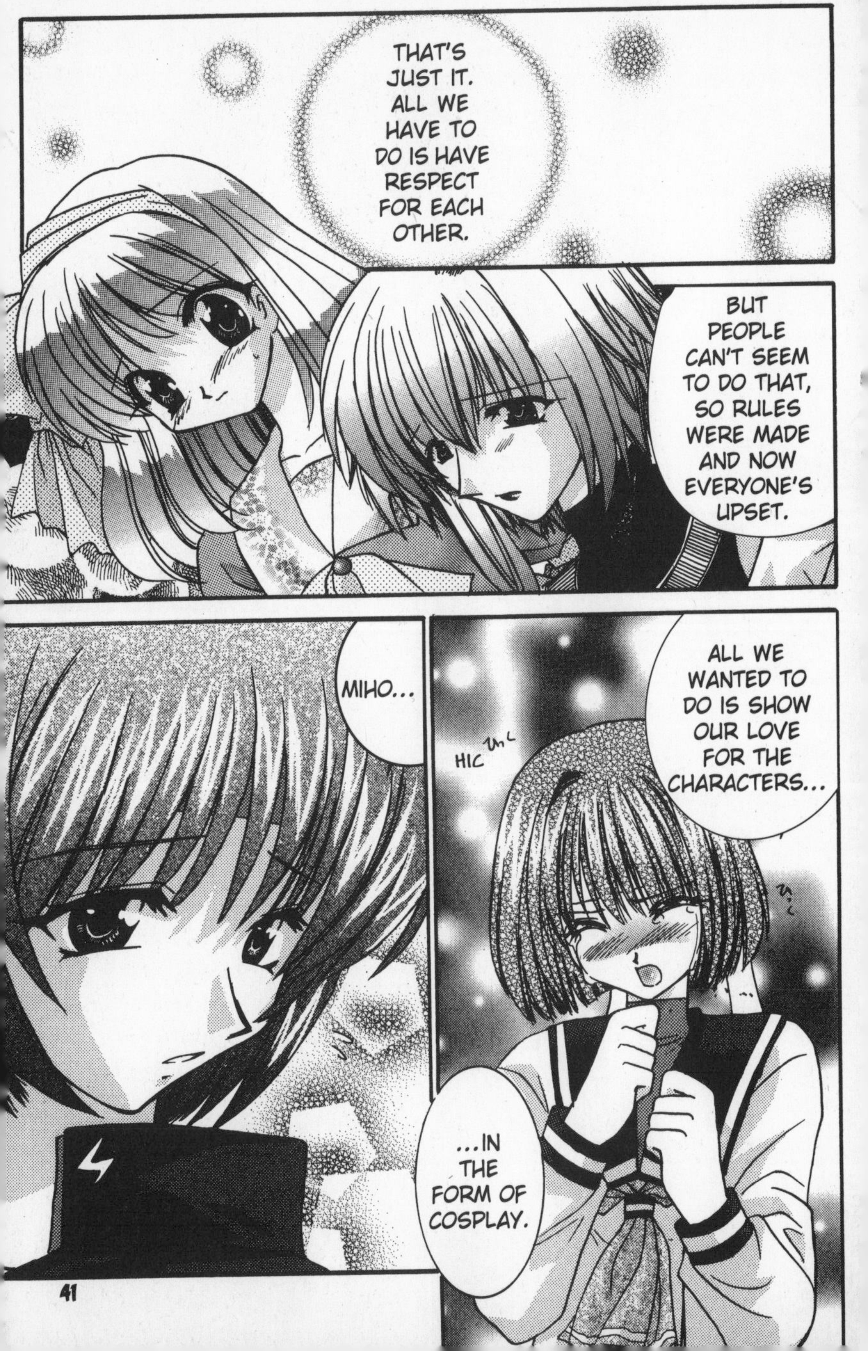
THAT'S JUST IT. ALL WE HAVE TO DO IS HAVE RESPECT FOR EACH OTHER.
BUT PEOPLE CAN'T SEEM TO DO THAT, SO RULES WERE MADE AND NOW EVERYONE'S UPSET.
ALL WE WANTED TO DO IS SHOW OUR LOVE FOR THE CHARACTERS...
HIC
...IN THE FORM OF COSPLAY.
MIHO...

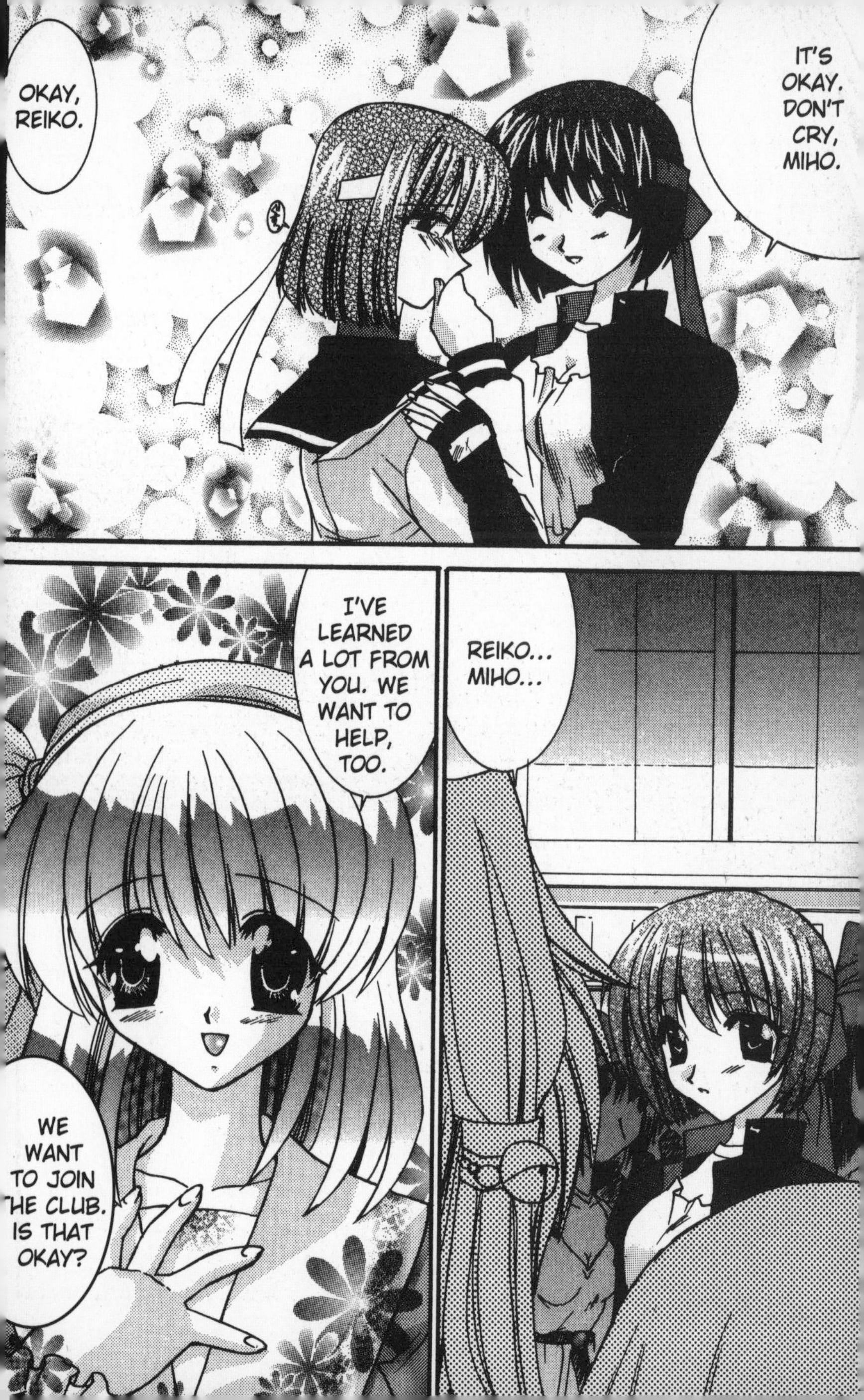
IT'S OKAY. DON'T CRY, MIHO.
OKAY, REIKO.
REIKO... MIHO...
I'VE LEARNED A LOT FROM YOU. WE WANT TO HELP, TOO.
WE WANT TO JOIN HE CLUB. IS THAT OKAY?

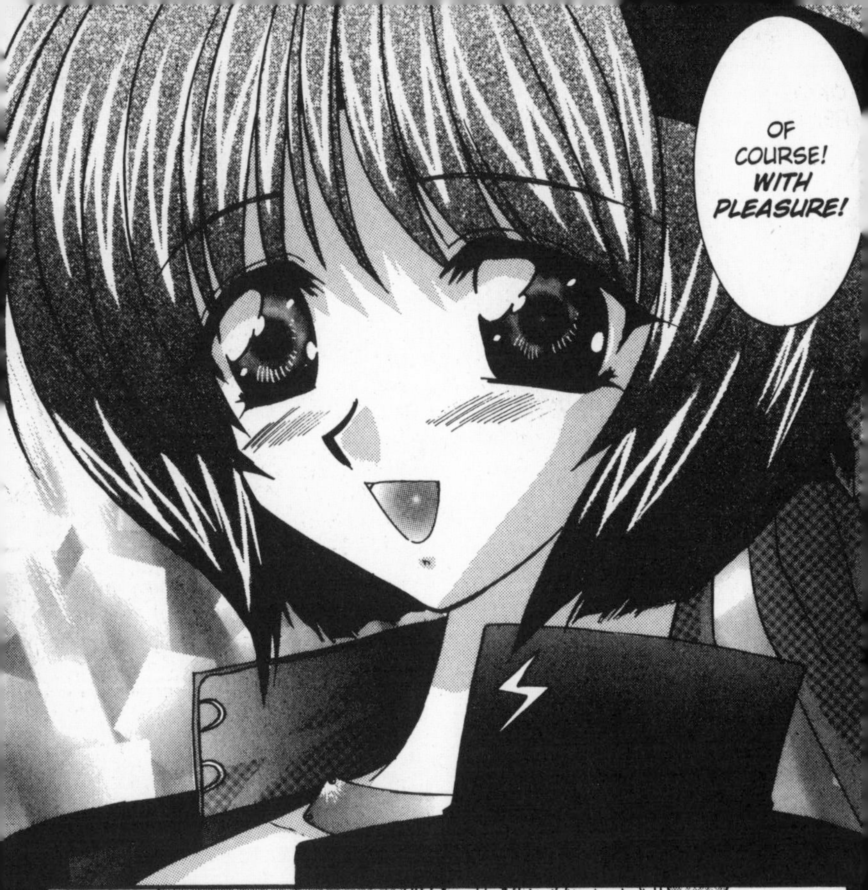
OF COURSE! WITH PLEASURE!

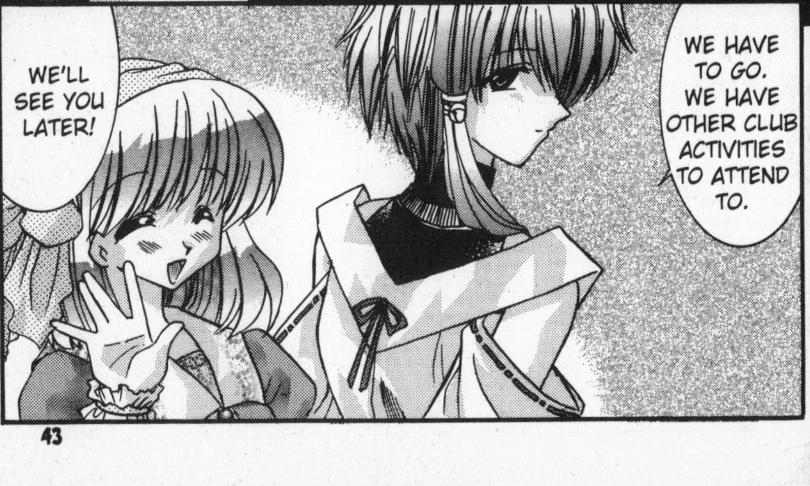
WE HAVE TO GO. WE HAVE OTHER CLUB ACTIVITIES TO ATTEND TO.
WE'LL SEE YOU LATER!

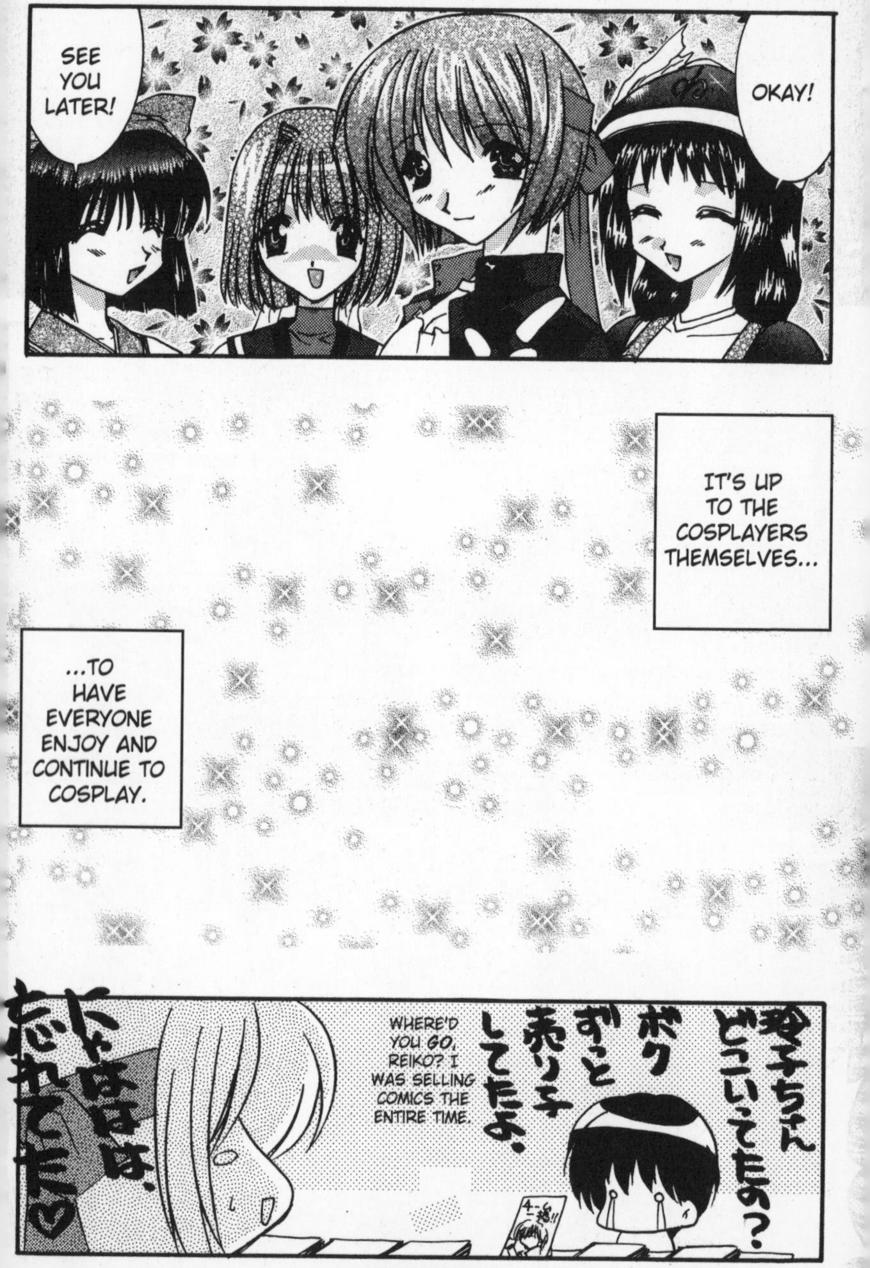
OKAY!
SEE YOU LATER!
IT'S UP TO THE COSPLAYERS THEMSELVES...
...TO HAVE EVERYONE ENJOY AND CONTINUE TO COSPLAY.
玲子ちゃんどこいってたの？ボクずっと売り子してたよ。
WHERE'D YOU GO, REIKO? I WAS SELLING COMICS THE ENTIRE TIME.
いやははは、忘れてた♡
END

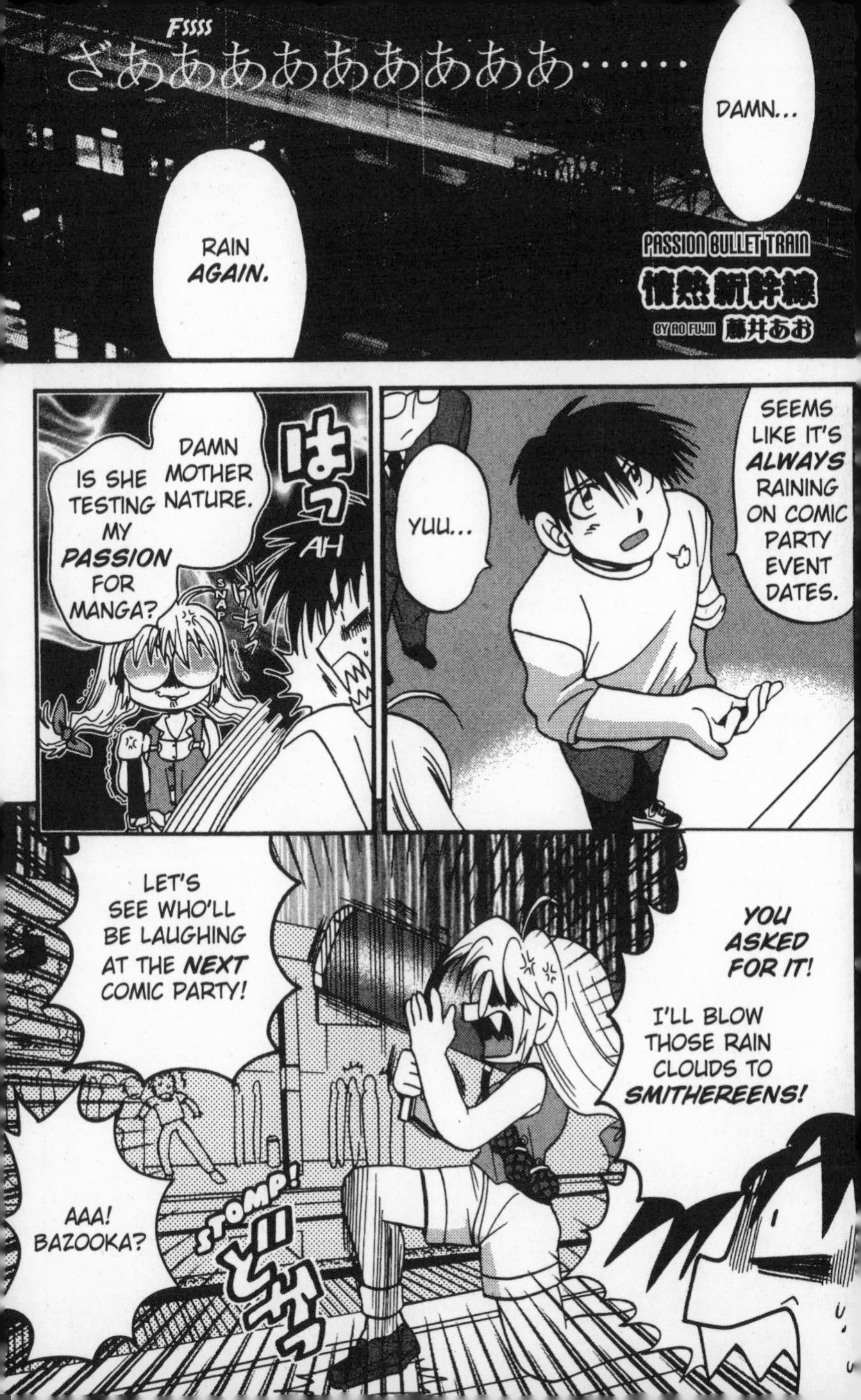FSSSS
ざあああああああああ……
DAMN…
RAIN AGAIN.
PASSION BULLET TRAIN
情熱新幹線
BY AO FUJII
藤井あお
SEEMS LIKE IT'S ALWAYS RAINING ON COMIC PARTY EVENT DATES.
YUU…
はっ
AH
DAMN MOTHER NATURE.
IS SHE TESTING MY PASSION FOR MANGA?
SNAP
YOU ASKED FOR IT!
I'LL BLOW THOSE RAIN CLOUDS TO SMITHEREENS!
LET'S SEE WHO'LL BE LAUGHING AT THE NEXT COMIC PARTY!
AAA! BAZOOKA?
STOMP!
どんっ

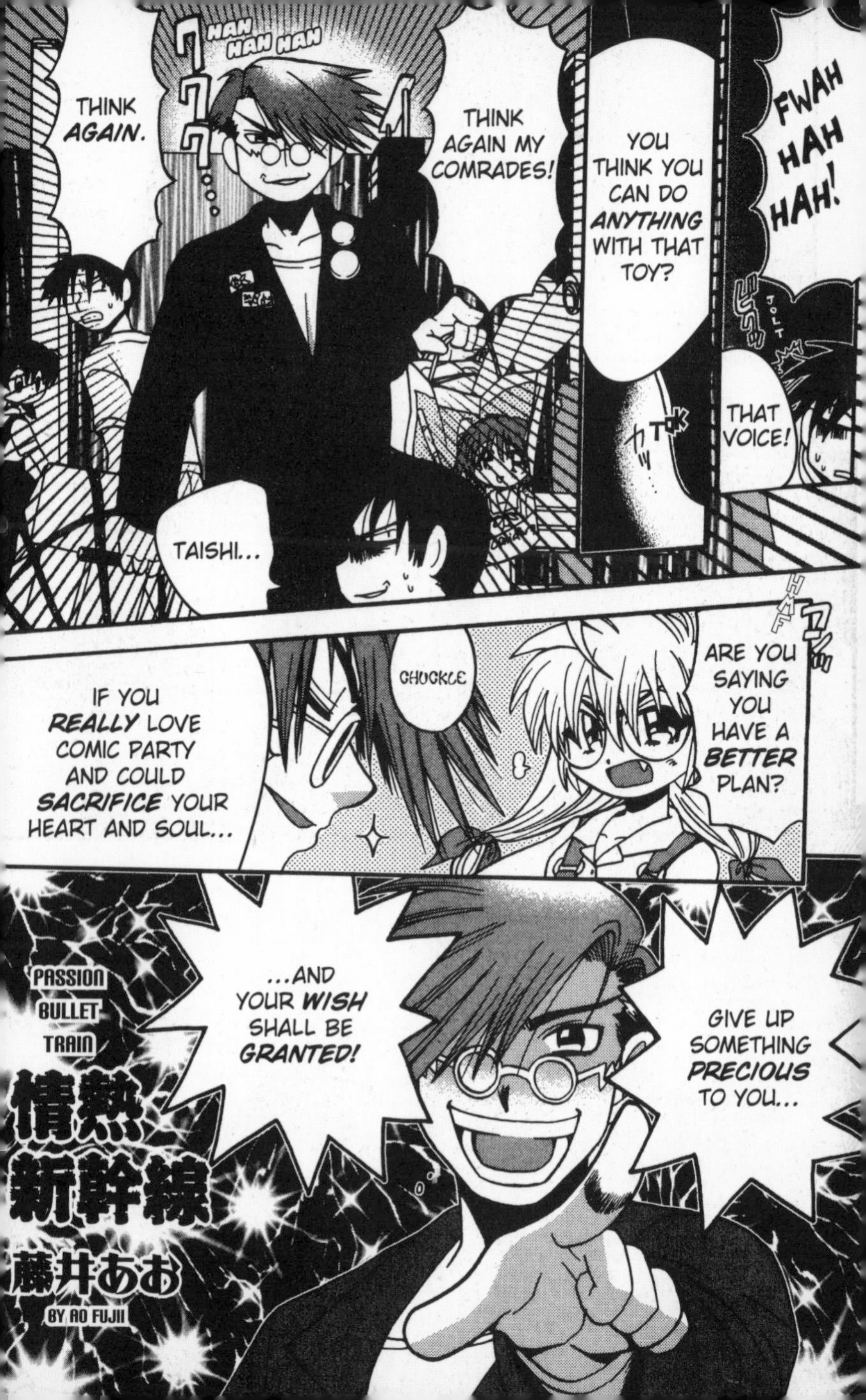
FWAH HAH HAH!
JOLT
THAT VOICE!
TOK
YOU THINK YOU CAN DO ANYTHING WITH THAT TOY?
THINK AGAIN MY COMRADES!
HAH HAH HAH HAH
THINK AGAIN.
TAISHI...
HMF
ARE YOU SAYING YOU HAVE A BETTER PLAN?
CHUCKLE
IF YOU REALLY LOVE COMIC PARTY AND COULD SACRIFICE YOUR HEART AND SOUL...
GIVE UP SOMETHING PRECIOUS TO YOU...
...AND YOUR WISH SHALL BE GRANTED!
PASSION BULLET TRAIN
情熱新幹線
藤井あお
BY AO FUJII

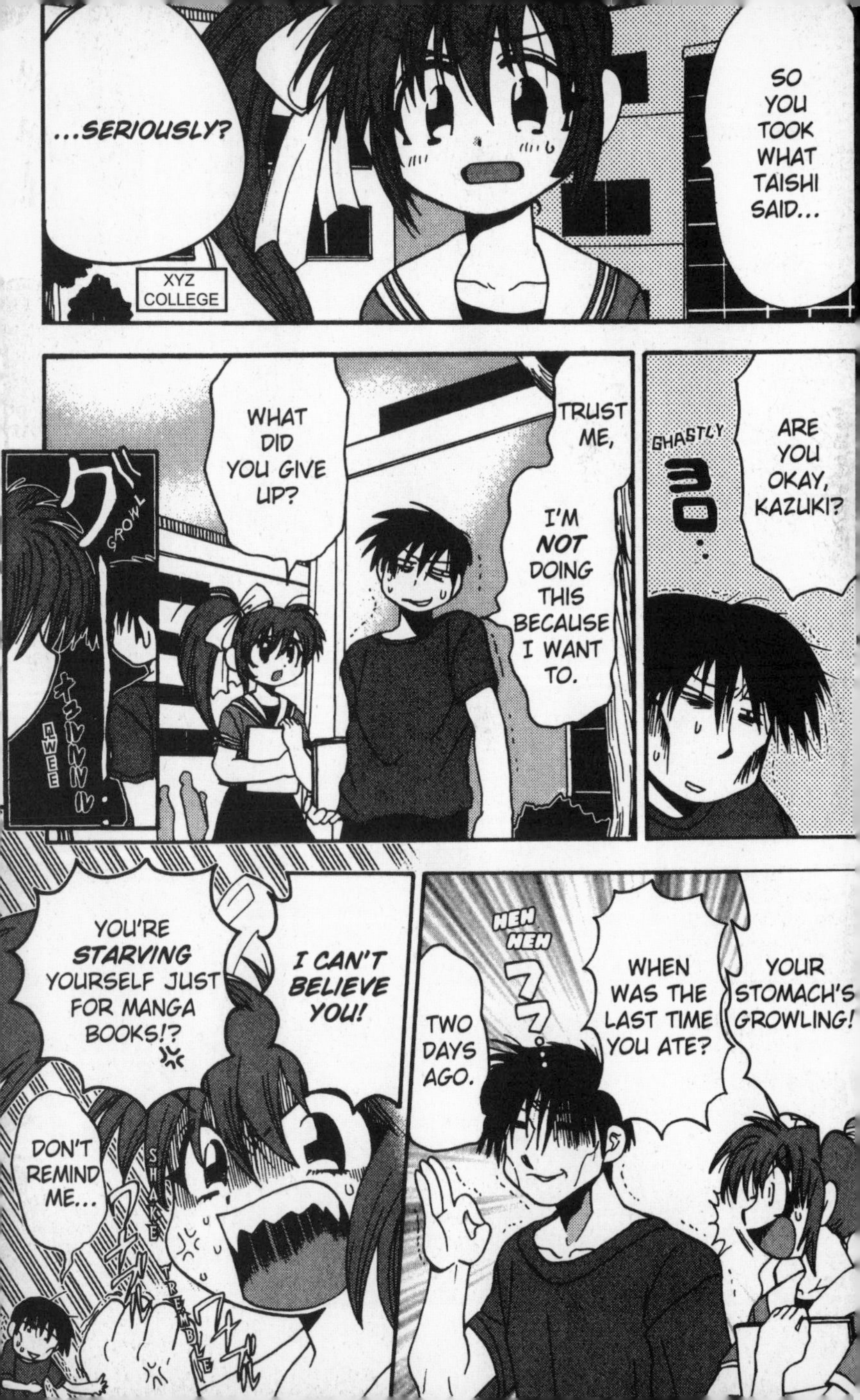
SO YOU TOOK WHAT TAISHI SAID...
...SERIOUSLY?
XYZ COLLEGE
ARE YOU OKAY, KAZUKI?
GHASTLY
TRUST ME, I'M *NOT* DOING THIS BECAUSE I WANT TO.
WHAT DID YOU GIVE UP?
GROWL
AWEEE
YOUR STOMACH'S GROWLING!
WHEN WAS THE LAST TIME YOU ATE?
HEH HEH
TWO DAYS AGO.
I CAN'T BELIEVE YOU!
YOU'RE **STARVING** YOURSELF JUST FOR MANGA BOOKS!?
DON'T REMIND ME...
SHAKE
TREMBLE

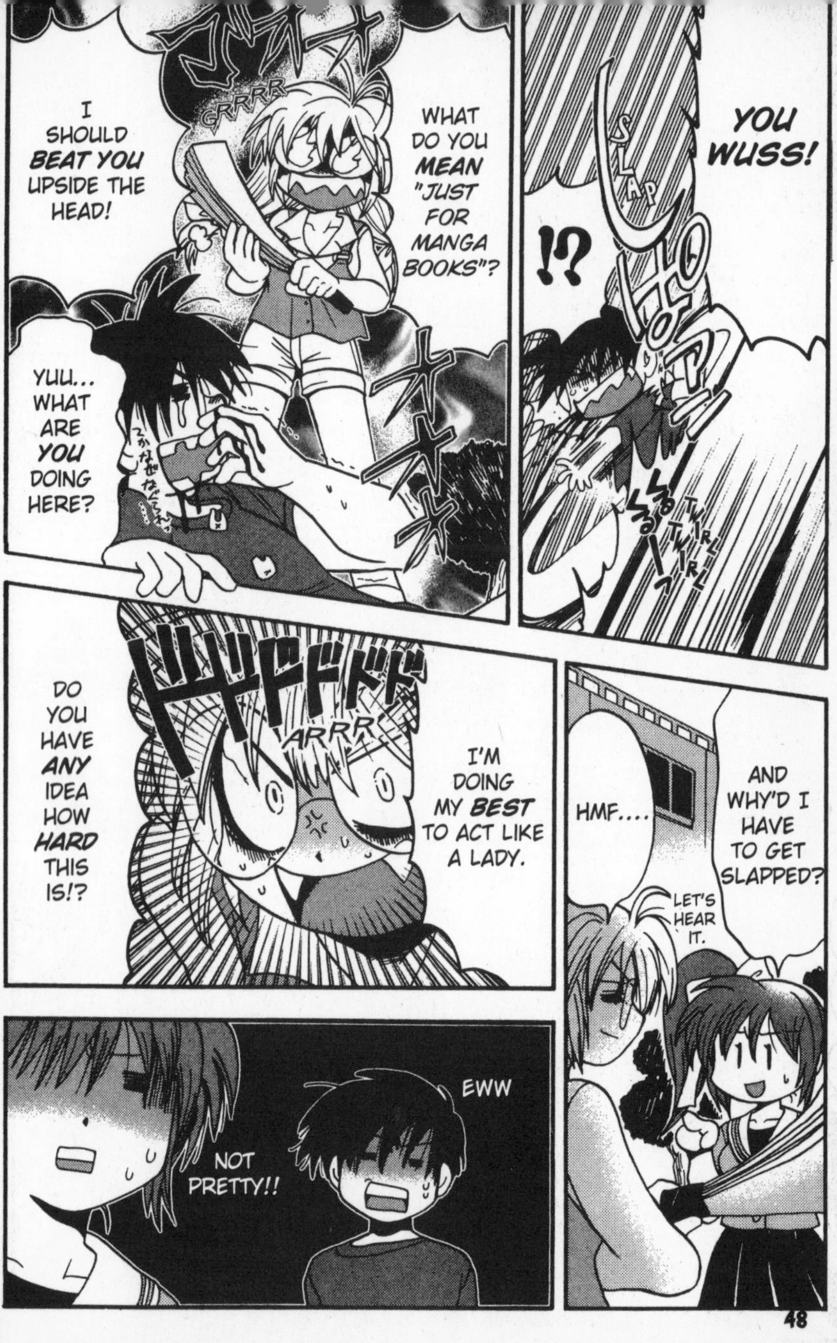
YOU WUSS!
SLAP
!?
TWIRL TWIRL
WHAT DO YOU MEAN "JUST FOR MANGA BOOKS"?
GRRRR
I SHOULD BEAT YOU UPSIDE THE HEAD!
YUU... WHAT ARE YOU DOING HERE?
AND WHY'D I HAVE TO GET SLAPPED?
LET'S HEAR IT.
HMF....
I'M DOING MY BEST TO ACT LIKE A LADY.
ARRR
DO YOU HAVE ANY IDEA HOW HARD THIS IS!?
EWW
NOT PRETTY!!

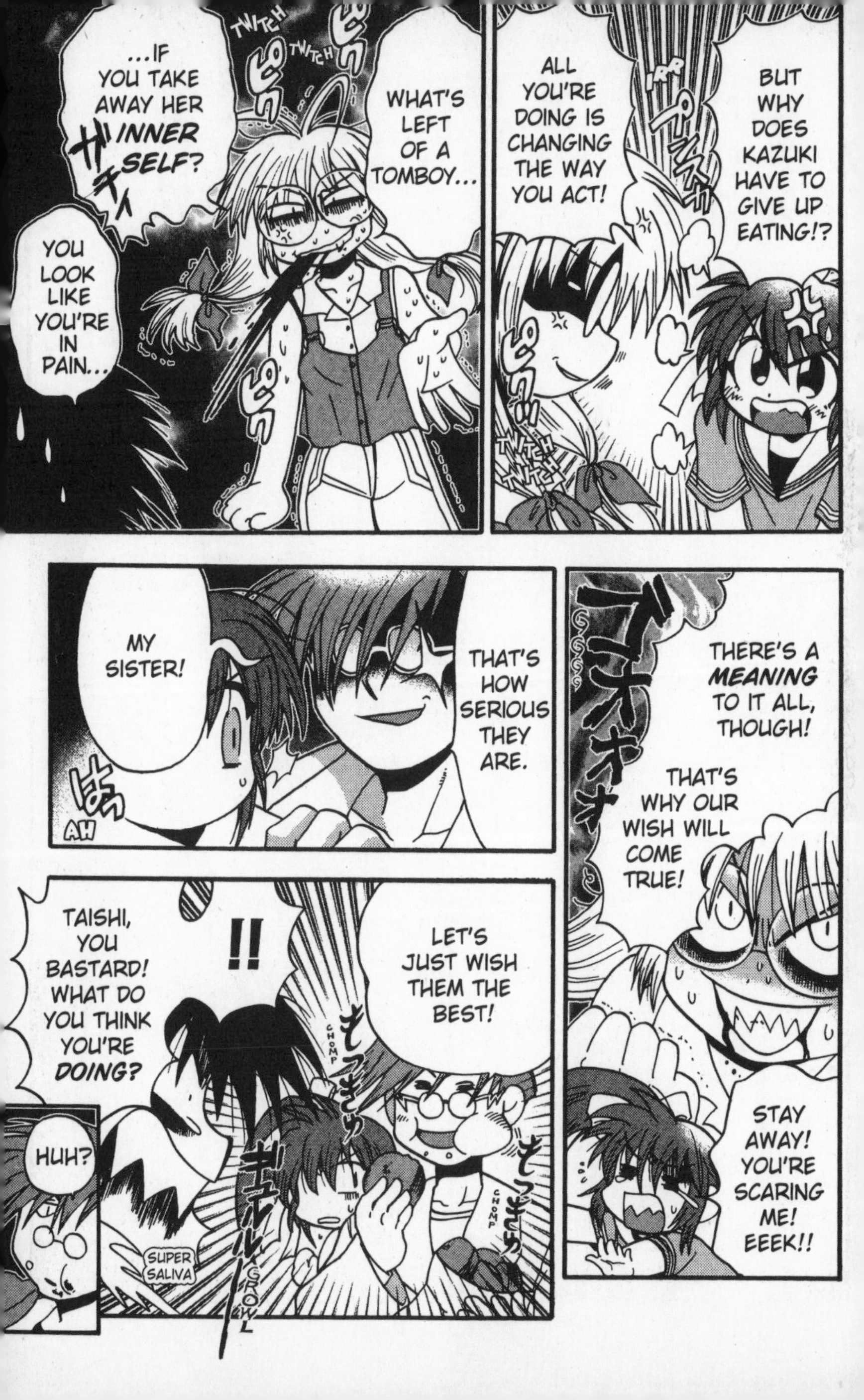
BUT WHY DOES KAZUKI HAVE TO GIVE UP EATING!?
IRR
ALL YOU'RE DOING IS CHANGING THE WAY YOU ACT!
TWITCH TWITCH
WHAT'S LEFT OF A TOMBOY...
TWITCH TWITCH
...IF YOU TAKE AWAY HER *INNER SELF*?
YOU LOOK LIKE YOU'RE IN PAIN...
THERE'S A *MEANING* TO IT ALL, THOUGH!
THAT'S WHY OUR WISH WILL COME TRUE!
STAY AWAY! YOU'RE SCARING ME! EEEK!!
THAT'S HOW SERIOUS THEY ARE.
MY SISTER!
AH
LET'S JUST WISH THEM THE BEST!
CHOMP
!!
TAISHI, YOU BASTARD! WHAT DO YOU THINK YOU'RE *DOING*?
CHOMP
GROWL
HUH?
SUPER SALIVA

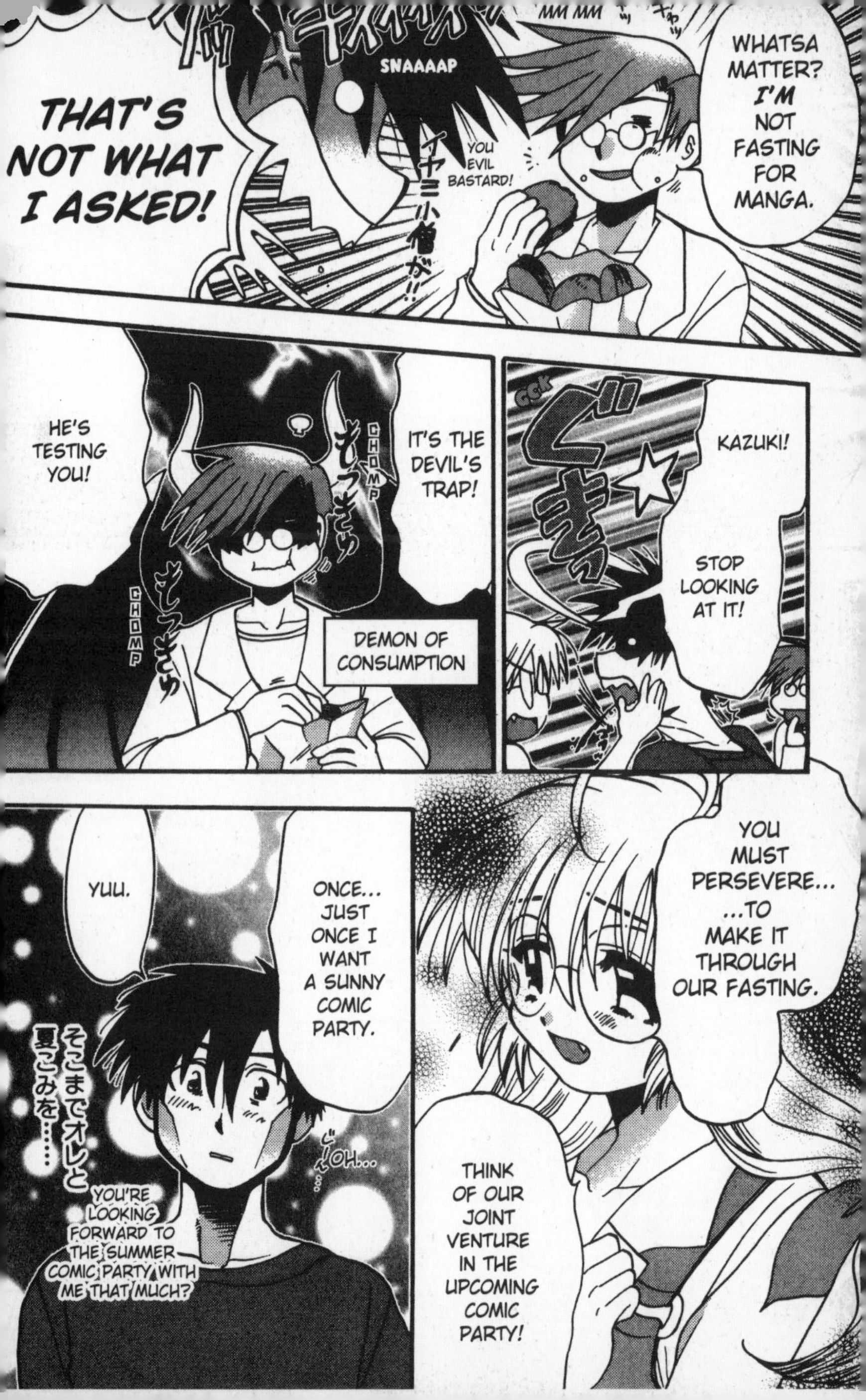
MM MM
WHATSA MATTER? I'M NOT FASTING FOR MANGA.
SNAAAAP
YOU EVIL BASTARD!
イヤミ小僧が!!
THAT'S NOT WHAT I ASKED!
GCK
KAZUKI!
STOP LOOKING AT IT!
IT'S THE DEVIL'S TRAP!
CHOMP
CHOMP
HE'S TESTING YOU!
DEMON OF CONSUMPTION
YOU MUST PERSEVERE... ...TO MAKE IT THROUGH OUR FASTING.
THINK OF OUR JOINT VENTURE IN THE UPCOMING COMIC PARTY!
ONCE... JUST ONCE I WANT A SUNNY COMIC PARTY.
YUU.
OH...
そこまでオレと夏こみを……
YOU'RE LOOKING FORWARD TO THE SUMMER COMIC PARTY WITH ME THAT MUCH?

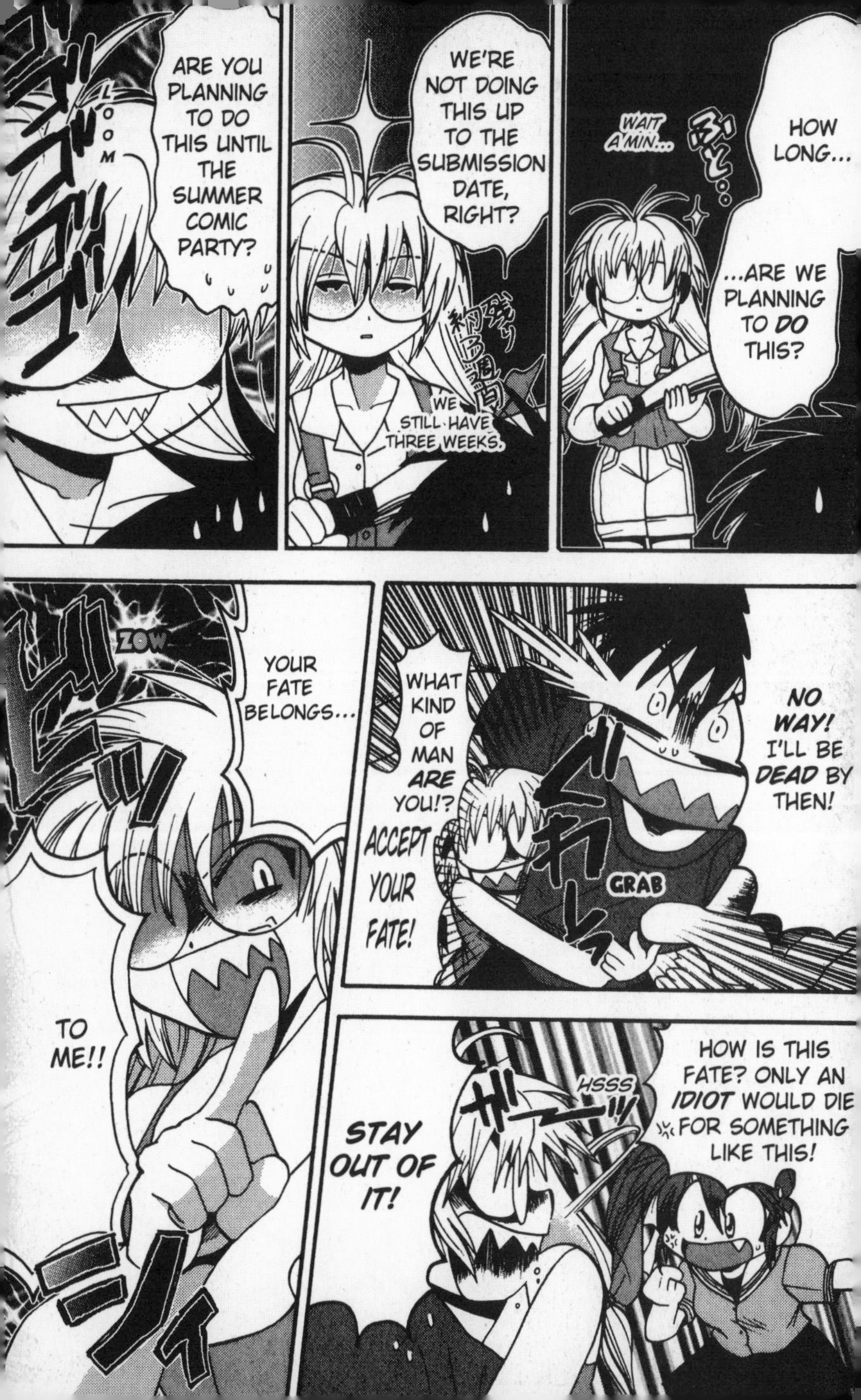
HOW LONG...
WAIT A MIN...
...ARE WE PLANNING TO DO THIS?
WE'RE NOT DOING THIS UP TO THE SUBMISSION DATE, RIGHT?
WE STILL HAVE THREE WEEKS.
ARE YOU PLANNING TO DO THIS UNTIL THE SUMMER COMIC PARTY?
LOOM
NO WAY! I'LL BE DEAD BY THEN!
WHAT KIND OF MAN ARE YOU!?
ACCEPT YOUR FATE!
GRAB
HOW IS THIS FATE? ONLY AN IDIOT WOULD DIE FOR SOMETHING LIKE THIS!
HSSS
STAY OUT OF IT!
ZOW
YOUR FATE BELONGS...
TO ME!!

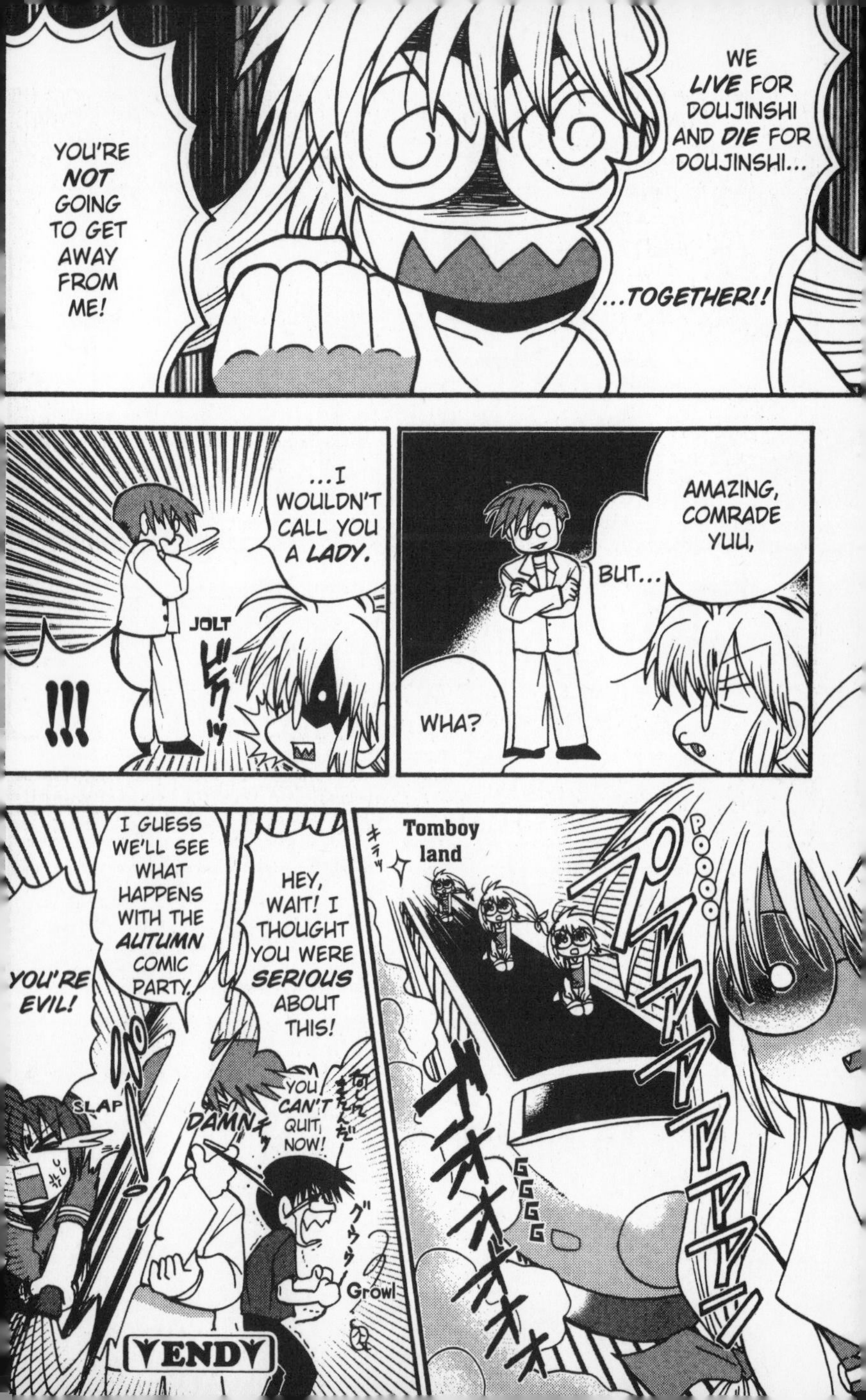
WE LIVE FOR DOUJINSHI AND DIE FOR DOUJINSHI...
...TOGETHER!!
YOU'RE NOT GOING TO GET AWAY FROM ME!
AMAZING, COMRADE YUU,
BUT...
WHA?
...I WOULDN'T CALL YOU A LADY.
JOLT
!!!
Tomboy land
POOOO
GGGG
HEY, WAIT! I THOUGHT YOU WERE SERIOUS ABOUT THIS!
I GUESS WE'LL SEE WHAT HAPPENS WITH THE AUTUMN COMIC PARTY.
YOU'RE EVIL!
SLAP
DAMN
YOU CAN'T QUIT NOW!
Growl
END

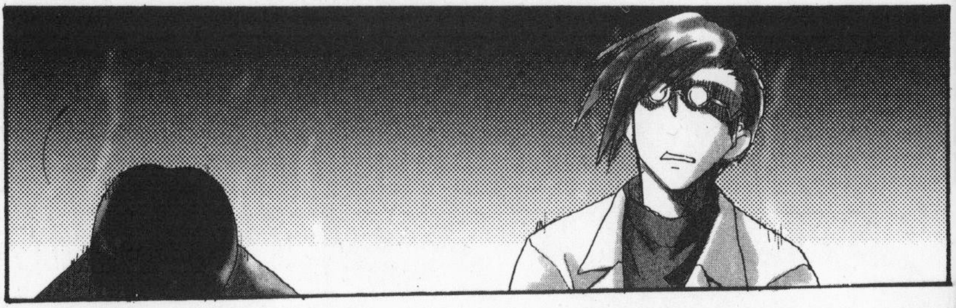

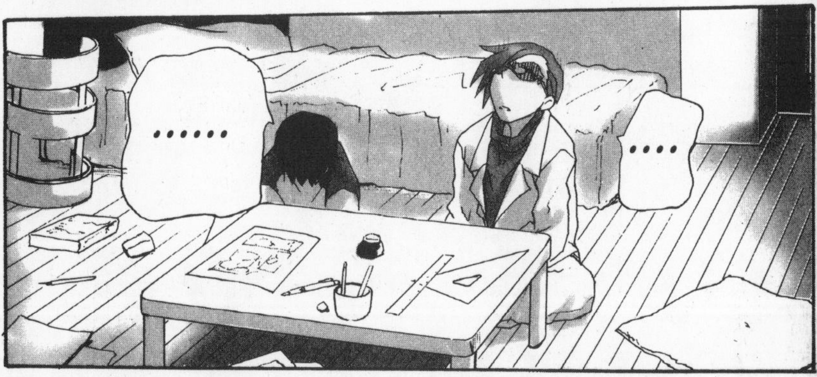
....
......

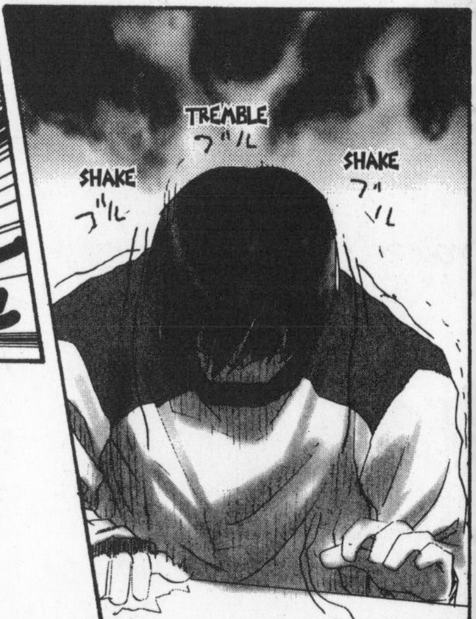
TREMBLE
ブル
SHAKE
ブル
SHAKE
ブル

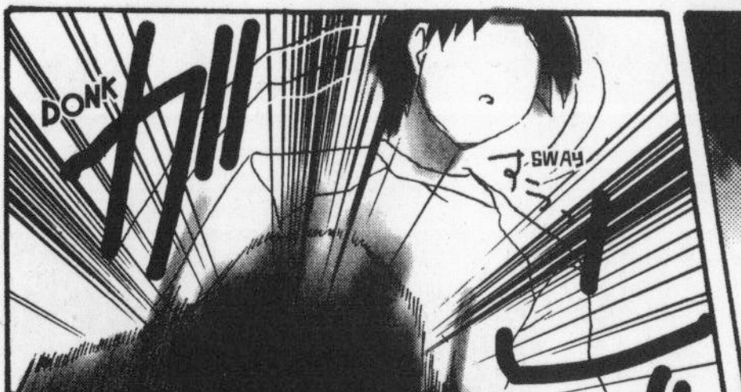
DONK
ガッ
SWAY

妙にリアルなお話
STRANGELY REALISTIC

むねきち
MUNEKICHI

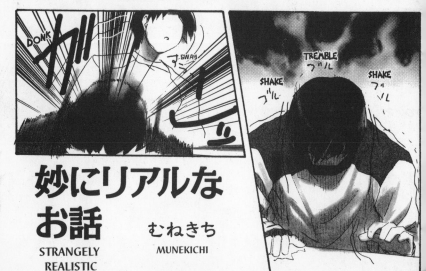

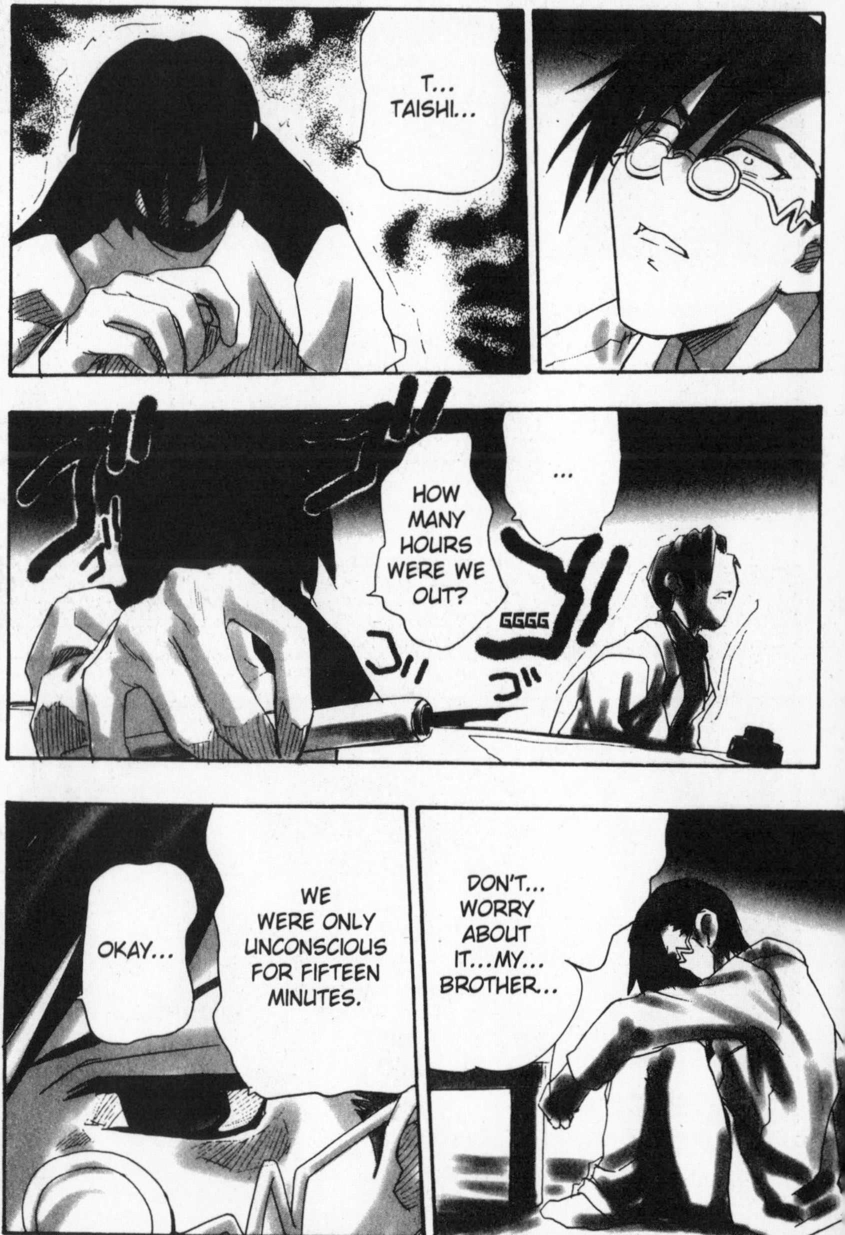
T... TAISHI...
...
HOW MANY HOURS WERE WE OUT?
GGGG
DON'T... WORRY ABOUT IT...MY... BROTHER...
WE WERE ONLY UNCONSCIOUS FOR FIFTEEN MINUTES.
OKAY...

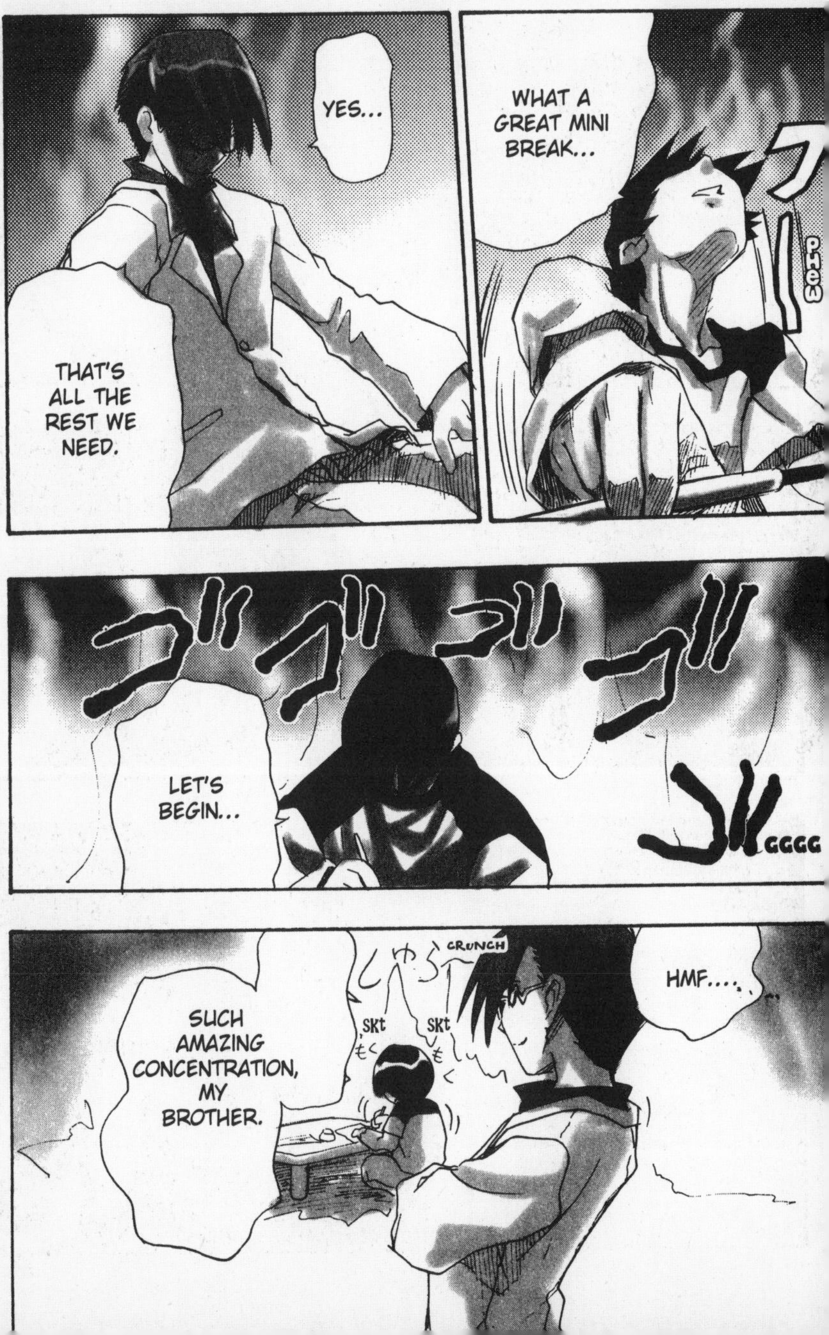
WHAT A GREAT MINI BREAK...
PHEW
YES...
THAT'S ALL THE REST WE NEED.
LET'S BEGIN...
GGGG
HMF....
CRUNCH
SKT
SKT
SUCH AMAZING CONCENTRATION, MY BROTHER.

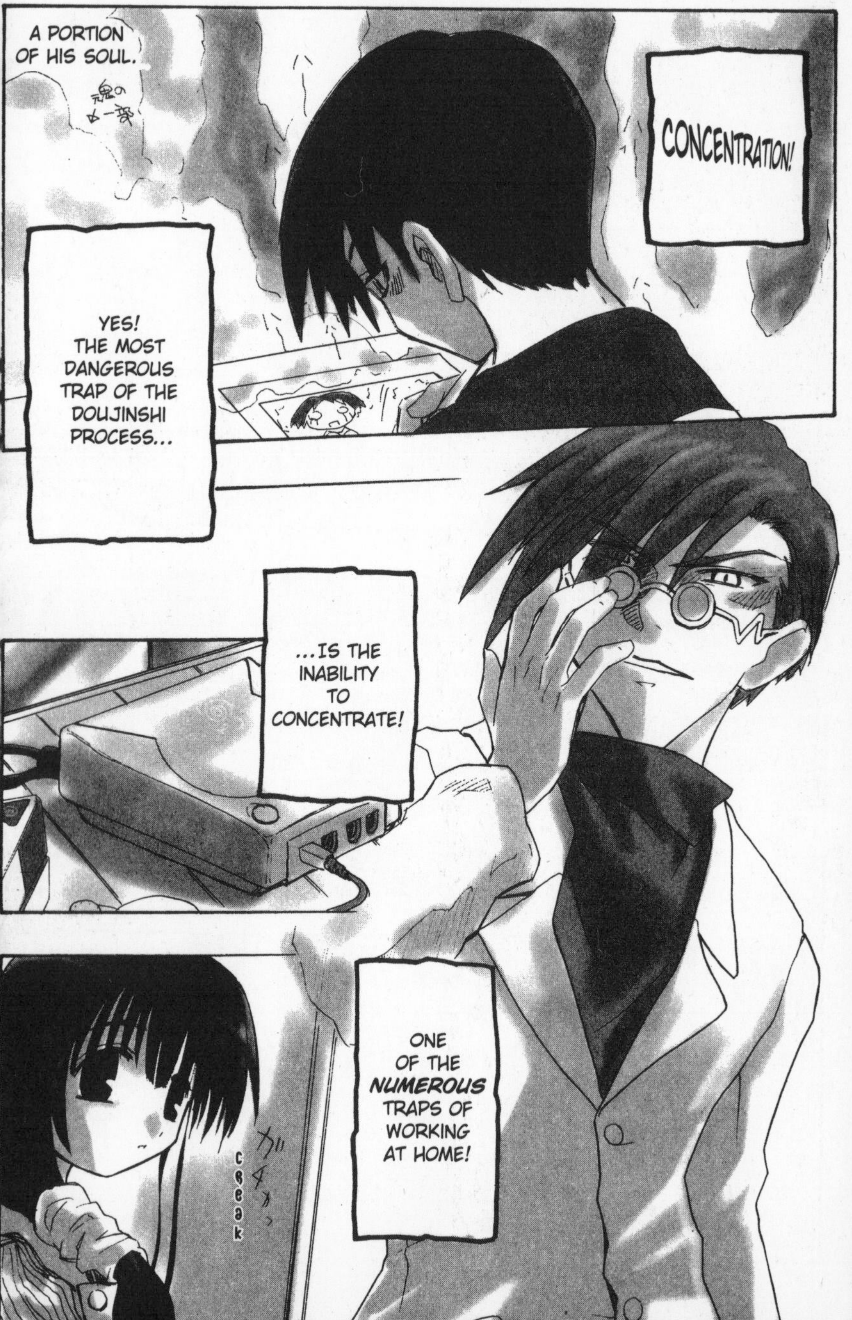
CONCENTRATION!
A PORTION OF HIS SOUL.
魂の一部
YES! THE MOST DANGEROUS TRAP OF THE DOUJINSHI PROCESS...
...IS THE INABILITY TO CONCENTRATE!
ONE OF THE ***NUMEROUS*** TRAPS OF WORKING AT HOME!
creak

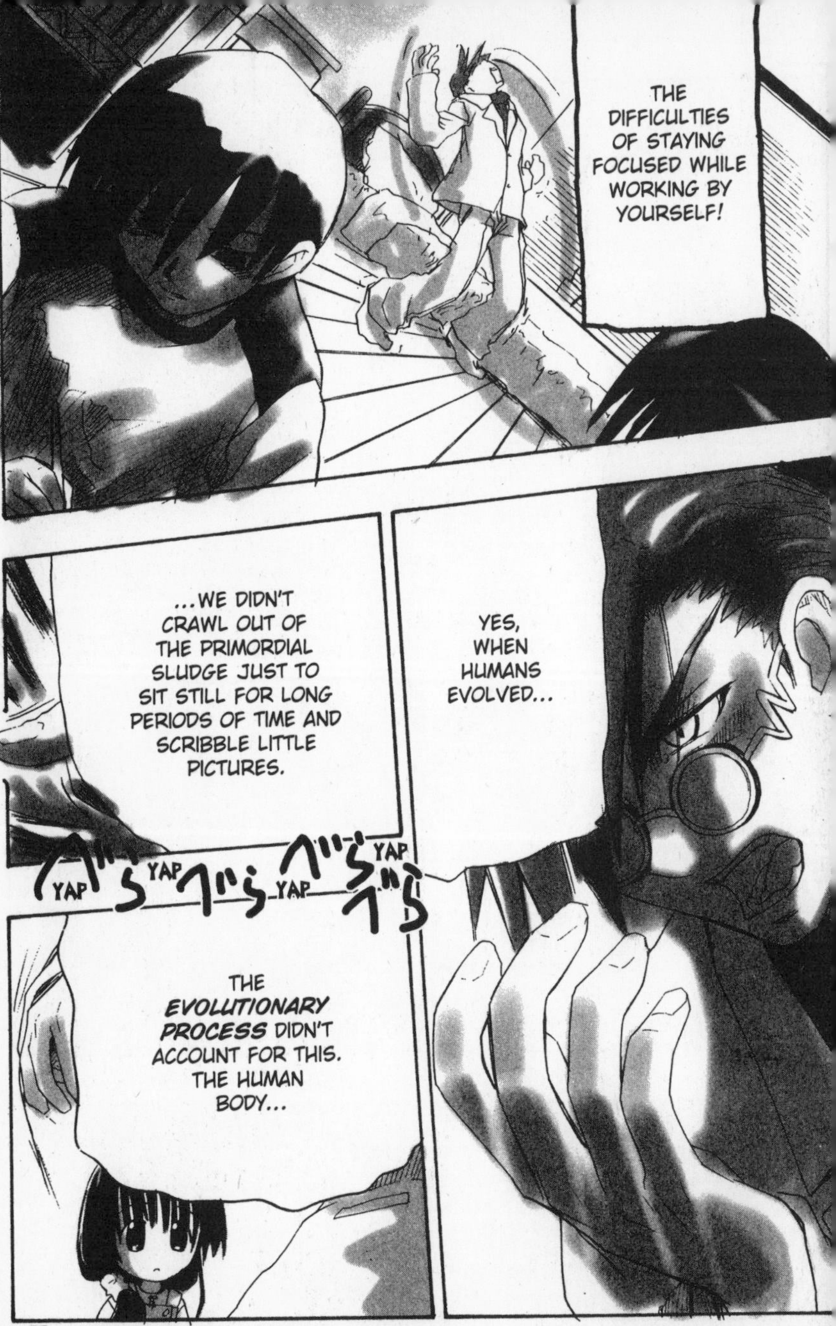
THE DIFFICULTIES OF STAYING FOCUSED WHILE WORKING BY YOURSELF!
YES, WHEN HUMANS EVOLVED...
...WE DIDN'T CRAWL OUT OF THE PRIMORDIAL SLUDGE JUST TO SIT STILL FOR LONG PERIODS OF TIME AND SCRIBBLE LITTLE PICTURES.
YAP YAP YAP YAP
THE *EVOLUTIONARY PROCESS* DIDN'T ACCOUNT FOR THIS. THE HUMAN BODY...

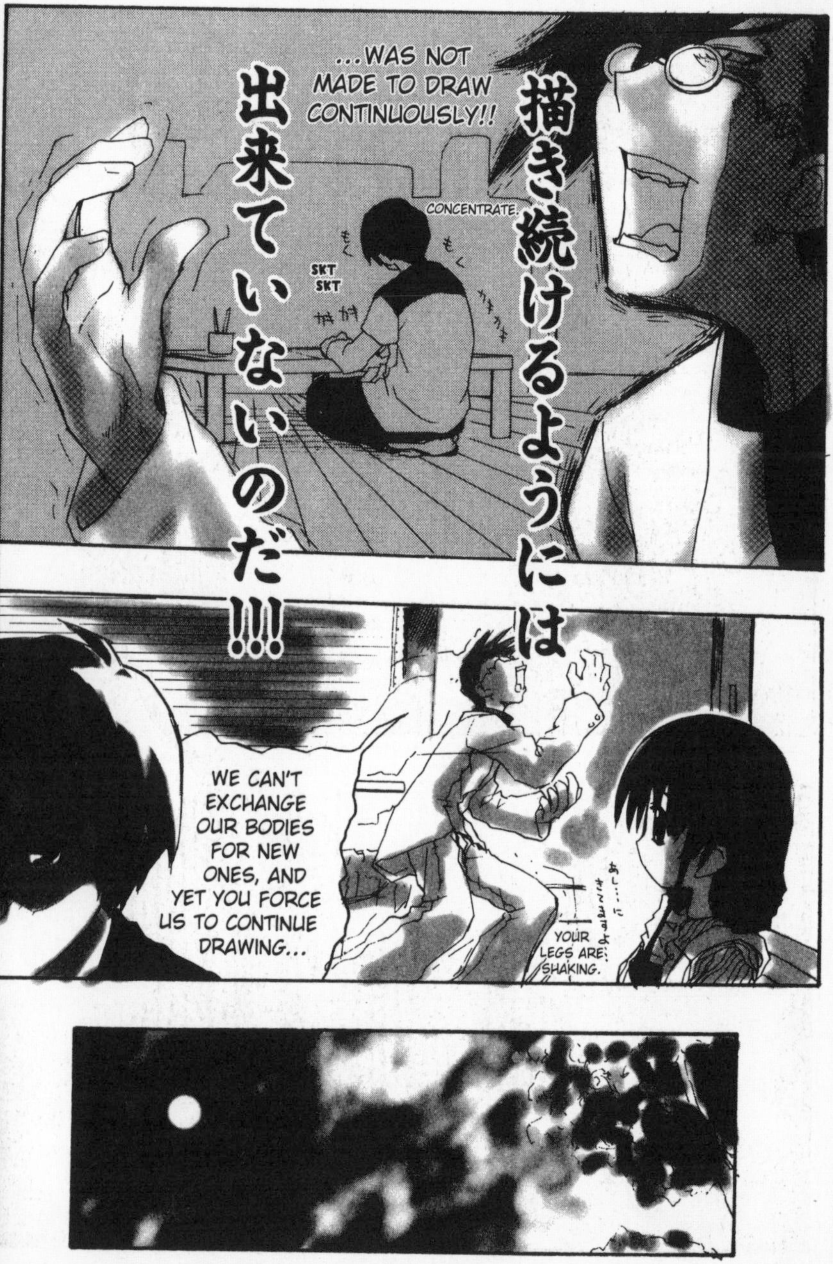
描き続けるようには
出来ていないのだ!!!
...WAS NOT MADE TO DRAW CONTINUOUSLY!!
CONCENTRATE.
もく もく
SKT SKT
WE CAN'T EXCHANGE OUR BODIES FOR NEW ONES, AND YET YOU FORCE US TO CONTINUE DRAWING...
あし…に きてますよ
YOUR LEGS ARE SHAKING.

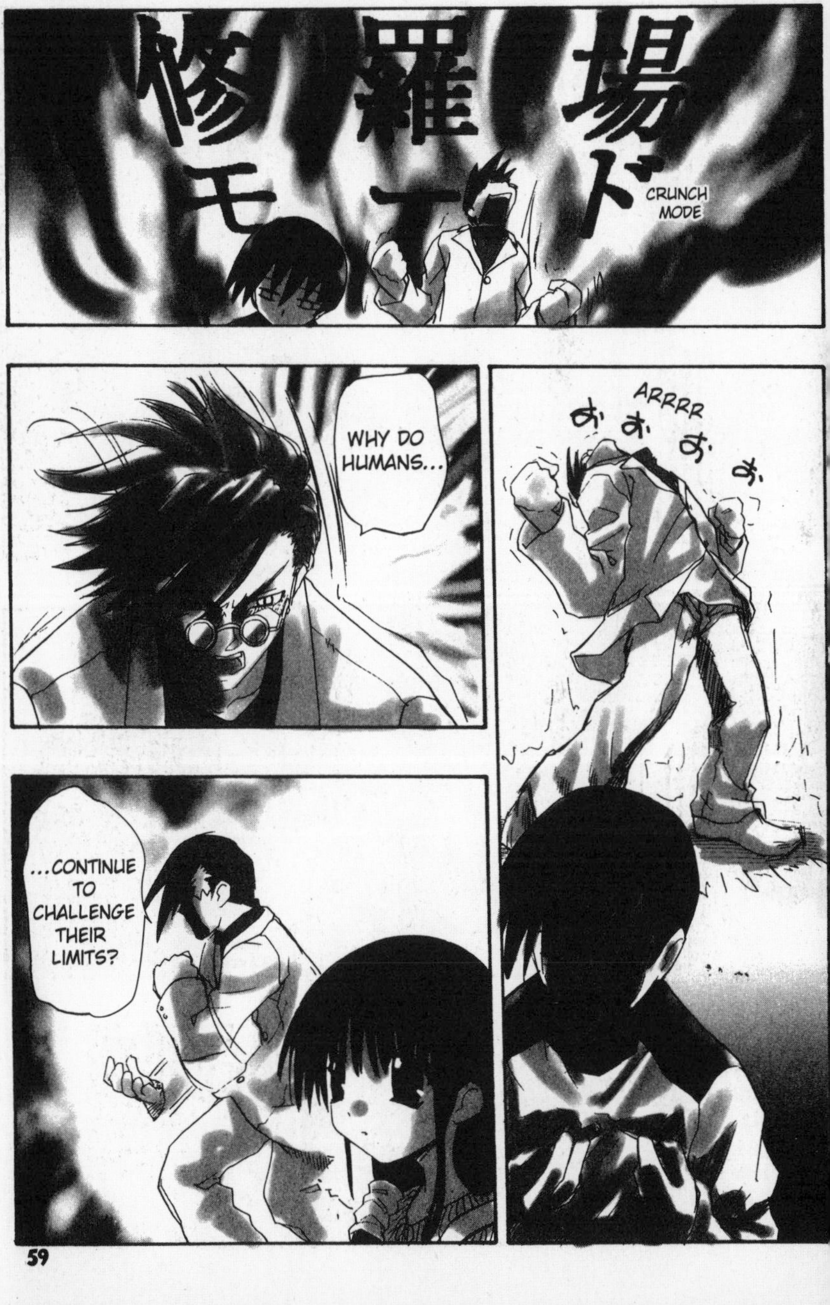
修羅場モード
CRUNCH MODE
ARRRR
おおおお
WHY DO HUMANS...
...CONTINUE TO CHALLENGE THEIR LIMITS?

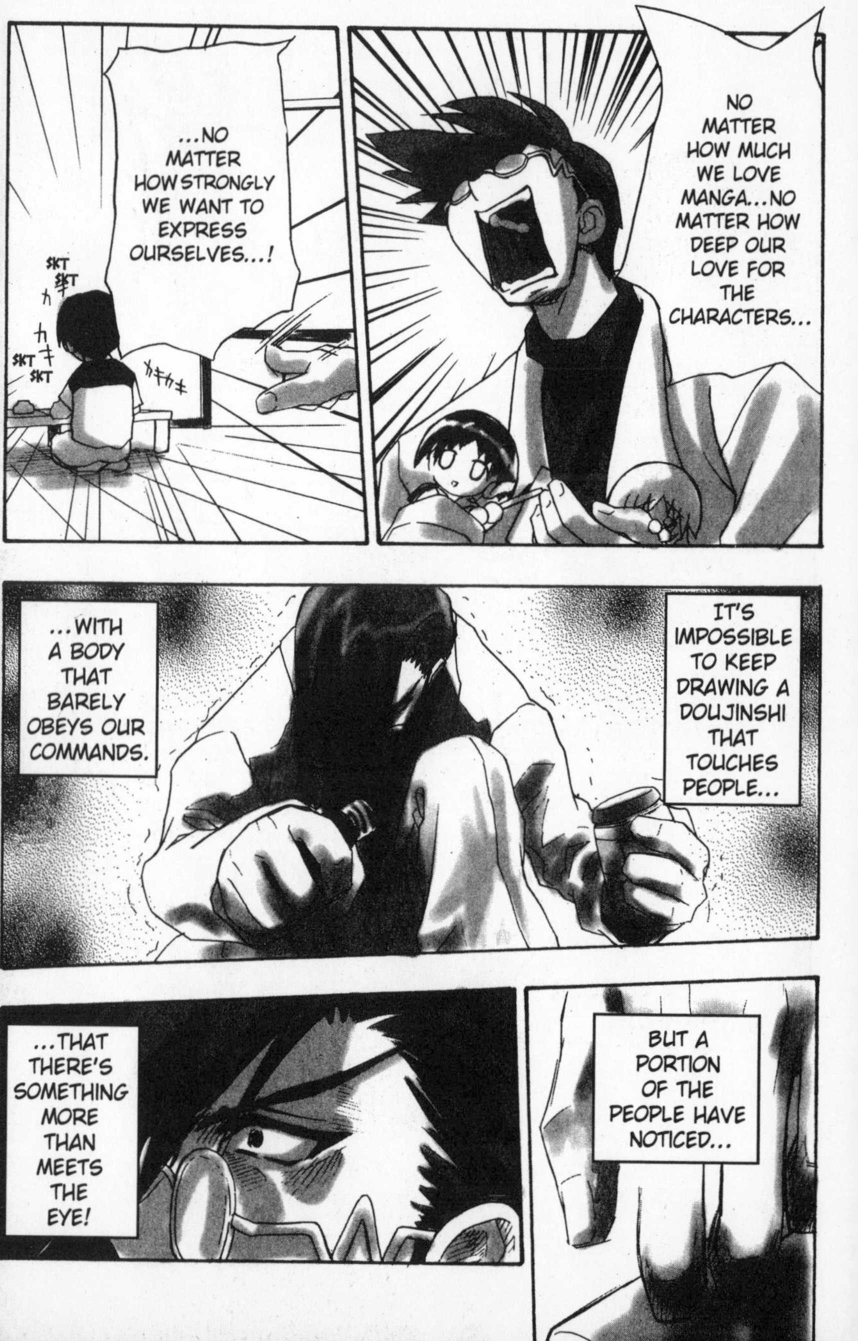

NO MATTER HOW MUCH WE LOVE MANGA...NO MATTER HOW DEEP OUR LOVE FOR THE CHARACTERS...
...NO MATTER HOW STRONGLY WE WANT TO EXPRESS OURSELVES...!
SKT SKT
SKT SKT
IT'S IMPOSSIBLE TO KEEP DRAWING A DOUJINSHI THAT TOUCHES PEOPLE...
...WITH A BODY THAT BARELY OBEYS OUR COMMANDS.
BUT A PORTION OF THE PEOPLE HAVE NOTICED...
...THAT THERE'S SOMETHING MORE THAN MEETS THE EYE!

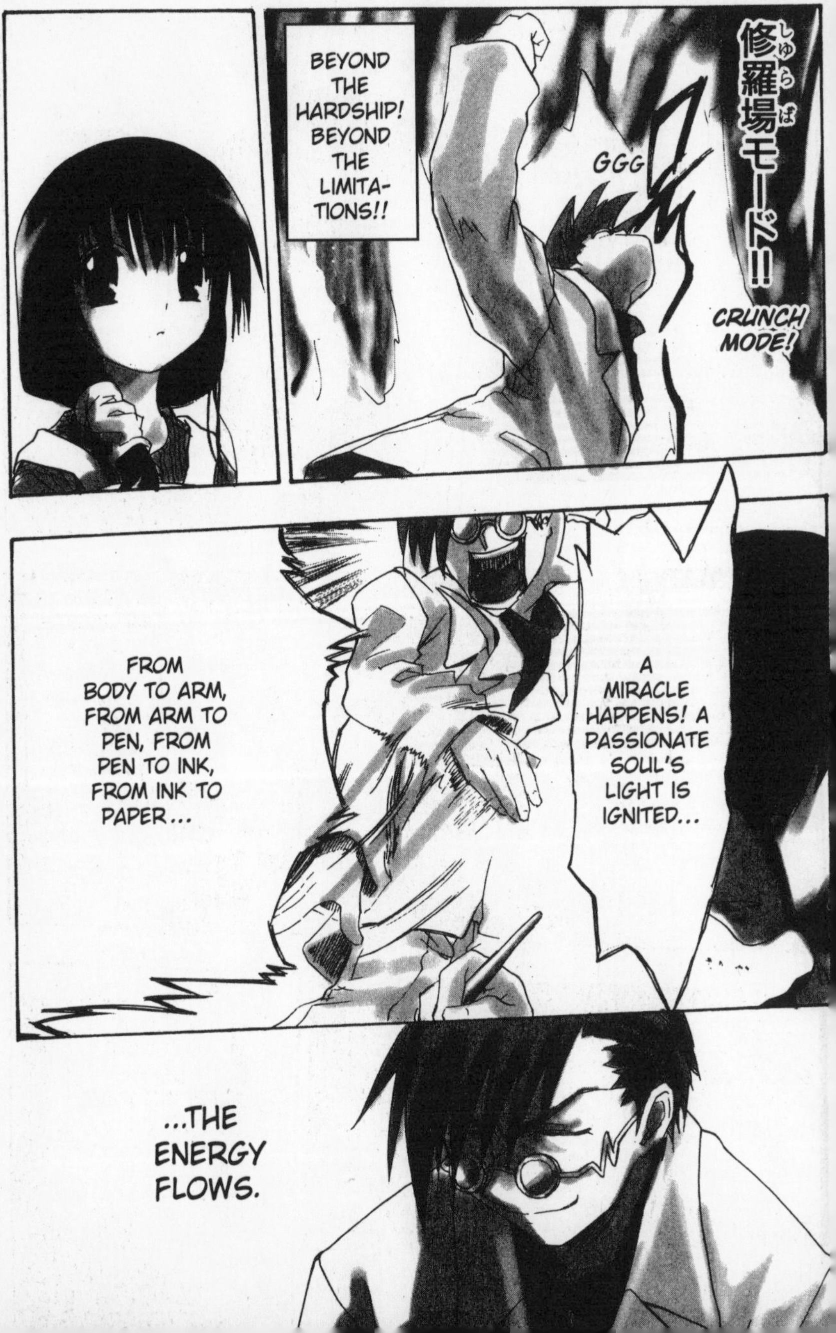
修羅場モード!!
CRUNCH MODE!
BEYOND THE HARDSHIP! BEYOND THE LIMITATIONS!!
GGG
A MIRACLE HAPPENS! A PASSIONATE SOUL'S LIGHT IS IGNITED...
FROM BODY TO ARM, FROM ARM TO PEN, FROM PEN TO INK, FROM INK TO PAPER...
...THE ENERGY FLOWS.

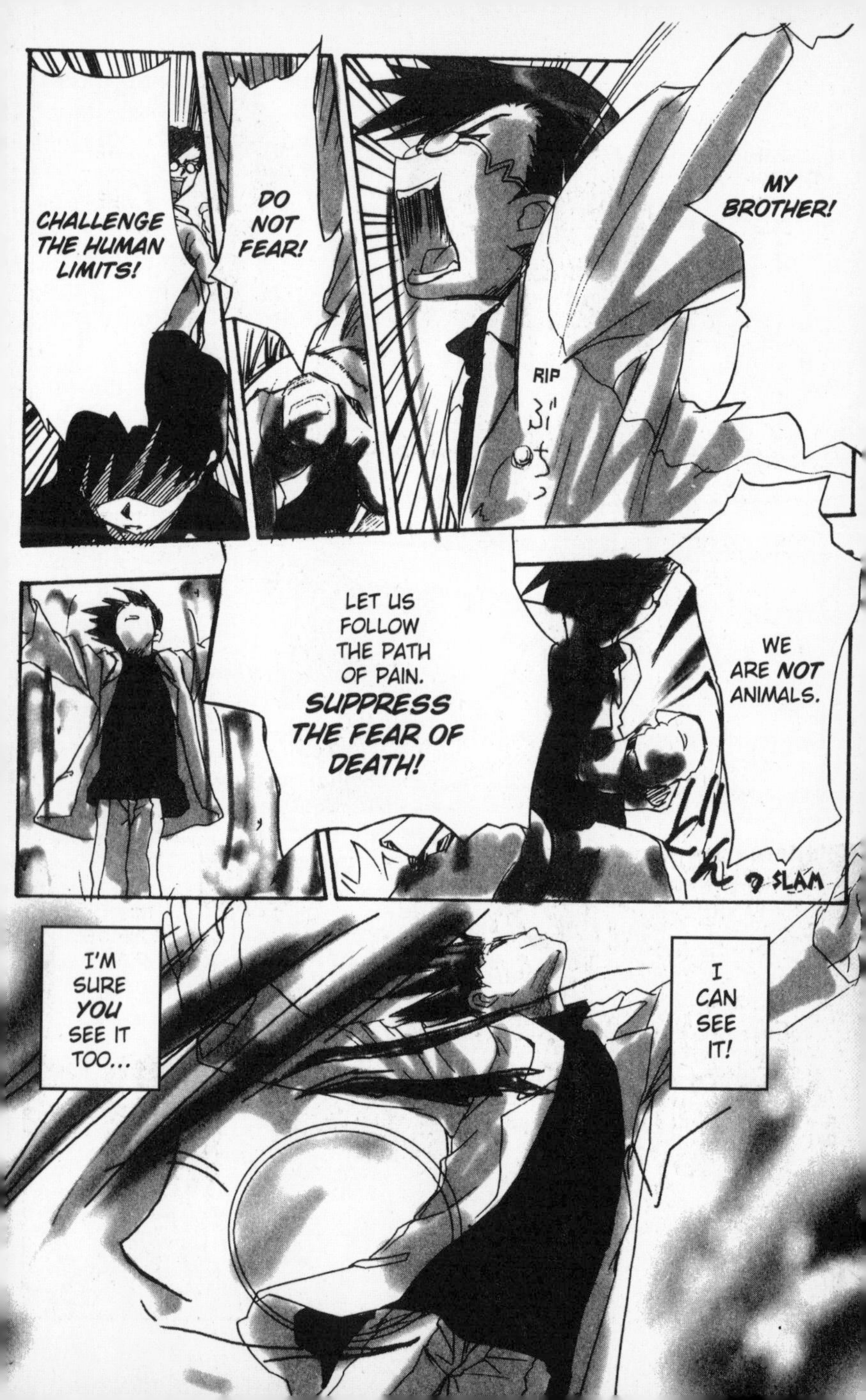
MY BROTHER!
RIP
DO NOT FEAR!
CHALLENGE THE HUMAN LIMITS!
WE ARE NOT ANIMALS.
SLAM
LET US FOLLOW THE PATH OF PAIN. SUPPRESS THE FEAR OF DEATH!
I CAN SEE IT!
I'M SURE YOU SEE IT TOO...

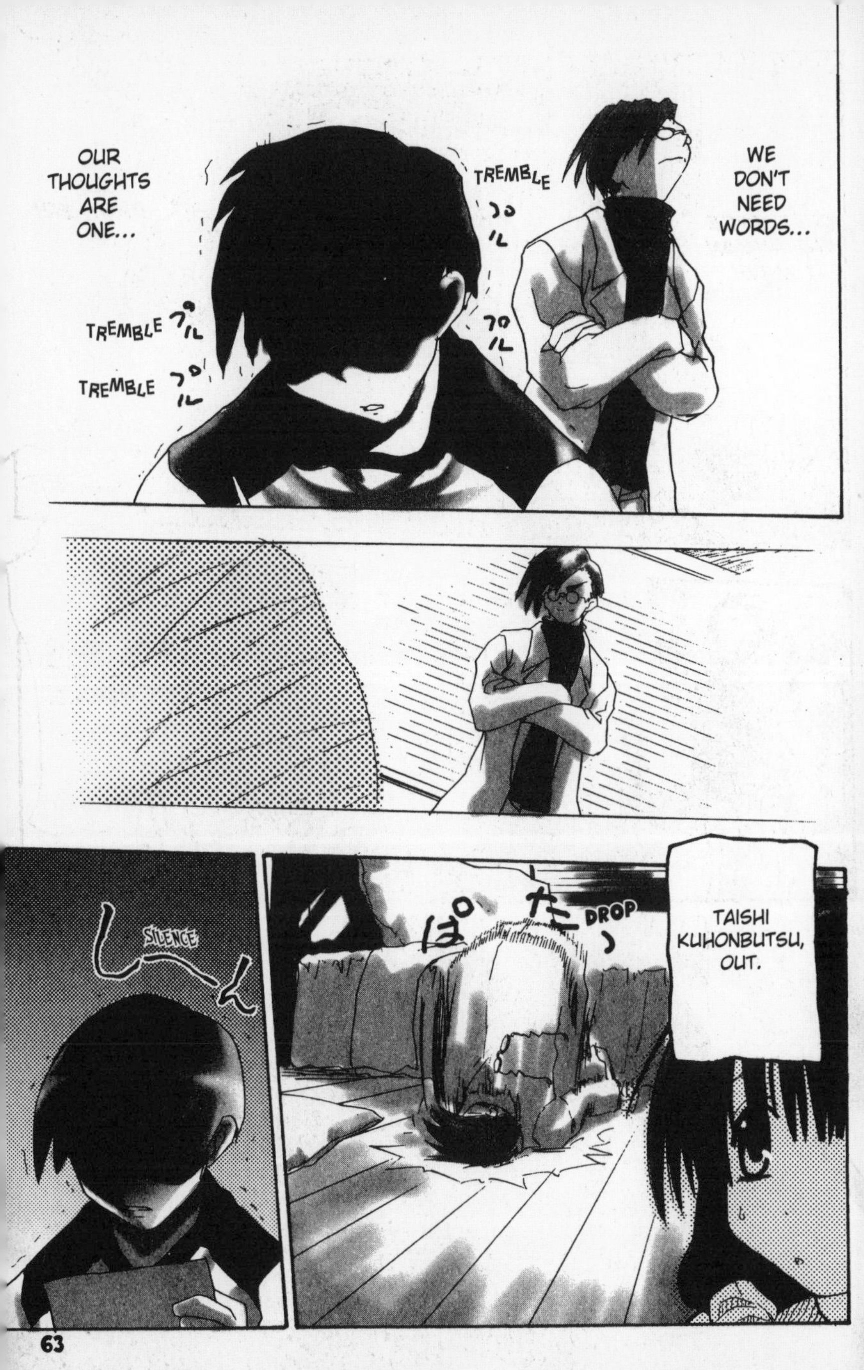
WE DON'T NEED WORDS...
TREMBLE
プル
OUR THOUGHTS ARE ONE...
プル
TREMBLE
プル
TREMBLE
プル
TREMBLE
TAISHI KUHONBUTSU, OUT.
ぱた
DROP
しーん
SILENCE

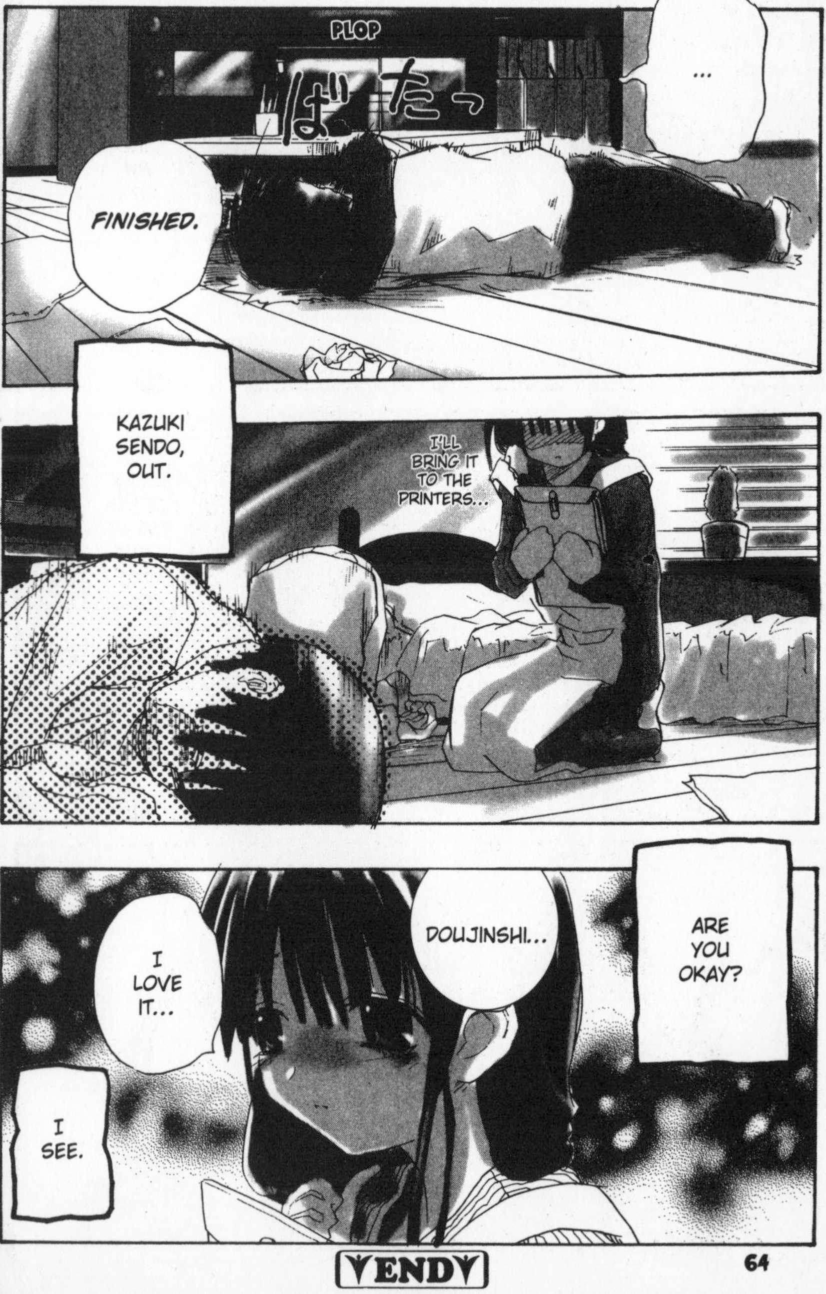
...
PLOP
ばたっ
FINISHED.
I'LL BRING IT TO THE PRINTERS...
KAZUKI SENDO, OUT.
ARE YOU OKAY?
DOUJINSHI...
I LOVE IT...
I SEE.

END

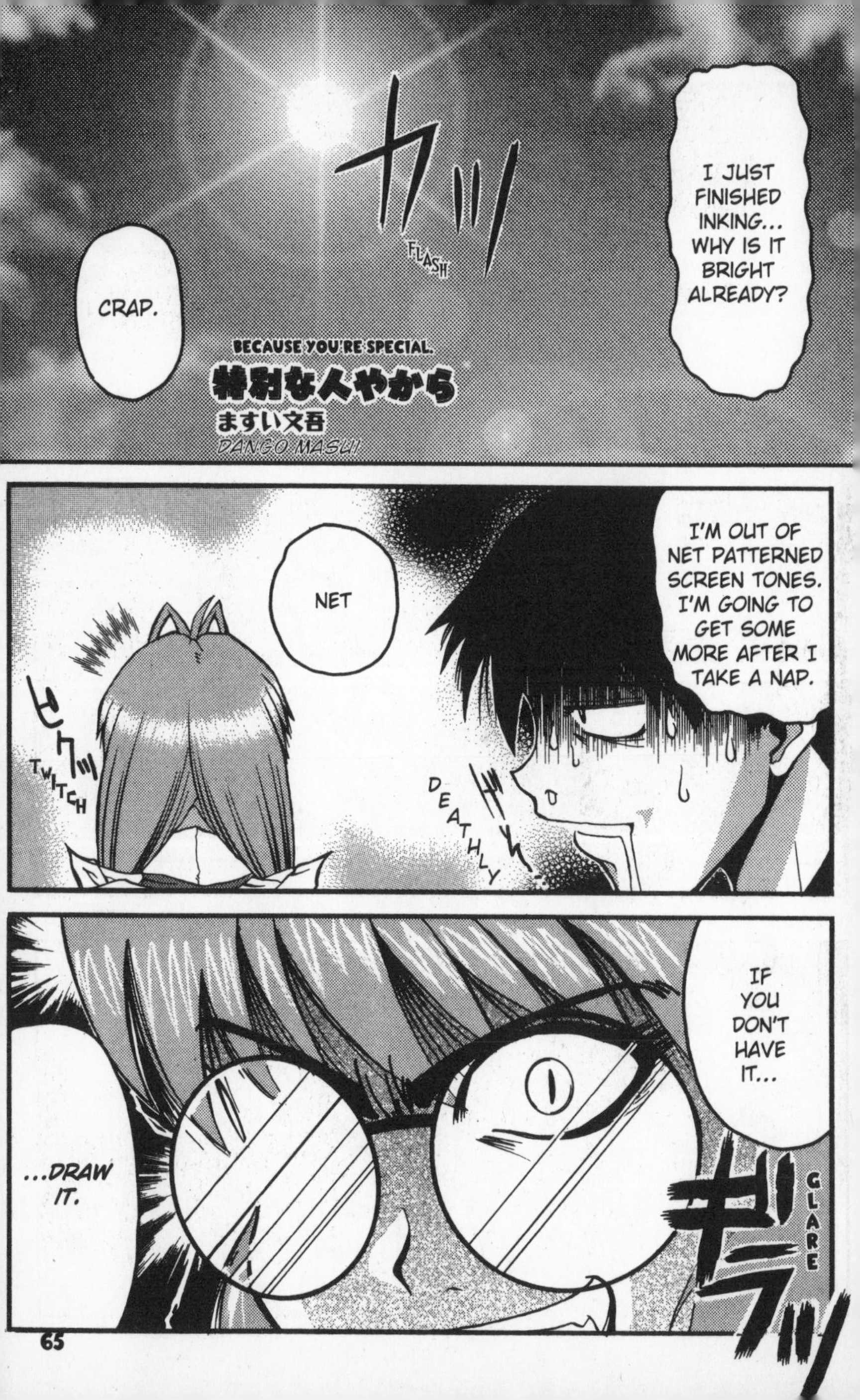

I JUST FINISHED INKING... WHY IS IT BRIGHT ALREADY?
カッ
FLASH
CRAP.
BECAUSE YOU'RE SPECIAL.
特別な人やから
ますい文吾
DANGO MASUI
I'M OUT OF NET PATTERNED SCREEN TONES. I'M GOING TO GET SOME MORE AFTER I TAKE A NAP.
NET
DEATHLY
ヒクッ
TWITCH
IF YOU DON'T HAVE IT...
ギラッ
GLARE
...DRAW IT.

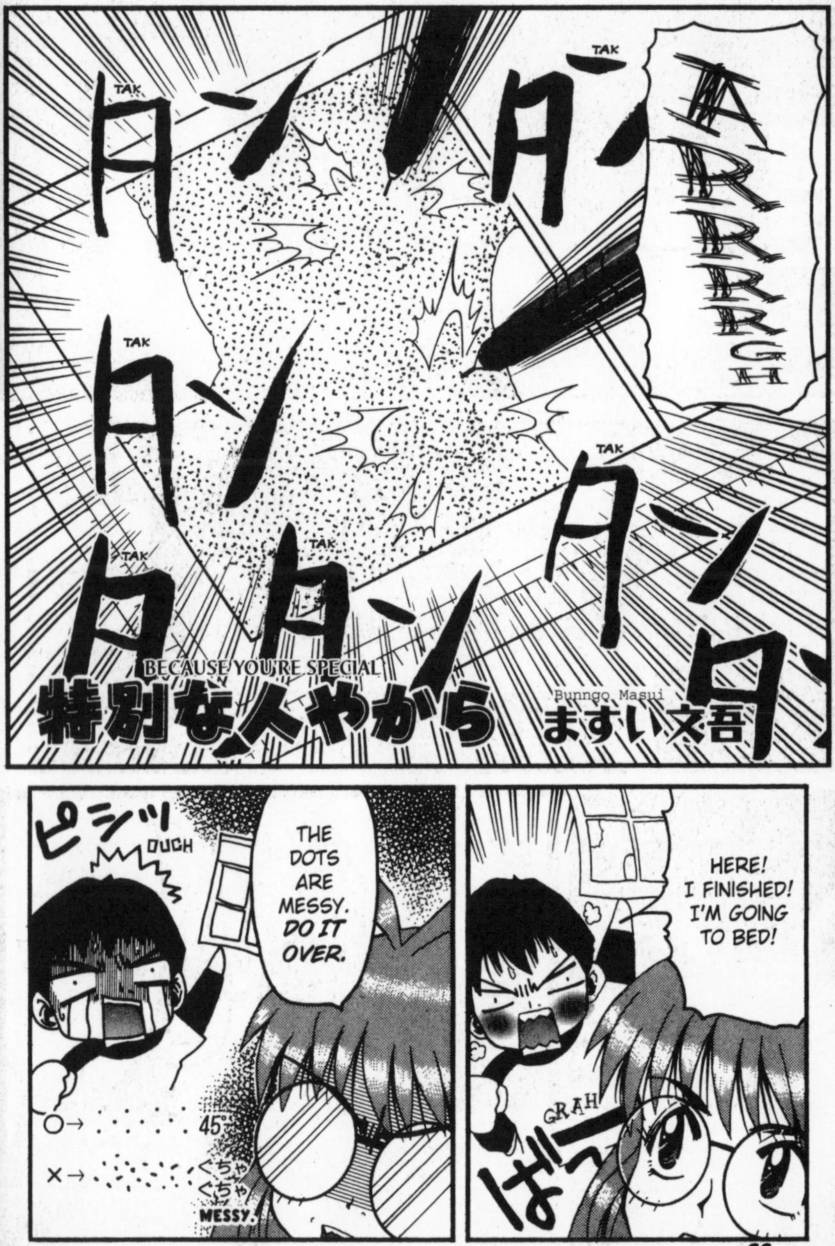
ARRRRRGH
TAK
TAK
TAK
TAK
TAK
TAK
BECAUSE YOU'RE SPECIAL
特別な人やから
Bunngo Masui
ますい文吾
HERE! I FINISHED! I'M GOING TO BED!
GRAH
ピシッ
OUCH
THE DOTS ARE MESSY. DO IT OVER.
○→
45°
×→
くちゃくちゃ
MESSY.

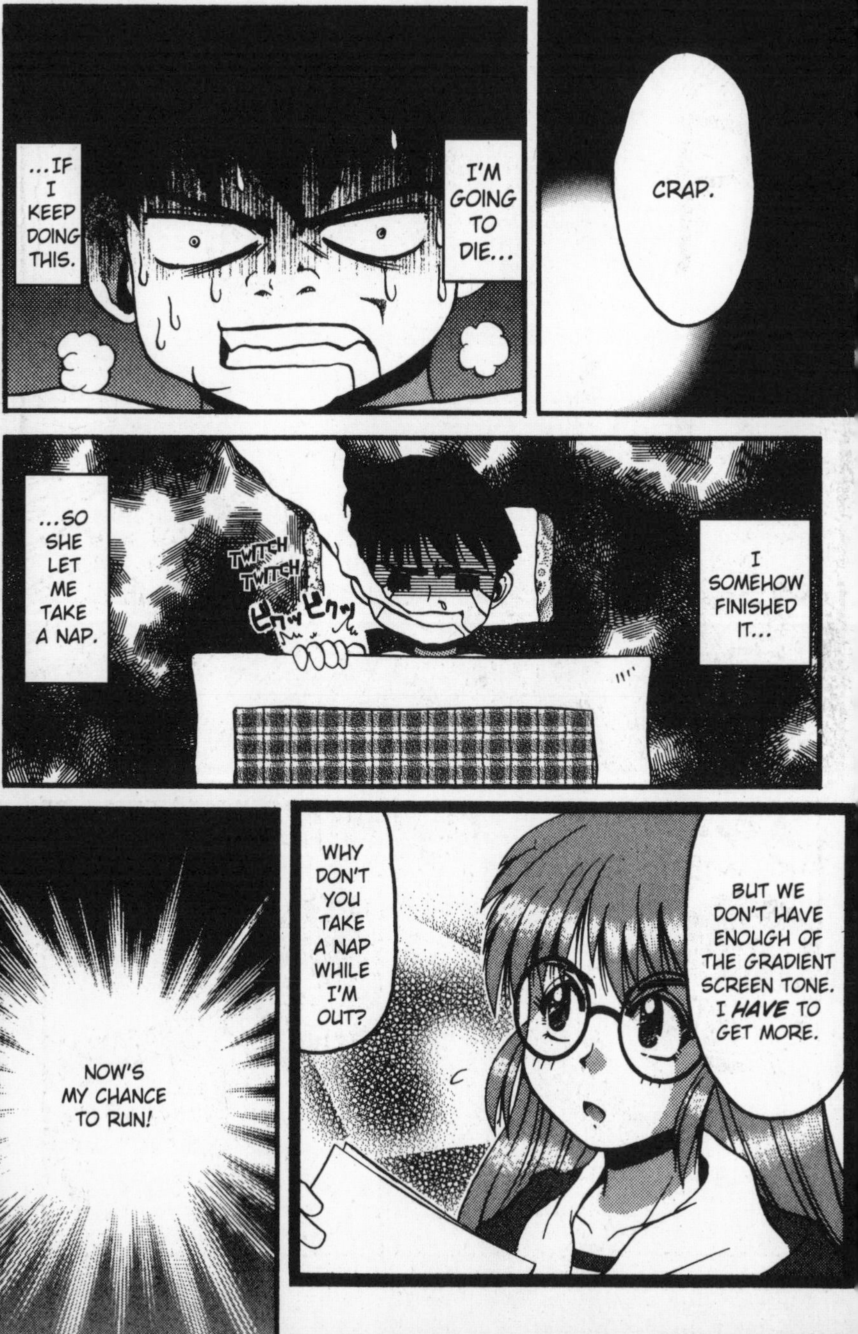
CRAP.
I'M GOING TO DIE...
...IF I KEEP DOING THIS.
I SOMEHOW FINISHED IT...
TWITCH TWITCH
ピクッピクッ
...SO SHE LET ME TAKE A NAP.
BUT WE DON'T HAVE ENOUGH OF THE GRADIENT SCREEN TONE. I *HAVE* TO GET MORE.
WHY DON'T YOU TAKE A NAP WHILE I'M OUT?
NOW'S MY CHANCE TO RUN!

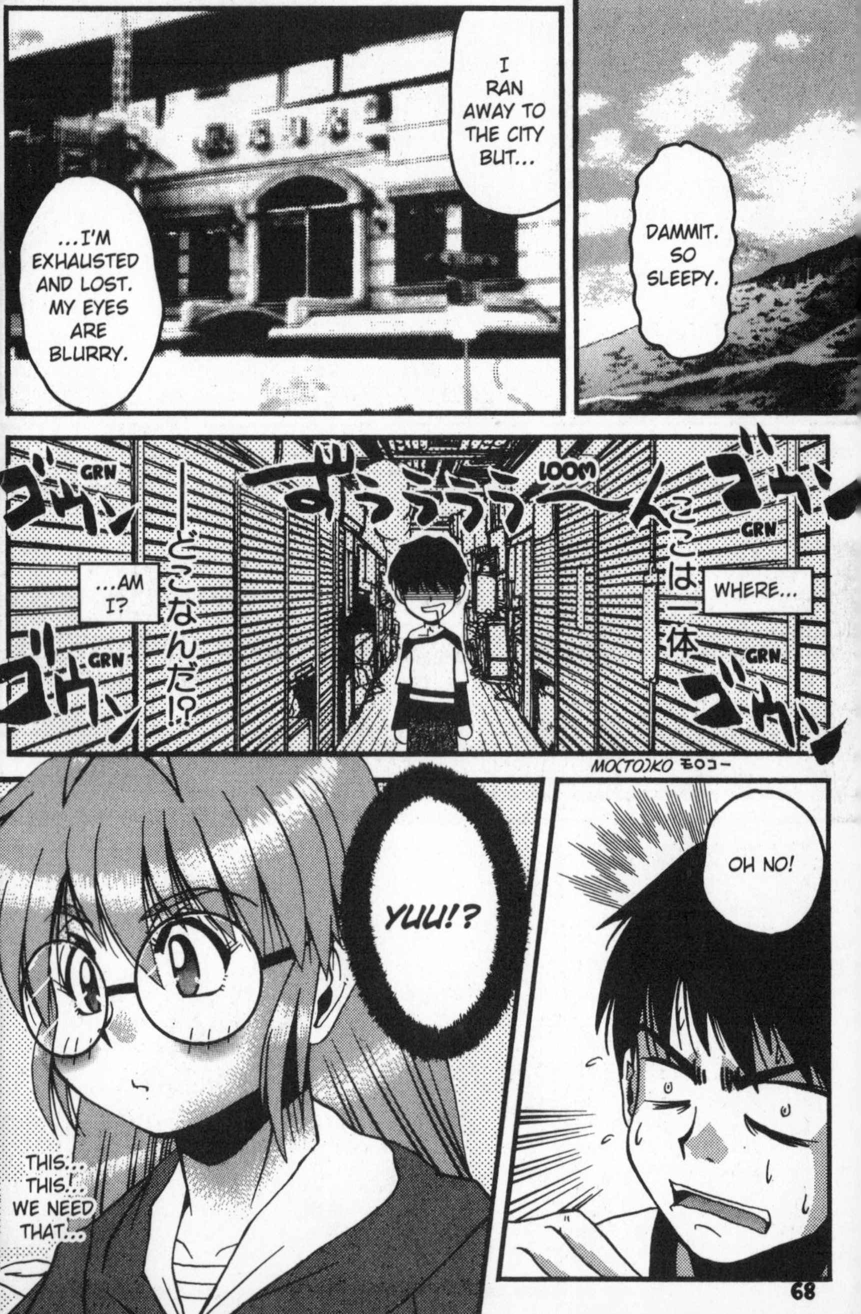
DAMMIT. SO SLEEPY.
I RAN AWAY TO THE CITY BUT...
...I'M EXHAUSTED AND LOST. MY EYES ARE BLURRY.
GRN
LOOM
GRN
ここは一体
WHERE...
どこなんだ!?
...AM I?
GRN
GRN
MO(TO)KO モロコー
OH NO!
YUU!?
THIS... THIS!.. WE NEED THAT...

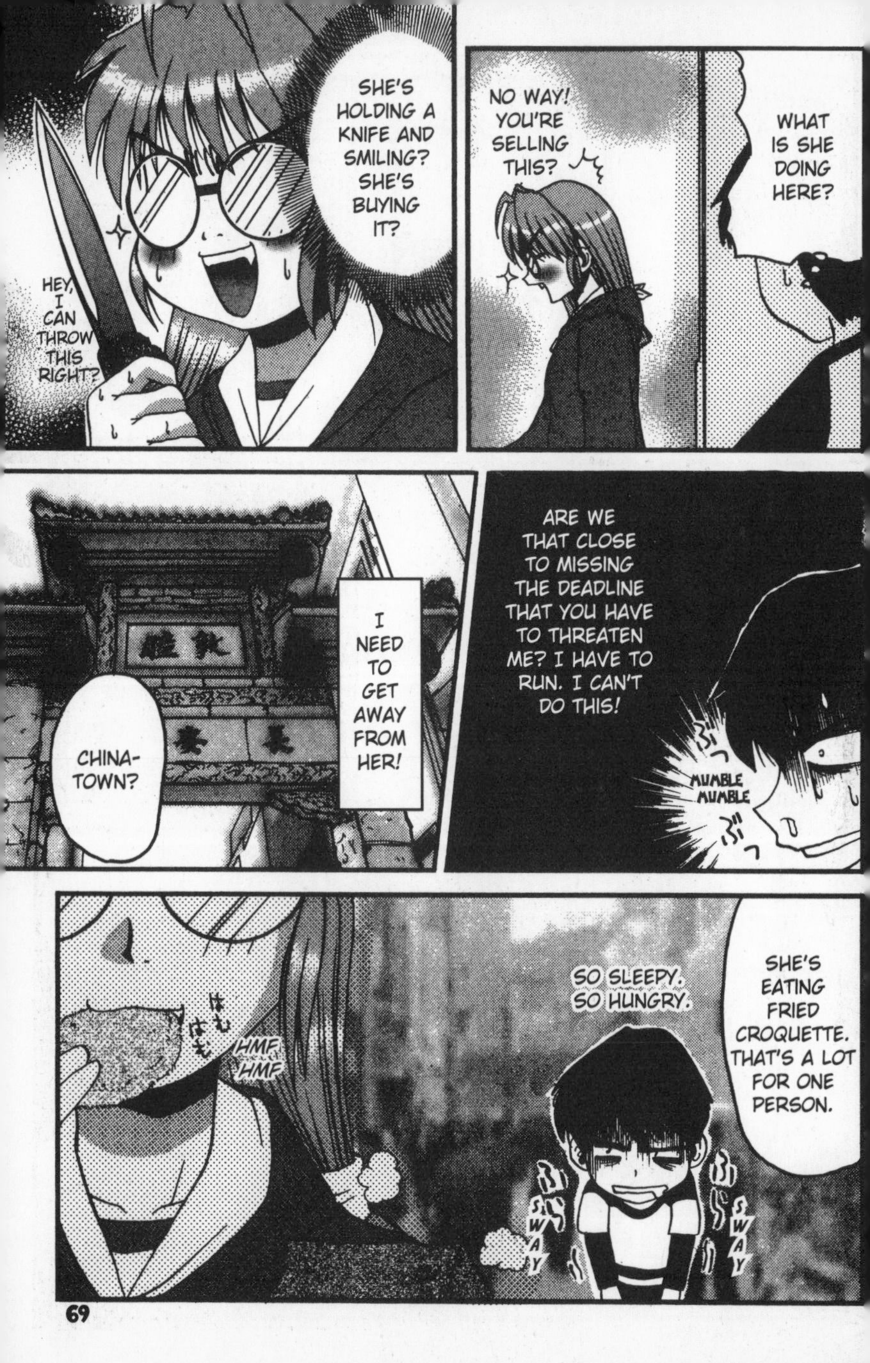
WHAT IS SHE DOING HERE?
NO WAY! YOU'RE SELLING THIS?
SHE'S HOLDING A KNIFE AND SMILING? SHE'S BUYING IT?
HEY, I CAN THROW THIS RIGHT?
ARE WE THAT CLOSE TO MISSING THE DEADLINE THAT YOU HAVE TO THREATEN ME? I HAVE TO RUN. I CAN'T DO THIS!
ぶつ
MUMBLE MUMBLE
ぶつ
I NEED TO GET AWAY FROM HER!
CHINA-TOWN?
SHE'S EATING FRIED CROQUETTE. THAT'S A LOT FOR ONE PERSON.
SO SLEEPY. SO HUNGRY.
SWAY
SWAY
はむ はむ
HMF HMF

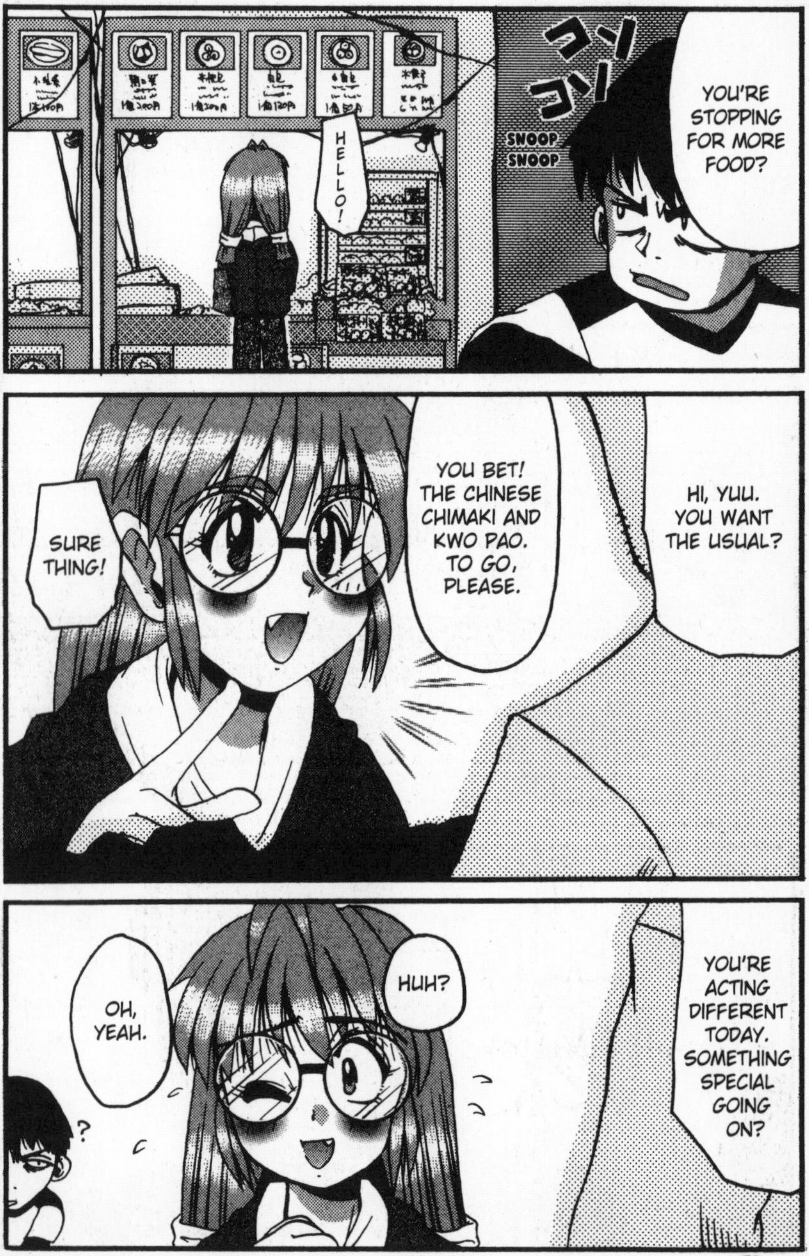
SNOOP SNOOP
YOU'RE STOPPING FOR MORE FOOD?
HELLO!
HI, YUU. YOU WANT THE USUAL?
YOU BET! THE CHINESE CHIMAKI AND KWO PAO. TO GO, PLEASE.
SURE THING!
YOU'RE ACTING DIFFERENT TODAY. SOMETHING SPECIAL GOING ON?
HUH?
OH, YEAH.
?

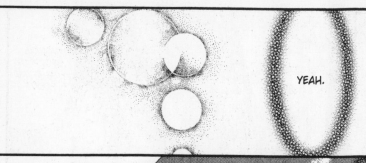

YEAH.

SOMEONE *SPECIAL*...

...IS VISITING ME.

HUH?

YOU...

I HAD NO *IDEA,* AND I...

YUU...

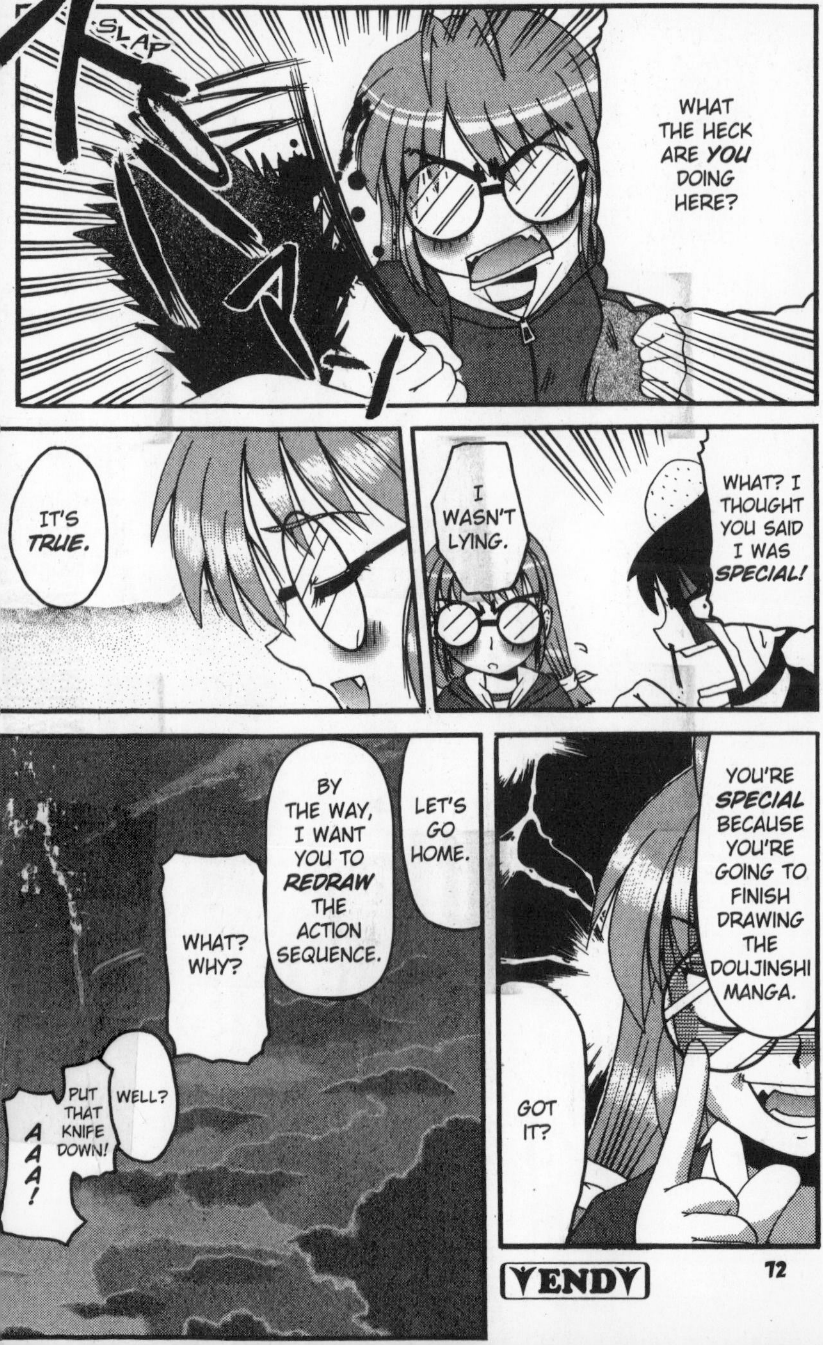
SLAP
WHAT THE HECK ARE YOU DOING HERE?
WHAT? I THOUGHT YOU SAID I WAS SPECIAL!
I WASN'T LYING.
IT'S TRUE.
YOU'RE SPECIAL BECAUSE YOU'RE GOING TO FINISH DRAWING THE DOUJINSHI MANGA.
GOT IT?
LET'S GO HOME.
BY THE WAY, I WANT YOU TO REDRAW THE ACTION SEQUENCE.
WHAT? WHY?
WELL?
PUT THAT KNIFE DOWN!
AAAA!
END

LIKE THE SUN'S RAYS.

ひだまりのように

中島 初美

Hatsumi Nakashima

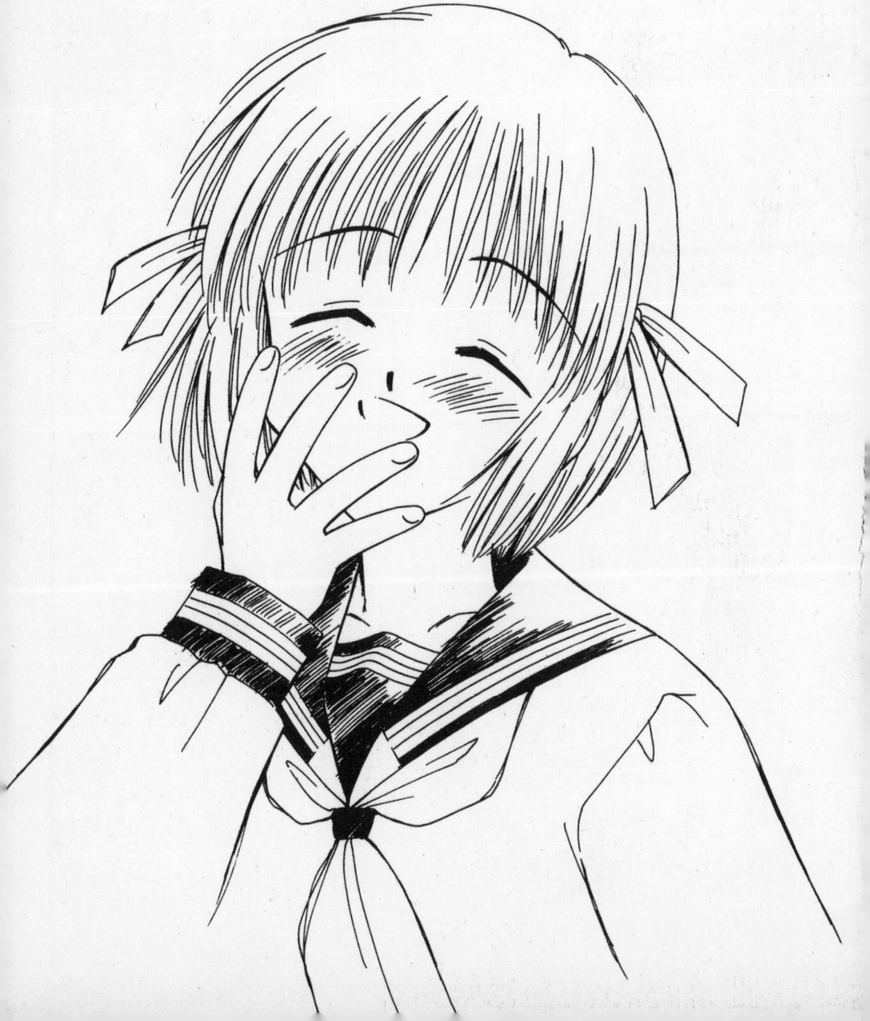

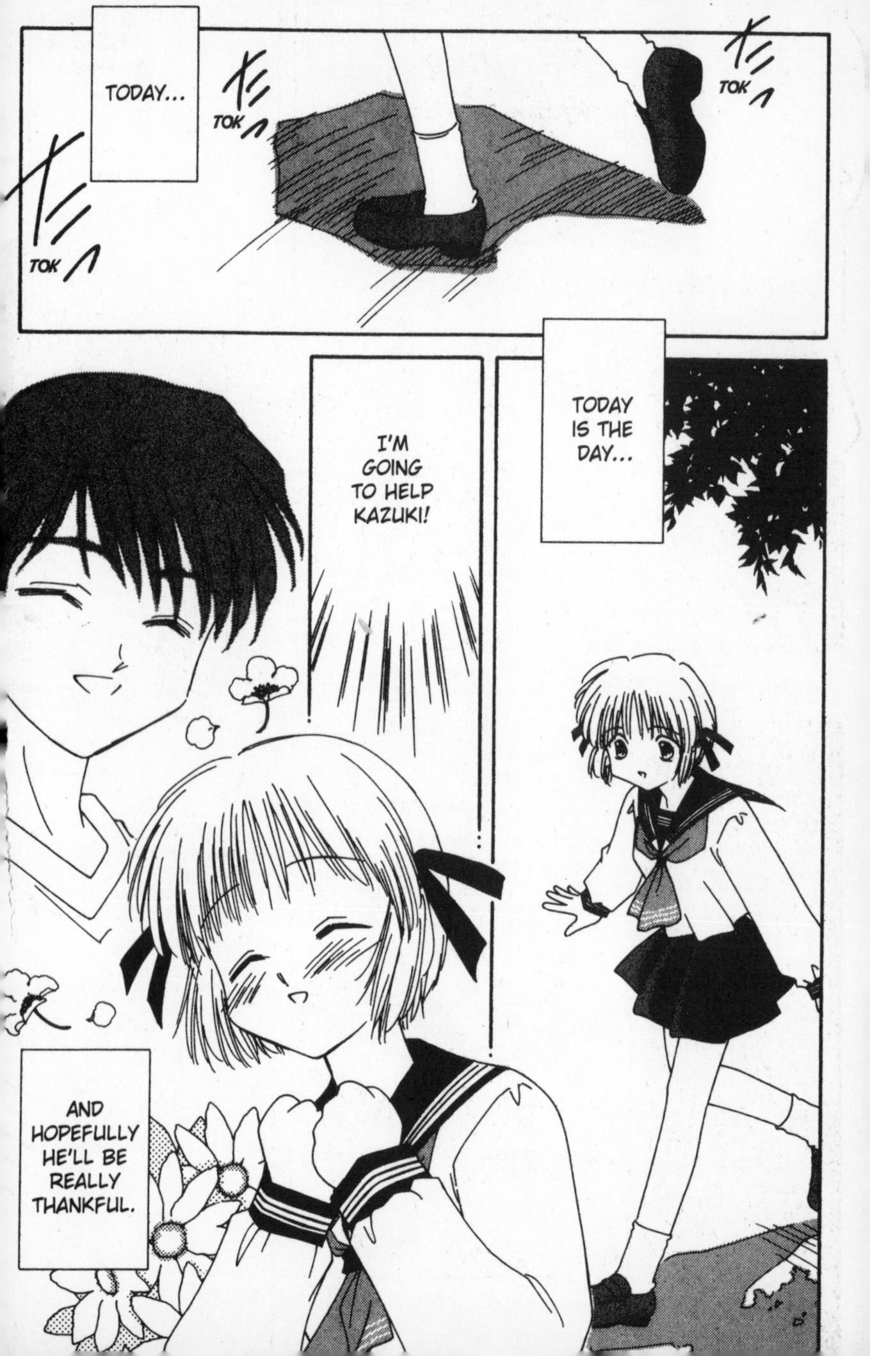
TOK
TOK
TODAY...
TOK
TODAY IS THE DAY...
I'M GOING TO HELP KAZUKI!
AND HOPEFULLY HE'LL BE REALLY THANKFUL.

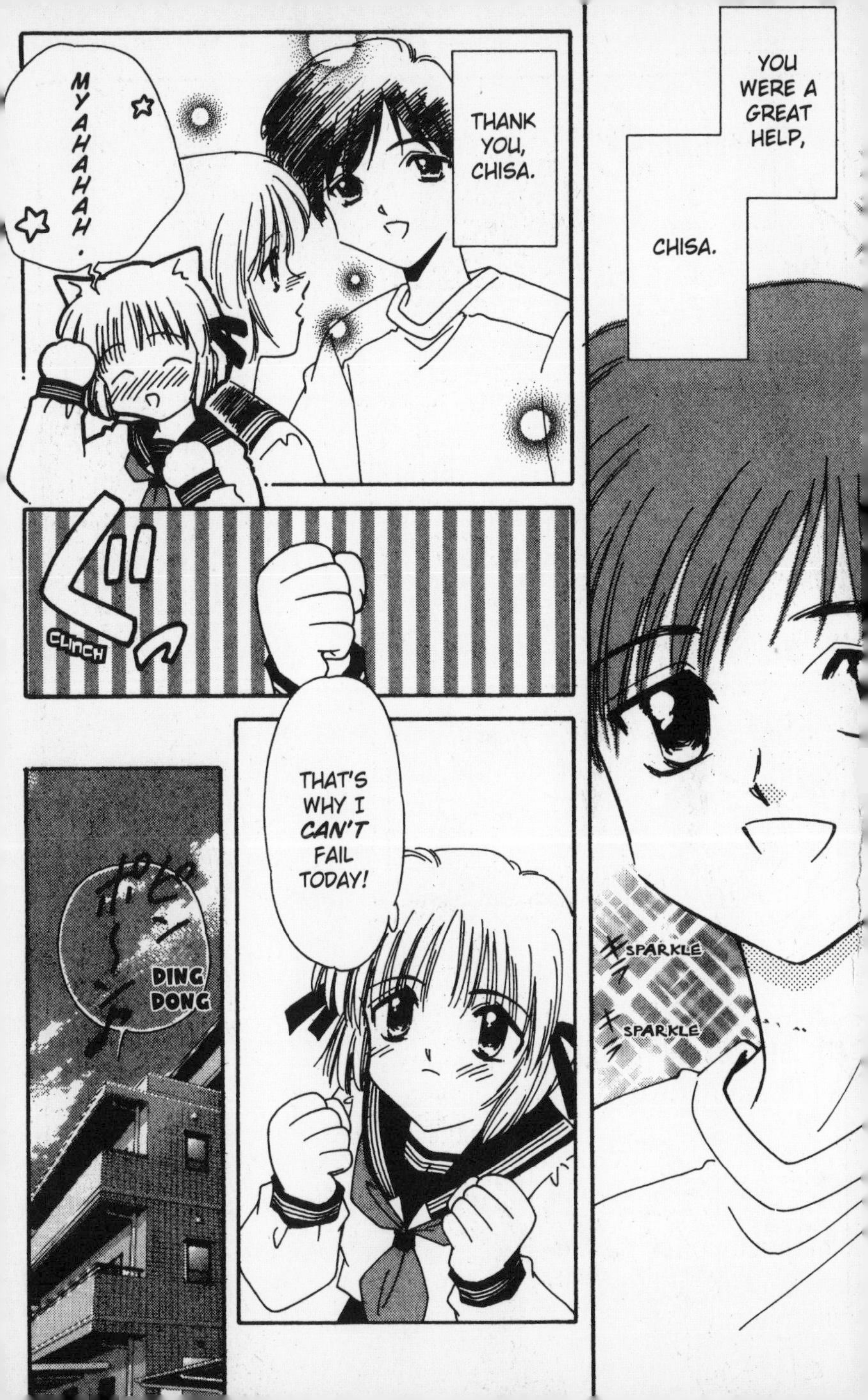
YOU WERE A GREAT HELP,
CHISA.
SPARKLE
SPARKLE
THANK YOU, CHISA.
MYAHAHAHAH.
CLINCH
THAT'S WHY I *CAN'T* FAIL TODAY!
DING DONG

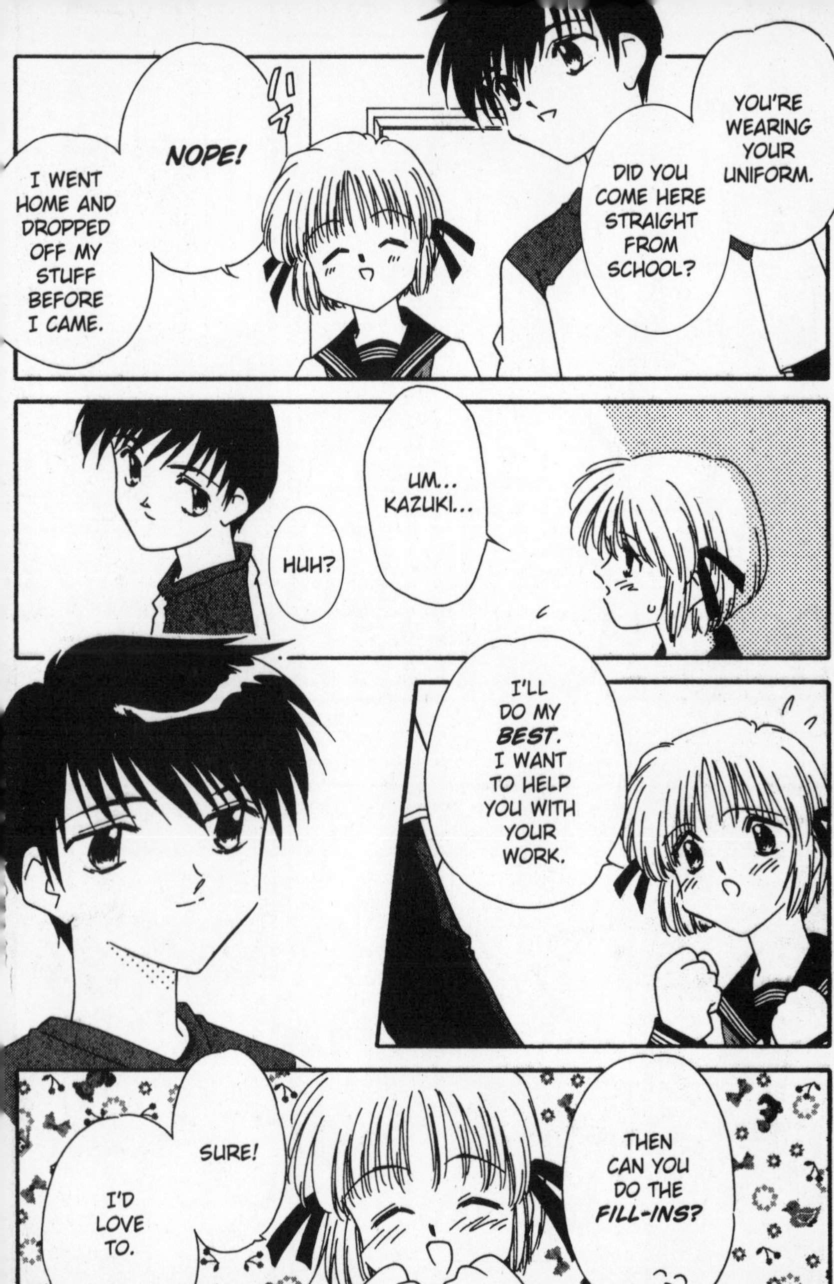
YOU'RE WEARING YOUR UNIFORM.
DID YOU COME HERE STRAIGHT FROM SCHOOL?
NOPE!
I WENT HOME AND DROPPED OFF MY STUFF BEFORE I CAME.
UM... KAZUKI...
HUH?
I'LL DO MY BEST. I WANT TO HELP YOU WITH YOUR WORK.
THEN CAN YOU DO THE FILL-INS?
SURE!
I'D LOVE TO.

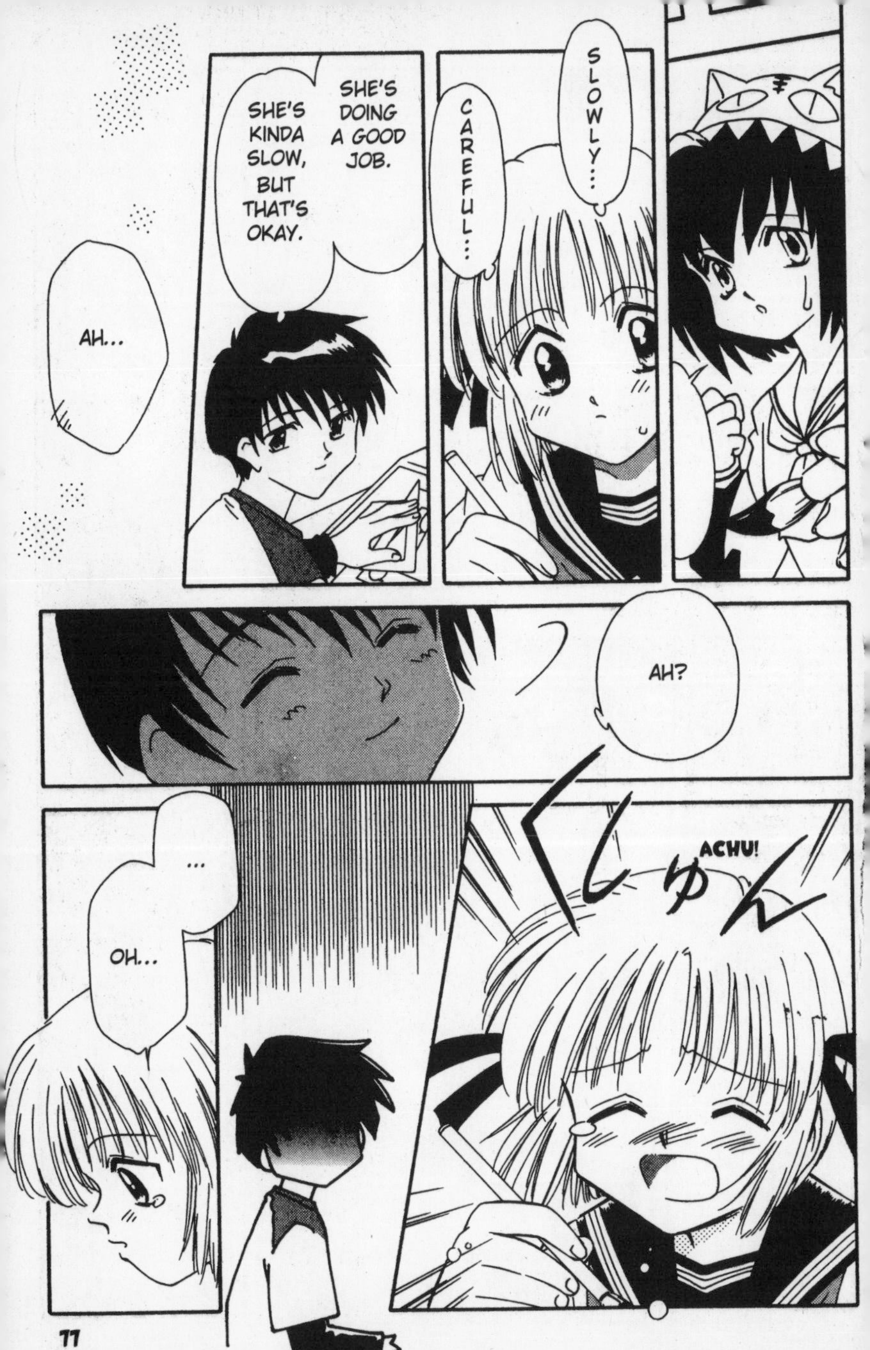
SLOWLY...
CAREFUL...
SHE'S DOING A GOOD JOB.
SHE'S KINDA SLOW, BUT THAT'S OKAY.
AH...
AH?
くしゅん
ACHU!
...
OH...

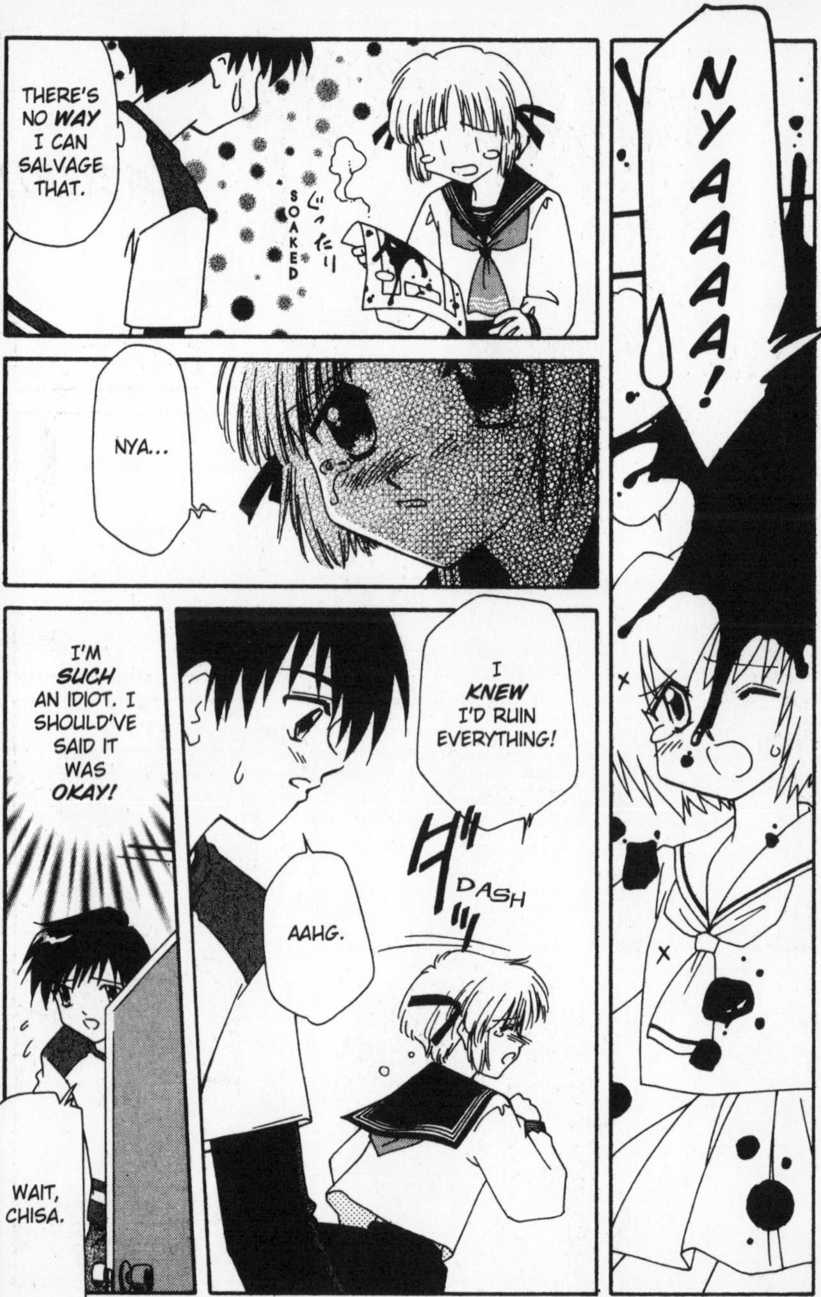
NYAAAAA!
THERE'S NO WAY I CAN SALVAGE THAT.
ぐったり
SOAKED
NYA...
I KNEW I'D RUIN EVERYTHING!
ダッ
DASH
AAHG.
I'M SUCH AN IDIOT. I SHOULD'VE SAID IT WAS OKAY!
WAIT, CHISA.

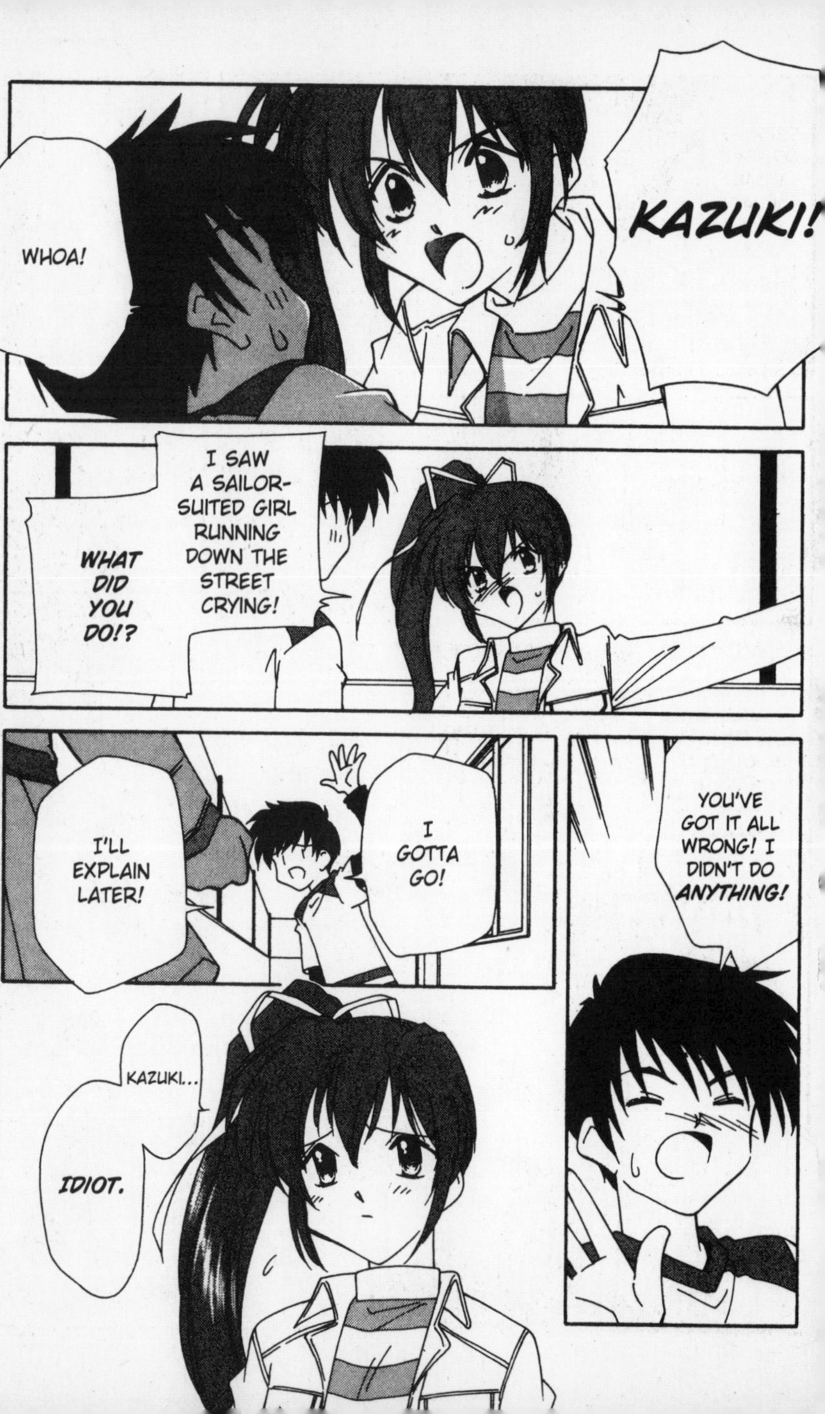
KAZUKI!
WHOA!
I SAW A SAILOR-SUITED GIRL RUNNING DOWN THE STREET CRYING!
WHAT DID YOU DO!?
YOU'VE GOT IT ALL WRONG! I DIDN'T DO ANYTHING!
I GOTTA GO!
I'LL EXPLAIN LATER!
KAZUKI...
IDIOT.

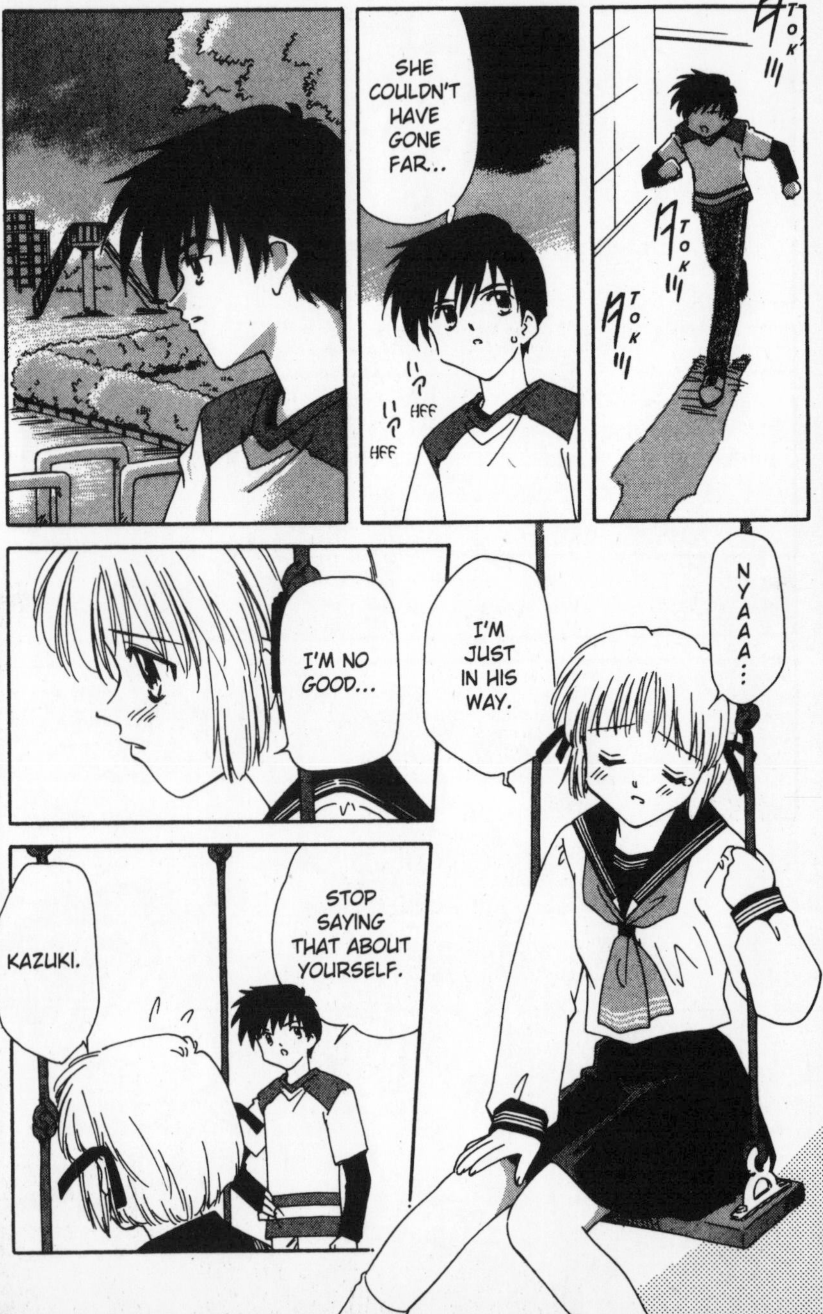
TOK
TOK
TOK
SHE COULDN'T HAVE GONE FAR..
HFF
HFF
NYAAAA...
I'M JUST IN HIS WAY.
I'M NO GOOD...
STOP SAYING THAT ABOUT YOURSELF.
KAZUKI.

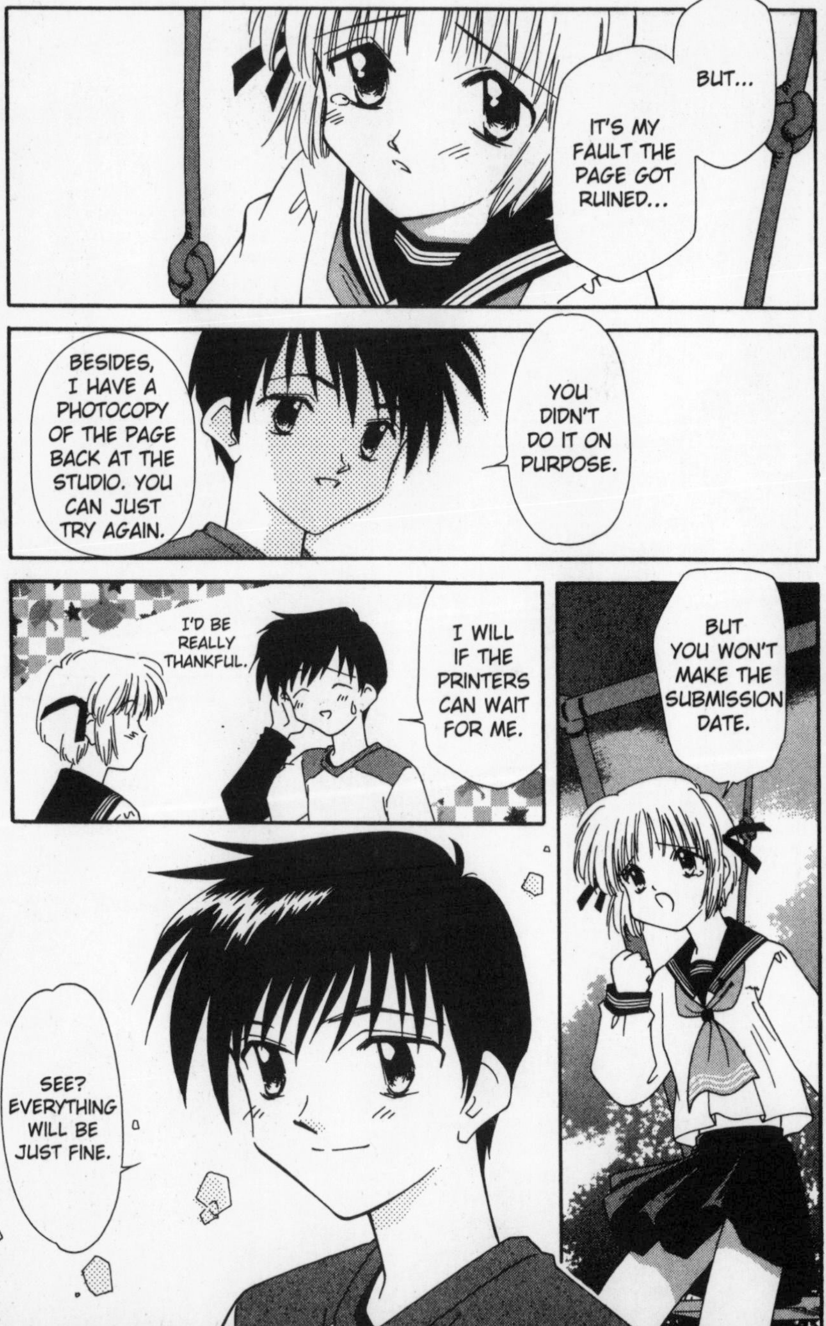
BUT...
IT'S MY FAULT THE PAGE GOT RUINED...
YOU DIDN'T DO IT ON PURPOSE.
BESIDES, I HAVE A PHOTOCOPY OF THE PAGE BACK AT THE STUDIO. YOU CAN JUST TRY AGAIN.
BUT YOU WON'T MAKE THE SUBMISSION DATE.
I WILL IF THE PRINTERS CAN WAIT FOR ME.
I'D BE REALLY THANKFUL.
SEE? EVERYTHING WILL BE JUST FINE.

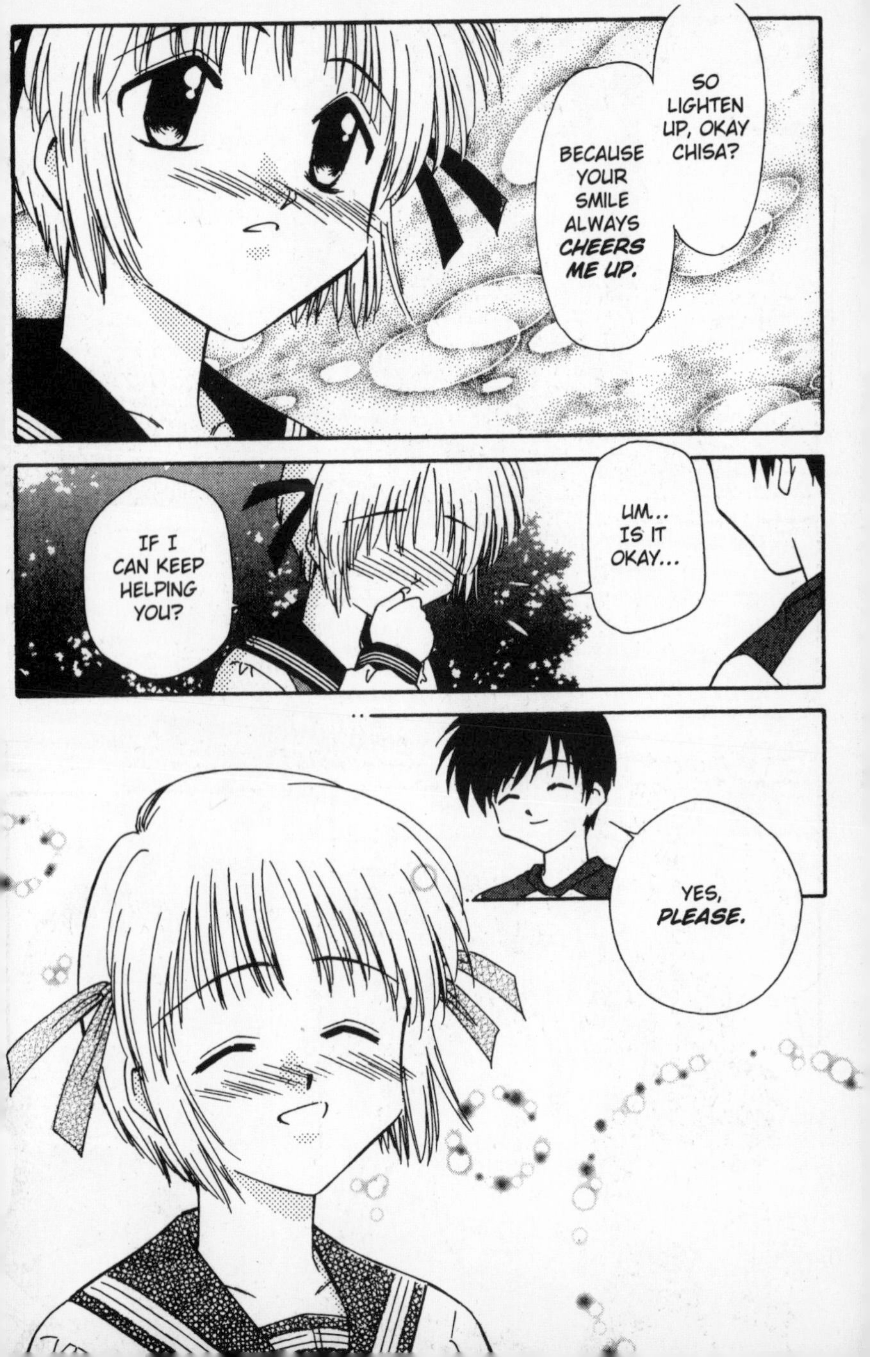
SO LIGHTEN UP, OKAY CHISA?
BECAUSE YOUR SMILE ALWAYS CHEERS ME UP.
UM... IS IT OKAY...
IF I CAN KEEP HELPING YOU?
YES, PLEASE.

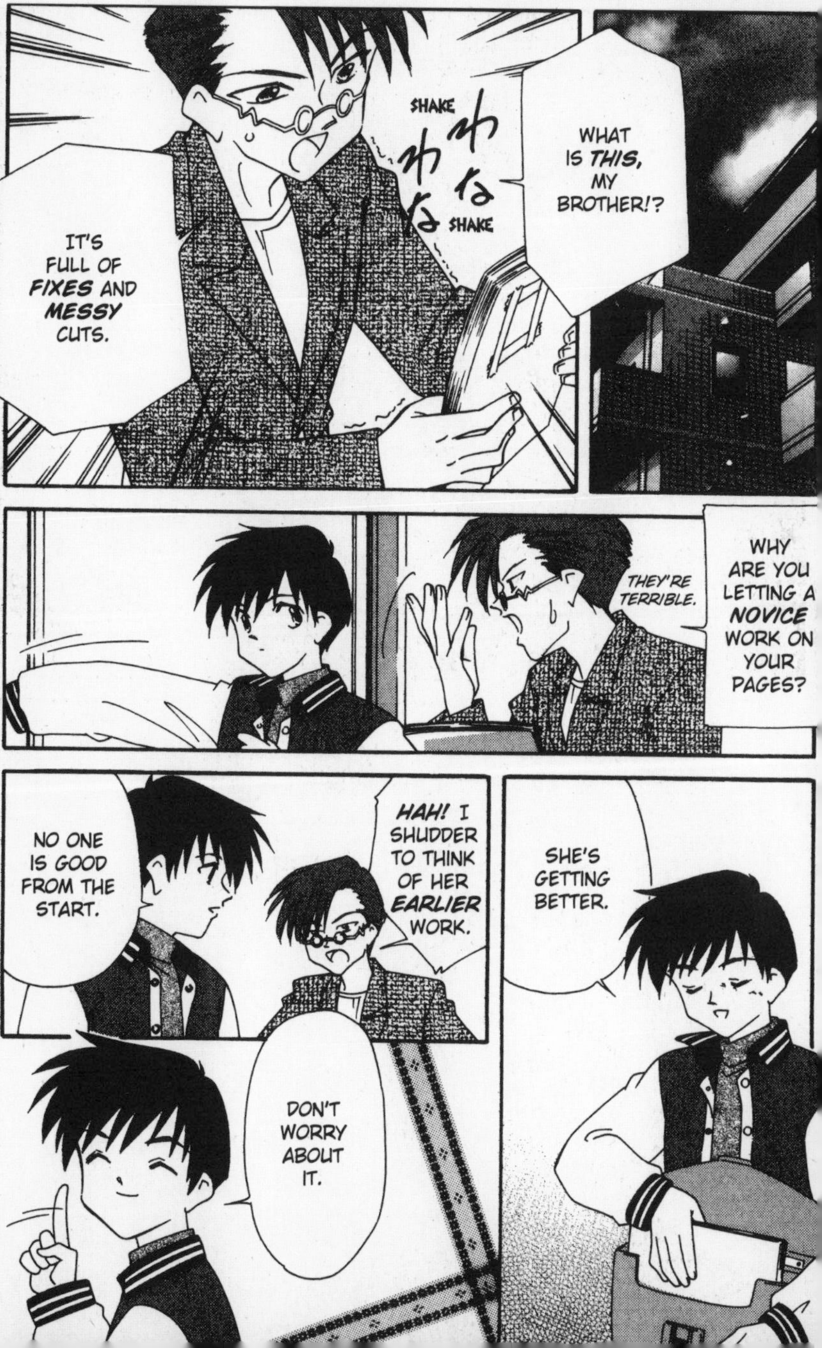
WHAT IS THIS, MY BROTHER!?
SHAKE
わなわな
SHAKE
IT'S FULL OF FIXES AND MESSY CUTS.
WHY ARE YOU LETTING A NOVICE WORK ON YOUR PAGES?
THEY'RE TERRIBLE.
SHE'S GETTING BETTER.
HAH! I SHUDDER TO THINK OF HER EARLIER WORK.
NO ONE IS GOOD FROM THE START.
DON'T WORRY ABOUT IT.

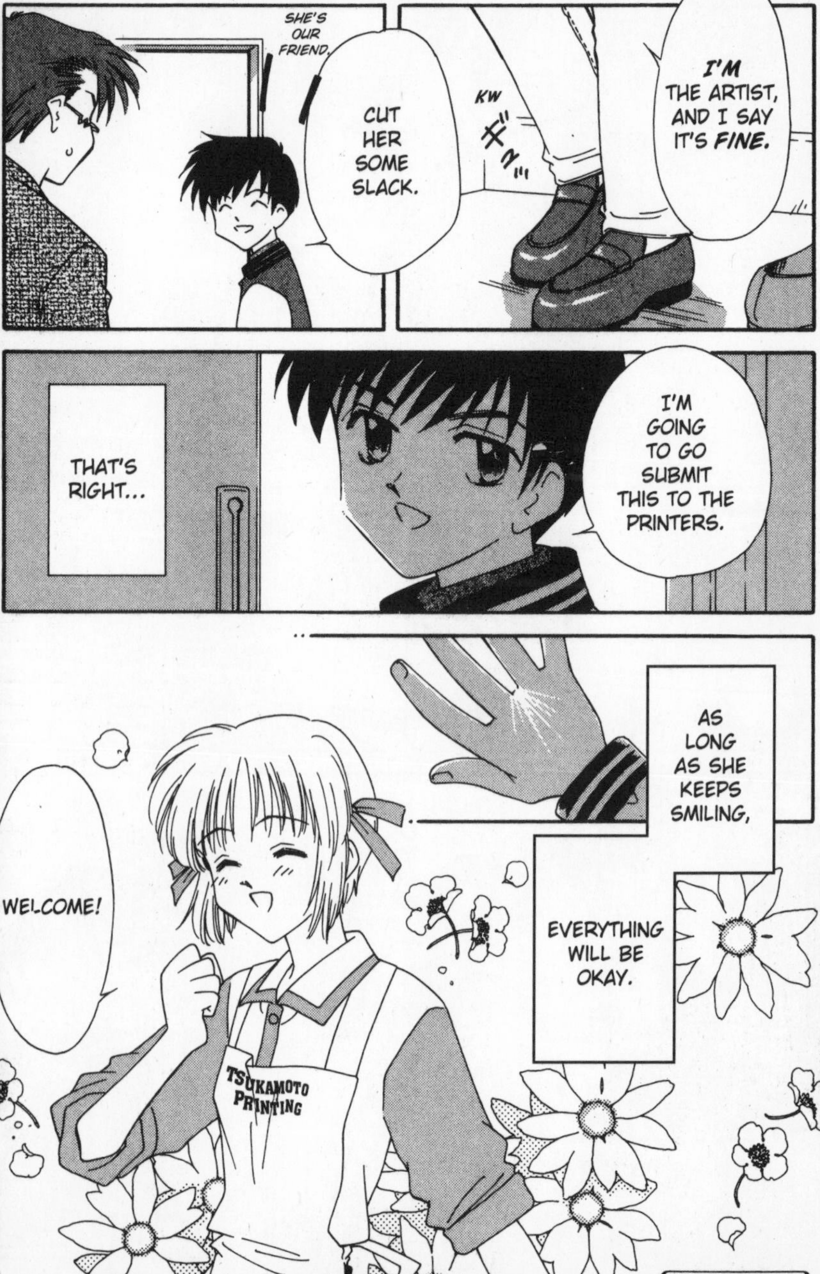

KW
I'M THE ARTIST, AND I SAY IT'S FINE.
CUT HER SOME SLACK.
SHE'S OUR FRIEND.
I'M GOING TO GO SUBMIT THIS TO THE PRINTERS.
THAT'S RIGHT...
AS LONG AS SHE KEEPS SMILING,
EVERYTHING WILL BE OKAY.
WELCOME!
TSUKAMOTO PRINTING
END

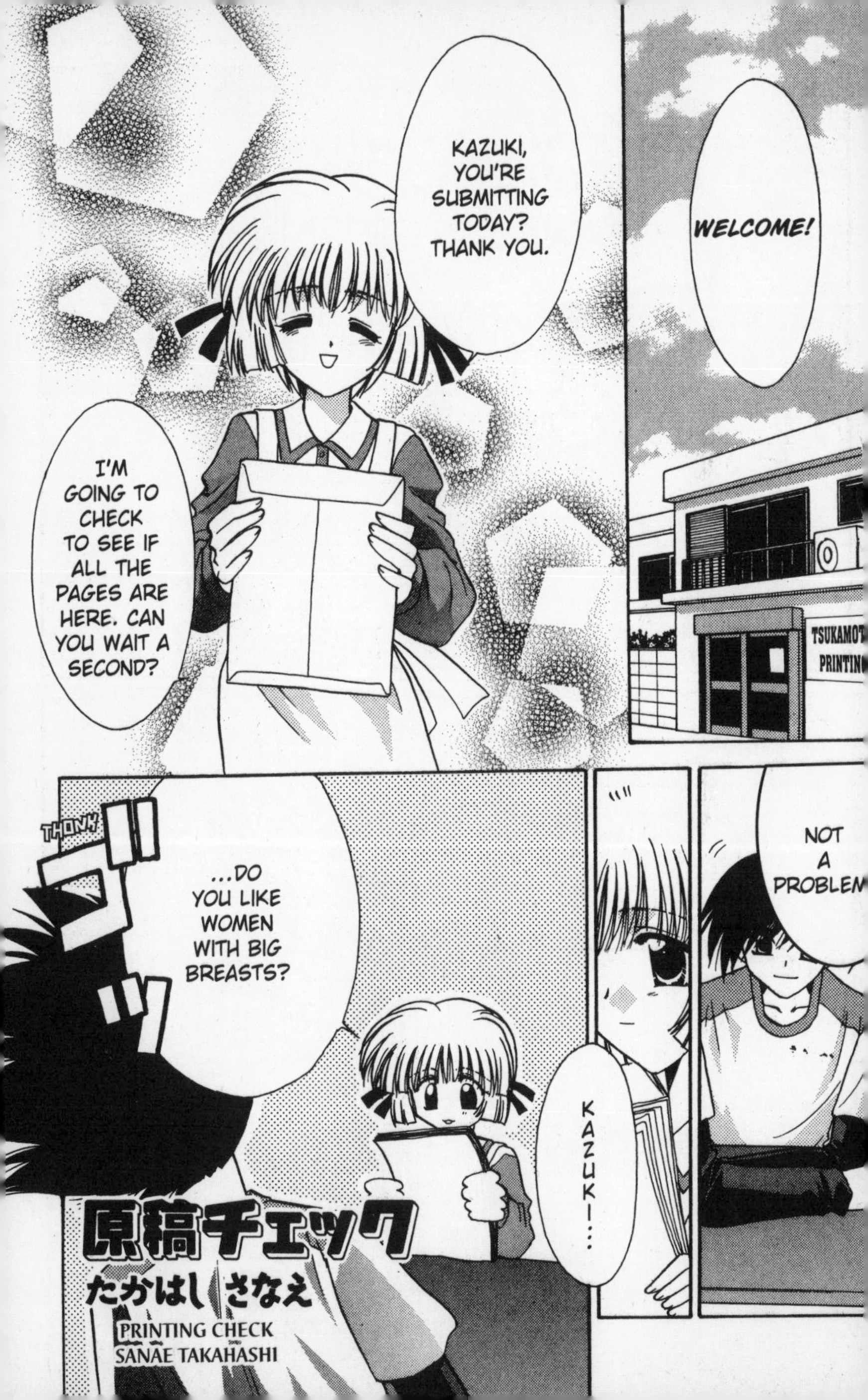
WELCOME!
TSUKAMOT PRINTIN
KAZUKI, YOU'RE SUBMITTING TODAY? THANK YOU.
I'M GOING TO CHECK TO SEE IF ALL THE PAGES ARE HERE. CAN YOU WAIT A SECOND?
NOT A PROBLEM
KAZUKI!...
THONK
...DO YOU LIKE WOMEN WITH BIG BREASTS?
原稿チェック
たかはし さなえ
PRINTING CHECK
SANAE TAKAHASHI

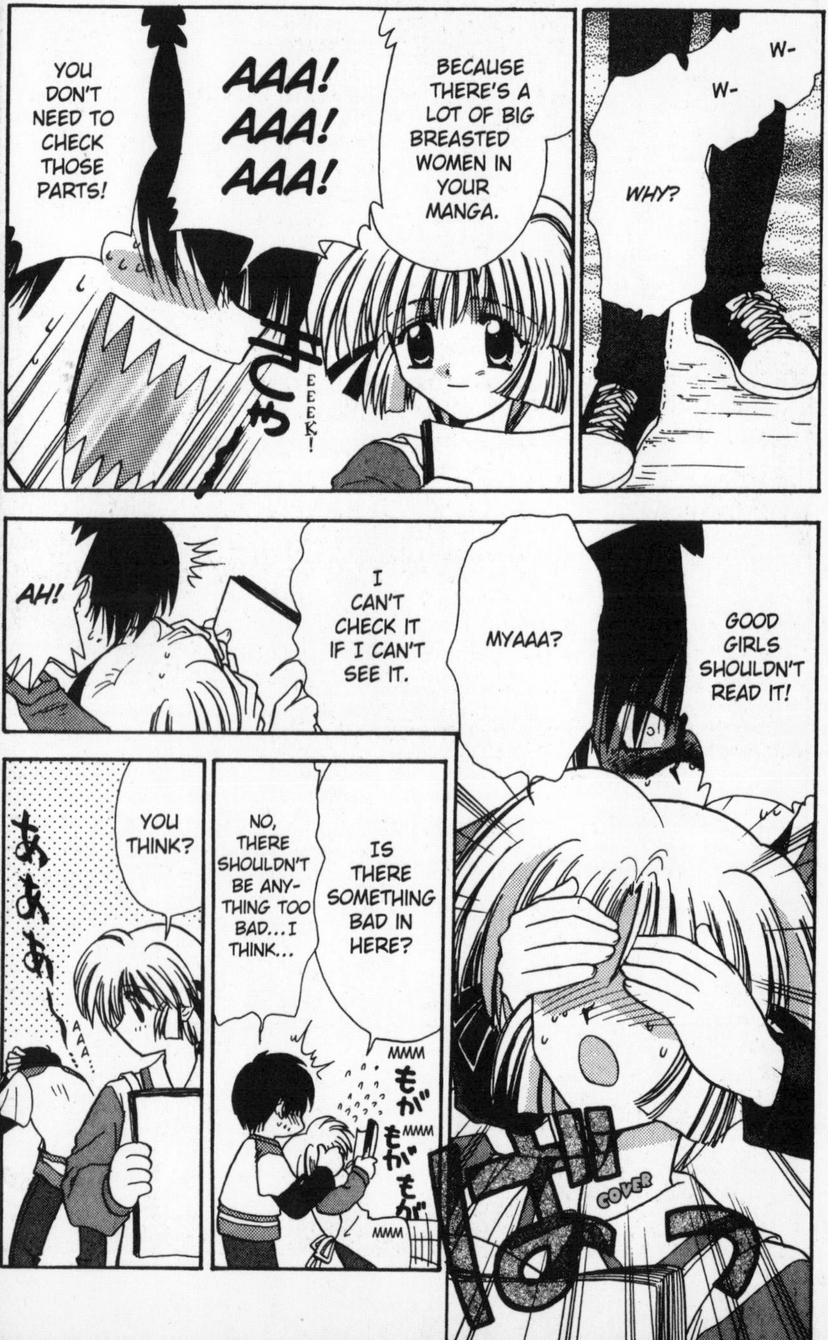
W-
W-
WHY?
BECAUSE THERE'S A LOT OF BIG BREASTED WOMEN IN YOUR MANGA.
AAA! AAA! AAA!
YOU DON'T NEED TO CHECK THOSE PARTS!
EEEK!
GOOD GIRLS SHOULDN'T READ IT!
MYAAA?
COVER
I CAN'T CHECK IT IF I CAN'T SEE IT.
AH!
IS THERE SOMETHING BAD IN HERE?
NO, THERE SHOULDN'T BE ANY-THING TOO BAD...I THINK...
MMM
もが
MMM
もが
もが
MMM
YOU THINK?
ああああ
AAA

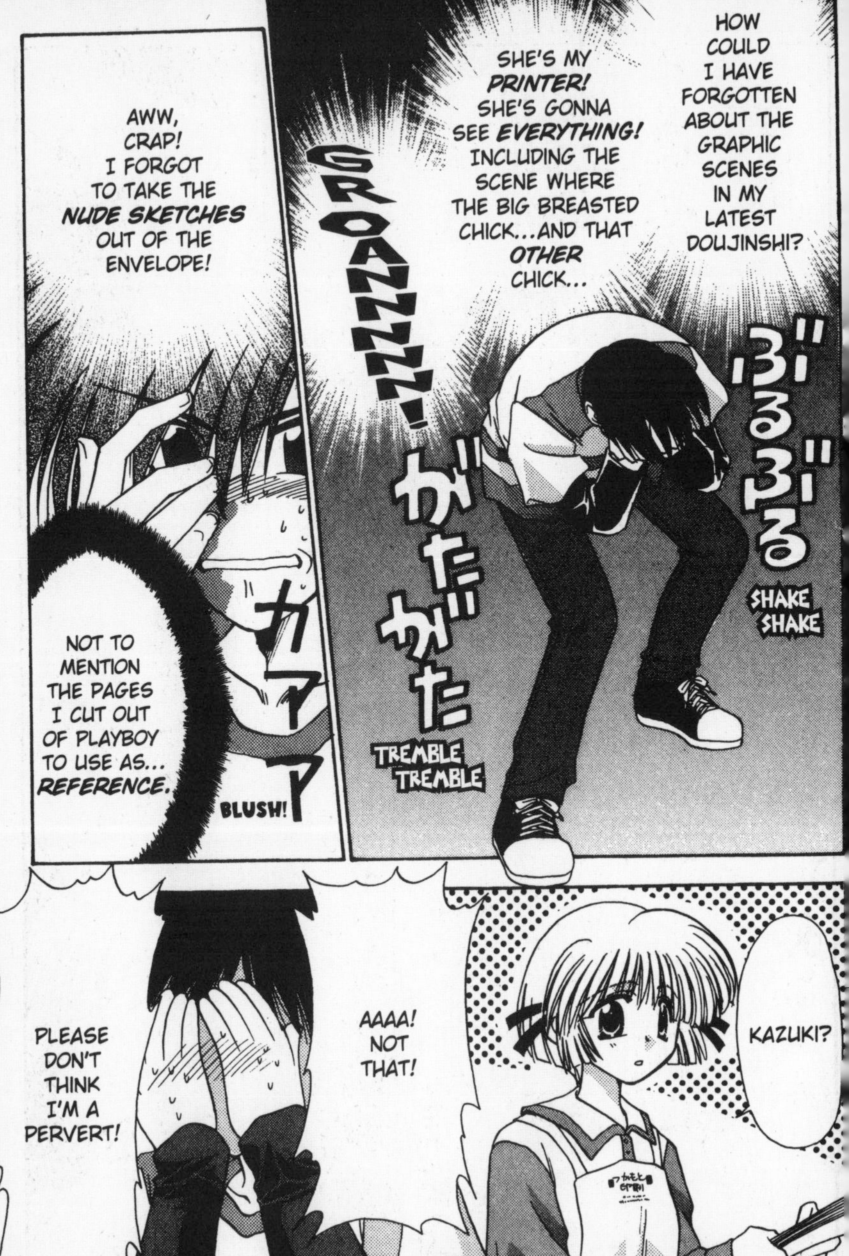
HOW COULD I HAVE FORGOTTEN ABOUT THE GRAPHIC SCENES IN MY LATEST DOUJINSHI?
SHE'S MY *PRINTER!* SHE'S GONNA SEE *EVERYTHING!* INCLUDING THE SCENE WHERE THE BIG BREASTED CHICK...AND THAT *OTHER* CHICK...
GROANNNN!
ぶるぶる
SHAKE SHAKE
がたがた
TREMBLE TREMBLE
AWW, CRAP! I FORGOT TO TAKE THE *NUDE SKETCHES* OUT OF THE ENVELOPE!
NOT TO MENTION THE PAGES I CUT OUT OF PLAYBOY TO USE AS... *REFERENCE.*
BLUSH!
KAZUKI?
AAAA! NOT THAT!
PLEASE DON'T THINK I'M A PERVERT!

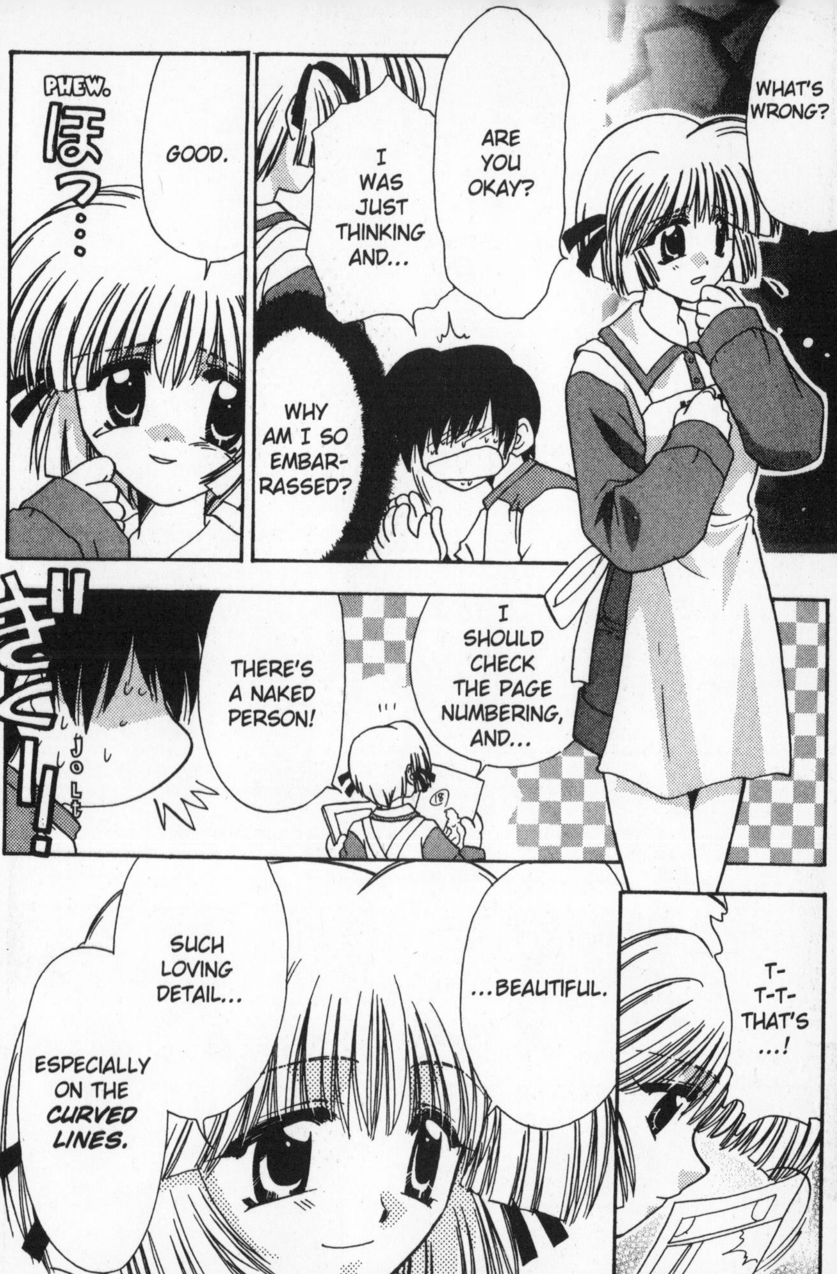
WHAT'S WRONG?
ARE YOU OKAY?
I WAS JUST THINKING AND...
WHY AM I SO EMBARRASSED?
GOOD.
PHEW.
ほっ…
I SHOULD CHECK THE PAGE NUMBERING, AND...
THERE'S A NAKED PERSON!
ぎくー!
JOLT
T- T-T- THAT'S ...!
...BEAUTIFUL.
SUCH LOVING DETAIL...
ESPECIALLY ON THE *CURVED LINES.*

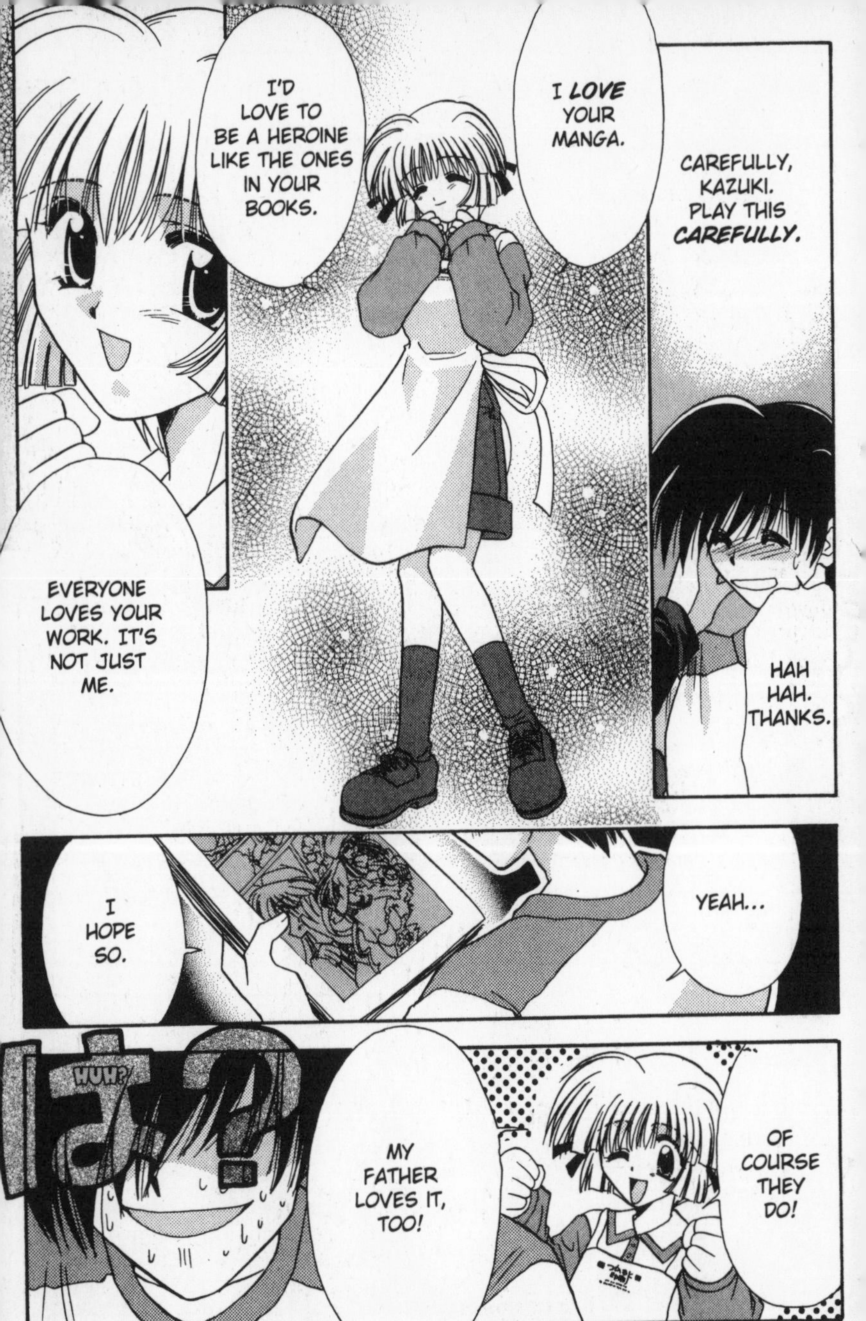
I *LOVE* YOUR MANGA.
CAREFULLY, KAZUKI. PLAY THIS *CAREFULLY.*
HAH HAH. THANKS.
I'D LOVE TO BE A HEROINE LIKE THE ONES IN YOUR BOOKS.
EVERYONE LOVES YOUR WORK. IT'S NOT JUST ME.
YEAH...
I HOPE SO.
OF COURSE THEY DO!
MY FATHER LOVES IT, TOO!
HUH?

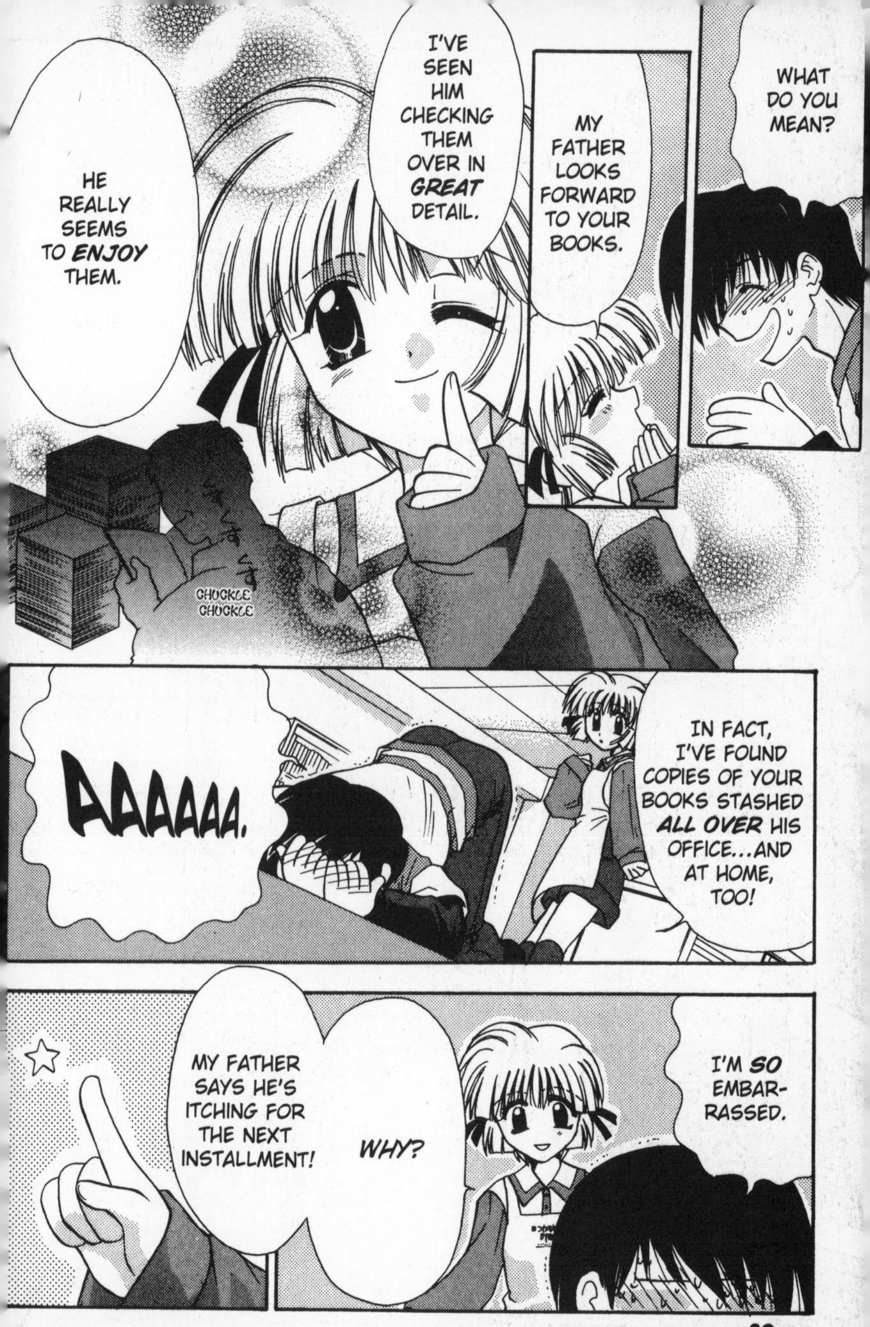
WHAT DO YOU MEAN?
MY FATHER LOOKS FORWARD TO YOUR BOOKS.
I'VE SEEN HIM CHECKING THEM OVER IN GREAT DETAIL.
HE REALLY SEEMS TO ENJOY THEM.
CHUCKLE CHUCKLE
IN FACT, I'VE FOUND COPIES OF YOUR BOOKS STASHED ALL OVER HIS OFFICE...AND AT HOME, TOO!
AAAAAA.
I'M SO EMBARRASSED.
WHY?
MY FATHER SAYS HE'S ITCHING FOR THE NEXT INSTALLMENT!

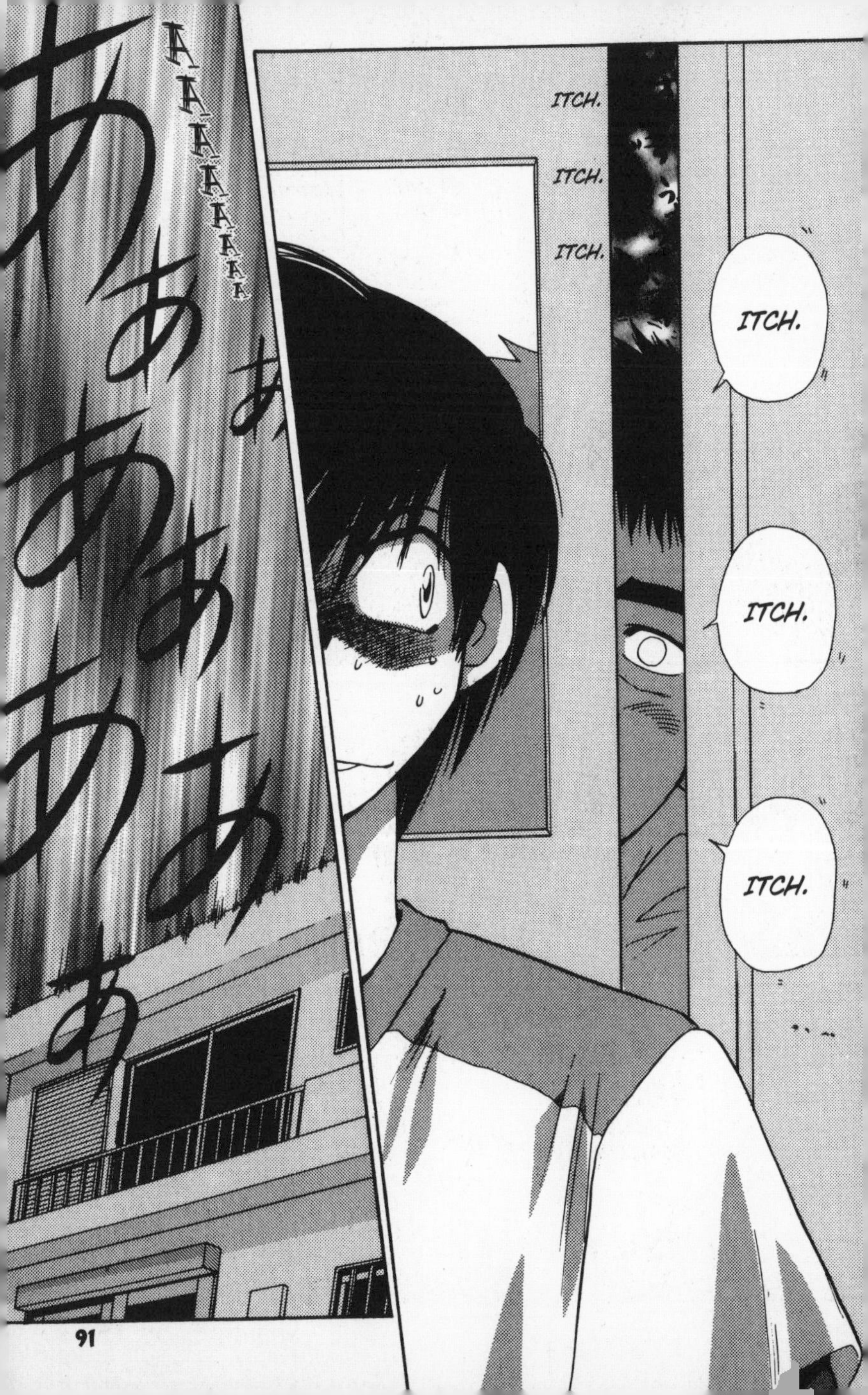
ITCH.
ITCH.
ITCH.
ITCH.
ITCH.
ITCH.
AAAAAAAAAA
ああああああああ

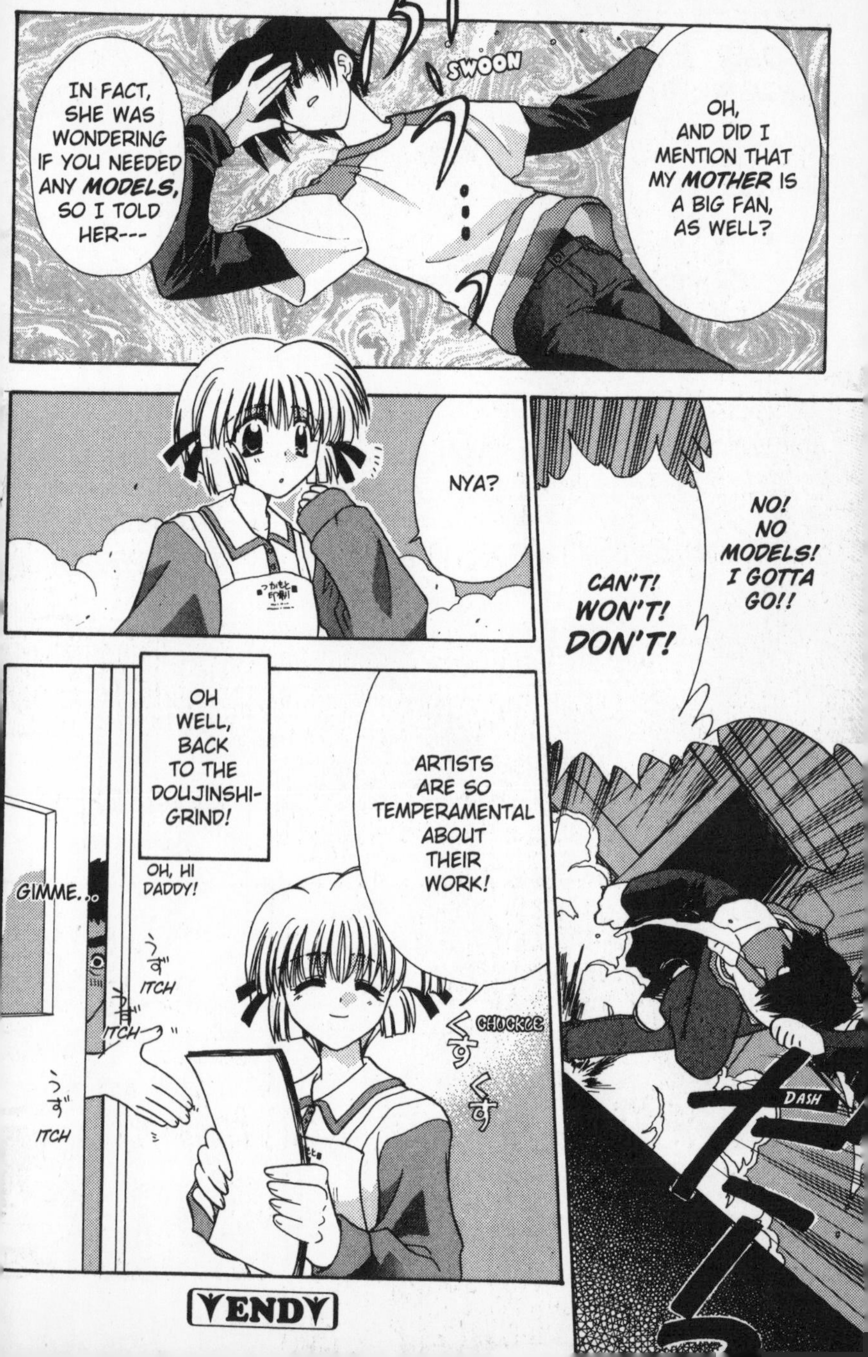

OH, AND DID I MENTION THAT MY **MOTHER** IS A BIG FAN, AS WELL?
SWOON
IN FACT, SHE WAS WONDERING IF YOU NEEDED ANY **MODELS**, SO I TOLD HER---
...
NO! NO MODELS! I GOTTA GO!!
CAN'T! WON'T! DON'T!
DASH
NYA?
ARTISTS ARE SO TEMPERAMENTAL ABOUT THEIR WORK!
OH WELL, BACK TO THE DOUJINSHI-GRIND!
くすくす
CHUCKLE
OH, HI DADDY!
GIMME...
うず
ITCH
うず
ITCH
うず
ITCH
END

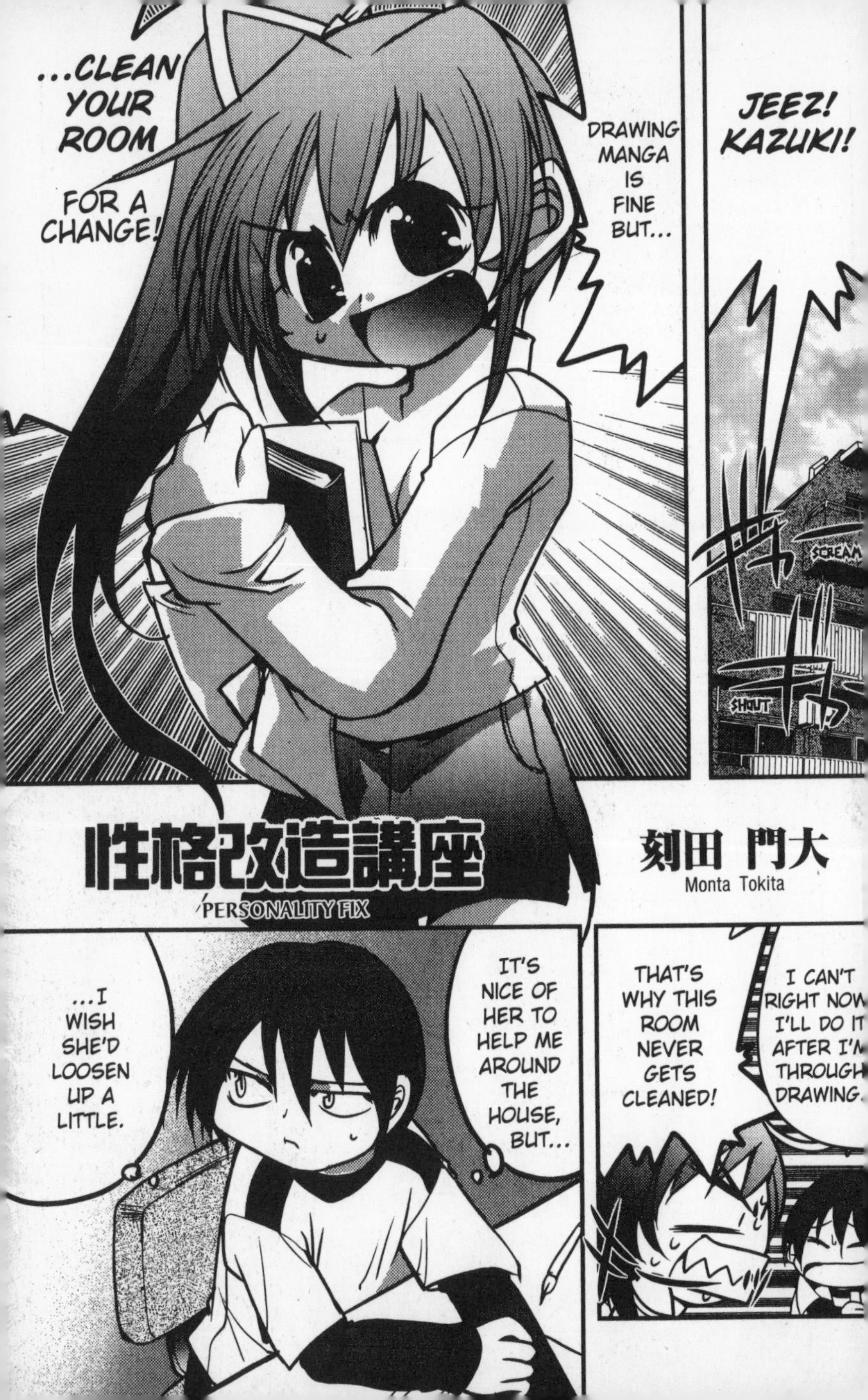
JEEZ! KAZUKI!
SCREAM
SHOUT
DRAWING MANGA IS FINE BUT...
...CLEAN YOUR ROOM FOR A CHANGE!
性格改造講座
PERSONALITY FIX
刻田 門大
Monta Tokita
I CAN'T RIGHT NOW I'LL DO IT AFTER I'M THROUGH DRAWING.
THAT'S WHY THIS ROOM NEVER GETS CLEANED!
IT'S NICE OF HER TO HELP ME AROUND THE HOUSE, BUT...
...I WISH SHE'D LOOSEN UP A LITTLE.

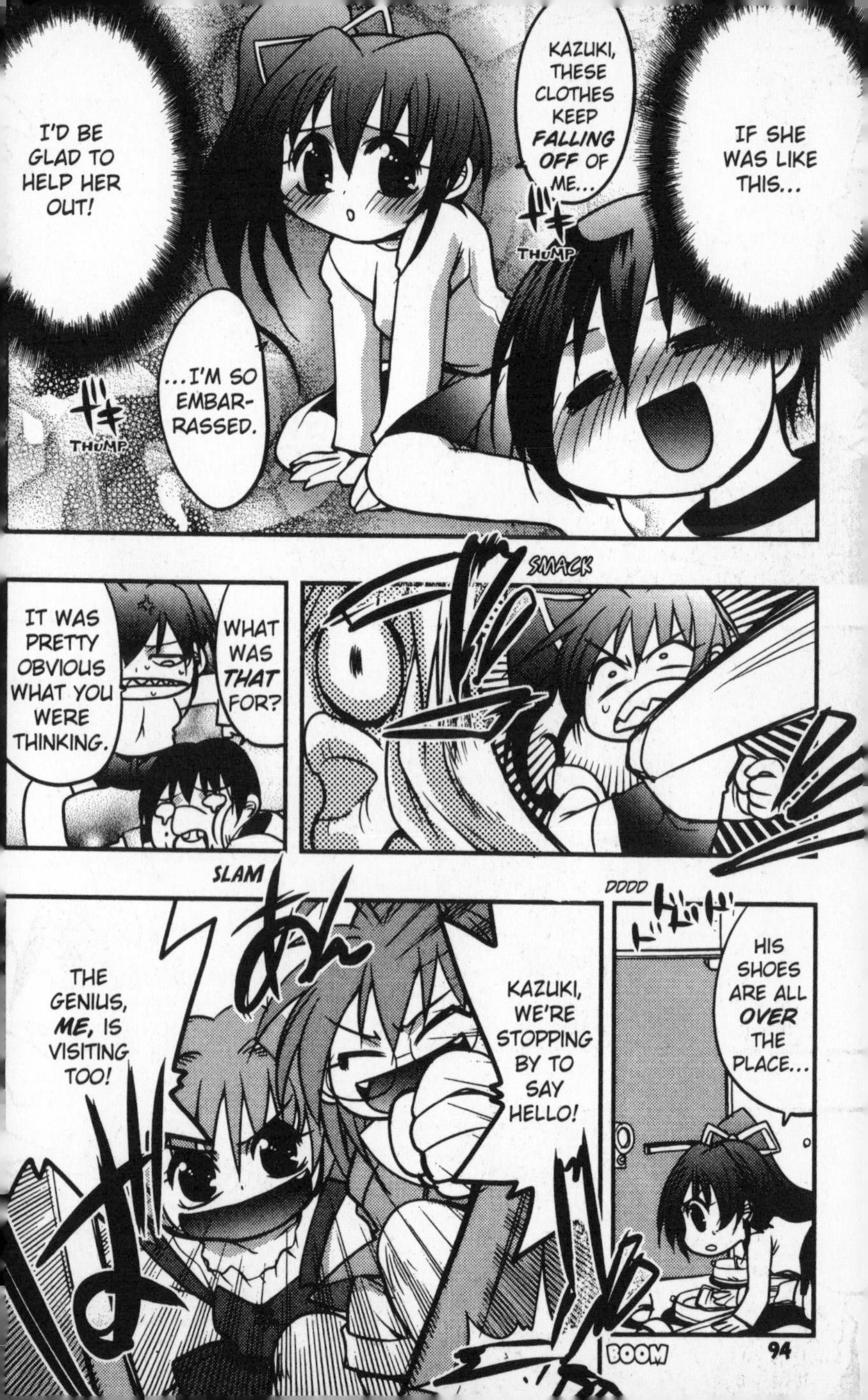
IF SHE WAS LIKE THIS...
KAZUKI, THESE CLOTHES KEEP FALLING OFF OF ME...
THUMP
I'D BE GLAD TO HELP HER OUT!
...I'M SO EMBARRASSED.
THUMP
SMACK
WHAT WAS THAT FOR?
IT WAS PRETTY OBVIOUS WHAT YOU WERE THINKING.
DDDD
HIS SHOES ARE ALL OVER THE PLACE...
BOOM
SLAM
KAZUKI, WE'RE STOPPING BY TO SAY HELLO!
THE GENIUS, ME, IS VISITING TOO!

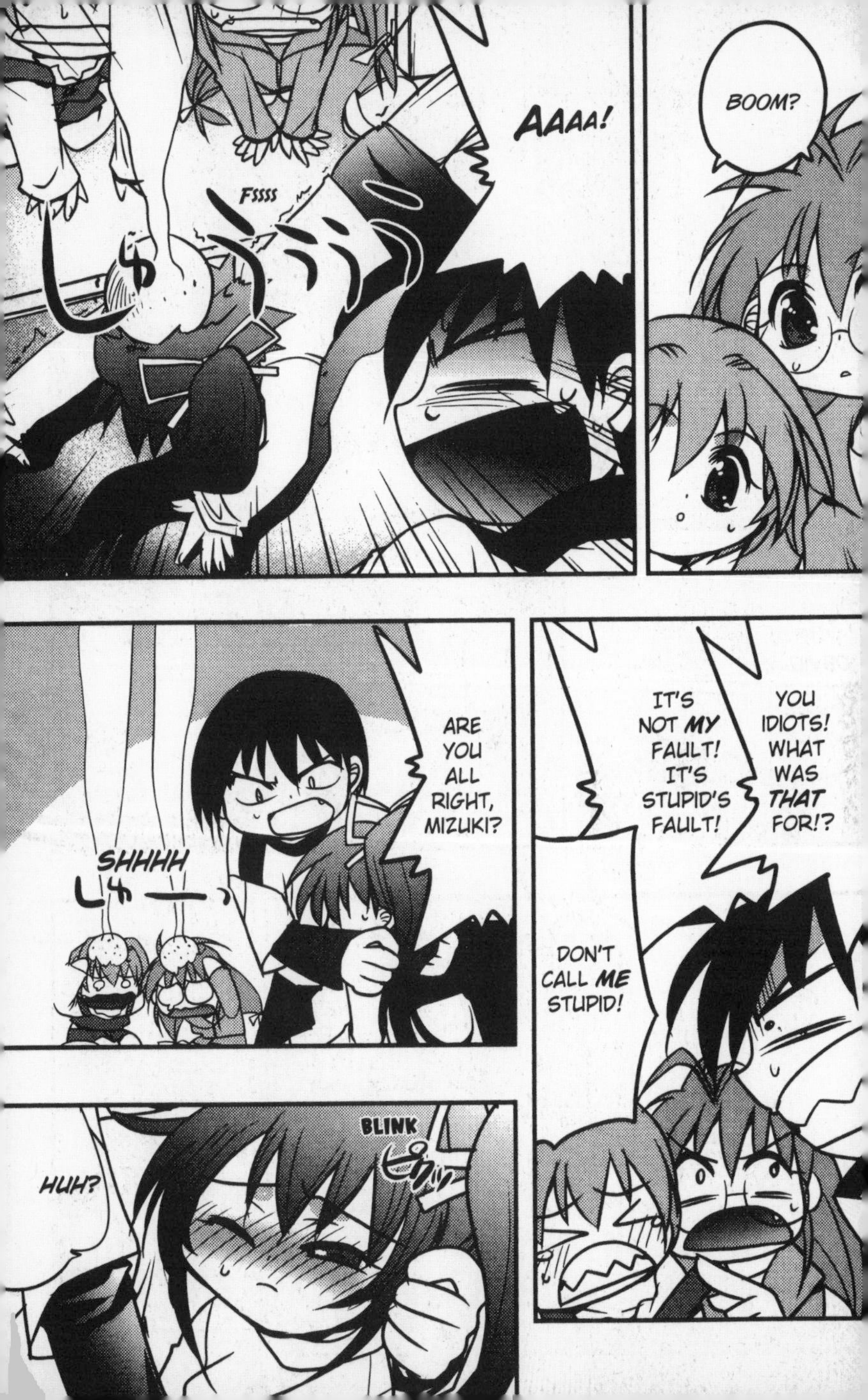
BOOM?
AAAA!
FSSSS
YOU IDIOTS! WHAT WAS THAT FOR!?
IT'S NOT MY FAULT! IT'S STUPID'S FAULT!
DON'T CALL ME STUPID!
ARE YOU ALL RIGHT, MIZUKI?
SHHHH
しゅーーっ
BLINK
HUH?

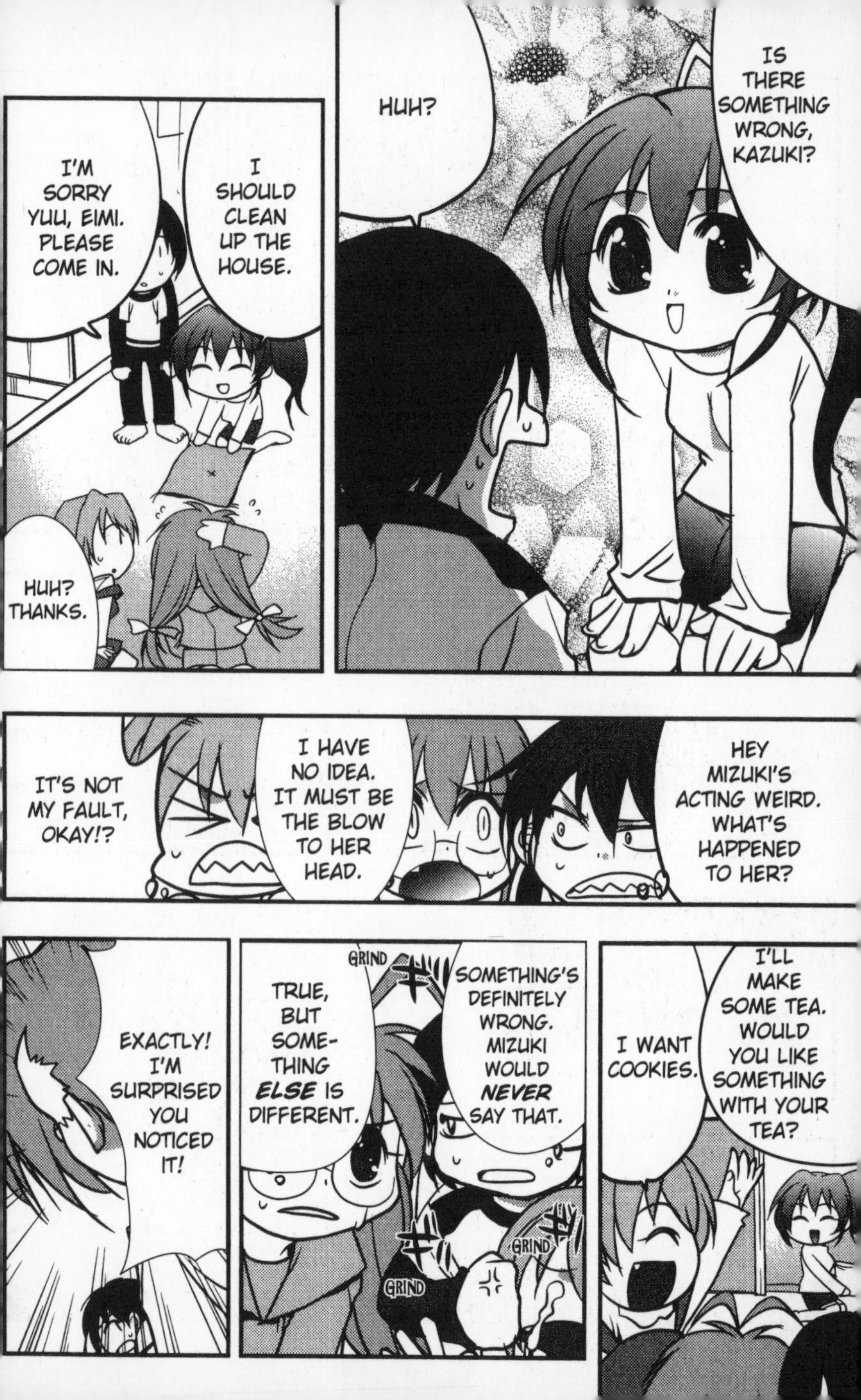
IS THERE SOMETHING WRONG, KAZUKI?
HUH?
I SHOULD CLEAN UP THE HOUSE.
I'M SORRY YUU, EIMI. PLEASE COME IN.
HUH? THANKS.
HEY MIZUKI'S ACTING WEIRD. WHAT'S HAPPENED TO HER?
I HAVE NO IDEA. IT MUST BE THE BLOW TO HER HEAD.
IT'S NOT MY FAULT, OKAY!?
I'LL MAKE SOME TEA. WOULD YOU LIKE SOMETHING WITH YOUR TEA?
I WANT COOKIES.
GRIND
SOMETHING'S DEFINITELY WRONG. MIZUKI WOULD *NEVER* SAY THAT.
TRUE, BUT SOMETHING *ELSE* IS DIFFERENT.
GRIND
GRIND
EXACTLY! I'M SURPRISED YOU NOTICED IT!

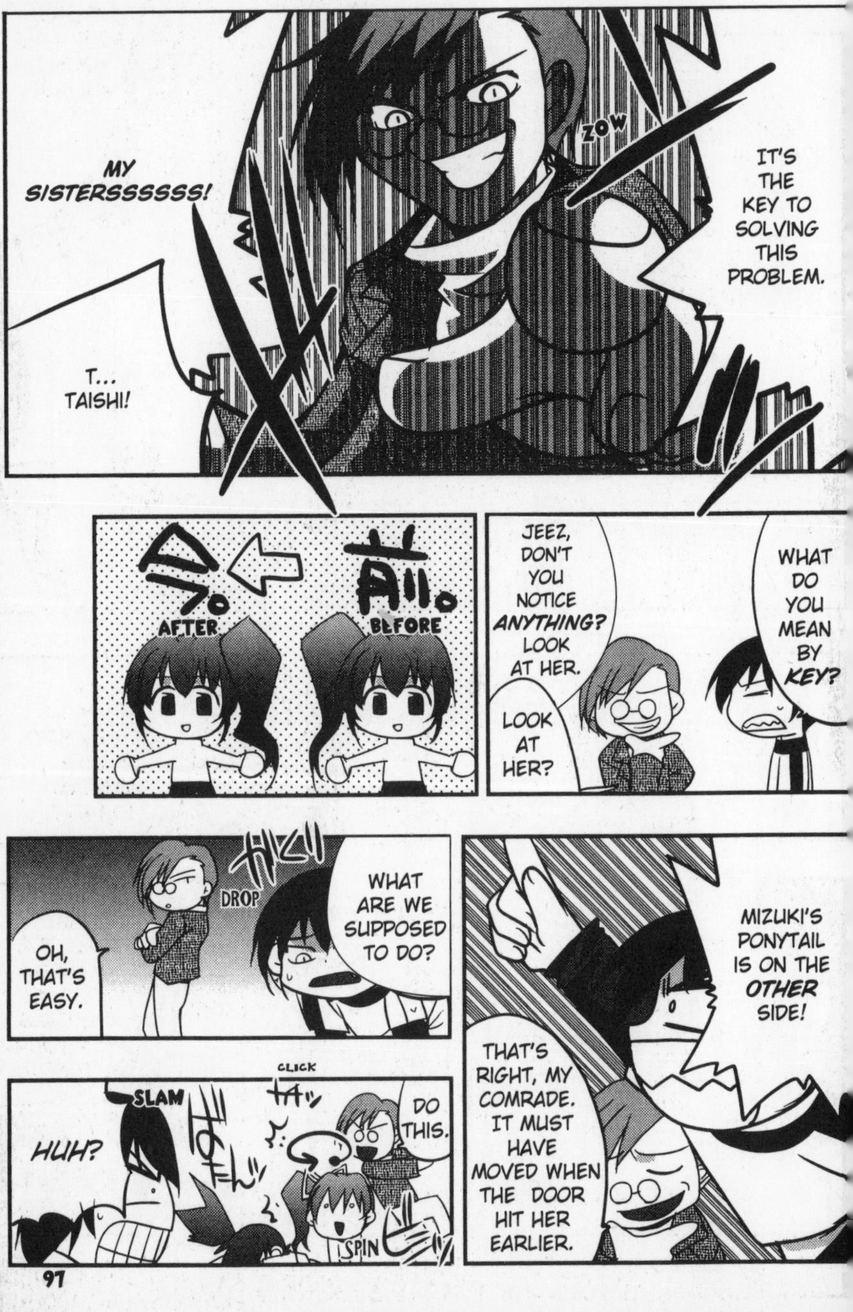
IT'S THE KEY TO SOLVING THIS PROBLEM.
ZOW
MY SISTERSSSSSS!
T... TAISHI!
WHAT DO YOU MEAN BY KEY?
JEEZ, DON'T YOU NOTICE ANYTHING? LOOK AT HER.
LOOK AT HER?
BEFORE
AFTER
MIZUKI'S PONYTAIL IS ON THE OTHER SIDE!
THAT'S RIGHT, MY COMRADE. IT MUST HAVE MOVED WHEN THE DOOR HIT HER EARLIER.
WHAT ARE WE SUPPOSED TO DO?
DROP
OH, THAT'S EASY.
CLICK
DO THIS.
SLAM
HUH?
SPIN

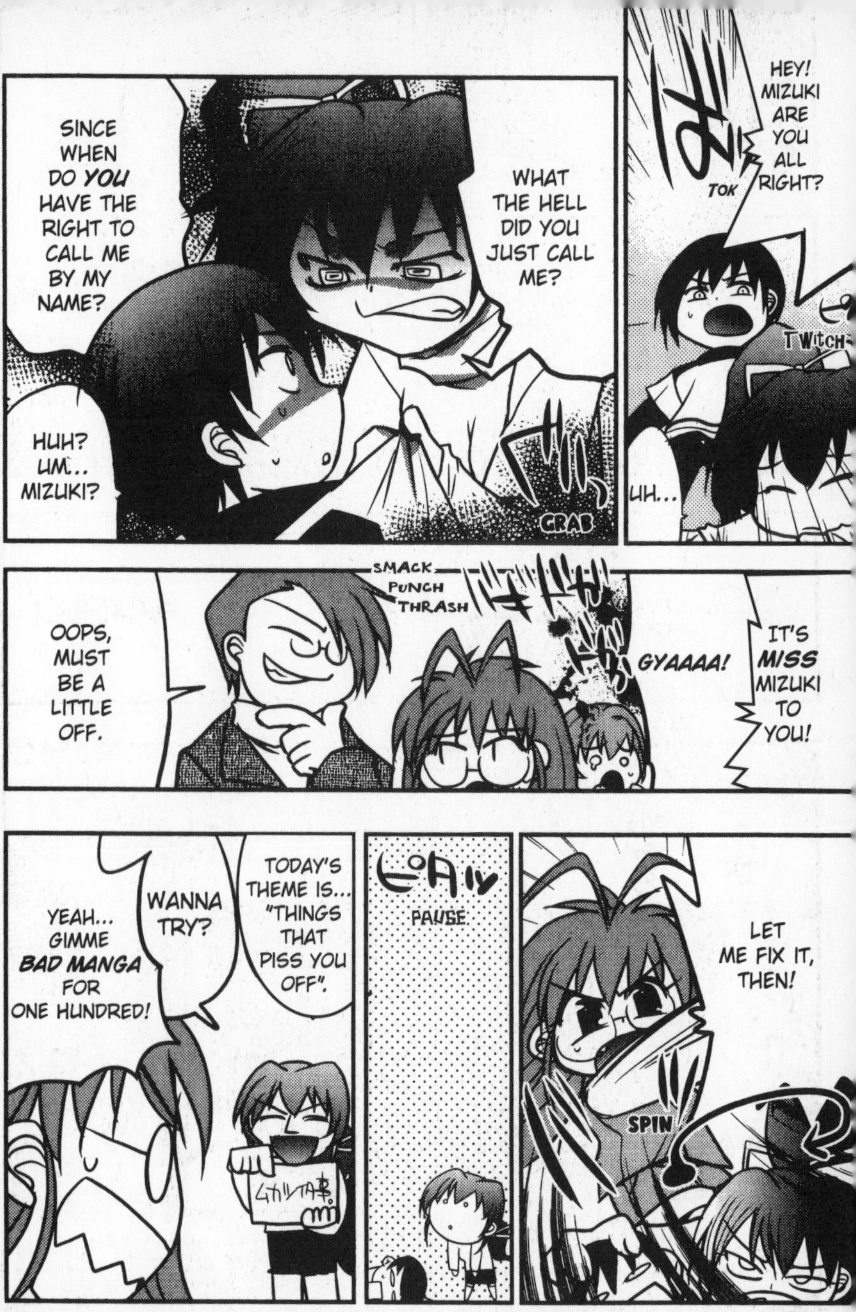
HEY! MIZUKI ARE YOU ALL RIGHT?
TOK
TWITCH
UH...
WHAT THE HELL DID YOU JUST CALL ME?
SINCE WHEN DO *YOU* HAVE THE RIGHT TO CALL ME BY MY NAME?
GRAB
HUH? UM... MIZUKI?
IT'S *MISS* MIZUKI TO YOU!
GYAAAA!
SMACK
PUNCH
THRASH
OOPS, MUST BE A LITTLE OFF.
LET ME FIX IT, THEN!
SPIN
PAUSE
TODAY'S THEME IS... "THINGS THAT PISS YOU OFF".
WANNA TRY?
YEAH... GIMME *BAD MANGA* FOR ONE HUNDRED!

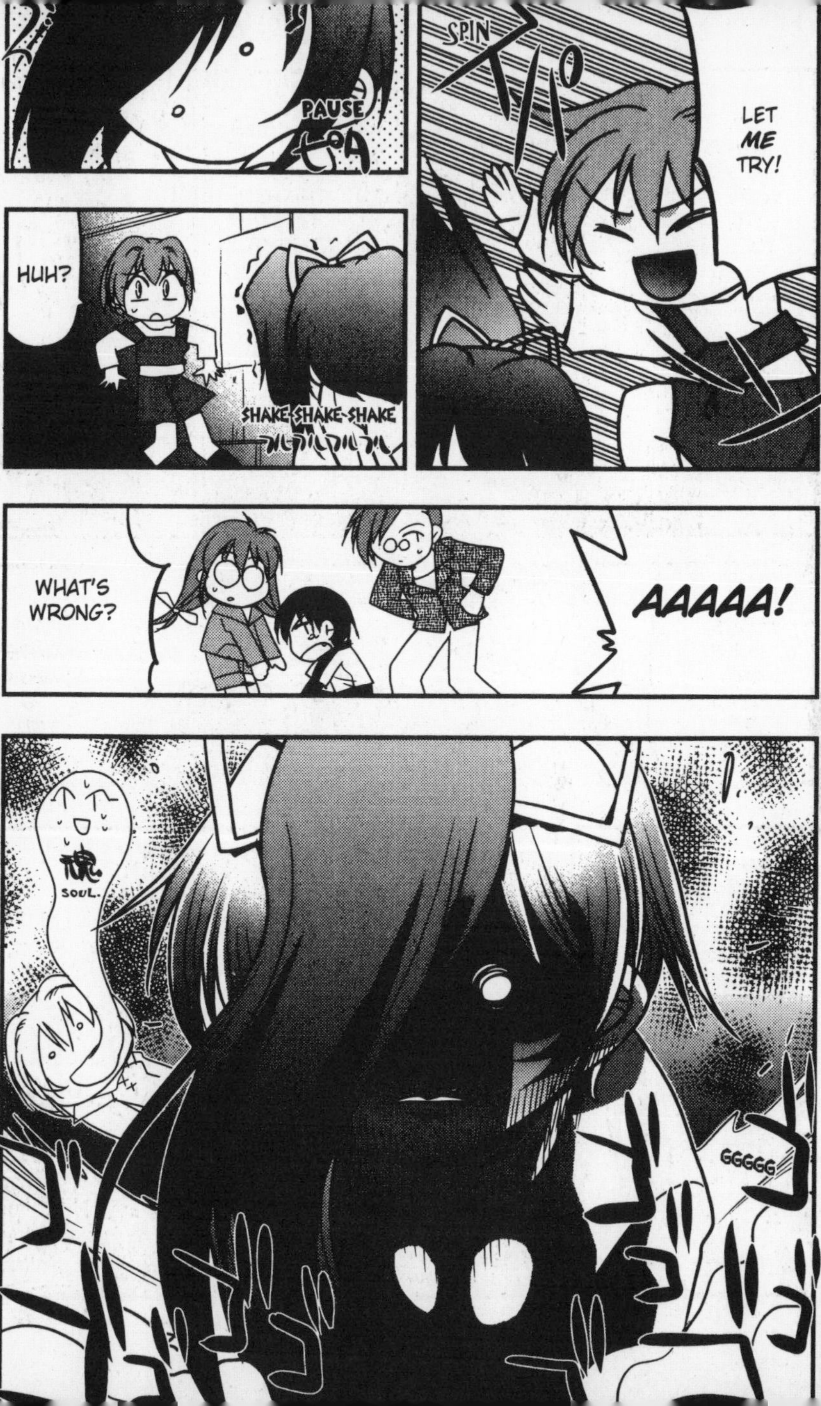
SPIN
LET ME TRY!
PAUSE
HUH?
SHAKE-SHAKE-SHAKE
AAAAA!
WHAT'S WRONG?
GGGGG
SOUL.

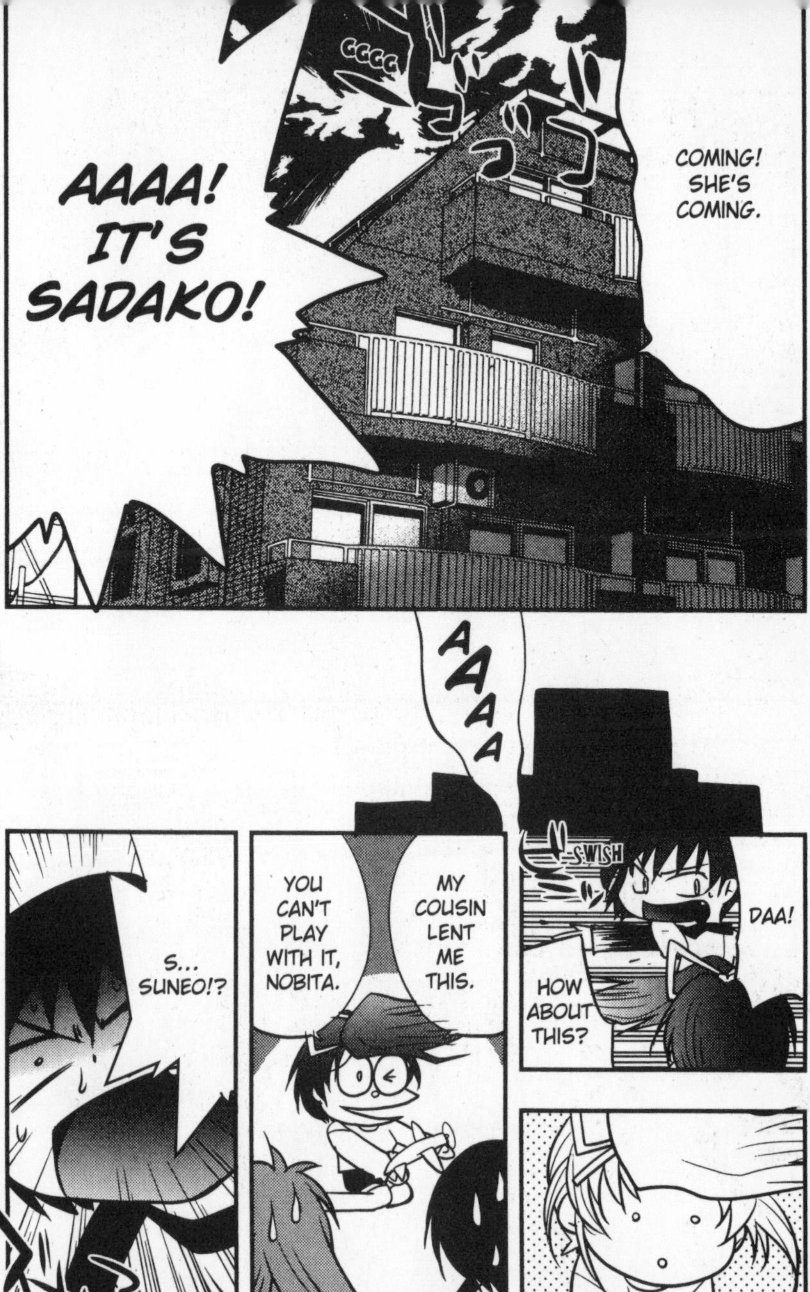
COMING! SHE'S COMING.
GGGG
AAAA! IT'S SADAKO!
AAAA
SWISH
DAA!
HOW ABOUT THIS?
MY COUSIN LENT ME THIS.
YOU CAN'T PLAY WITH IT, NOBITA.
S... SUNEO!?
NO WAY!
END

Sadako- The Ghost from the Japanese film "RINGU"

The End of Comic Party?

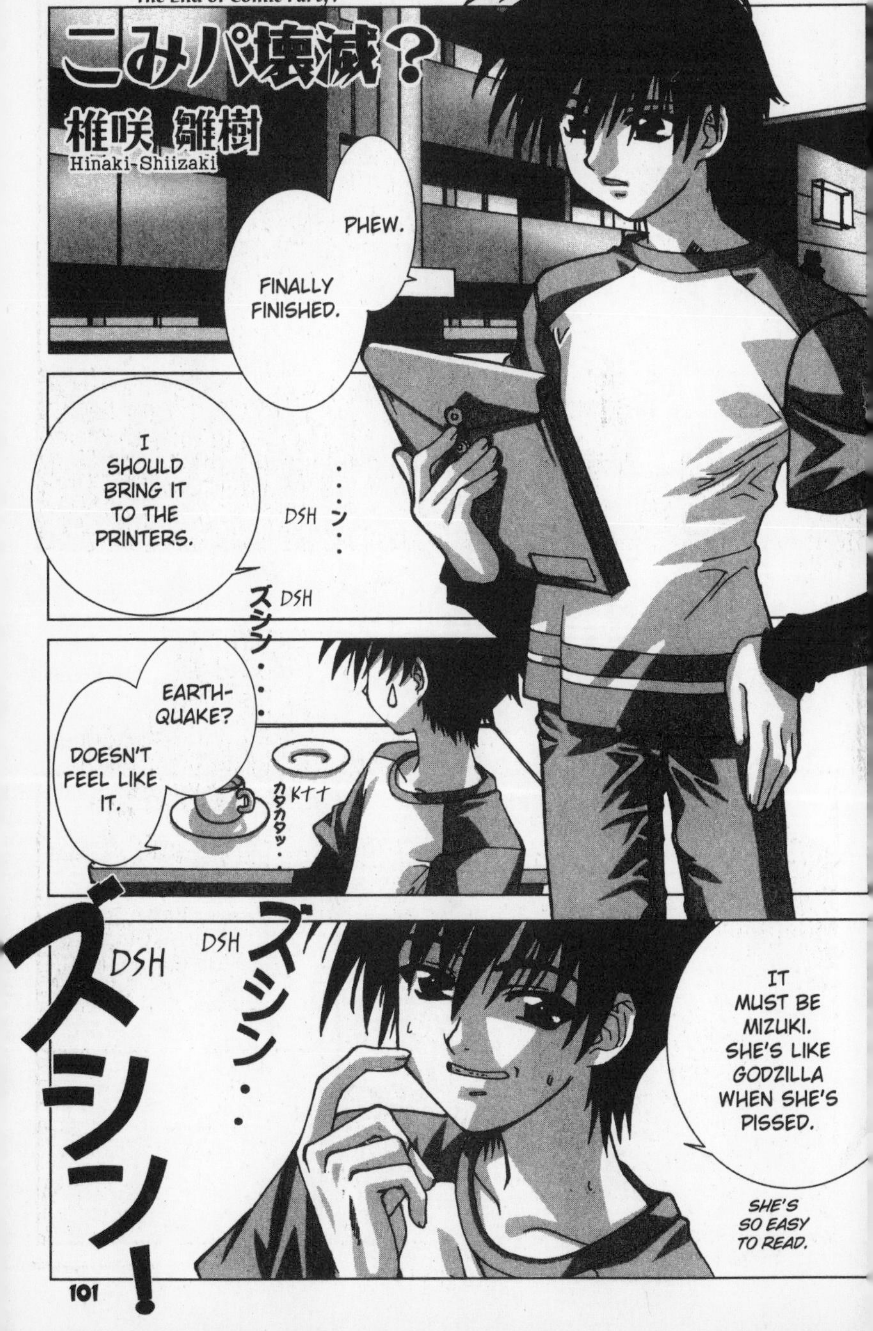

こみパ壊滅？
椎咲雛樹
Hinaki-Shiizaki
PHEW.
FINALLY FINISHED.
DSH
・・・ン・・・
I SHOULD BRING IT TO THE PRINTERS.
DSH
ズシン・・・
EARTH-QUAKE?
DOESN'T FEEL LIKE IT.
KTT
カタカタッ・
IT MUST BE MIZUKI. SHE'S LIKE GODZILLA WHEN SHE'S PISSED.
SHE'S SO EASY TO READ.
DSH
ズシン・・
DSH
ズシン！

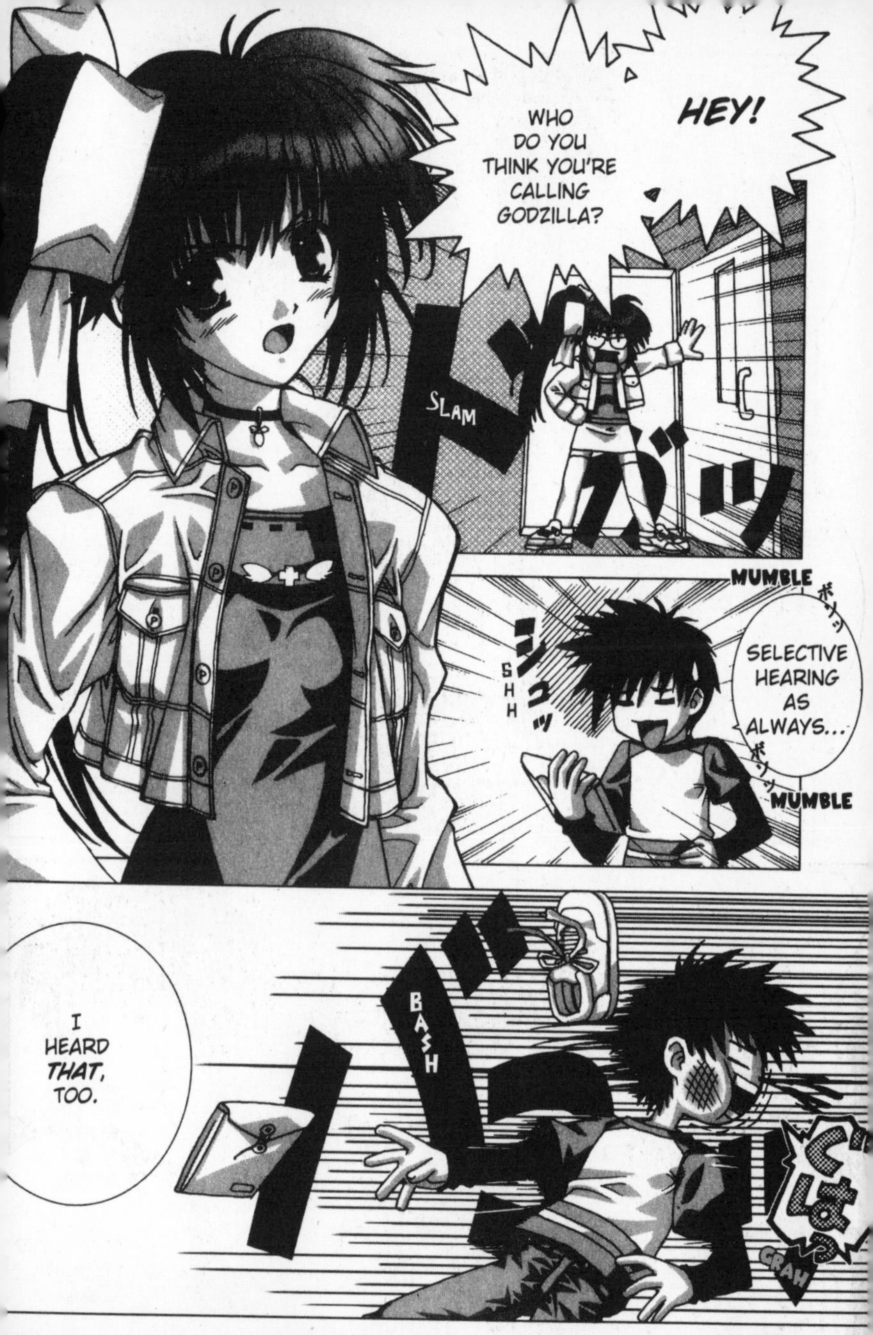
HEY!
WHO DO YOU THINK YOU'RE CALLING GODZILLA?
SLAM
MUMBLE
SHH
SELECTIVE HEARING AS ALWAYS...
MUMBLE
ぐはっ
GRAH
BASH
I HEARD *THAT*, TOO.

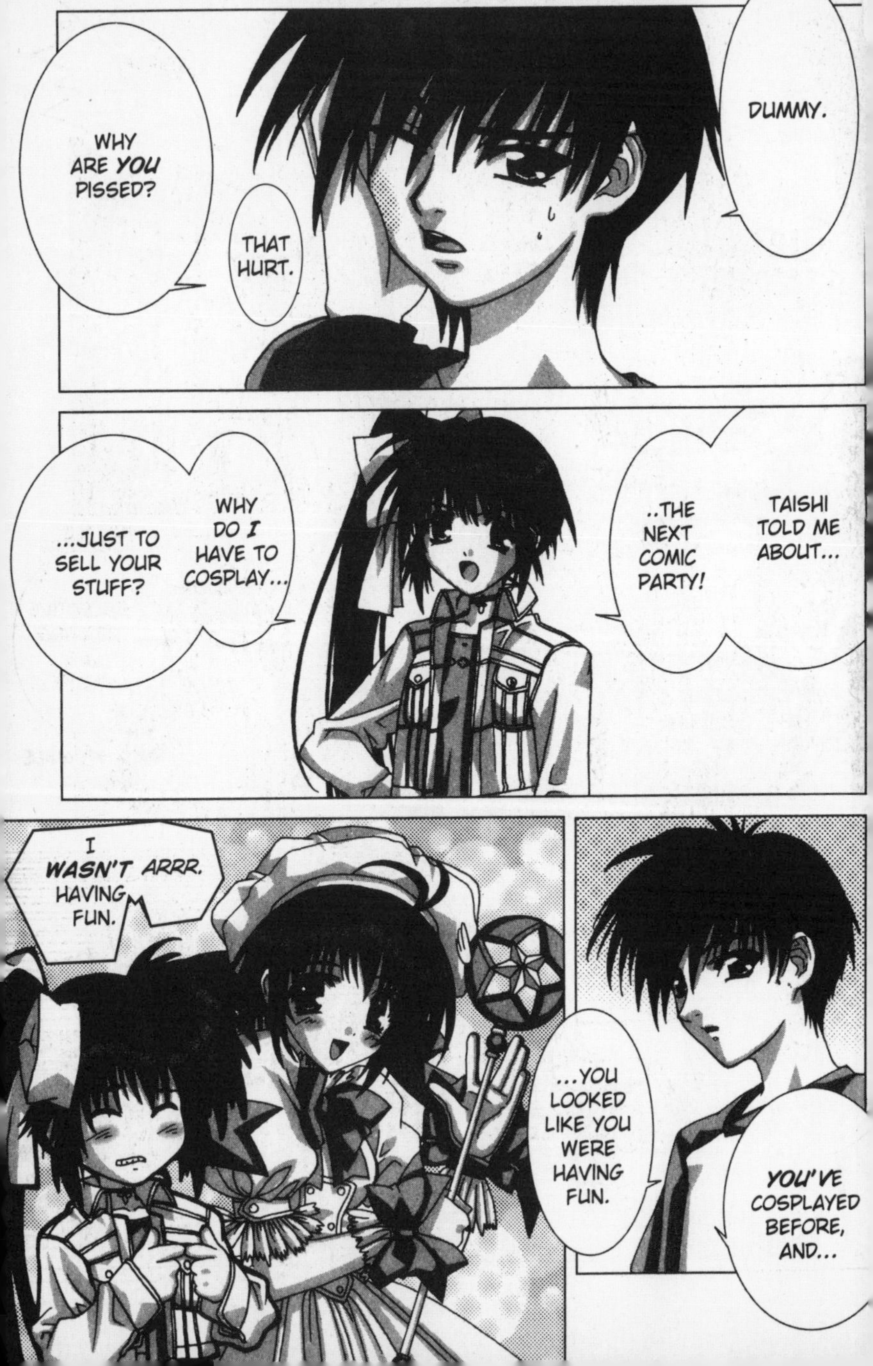
DUMMY.
THAT HURT.
WHY ARE *YOU* PISSED?
TAISHI TOLD ME ABOUT...
..THE NEXT COMIC PARTY!
WHY DO *I* HAVE TO COSPLAY...
...JUST TO SELL YOUR STUFF?
YOU'VE COSPLAYED BEFORE, AND...
...YOU LOOKED LIKE YOU WERE HAVING FUN.
I *WASN'T* HAVING FUN.
ARRR.

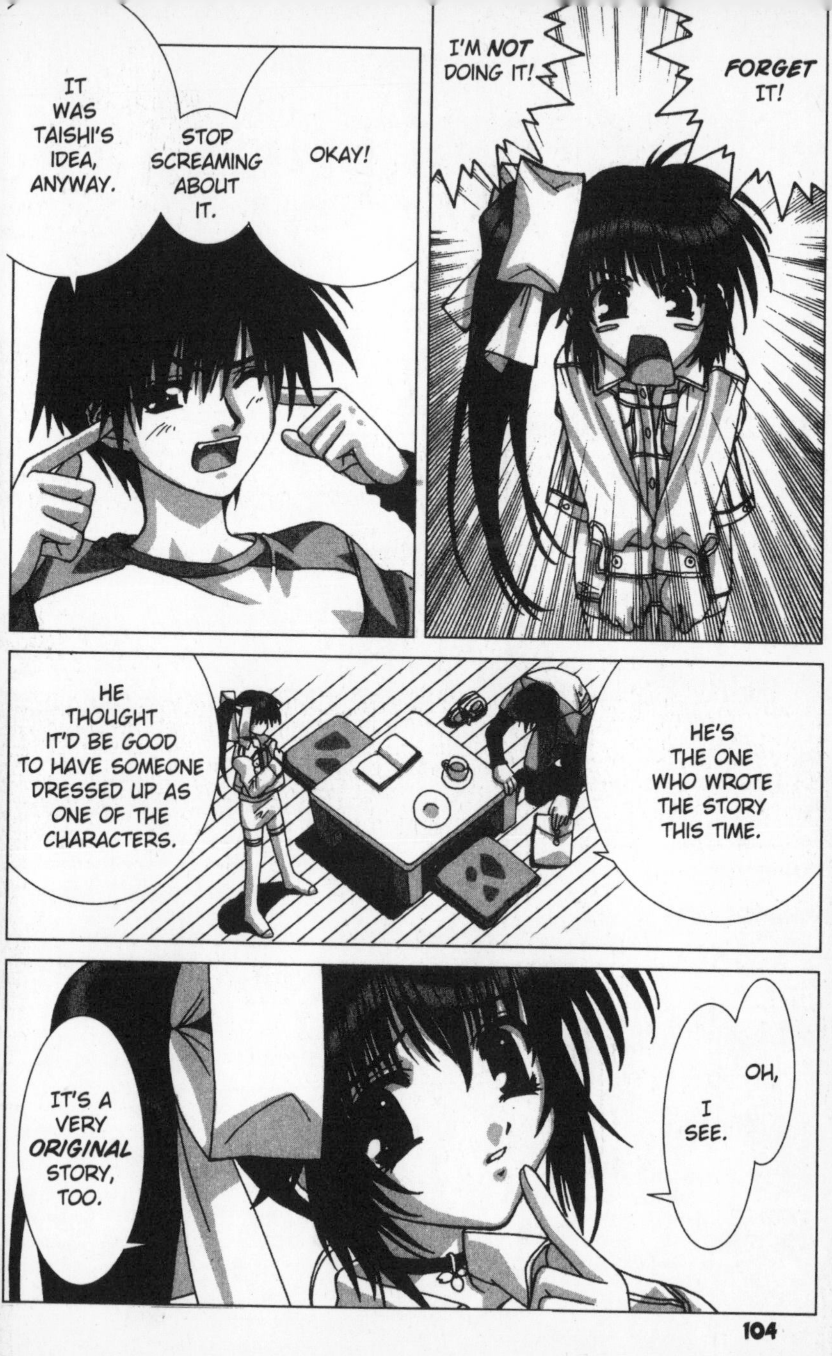

FORGET IT!
I'M **NOT** DOING IT!
OKAY!
STOP SCREAMING ABOUT IT.
IT WAS TAISHI'S IDEA, ANYWAY.
HE'S THE ONE WHO WROTE THE STORY THIS TIME.
HE THOUGHT IT'D BE GOOD TO HAVE SOMEONE DRESSED UP AS ONE OF THE CHARACTERS.
OH, I SEE.
IT'S A VERY **ORIGINAL** STORY, TOO.

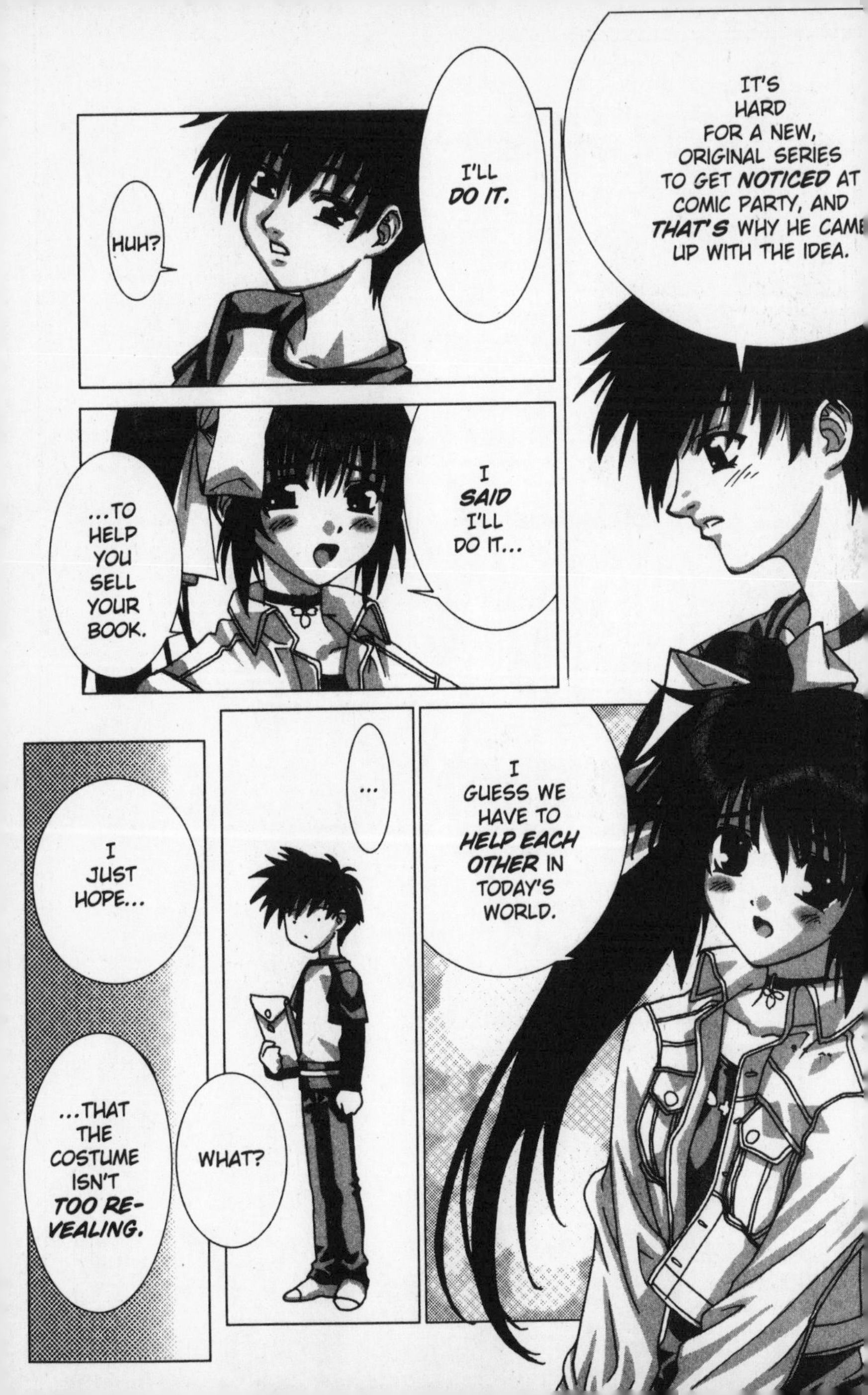
IT'S HARD FOR A NEW, ORIGINAL SERIES TO GET *NOTICED* AT COMIC PARTY, AND *THAT'S* WHY HE CAME UP WITH THE IDEA.
I'LL *DO IT.*
HUH?
I *SAID* I'LL DO IT...
...TO HELP YOU SELL YOUR BOOK.
I GUESS WE HAVE TO *HELP EACH OTHER* IN TODAY'S WORLD.
...
WHAT?
I JUST HOPE...
...THAT THE COSTUME ISN'T *TOO RE-VEALING.*

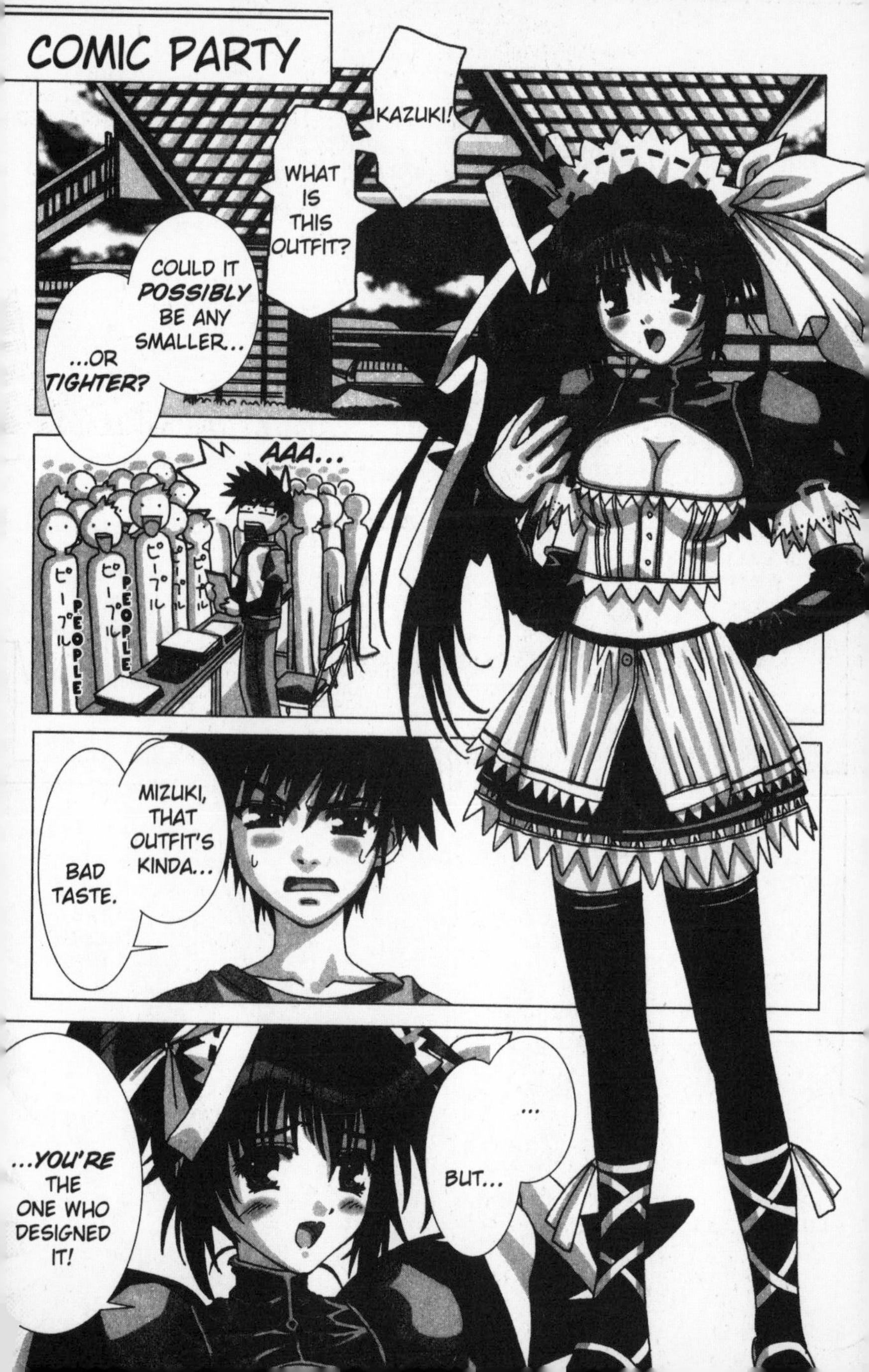
COMIC PARTY
KAZUKI!
WHAT IS THIS OUTFIT?
COULD IT *POSSIBLY* BE ANY SMALLER...
...OR *TIGHTER?*
AAA...
ピープル PEOPLE
ピープル PEOPLE
MIZUKI, THAT OUTFIT'S KINDA...
BAD TASTE.
...
BUT...
...*YOU'RE* THE ONE WHO DESIGNED IT!

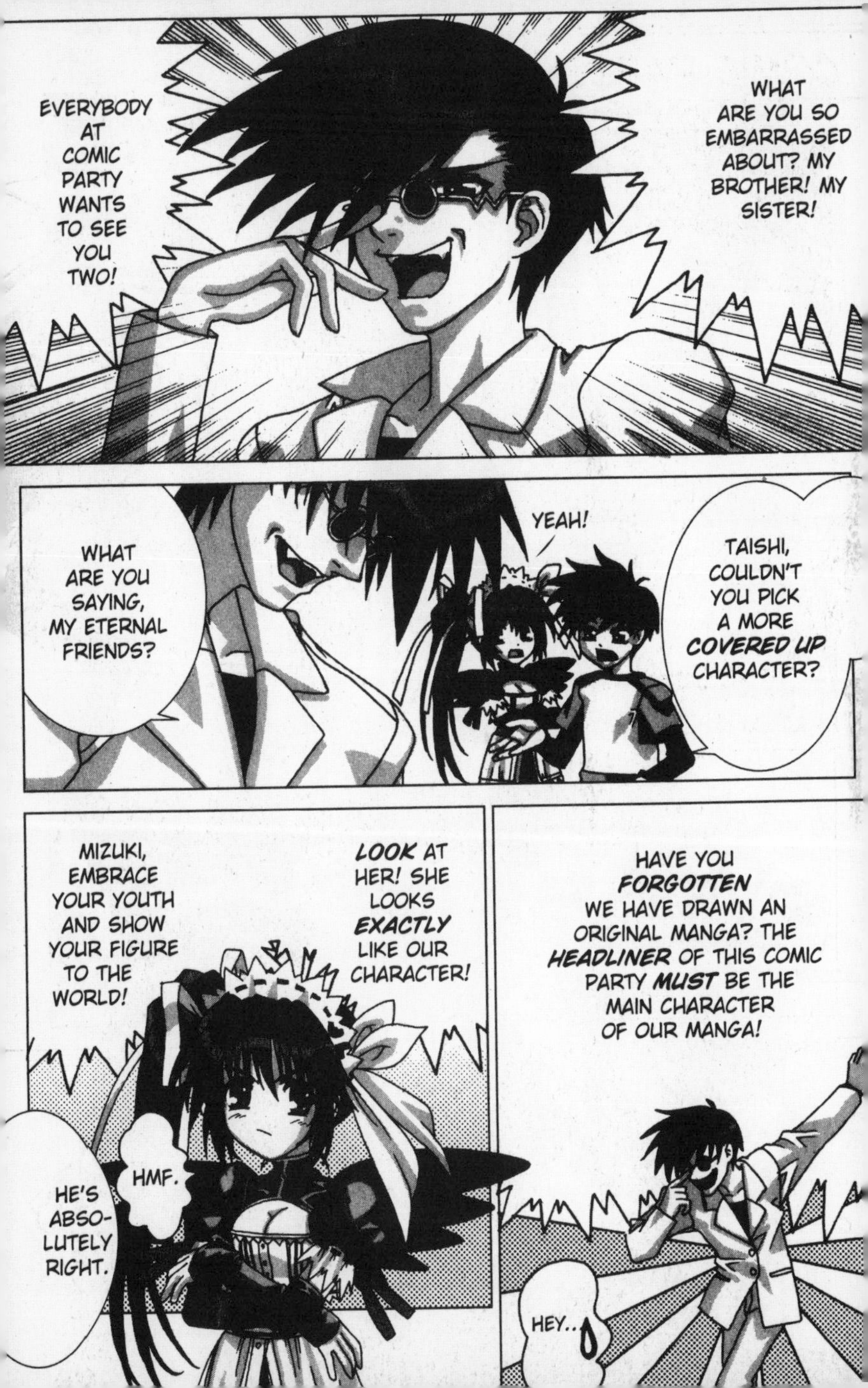
WHAT ARE YOU SO EMBARRASSED ABOUT? MY BROTHER! MY SISTER!
EVERYBODY AT COMIC PARTY WANTS TO SEE YOU TWO!
TAISHI, COULDN'T YOU PICK A MORE *COVERED UP* CHARACTER?
YEAH!
WHAT ARE YOU SAYING, MY ETERNAL FRIENDS?
HAVE YOU *FORGOTTEN* WE HAVE DRAWN AN ORIGINAL MANGA? THE *HEADLINER* OF THIS COMIC PARTY *MUST* BE THE MAIN CHARACTER OF OUR MANGA!
HEY..
LOOK AT HER! SHE LOOKS *EXACTLY* LIKE OUR CHARACTER!
MIZUKI, EMBRACE YOUR YOUTH AND SHOW YOUR FIGURE TO THE WORLD!
HMF.
HE'S ABSOLUTELY RIGHT.

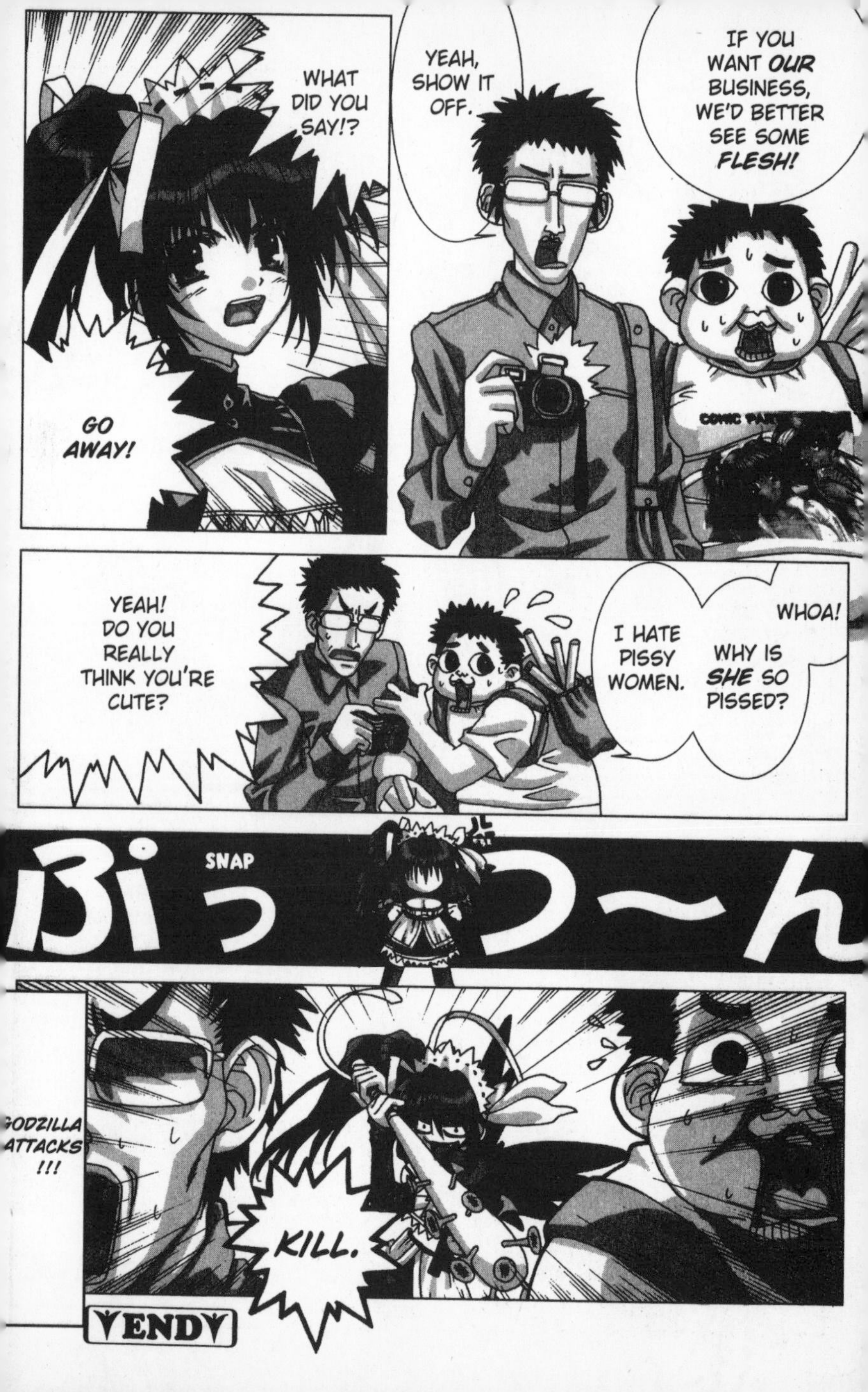
IF YOU WANT OUR BUSINESS, WE'D BETTER SEE SOME FLESH!
YEAH, SHOW IT OFF.
WHAT DID YOU SAY!?
GO AWAY!
WHOA!
WHY IS SHE SO PISSED?
I HATE PISSY WOMEN.
YEAH! DO YOU REALLY THINK YOU'RE CUTE?
ぷっつ～ん
SNAP
GODZILLA ATTACKS !!!
KILL.
END

BEST!

胡せんり

Senri Ebisu

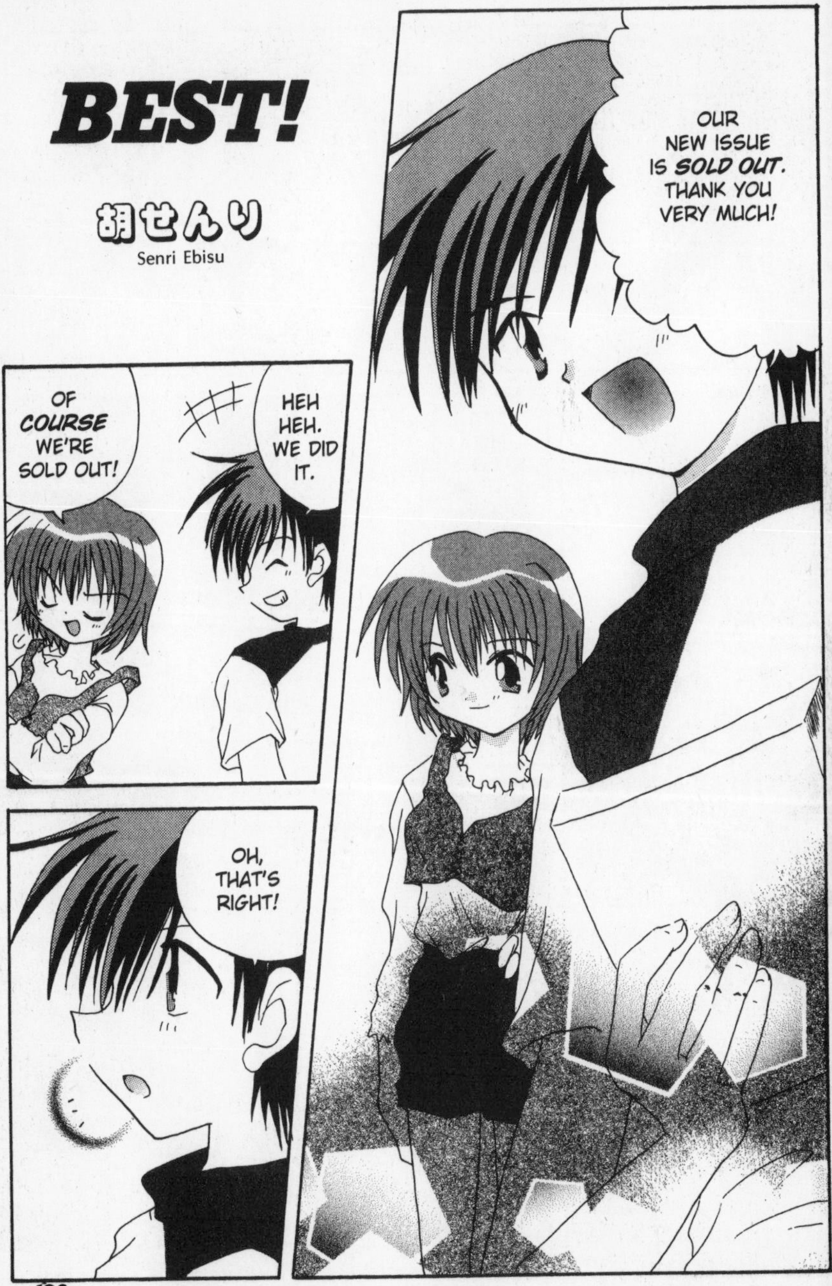

OUR NEW ISSUE IS ***SOLD OUT***. THANK YOU VERY MUCH!
HEH HEH. WE DID IT.
OF ***COURSE*** WE'RE SOLD OUT!
OH, THAT'S RIGHT!

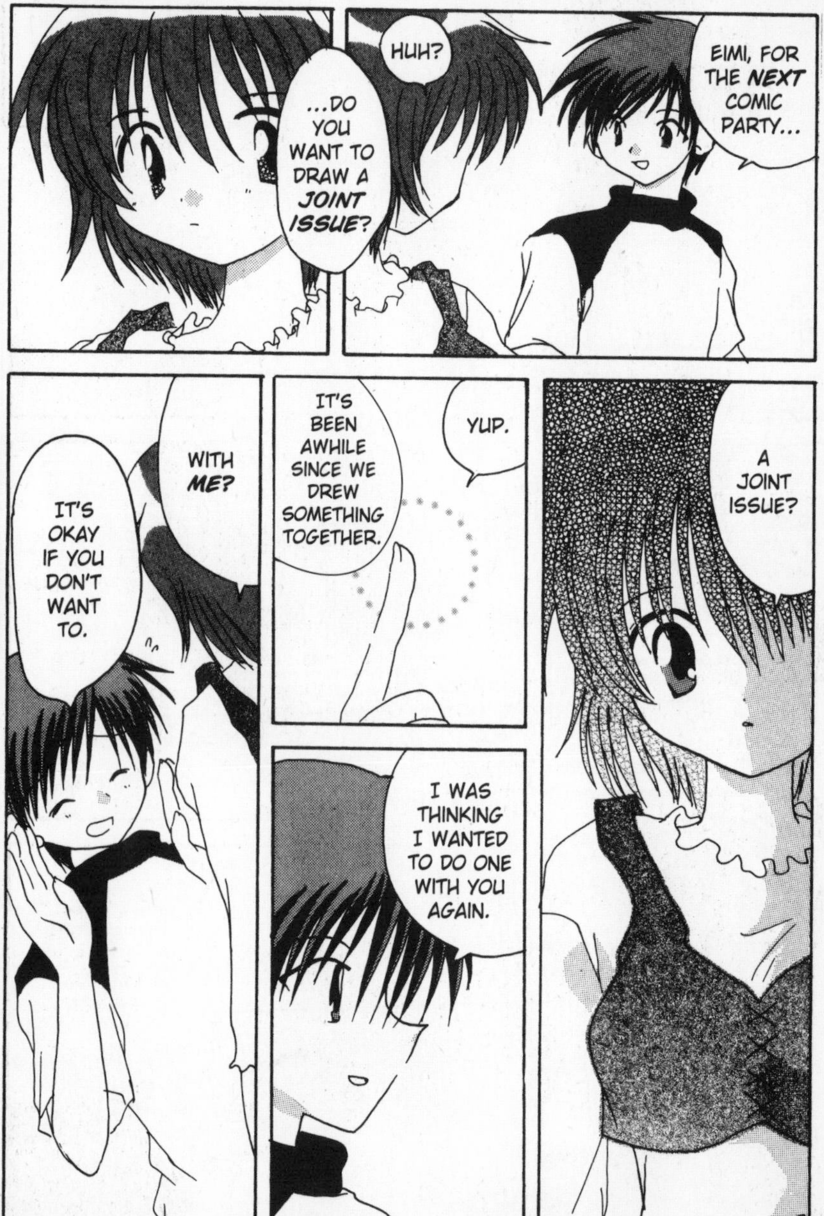
EIMI, FOR THE NEXT COMIC PARTY...
HUH?
...DO YOU WANT TO DRAW A JOINT ISSUE?
A JOINT ISSUE?
YUP.
IT'S BEEN AWHILE SINCE WE DREW SOMETHING TOGETHER.
I WAS THINKING I WANTED TO DO ONE WITH YOU AGAIN.
WITH ME?
IT'S OKAY IF YOU DON'T WANT TO.

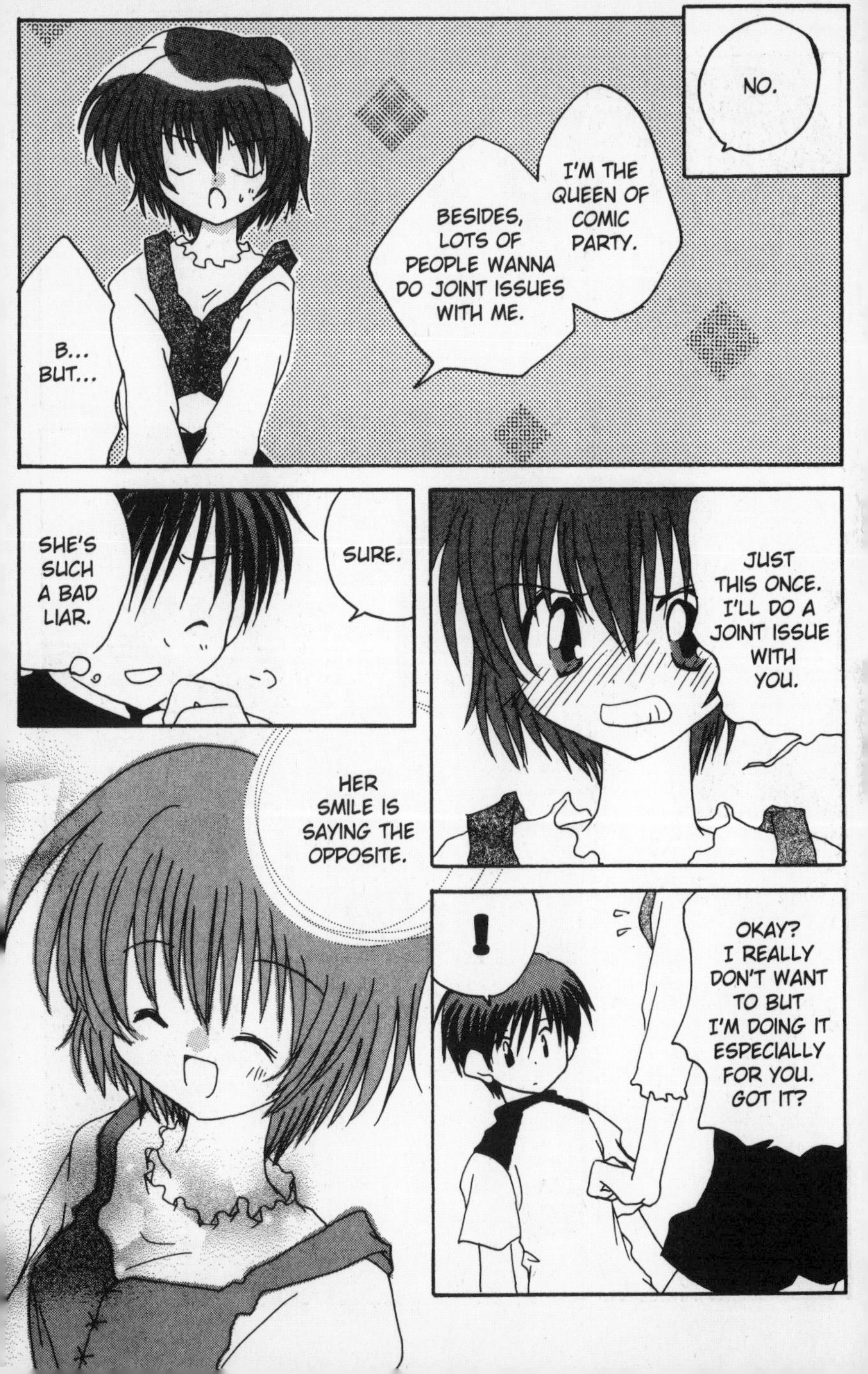
NO.
I'M THE QUEEN OF COMIC PARTY.
BESIDES, LOTS OF PEOPLE WANNA DO JOINT ISSUES WITH ME.
B... BUT...
JUST THIS ONCE. I'LL DO A JOINT ISSUE WITH YOU.
SURE.
SHE'S SUCH A BAD LIAR.
OKAY? I REALLY DON'T WANT TO BUT I'M DOING IT ESPECIALLY FOR YOU. GOT IT?
!
HER SMILE IS SAYING THE OPPOSITE.

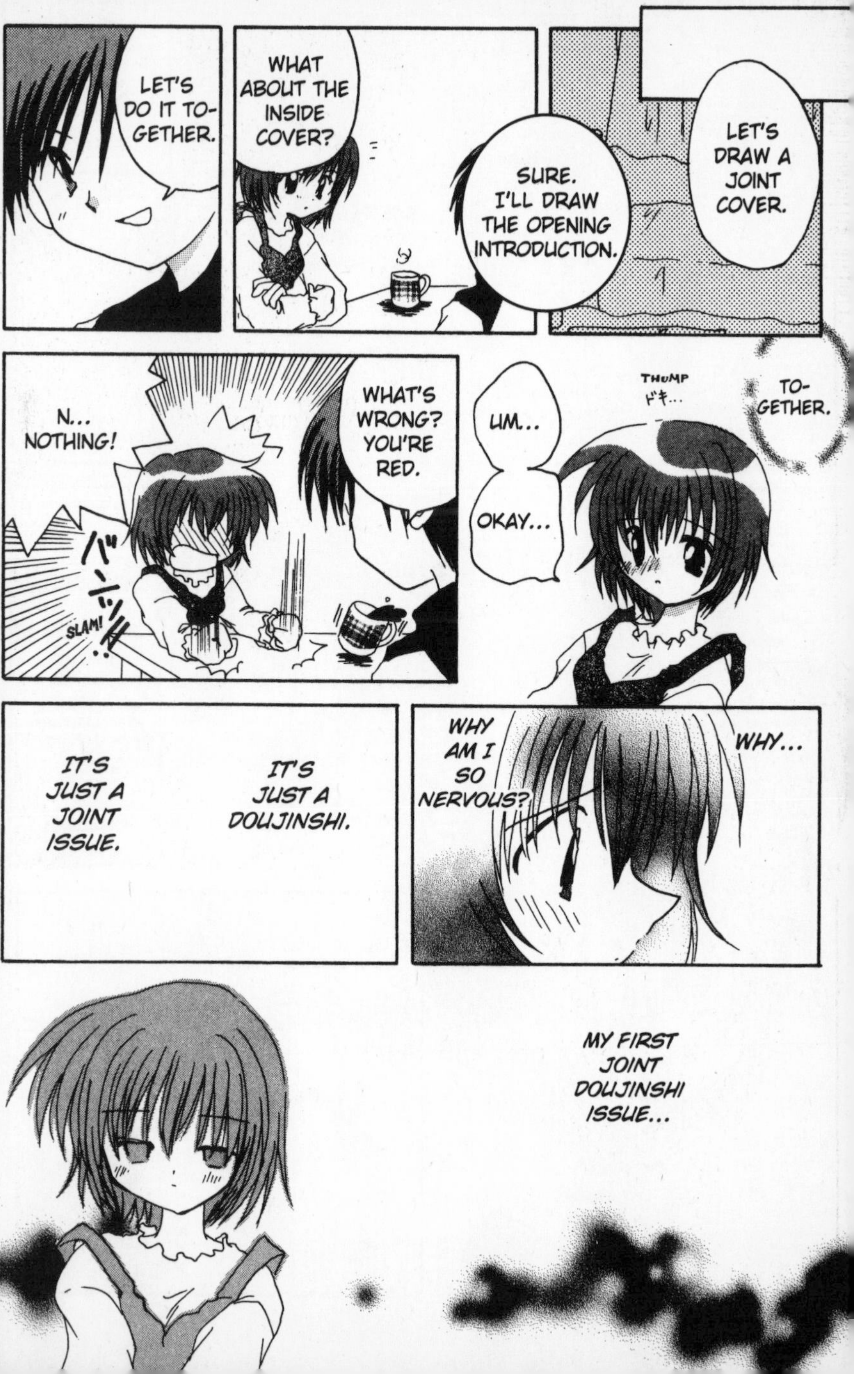
LET'S DRAW A JOINT COVER.
SURE. I'LL DRAW THE OPENING INTRODUCTION.
WHAT ABOUT THE INSIDE COVER?
LET'S DO IT TO-GETHER.
TO-GETHER.
THUMP ドキ...
UM...
OKAY...
WHAT'S WRONG? YOU'RE RED.
N... NOTHING!
バンッ
SLAM!
WHY...
WHY AM I SO NERVOUS?
IT'S JUST A DOUJINSHI.
IT'S JUST A JOINT ISSUE.
MY FIRST JOINT DOUJINSHI ISSUE...

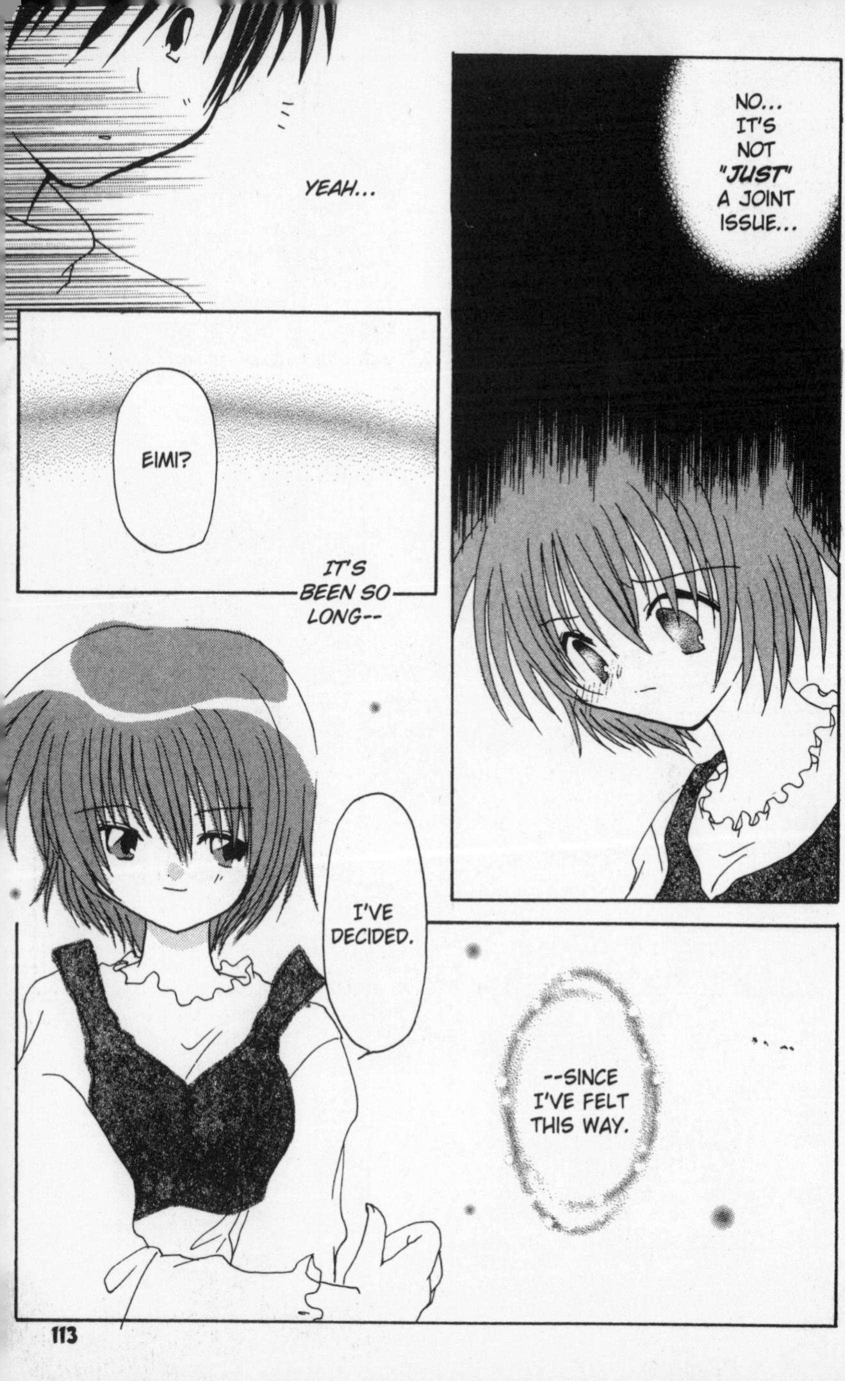
NO... IT'S NOT "JUST" A JOINT ISSUE...
YEAH...
EIMI?
IT'S BEEN SO LONG--
I'VE DECIDED.
--SINCE I'VE FELT THIS WAY.

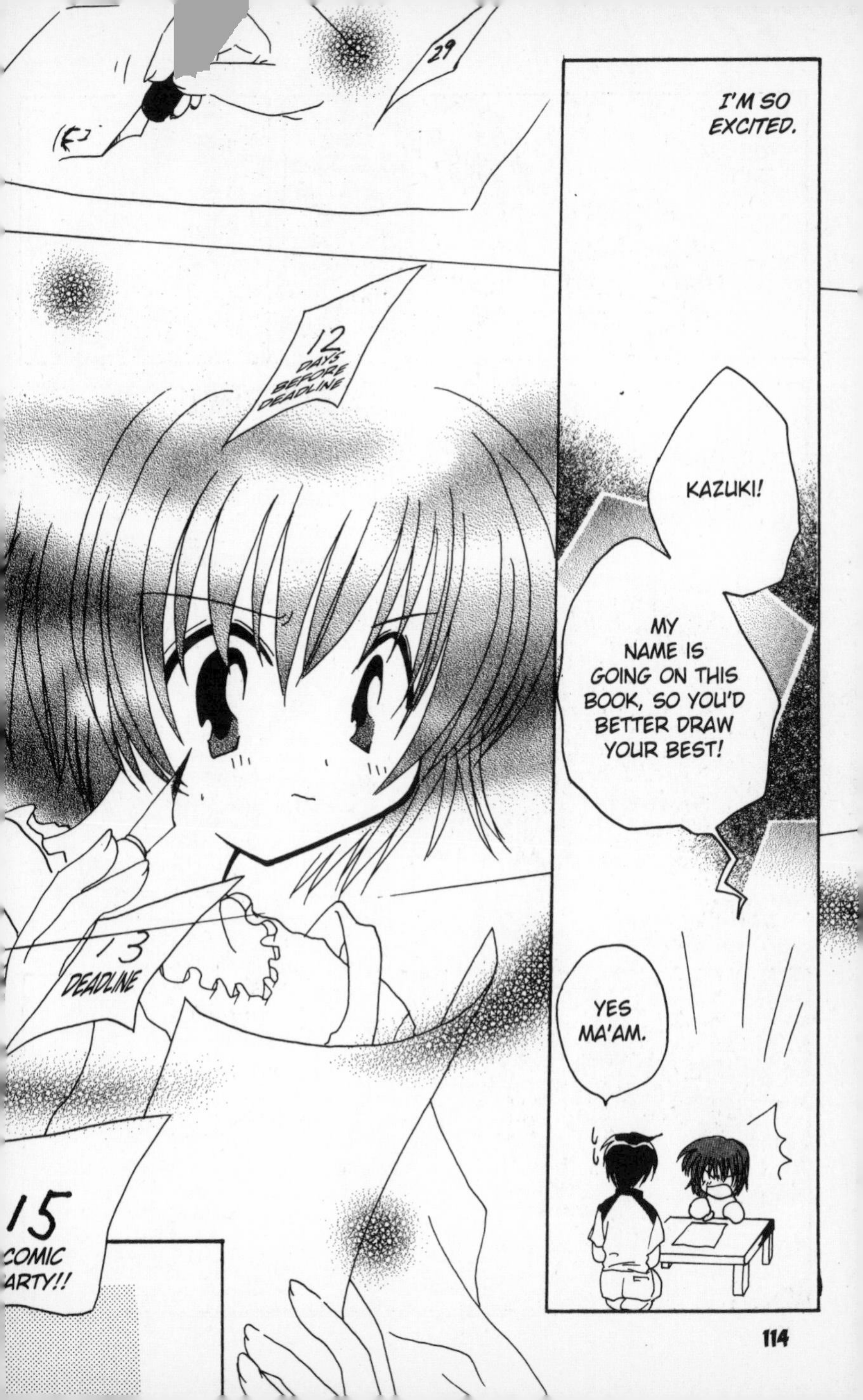
I'M SO EXCITED.
KAZUKI!
MY NAME IS GOING ON THIS BOOK, SO YOU'D BETTER DRAW YOUR BEST!
YES MA'AM.
29
12 DAYS BEFORE DEADLINE
13 DEADLINE
15 COMIC
ARTY!!

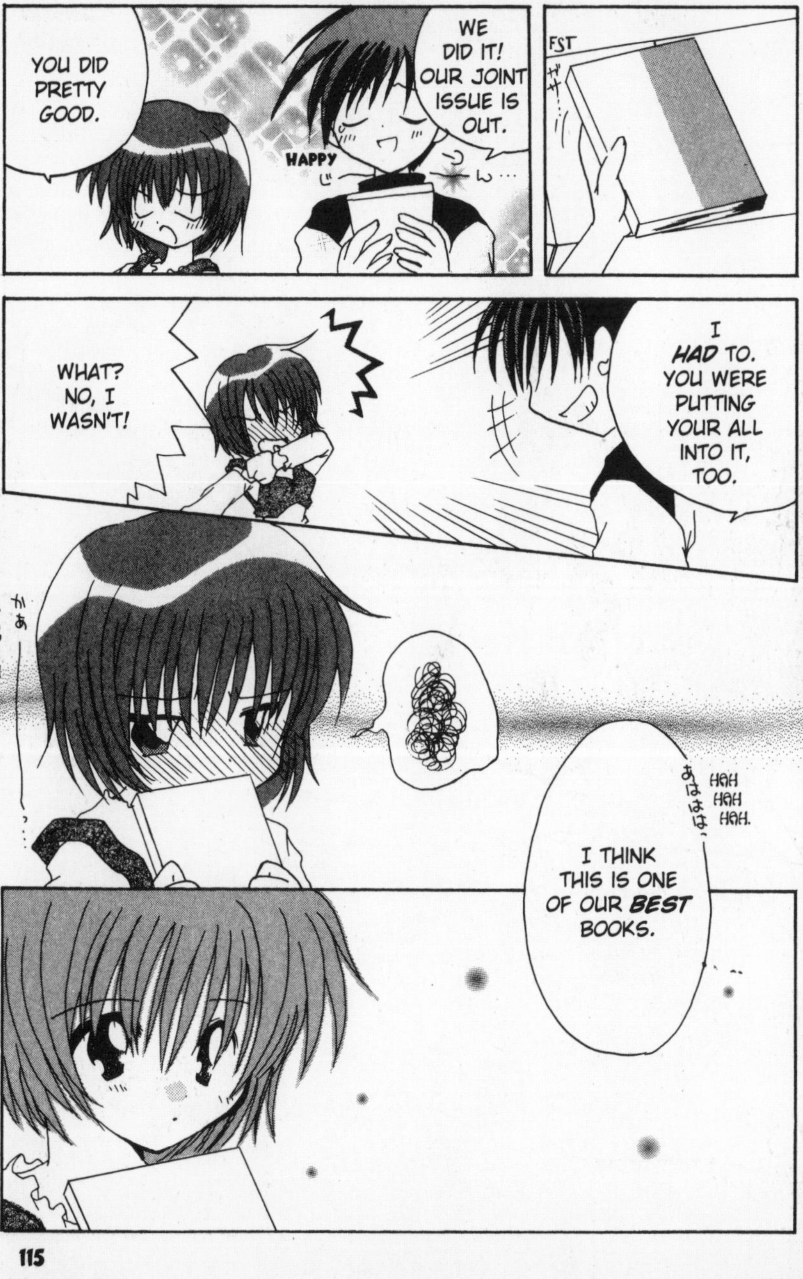
FST
WE DID IT! OUR JOINT ISSUE IS OUT.
HAPPY
YOU DID PRETTY GOOD.
I HAD TO. YOU WERE PUTTING YOUR ALL INTO IT, TOO.
WHAT? NO, I WASN'T!
HAH HAH HAH.
I THINK THIS IS ONE OF OUR BEST BOOKS.
BLUSH

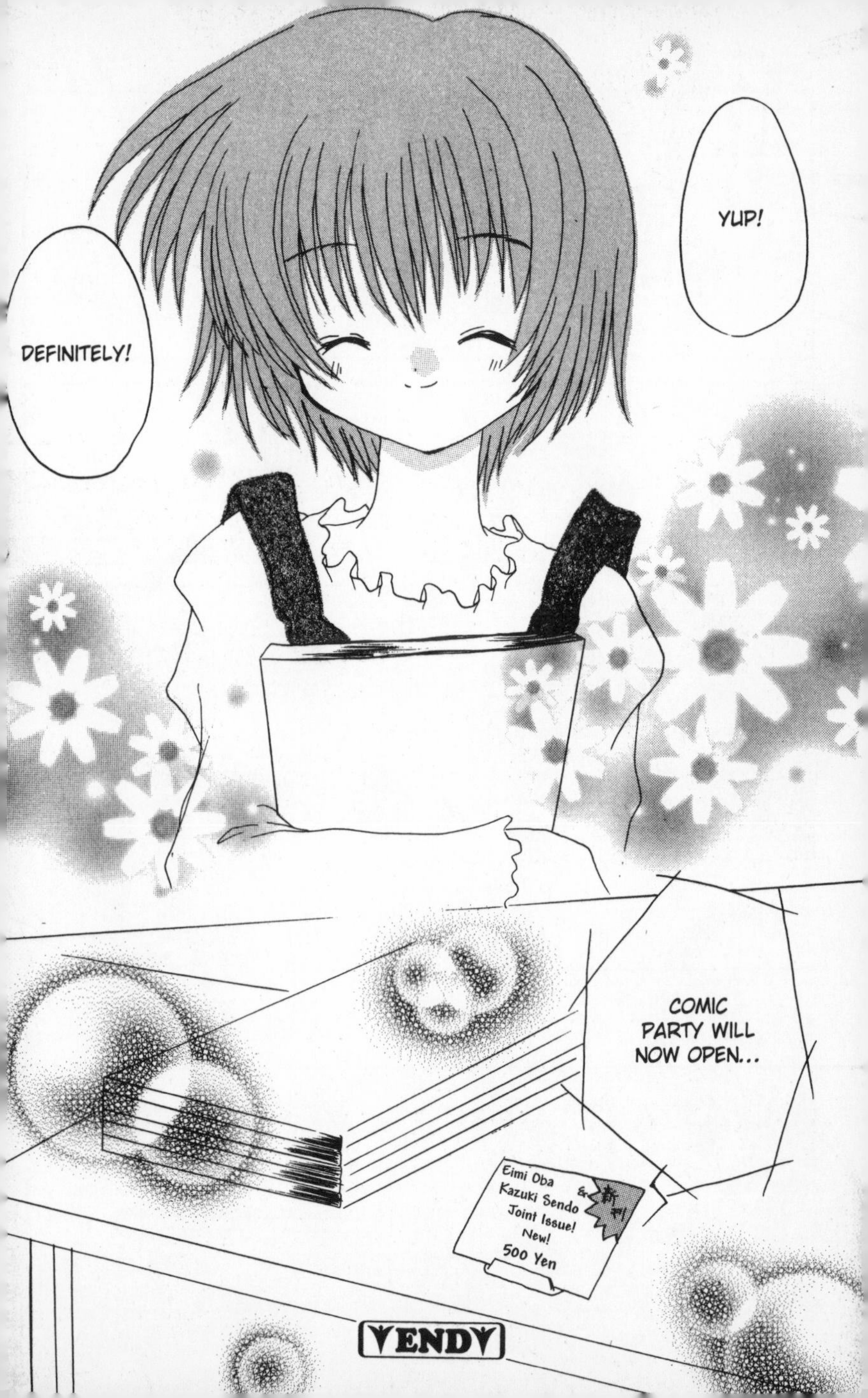
YUP!
DEFINITELY!
COMIC PARTY WILL NOW OPEN...
Eimi Oba & Kazuki Sendo Joint Issue! New! 500 Yen
END

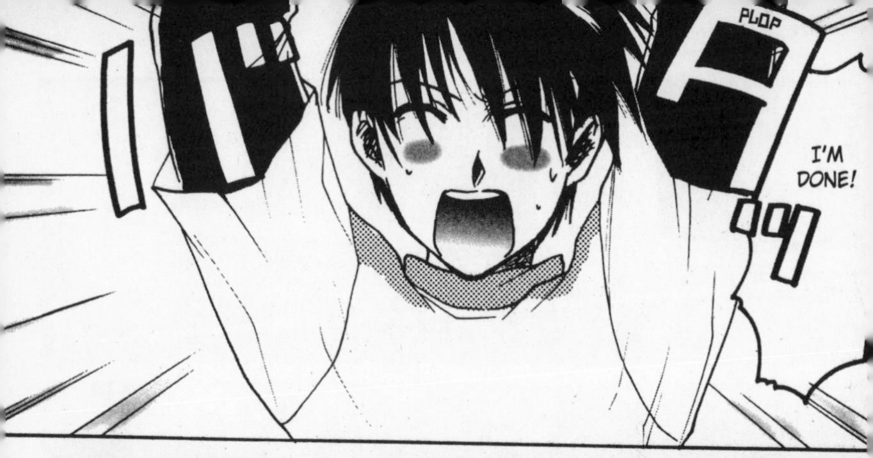
PLOP
I'M DONE!

THE OTHER DOUJIN WORLD?

もう一つの同人ワールド!?

天下 泰平
Taihei Tenka

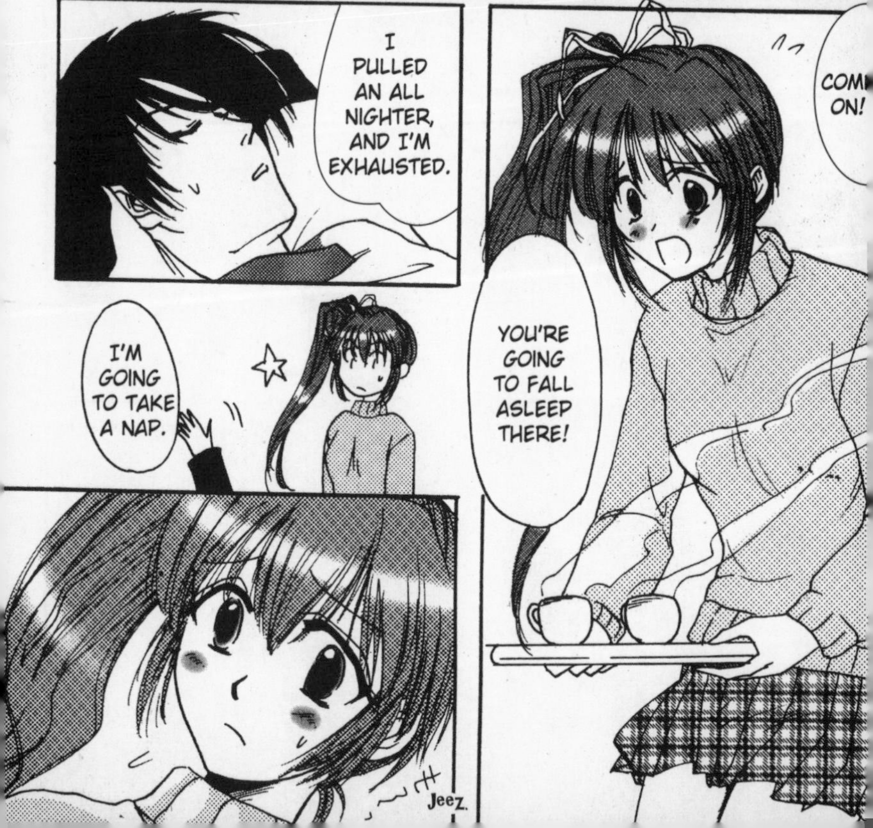
COM
ON!
YOU'RE GOING TO FALL ASLEEP THERE!
I PULLED AN ALL NIGHTER, AND I'M EXHAUSTED.
I'M GOING TO TAKE A NAP.
Jeez.

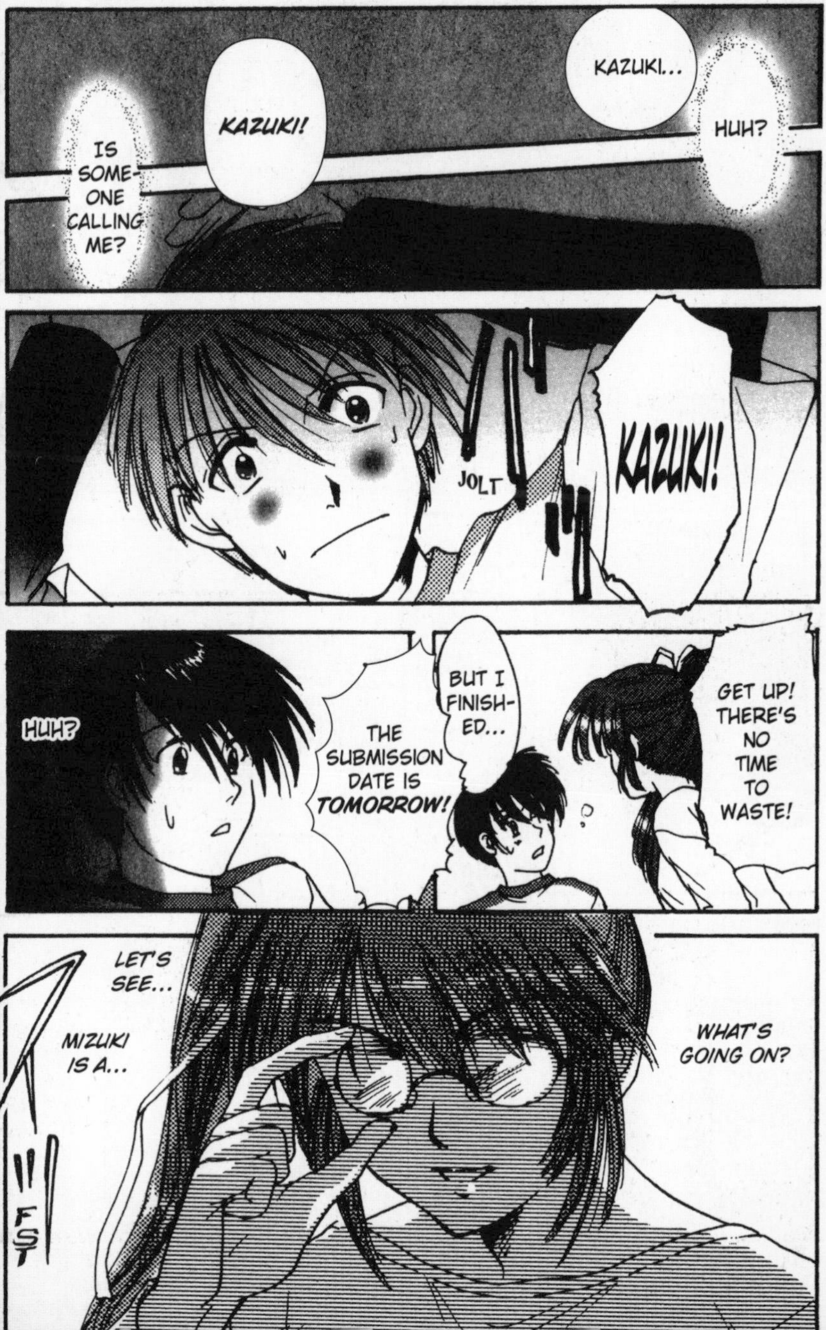
KAZUKI...
HUH?
KAZUKI!
IS SOME-ONE CALLING ME?
KAZUKI!
JOLT
GET UP! THERE'S NO TIME TO WASTE!
BUT I FINISH-ED...
THE SUBMISSION DATE IS TOMORROW!
HUH?
WHAT'S GOING ON?
LET'S SEE...
MIZUKI IS A...
FST

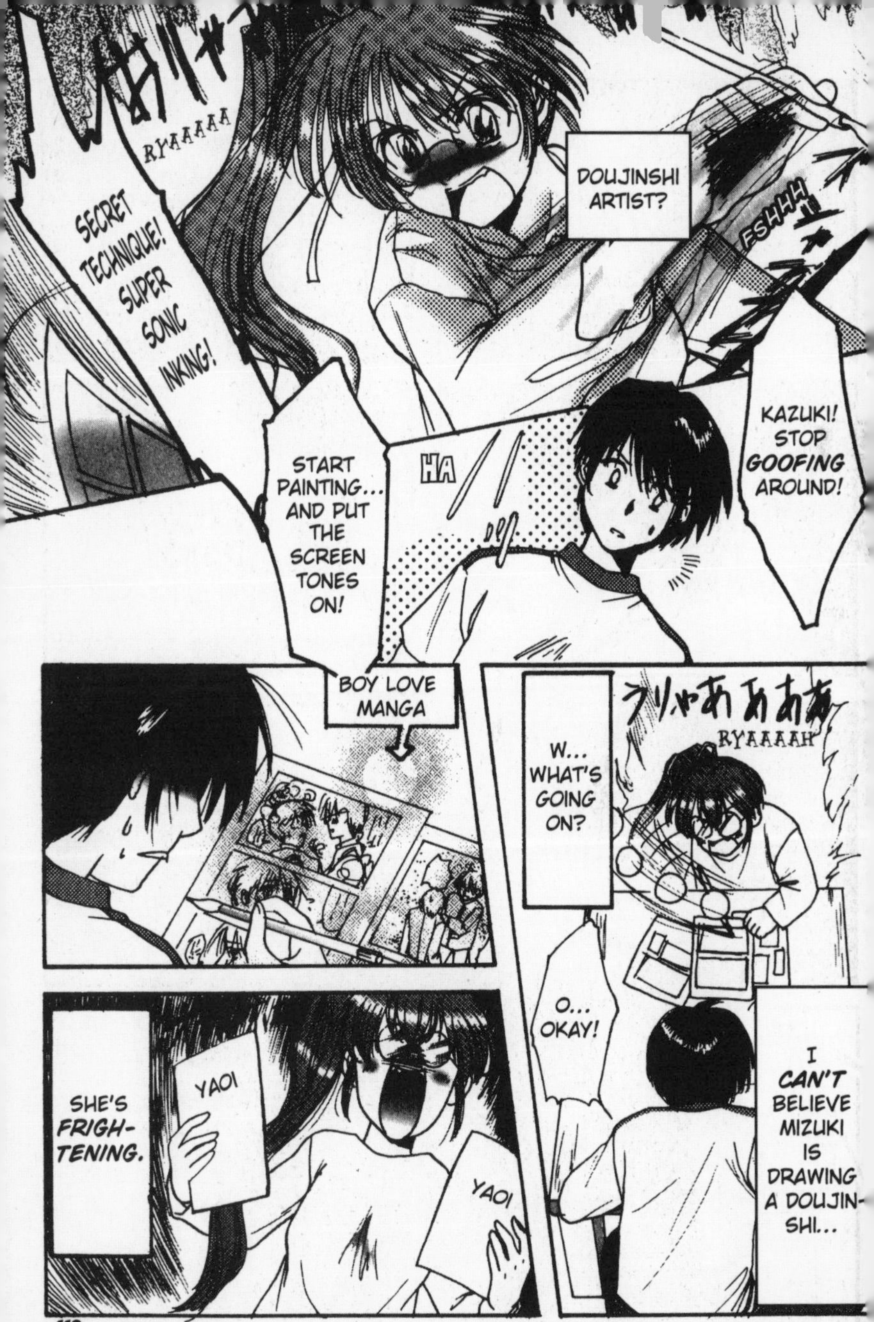
DOUJINSHI ARTIST?
FSHHH
RYAAAAA
SECRET TECHNIQUE! SUPER SONIC INKING!
KAZUKI! STOP *GOOFING* AROUND!
HA
START PAINTING... AND PUT THE SCREEN TONES ON!
RYAAAAH
W... WHAT'S GOING ON?
O... OKAY!
I *CAN'T* BELIEVE MIZUKI IS DRAWING A DOUJIN-SHI...
BOY LOVE MANGA
SHE'S *FRIGH-TENING.*
YAOI
YAOI

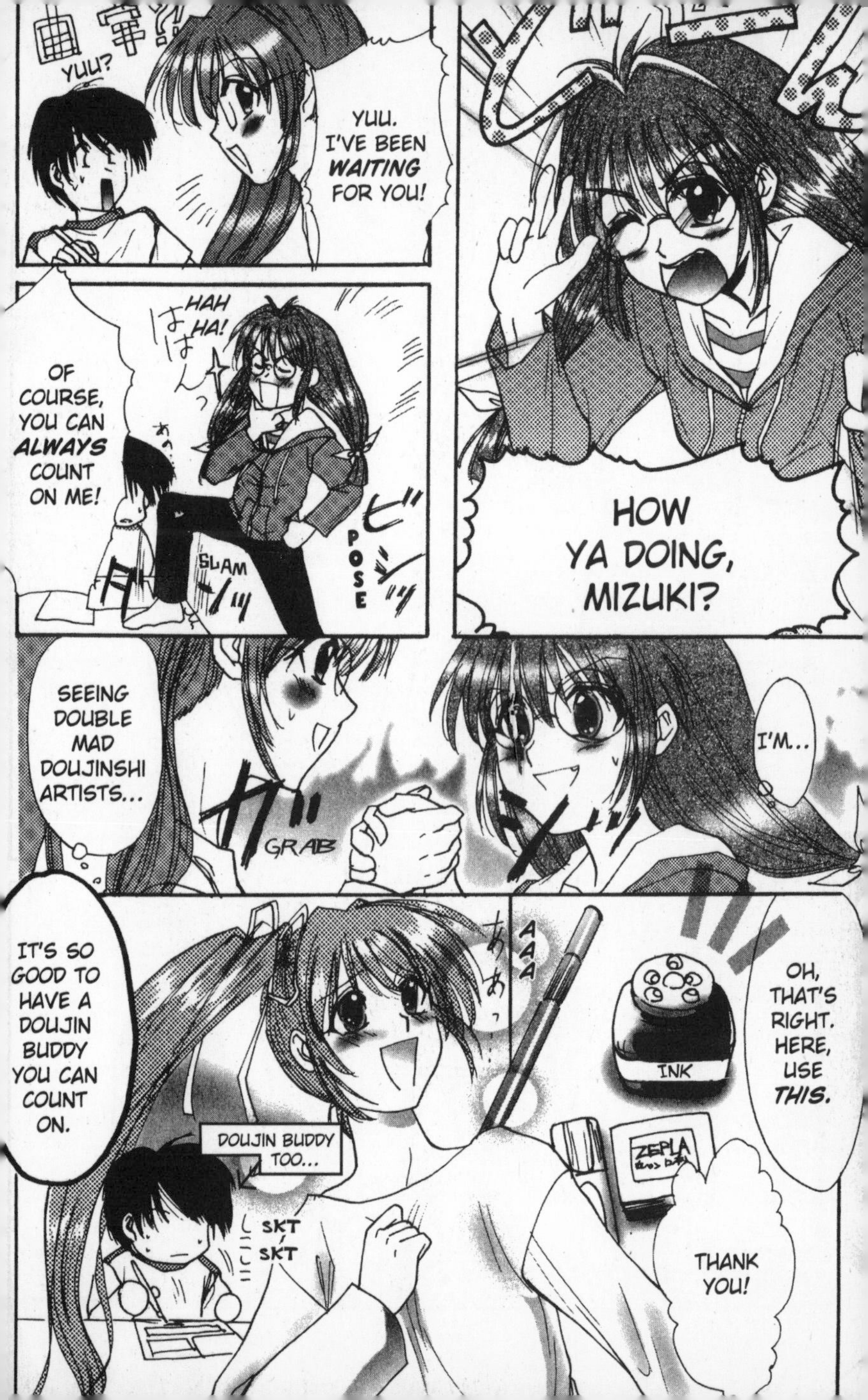
HOW YA DOING, MIZUKI?
YUU?
YUU. I'VE BEEN *WAITING* FOR YOU!
HAH HA!
POSE
SLAM
OF COURSE, YOU CAN *ALWAYS* COUNT ON ME!
I'M...
GRAB
SEEING DOUBLE MAD DOUJINSHI ARTISTS...
OH, THAT'S RIGHT. HERE, USE *THIS.*
INK
ZEPLA
THANK YOU!
AAA
IT'S SO GOOD TO HAVE A DOUJIN BUDDY YOU CAN COUNT ON.
DOUJIN BUDDY TOO...
SKT SKT

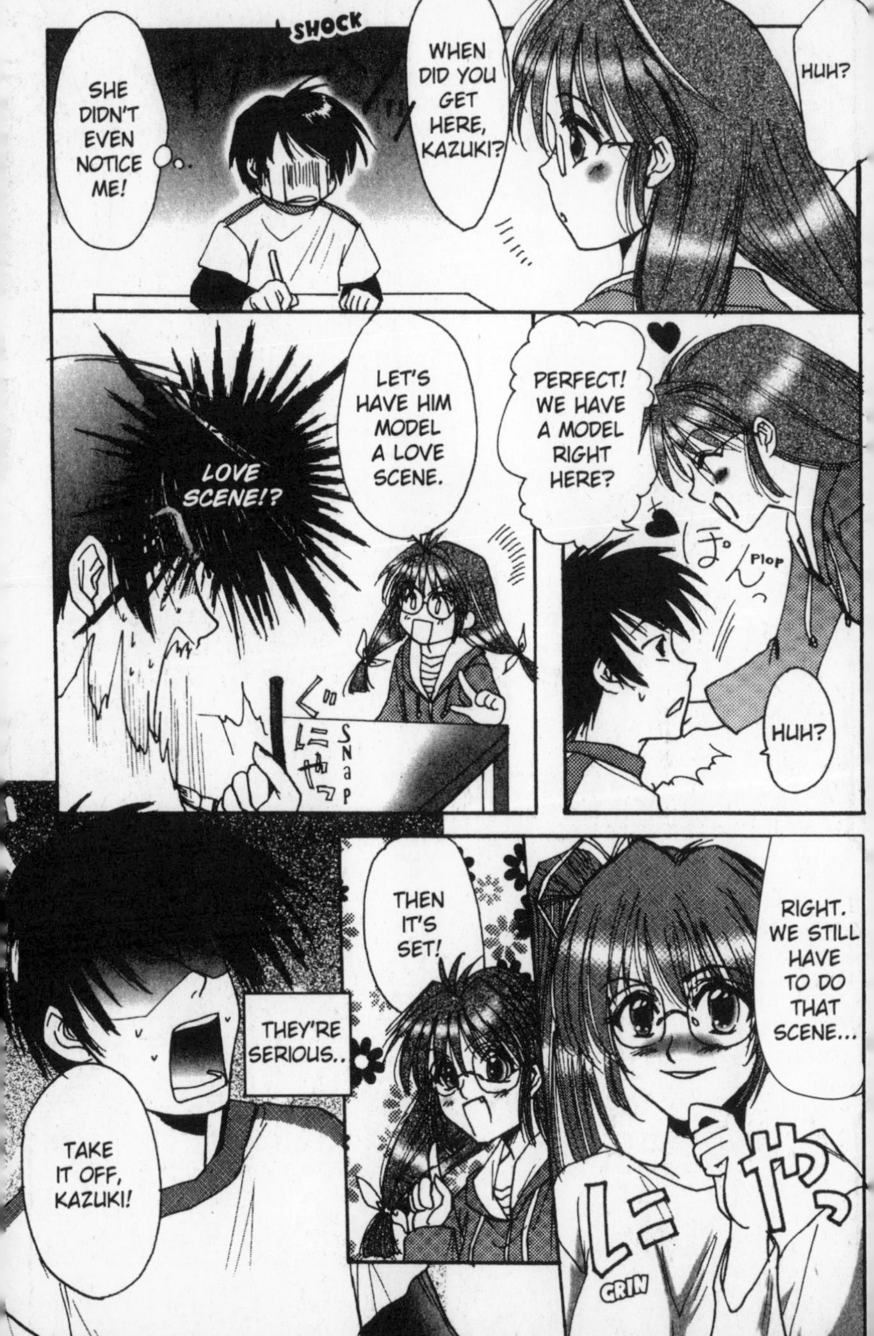
HUH?
WHEN DID YOU GET HERE, KAZUKI?
SHOCK
SHE DIDN'T EVEN NOTICE ME!
PERFECT! WE HAVE A MODEL RIGHT HERE?
Plop
HUH?
LET'S HAVE HIM MODEL A LOVE SCENE.
LOVE SCENE!?
Snap
RIGHT. WE STILL HAVE TO DO THAT SCENE...
GRIN
THEN IT'S SET!
THEY'RE SERIOUS..
TAKE IT OFF, KAZUKI!

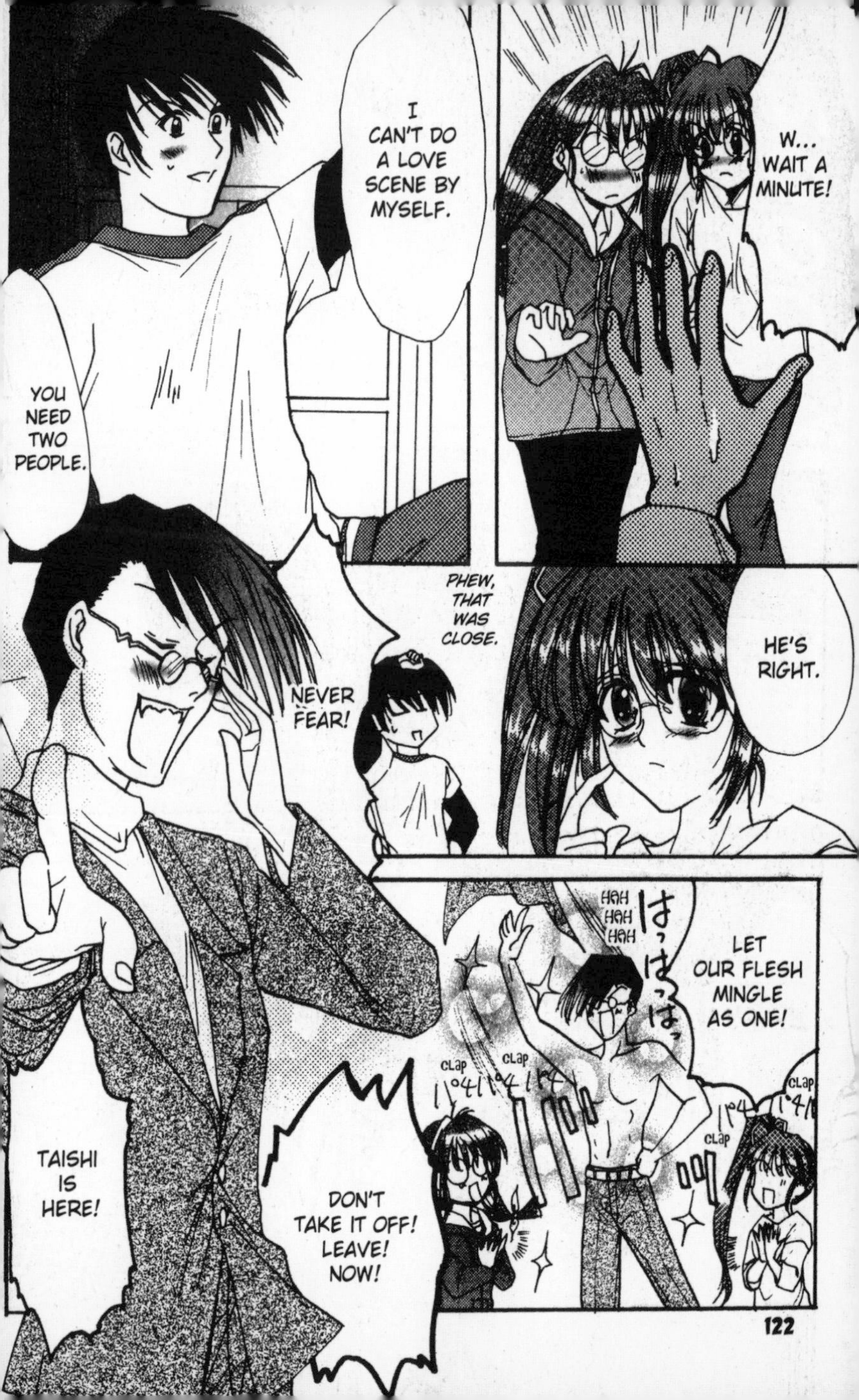
W... WAIT A MINUTE!
I CAN'T DO A LOVE SCENE BY MYSELF.
YOU NEED TWO PEOPLE.
HE'S RIGHT.
PHEW, THAT WAS CLOSE.
NEVER FEAR!
TAISHI IS HERE!
HAH HAH HAH
はっはっはっ
LET OUR FLESH MINGLE AS ONE!
CLAP
CLAP
CLAP
CLAP
DON'T TAKE IT OFF! LEAVE! NOW!

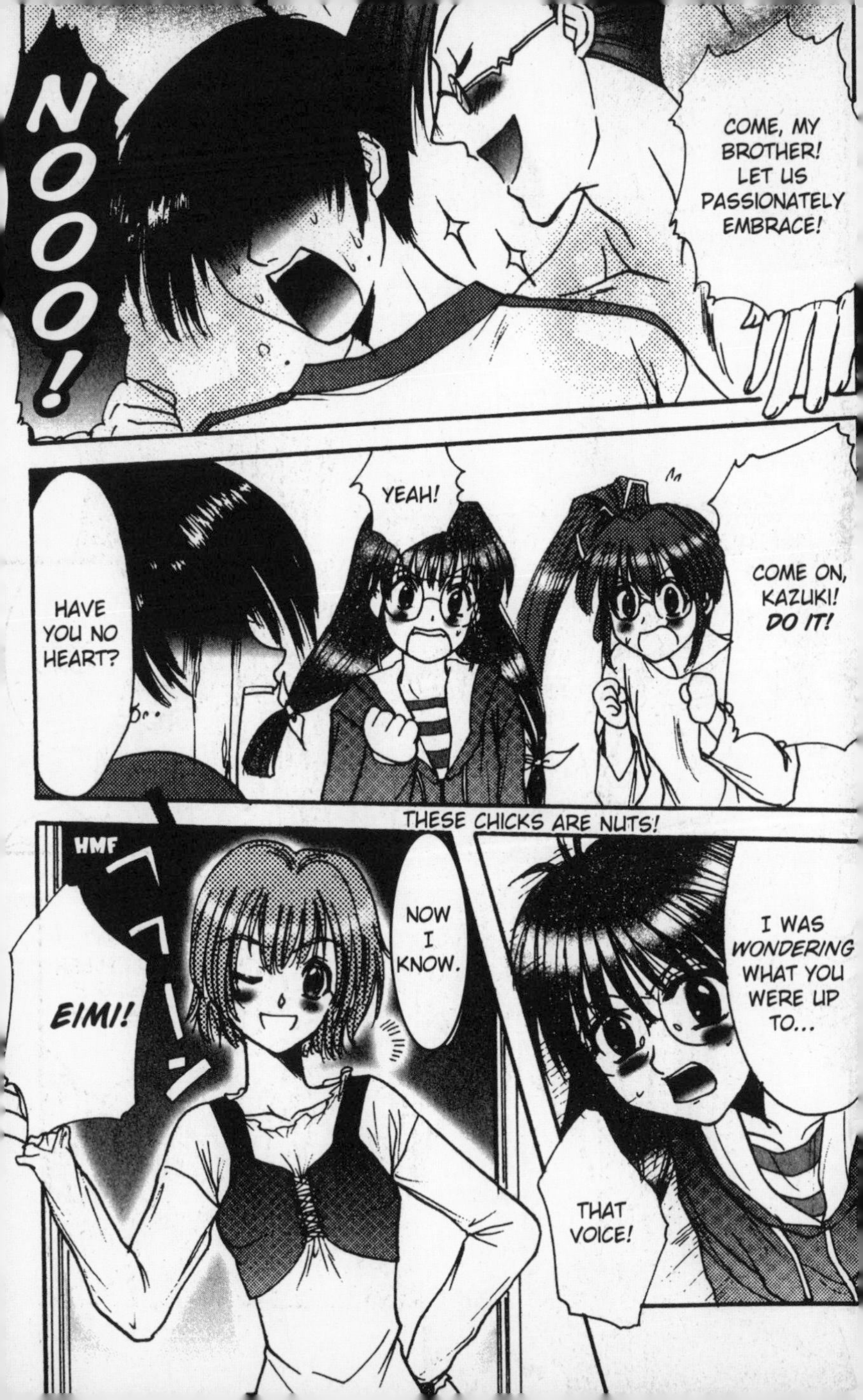
COME, MY BROTHER! LET US PASSIONATELY EMBRACE!
NOOOO!
COME ON, KAZUKI! DO IT!
YEAH!
HAVE YOU NO HEART?
THESE CHICKS ARE NUTS!
I WAS WONDERING WHAT YOU WERE UP TO...
THAT VOICE!
NOW I KNOW.
HMF
EIMI!

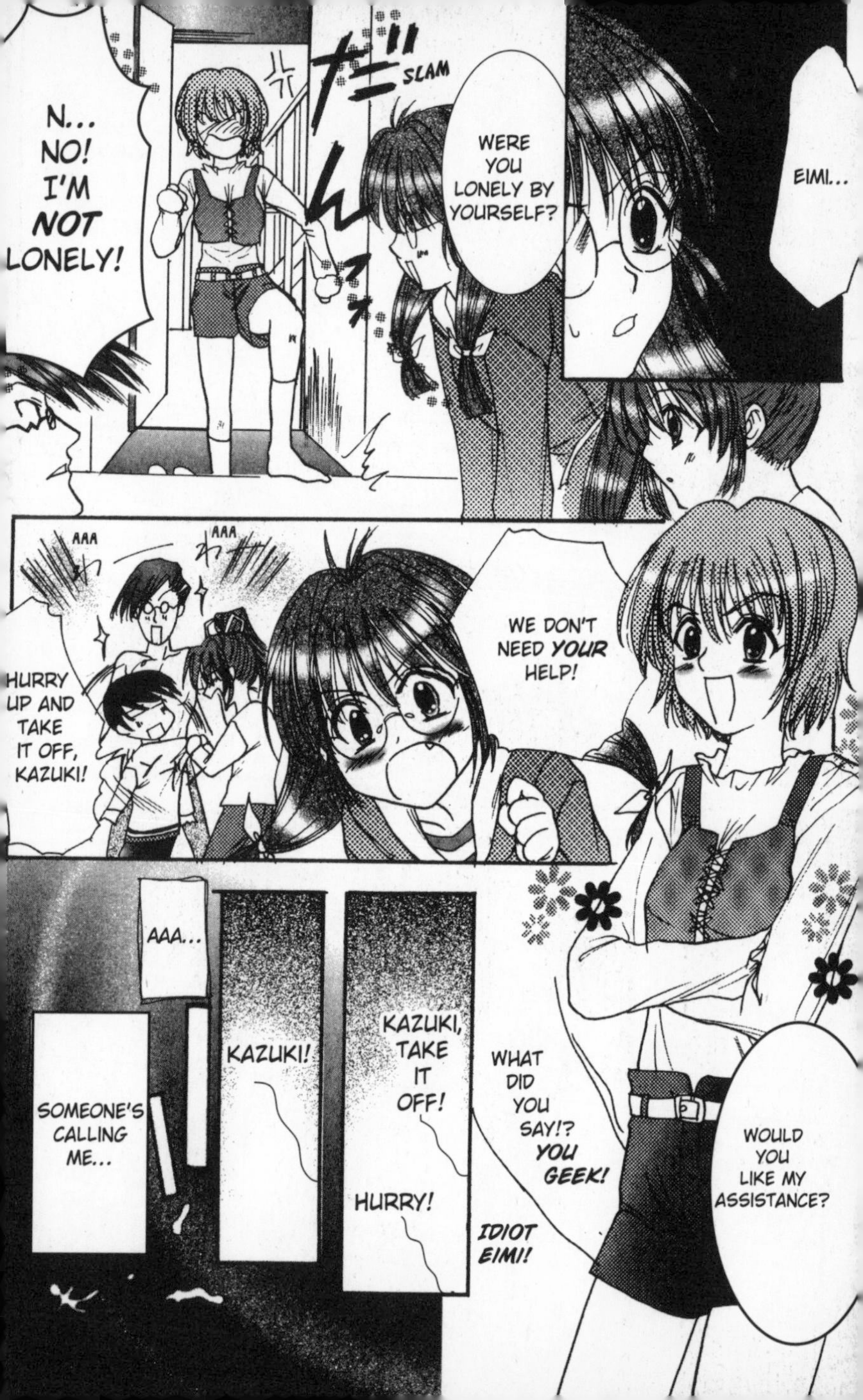
EIMI...
WERE YOU LONELY BY YOURSELF?
SLAM
N... NO! I'M NOT LONELY!
WOULD YOU LIKE MY ASSISTANCE?
WE DON'T NEED YOUR HELP!
AAA
AAA
HURRY UP AND TAKE IT OFF, KAZUKI!
WHAT DID YOU SAY!? YOU GEEK!
IDIOT EIMI!
KAZUKI, TAKE IT OFF!
HURRY!
KAZUKI!
AAA...
SOMEONE'S CALLING ME...

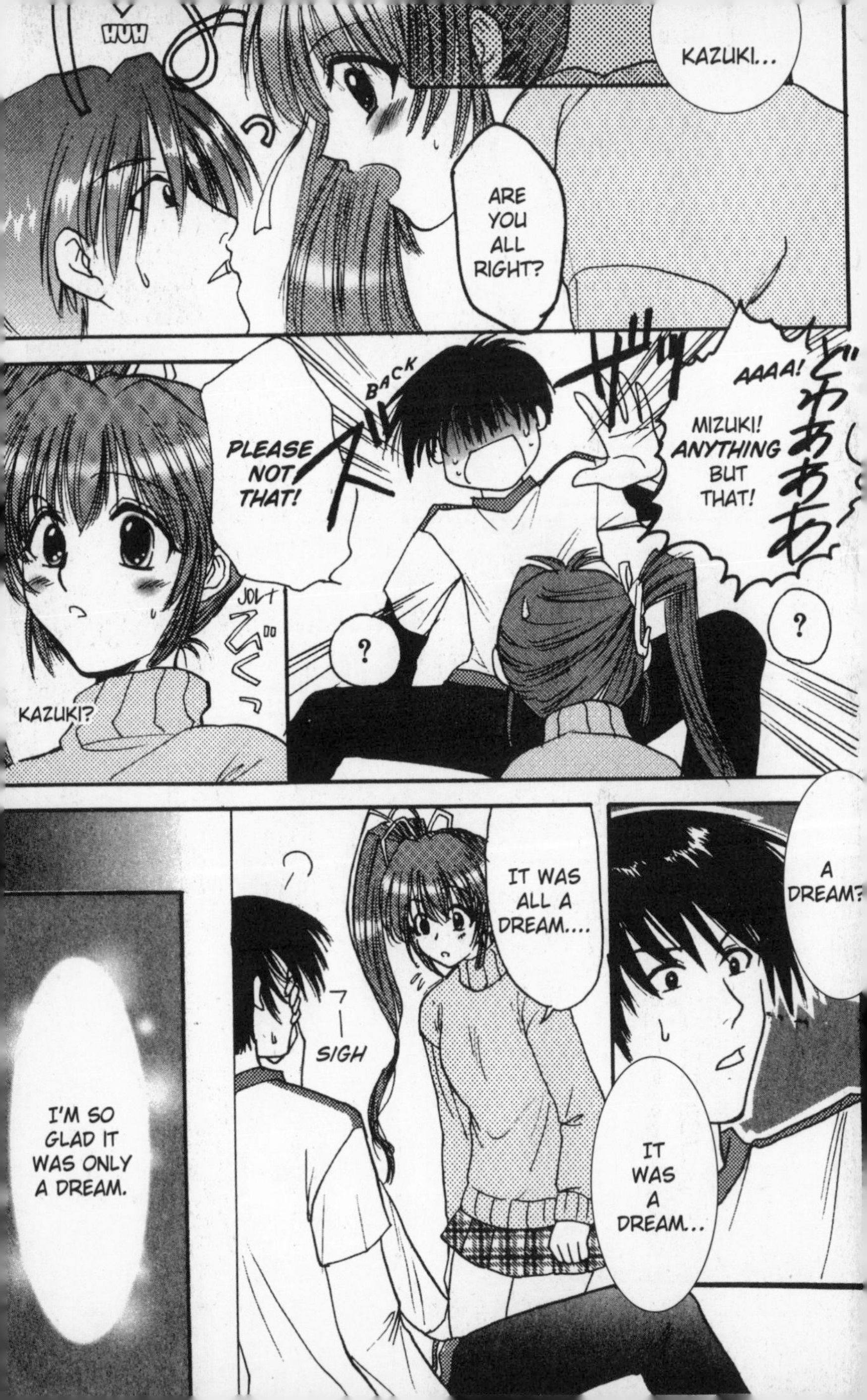
KAZUKI...
ARE YOU ALL RIGHT?
HUH
AAAA!
どわあああ
MIZUKI! ANYTHING BUT THAT!
BACK
PLEASE NOT THAT!
?
?
JOLT
KAZUKI?
A DREAM?
IT WAS A DREAM...
IT WAS ALL A DREAM....
SIGH
I'M SO GLAD IT WAS ONLY A DREAM.

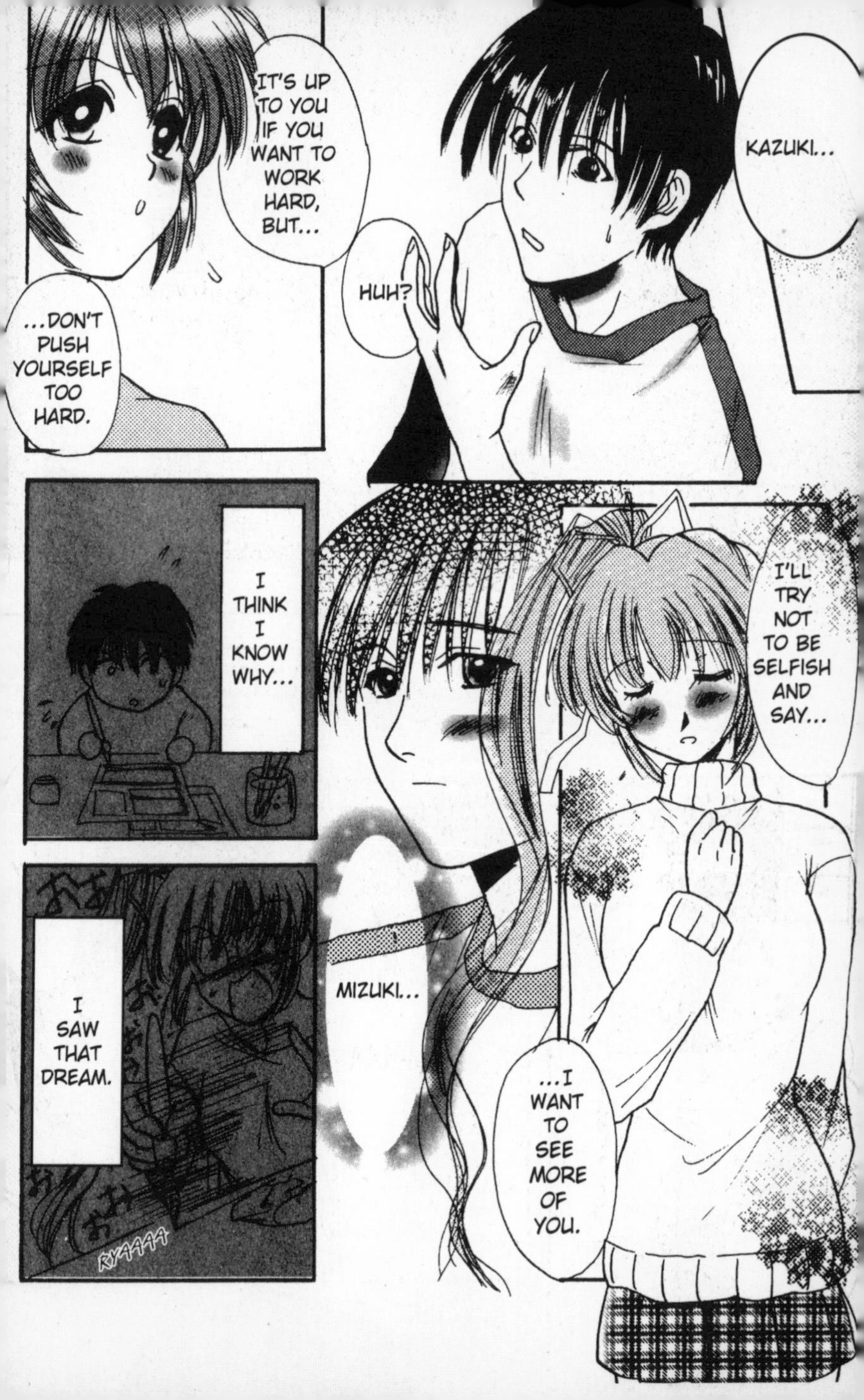
KAZUKI...
HUH?
IT'S UP TO YOU IF YOU WANT TO WORK HARD, BUT...
...DON'T PUSH YOURSELF TOO HARD.
I'LL TRY NOT TO BE SELFISH AND SAY...
...I WANT TO SEE MORE OF YOU.
MIZUKI...
I THINK I KNOW WHY...
I SAW THAT DREAM.
RYAAAA

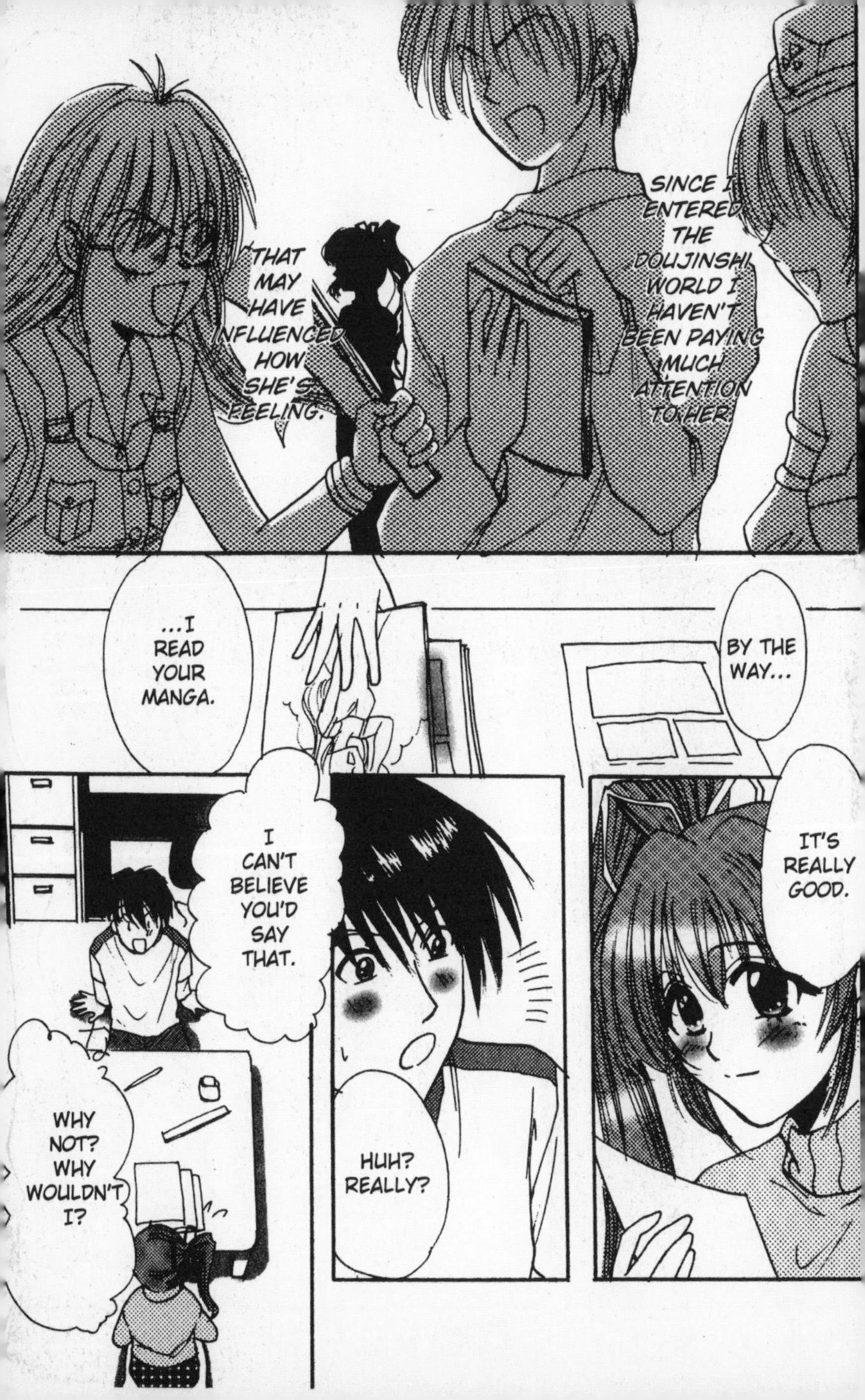
SINCE I ENTERED THE DOUJINSHI WORLD I HAVEN'T BEEN PAYING MUCH ATTENTION TO HER.
THAT MAY HAVE INFLUENCED HOW SHE'S FEELING.
BY THE WAY...
...I READ YOUR MANGA.
IT'S REALLY GOOD.
HUH? REALLY?
I CAN'T BELIEVE YOU'D SAY THAT.
WHY NOT? WHY WOULDN'T I?

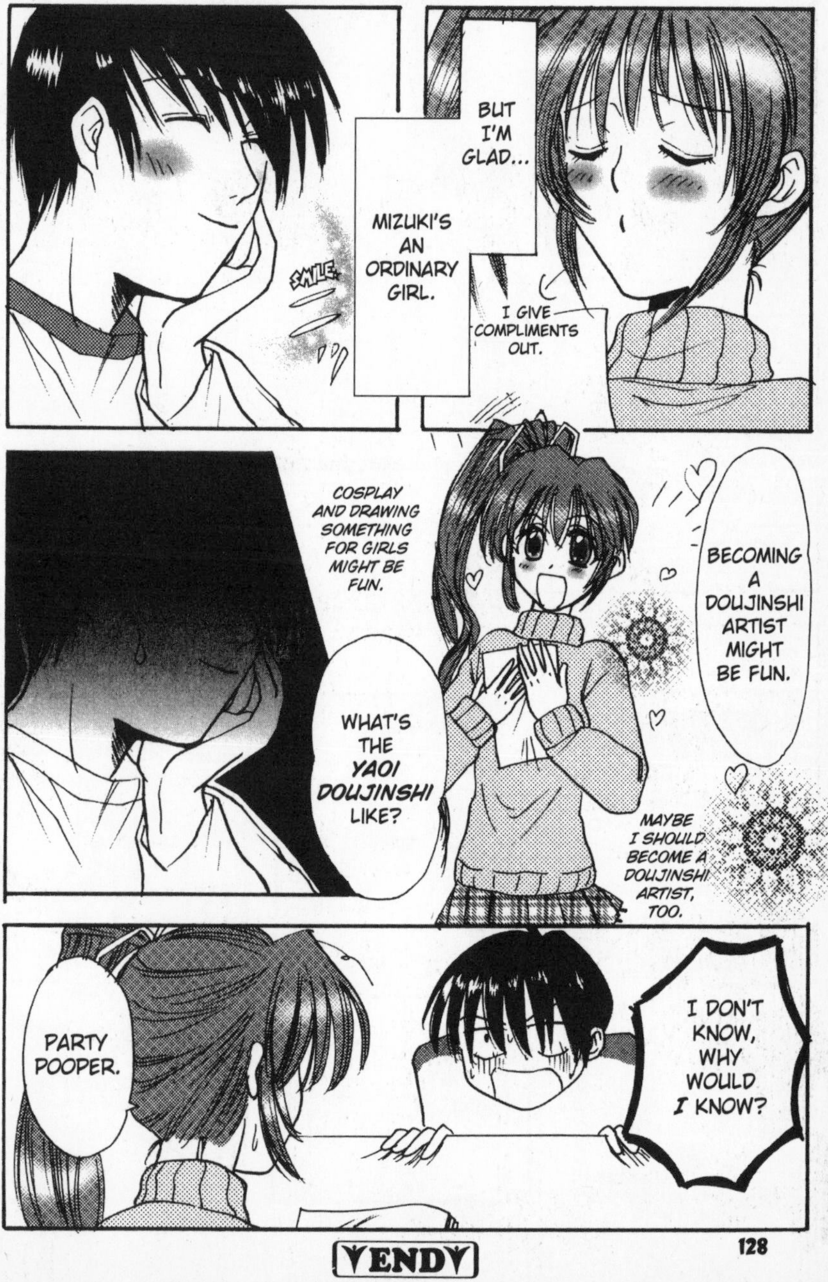
BUT I'M GLAD...
MIZUKI'S AN ORDINARY GIRL.
I GIVE COMPLIMENTS OUT.
SMILE
BECOMING A DOUJINSHI ARTIST MIGHT BE FUN.
COSPLAY AND DRAWING SOMETHING FOR GIRLS MIGHT BE FUN.
MAYBE I SHOULD BECOME A DOUJINSHI ARTIST, TOO.
WHAT'S THE *YAOI DOUJINSHI* LIKE?
I DON'T KNOW, WHY WOULD *I* KNOW?
PARTY POOPER.

END

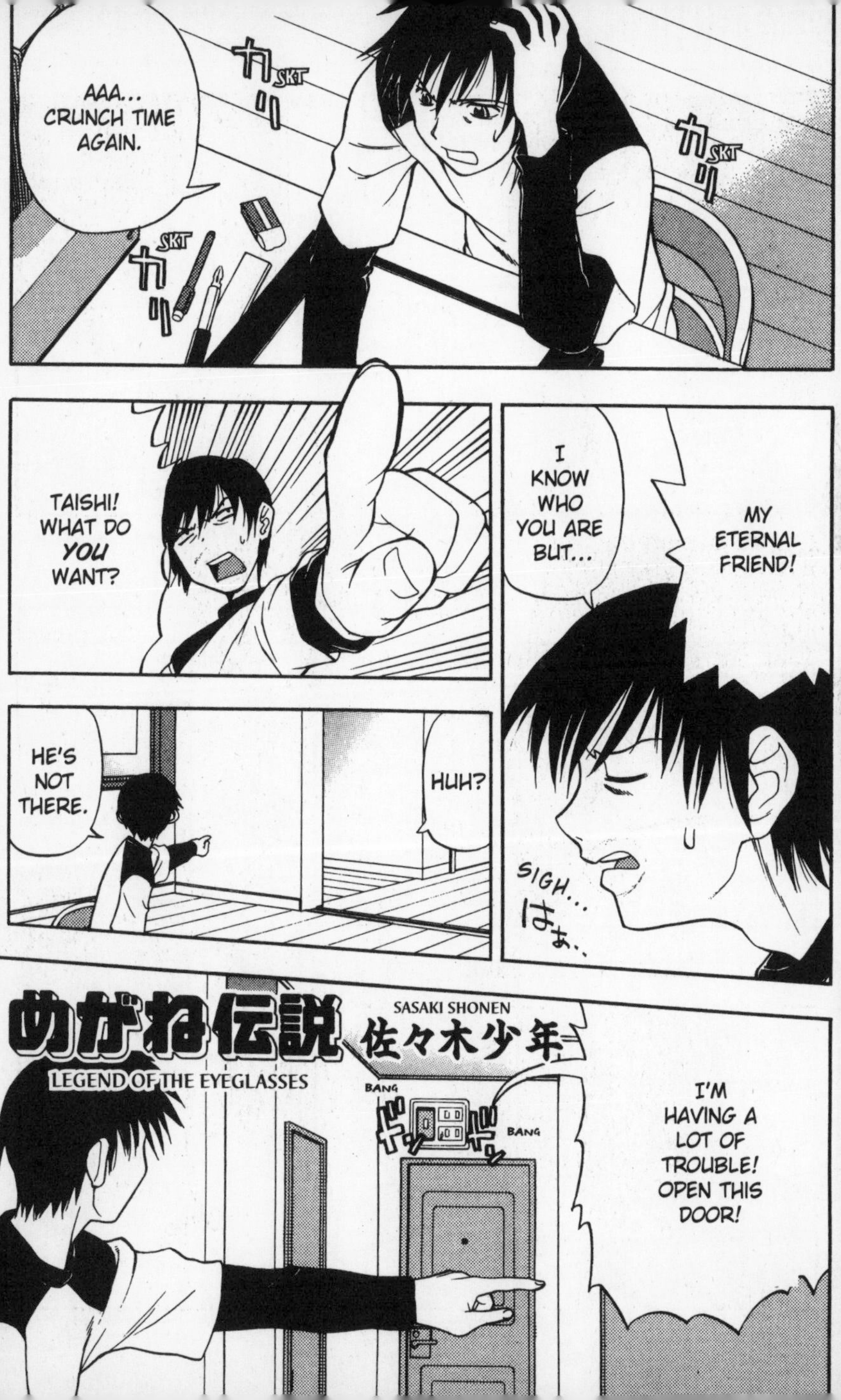
AAA... CRUNCH TIME AGAIN.
カ SKT リ
カ SKT リ
SKT カ リ
MY ETERNAL FRIEND!
I KNOW WHO YOU ARE BUT...
SIGH... はぁ..
TAISHI! WHAT DO *YOU* WANT?
HUH?
HE'S NOT THERE.
I'M HAVING A LOT OF TROUBLE! OPEN THIS DOOR!
BANG ドッ
BANG ドッ
めがね伝説
SASAKI SHONEN
佐々木少年
LEGEND OF THE EYEGLASSES

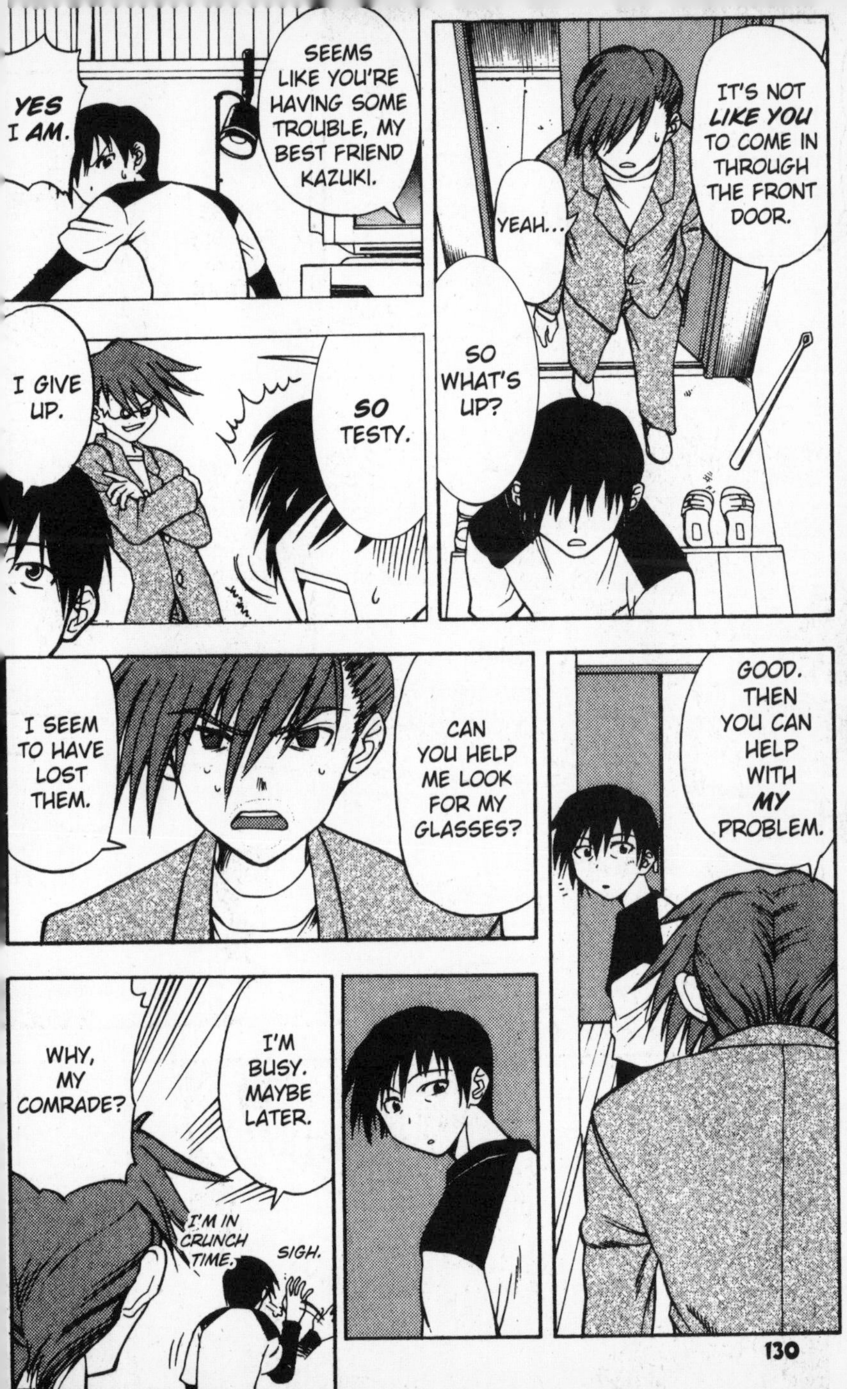
IT'S NOT LIKE YOU TO COME IN THROUGH THE FRONT DOOR.
YEAH...
SO WHAT'S UP?
SEEMS LIKE YOU'RE HAVING SOME TROUBLE, MY BEST FRIEND KAZUKI.
YES I AM.
SO TESTY.
I GIVE UP.
GOOD. THEN YOU CAN HELP WITH MY PROBLEM.
CAN YOU HELP ME LOOK FOR MY GLASSES?
I SEEM TO HAVE LOST THEM.
I'M BUSY. MAYBE LATER.
WHY, MY COMRADE?
I'M IN CRUNCH TIME.
SIGH.

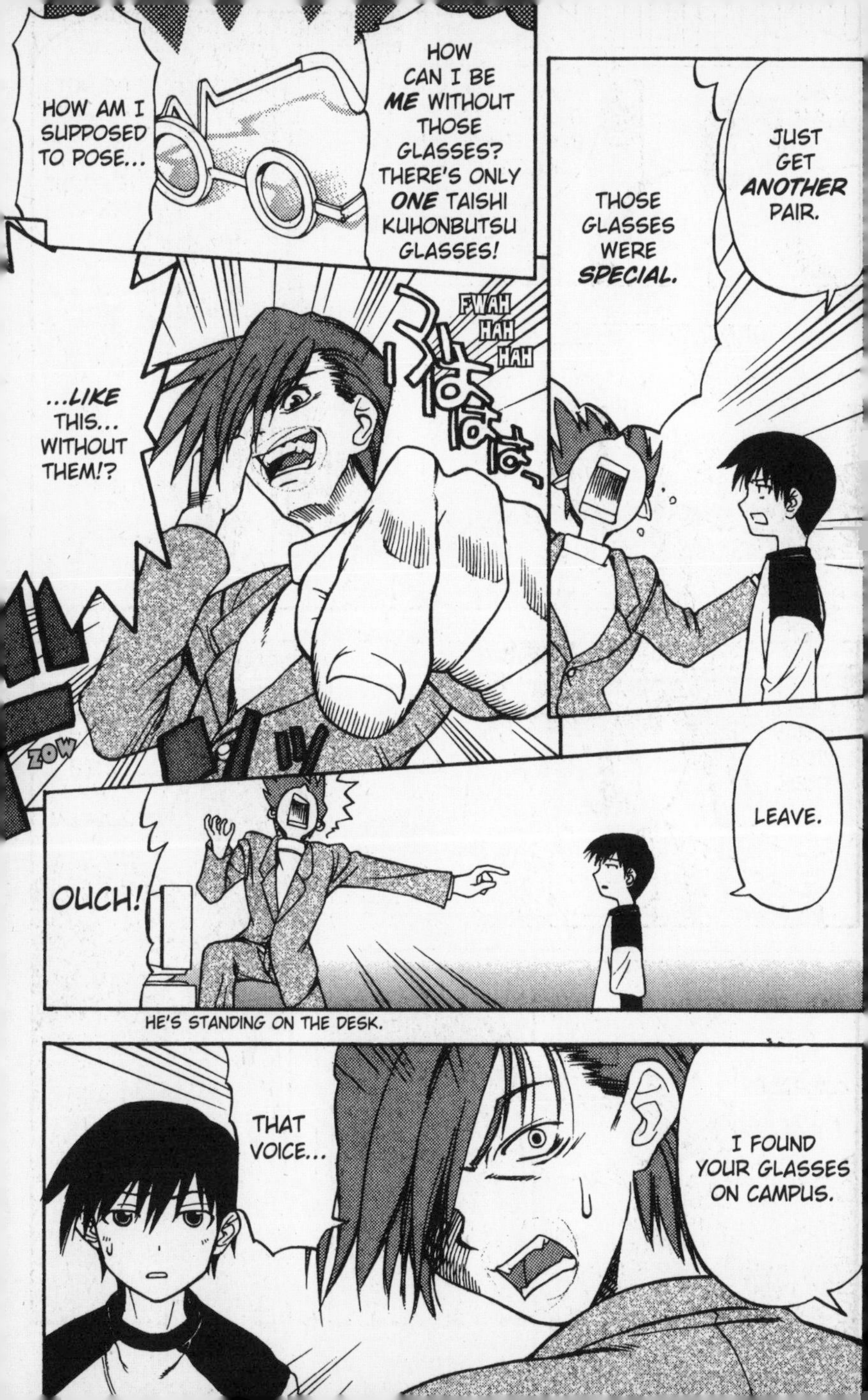
JUST GET *ANOTHER* PAIR.
THOSE GLASSES WERE *SPECIAL.*
HOW CAN I BE *ME* WITHOUT THOSE GLASSES? THERE'S ONLY *ONE* TAISHI KUHONBUTSU GLASSES!
HOW AM I SUPPOSED TO POSE...
FWAH HAH HAH
...*LIKE* THIS... WITHOUT THEM!?
ZOW
LEAVE.
OUCH!
HE'S STANDING ON THE DESK.
I FOUND YOUR GLASSES ON CAMPUS.
THAT VOICE...

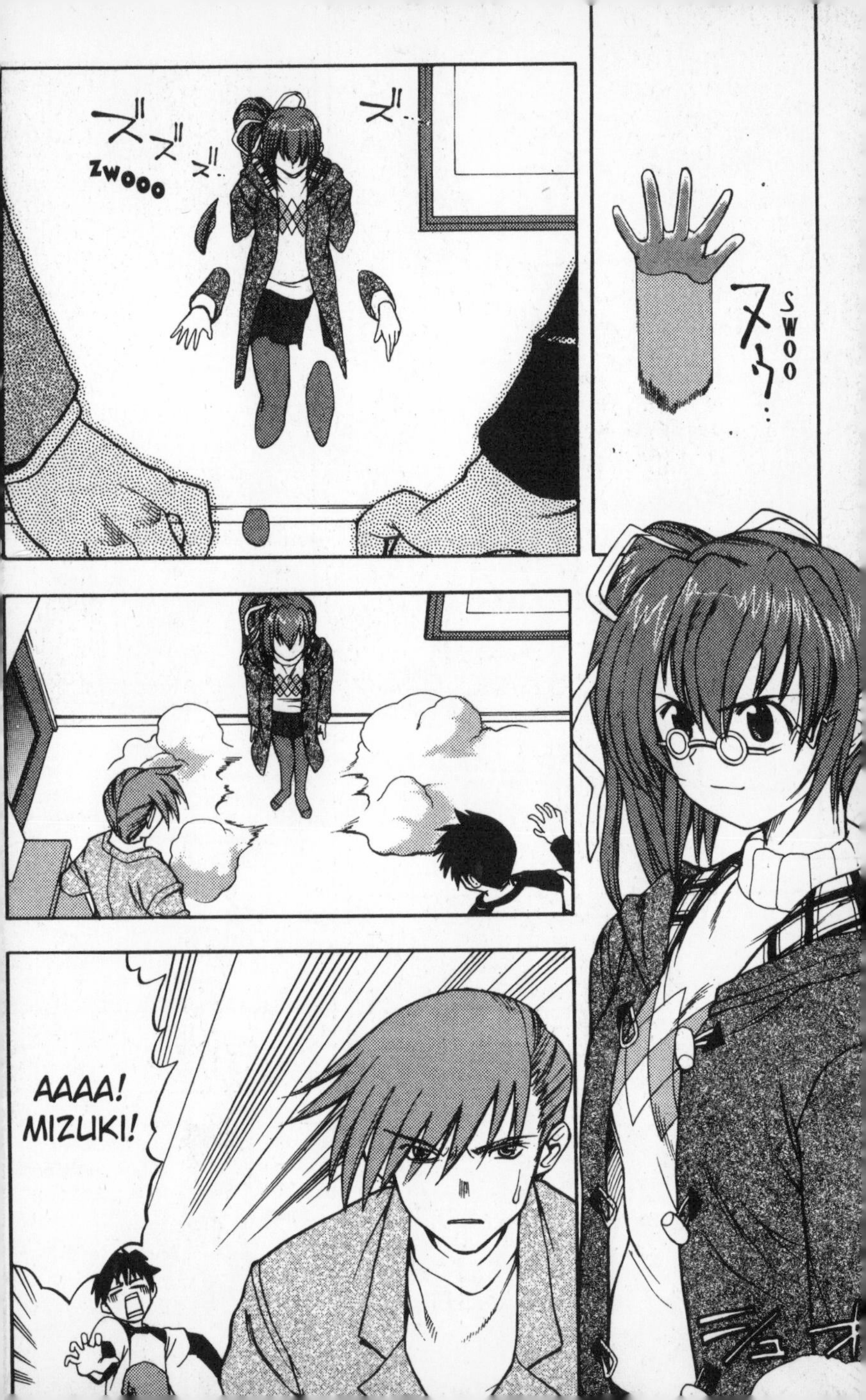
スッ…
SWOO
ズズズ…
ZWOOO
ズ…
AAAA! MIZUKI!

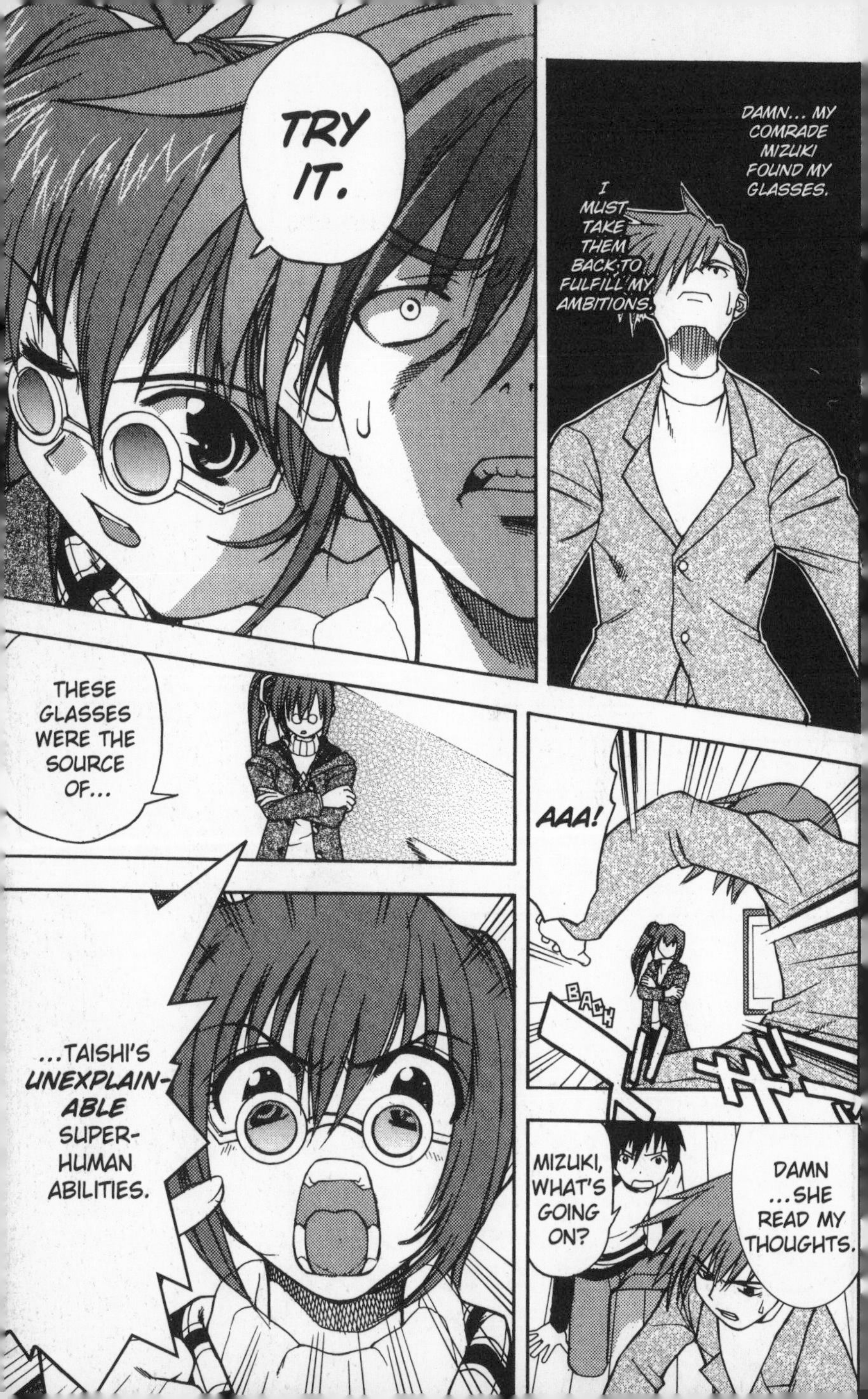
DAMN... MY COMRADE MIZUKI FOUND MY GLASSES.
I MUST TAKE THEM BACK TO FULFILL MY AMBITIONS.
TRY IT.
THESE GLASSES WERE THE SOURCE OF...
...TAISHI'S UNEXPLAINABLE SUPERHUMAN ABILITIES.
AAA!
BACH
MIZUKI, WHAT'S GOING ON?
DAMN ...SHE READ MY THOUGHTS.

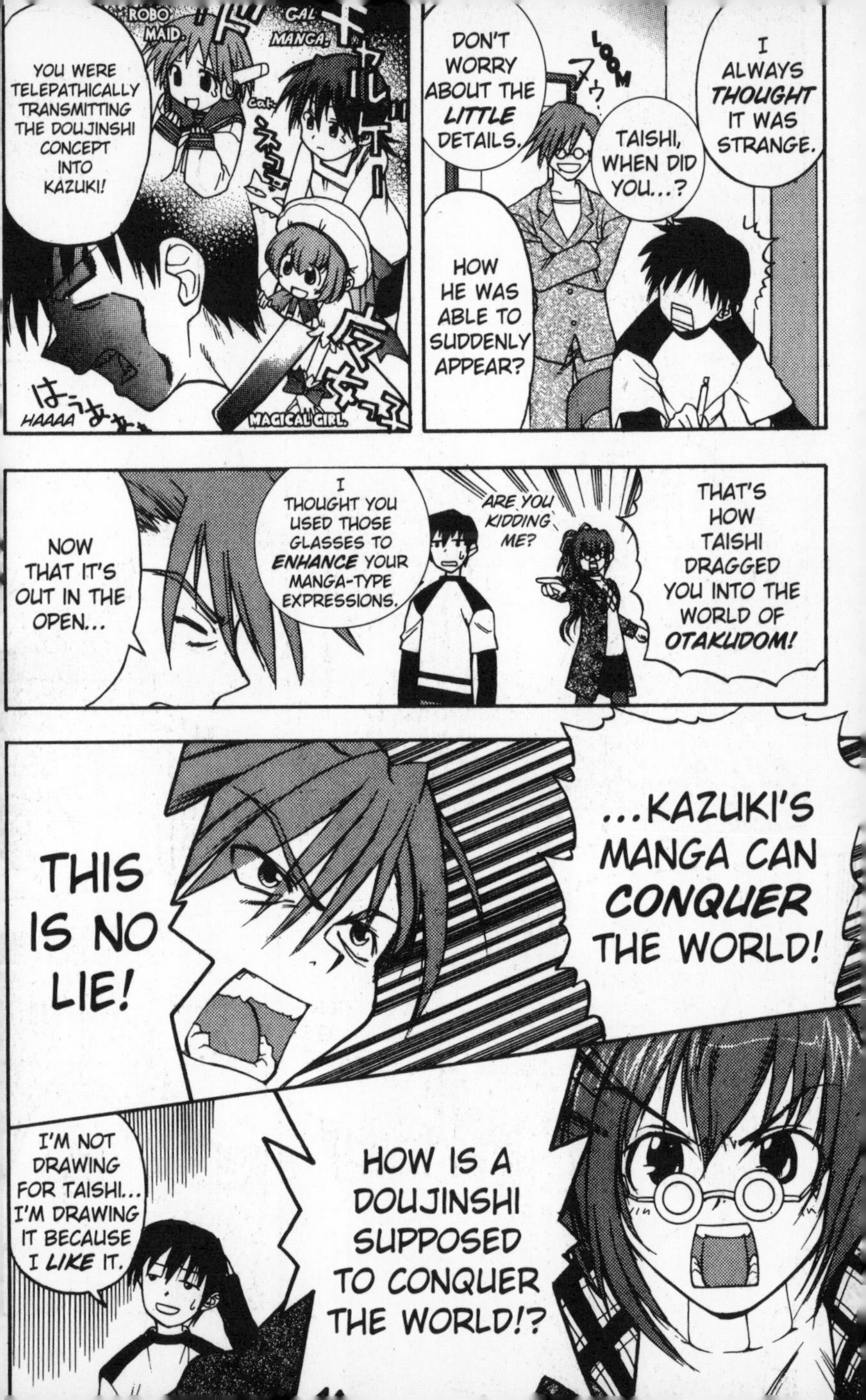
I ALWAYS THOUGHT IT WAS STRANGE.
TAISHI, WHEN DID YOU...?
VOOM
DON'T WORRY ABOUT THE LITTLE DETAILS.
HOW HE WAS ABLE TO SUDDENLY APPEAR?
GAL MANGA.
ROBO MAID.
CAT
YOU WERE TELEPATHICALLY TRANSMITTING THE DOUJINSHI CONCEPT INTO KAZUKI!
MAGICAL GIRL.
HAAAA
THAT'S HOW TAISHI DRAGGED YOU INTO THE WORLD OF OTAKUDOM!
ARE YOU KIDDING ME?
I THOUGHT YOU USED THOSE GLASSES TO ENHANCE YOUR MANGA-TYPE EXPRESSIONS.
NOW THAT IT'S OUT IN THE OPEN...
...KAZUKI'S MANGA CAN CONQUER THE WORLD!
THIS IS NO LIE!
HOW IS A DOUJINSHI SUPPOSED TO CONQUER THE WORLD!?
I'M NOT DRAWING FOR TAISHI... I'M DRAWING IT BECAUSE I LIKE IT.

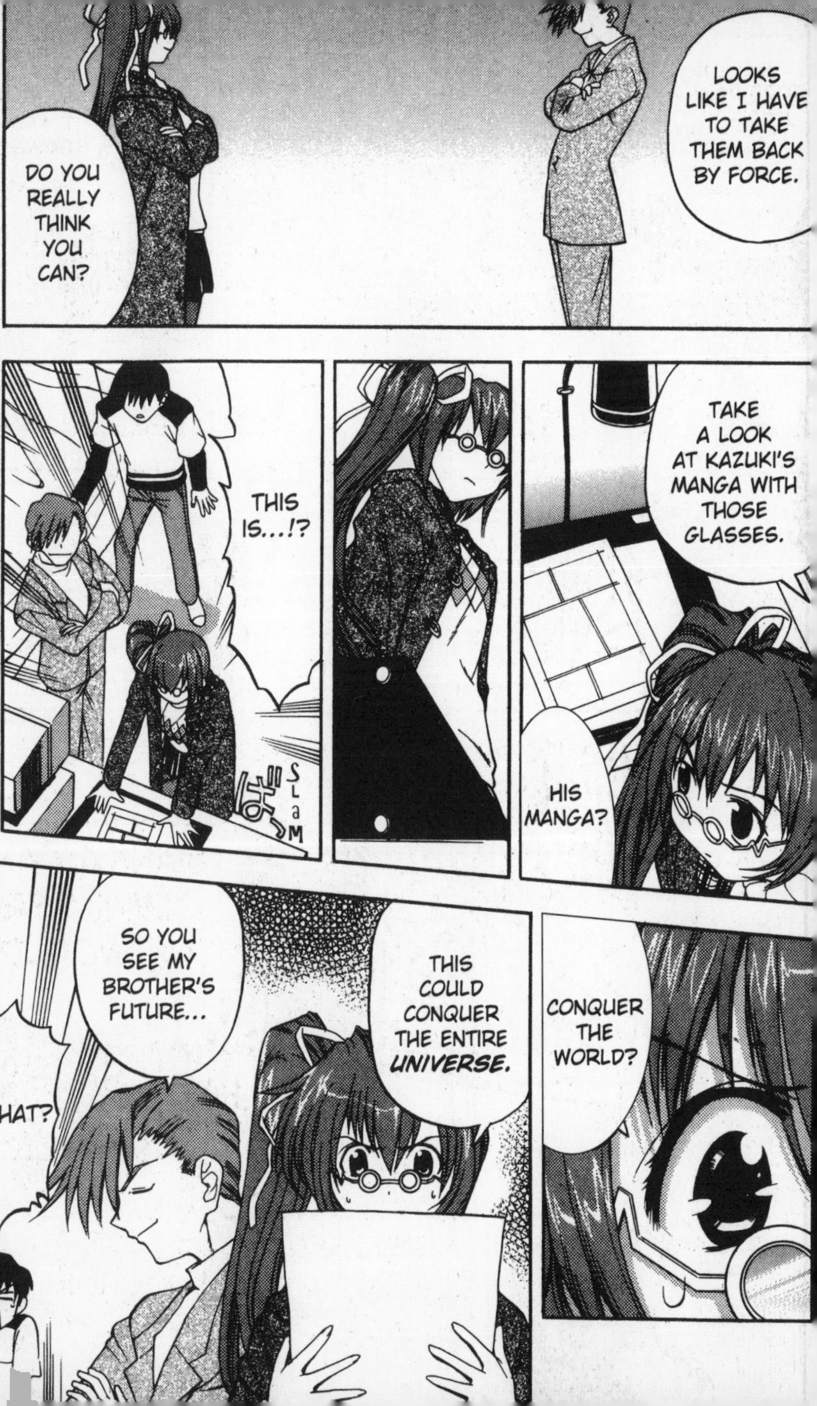
LOOKS LIKE I HAVE TO TAKE THEM BACK BY FORCE.
DO YOU REALLY THINK YOU CAN?
TAKE A LOOK AT KAZUKI'S MANGA WITH THOSE GLASSES.
HIS MANGA?
THIS IS...!?
ばっ
SLaM
CONQUER THE WORLD?
THIS COULD CONQUER THE ENTIRE UNIVERSE.
SO YOU SEE MY BROTHER'S FUTURE...
WHAT?

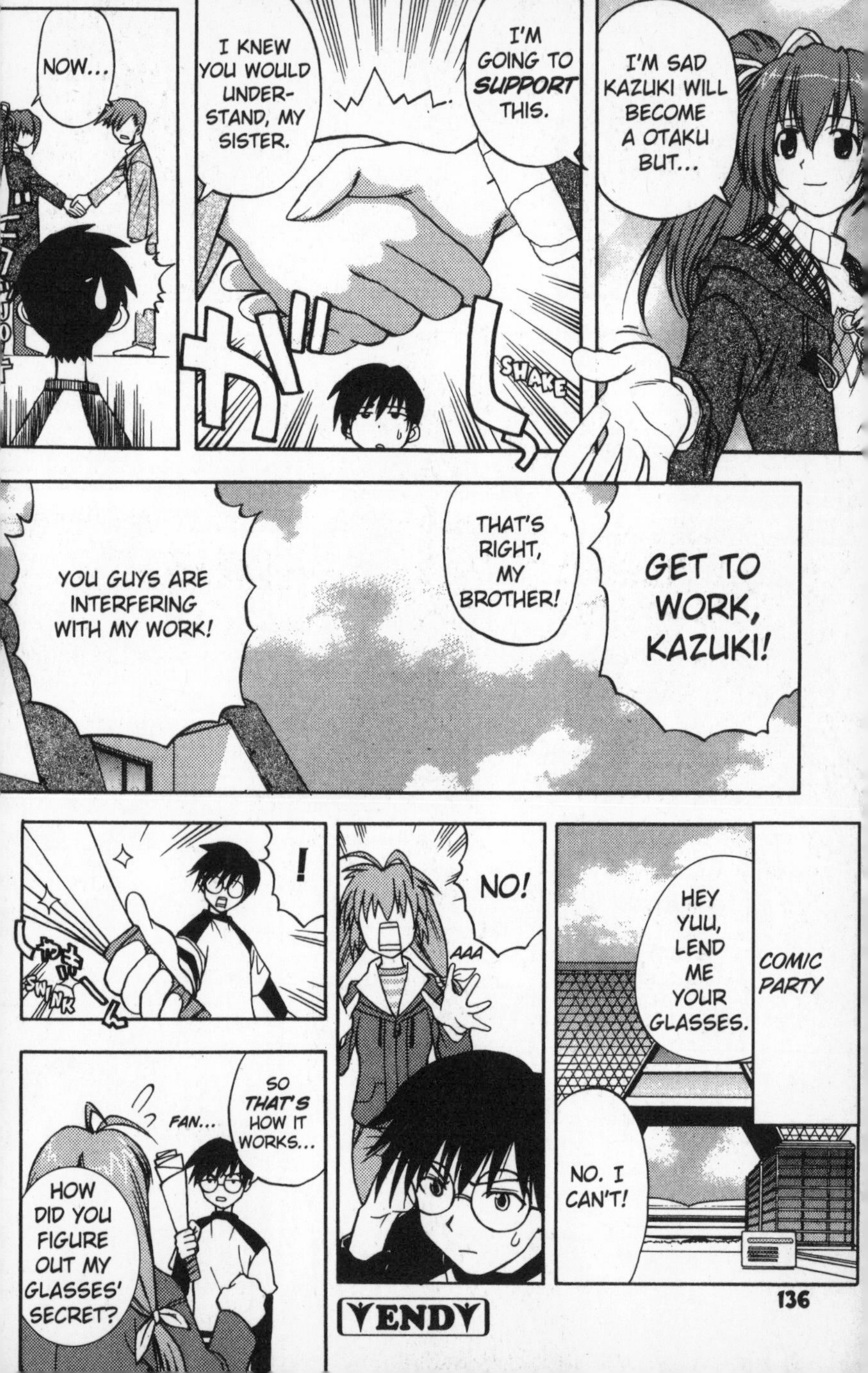
I'M SAD KAZUKI WILL BECOME A OTAKU BUT...
I'M GOING TO *SUPPORT* THIS.
I KNEW YOU WOULD UNDER-STAND, MY SISTER.
SHAKE
NOW...
GET TO WORK, KAZUKI!
THAT'S RIGHT, MY BROTHER!
YOU GUYS ARE INTERFERING WITH MY WORK!
COMIC PARTY
HEY YUU, LEND ME YOUR GLASSES.
NO. I CAN'T!
NO!
AAA
!
SWINK
SO *THAT'S* HOW IT WORKS...
FAN...
HOW DID YOU FIGURE OUT MY GLASSES' SECRET?
END

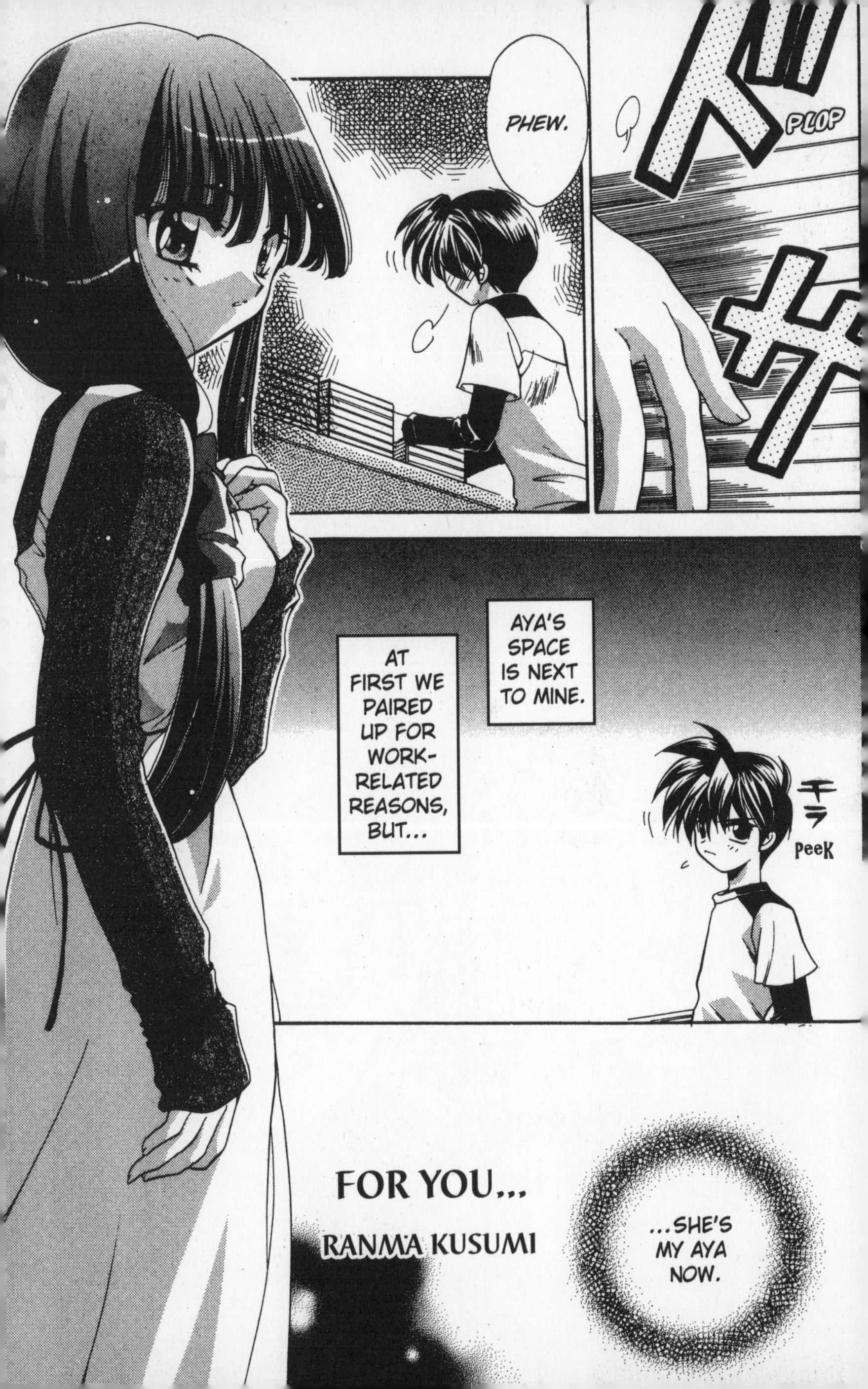
PLOP
PHEW.
AYA'S SPACE IS NEXT TO MINE.
AT FIRST WE PAIRED UP FOR WORK-RELATED REASONS, BUT...
PeeK
FOR YOU...
RANMA KUSUMI
...SHE'S MY AYA NOW.

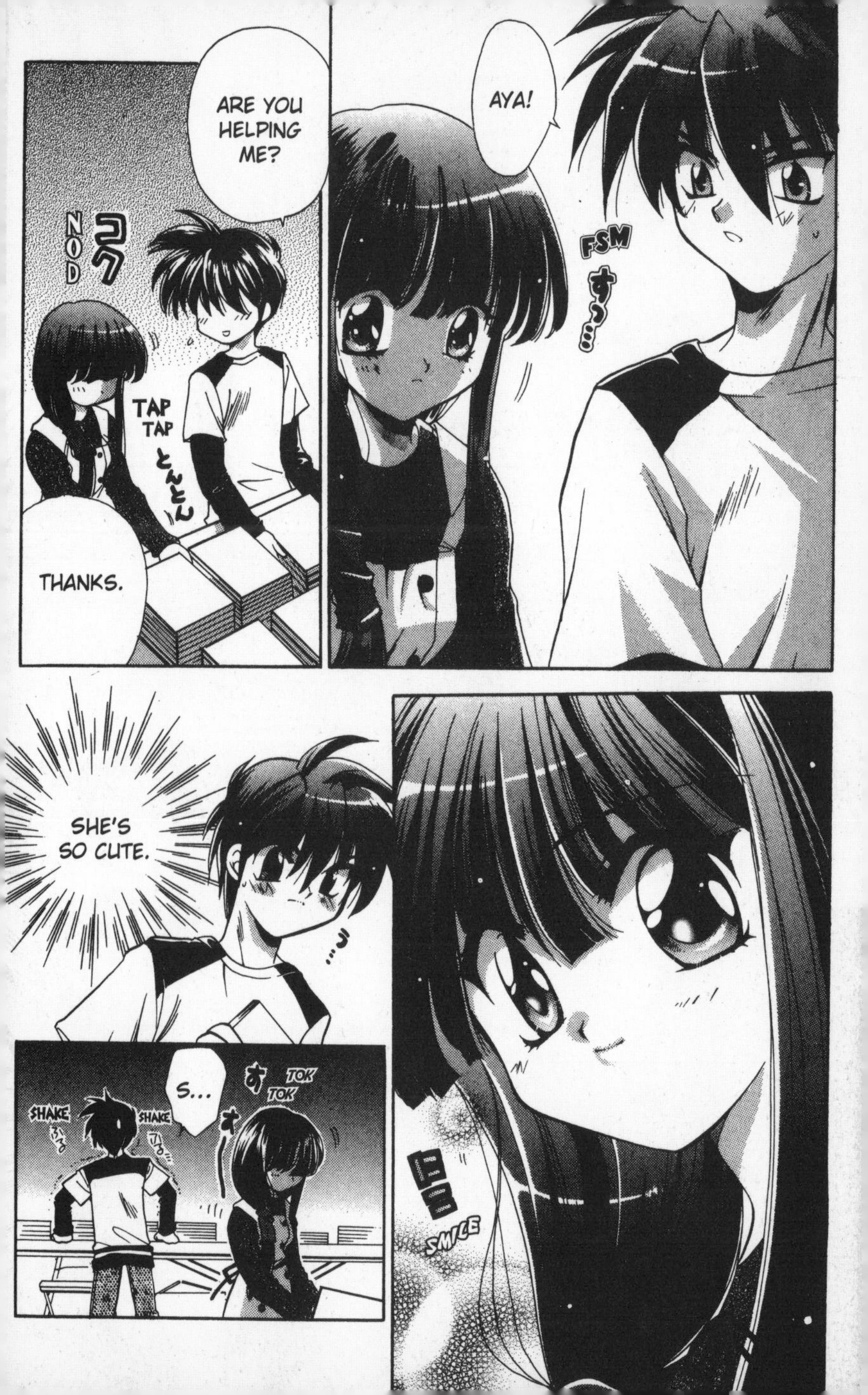
AYA!
FSM
すっ…
ARE YOU HELPING ME?
NOD
コク
TAP TAP
とんとん
THANKS.
SMILE
SHE'S SO CUTE.
S...
TOK TOK
SHAKE
SHAKE

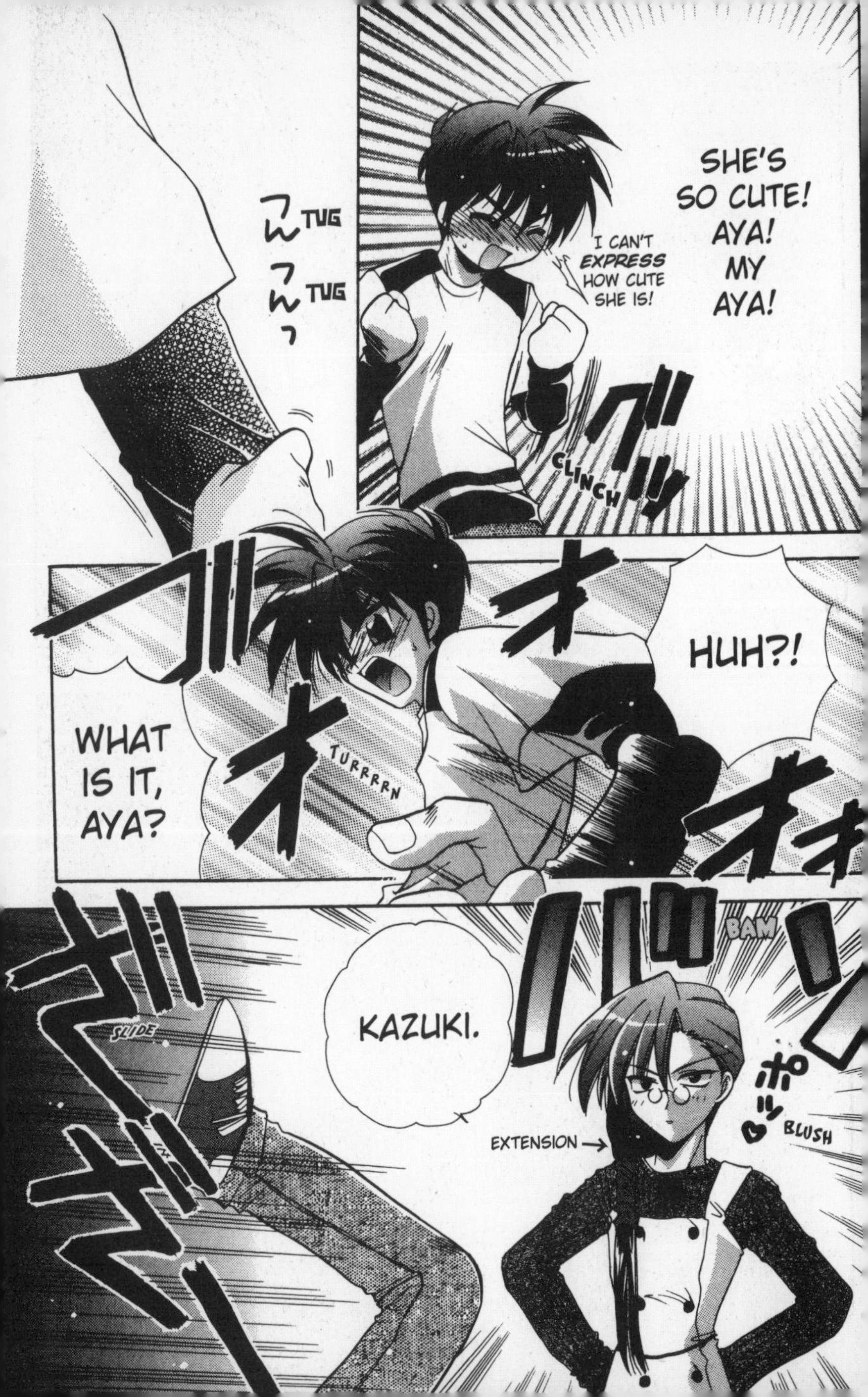
SHE'S SO CUTE! AYA! MY AYA!
I CAN'T EXPRESS HOW CUTE SHE IS!
CLINCH
TUG
TUG
HUH?!
TURRRRRN
WHAT IS IT, AYA?
BAM
BLUSH
EXTENSION →
KAZUKI.
SLIDE

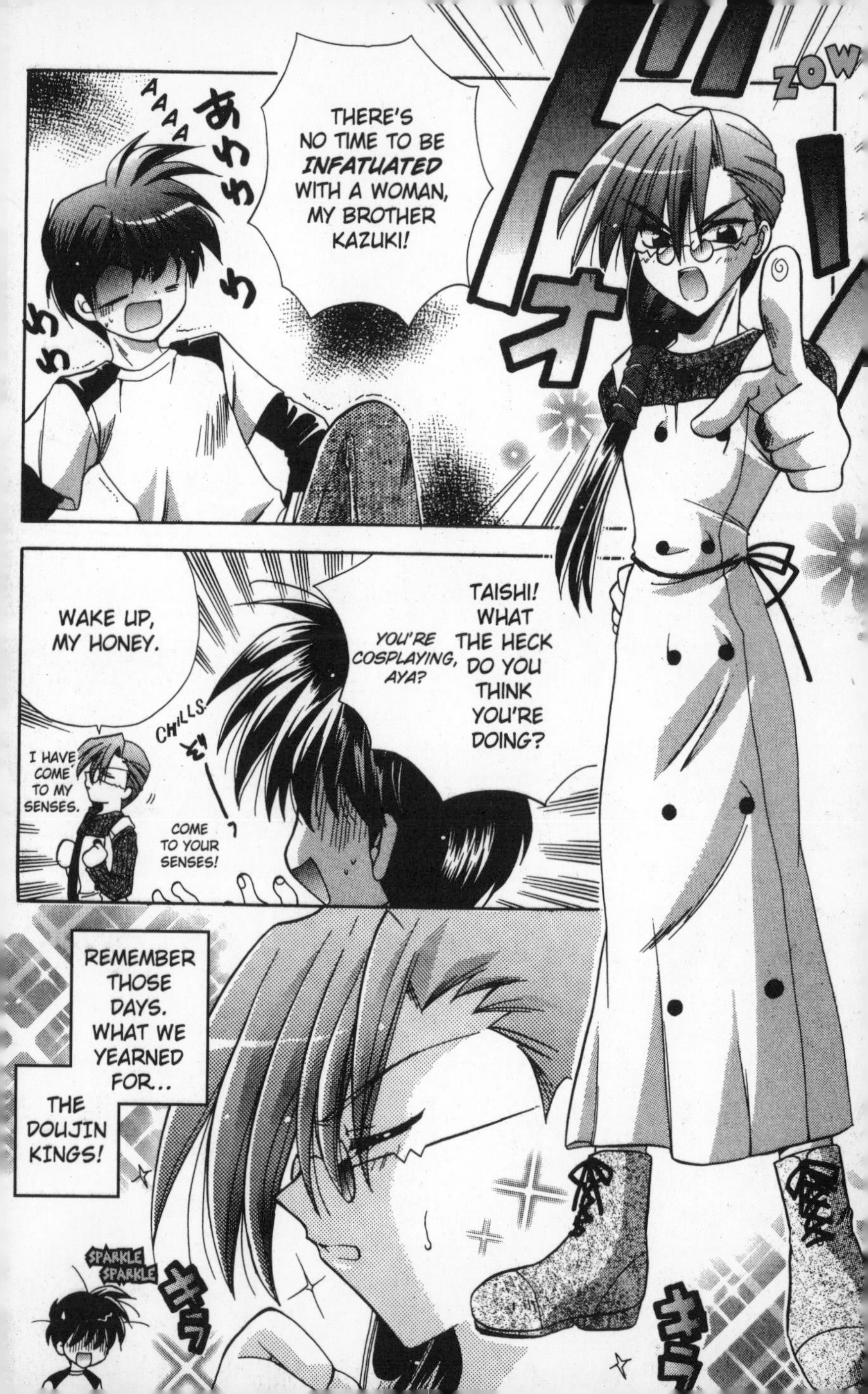
ZOW
THERE'S NO TIME TO BE *INFATUATED* WITH A WOMAN, MY BROTHER KAZUKI!
AAAA
TAISHI! WHAT THE HECK DO YOU THINK YOU'RE DOING?
YOU'RE COSPLAYING, AYA?
WAKE UP, MY HONEY.
CHILLS
I HAVE COME TO MY SENSES.
COME TO YOUR SENSES!
REMEMBER THOSE DAYS. WHAT WE YEARNED FOR...
THE DOUJIN KINGS!
SPARKLE SPARKLE

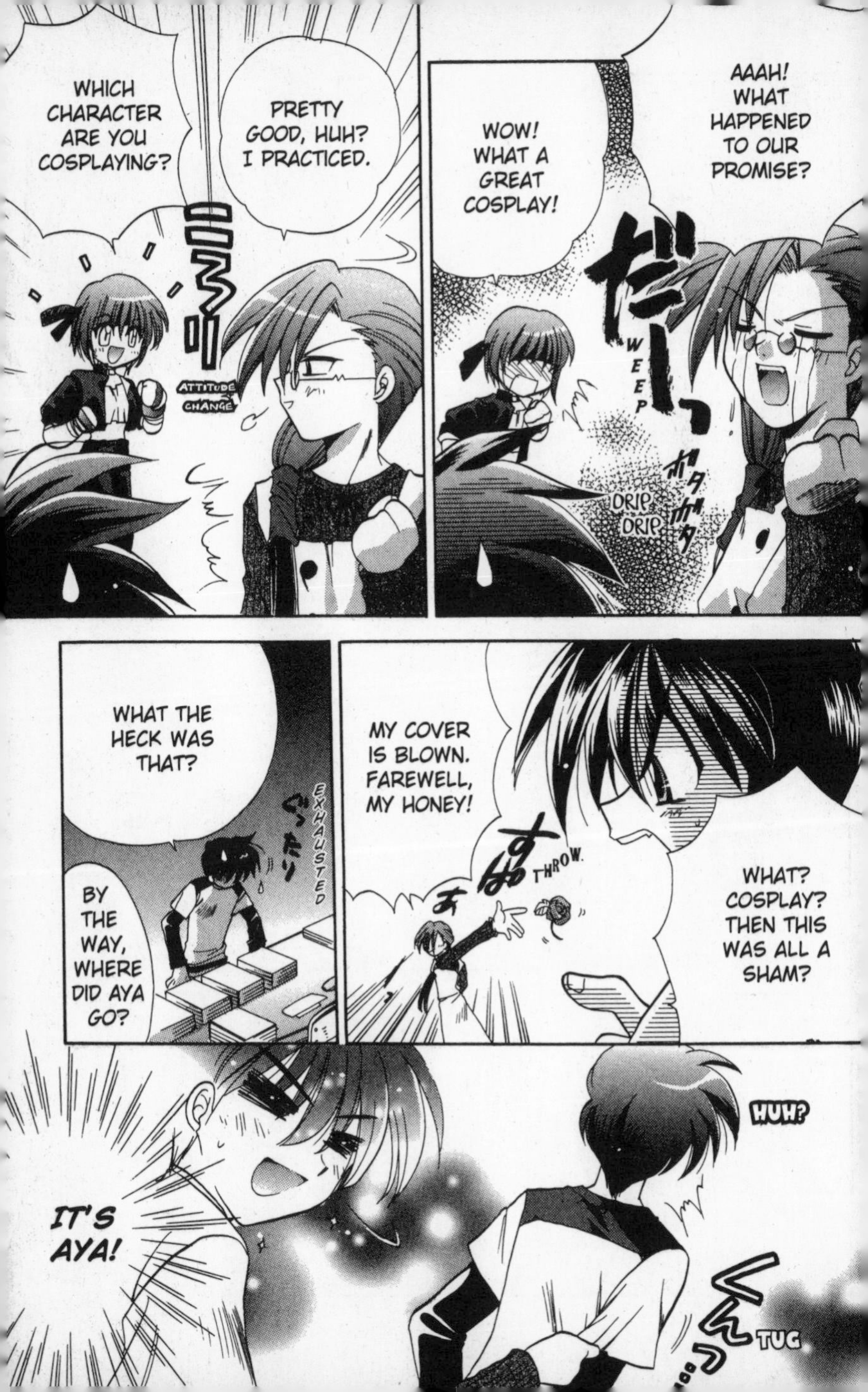
AAAH! WHAT HAPPENED TO OUR PROMISE?
WOW! WHAT A GREAT COSPLAY!
WEEP
DRIP DRIP
PRETTY GOOD, HUH? I PRACTICED.
ATTITUDE CHANGE
WHICH CHARACTER ARE YOU COSPLAYING?
MY COVER IS BLOWN. FAREWELL, MY HONEY!
THROW
WHAT? COSPLAY? THEN THIS WAS ALL A SHAM?
WHAT THE HECK WAS THAT?
EXHAUSTED
BY THE WAY, WHERE DID AYA GO?
HUH?
TUG
IT'S AYA!

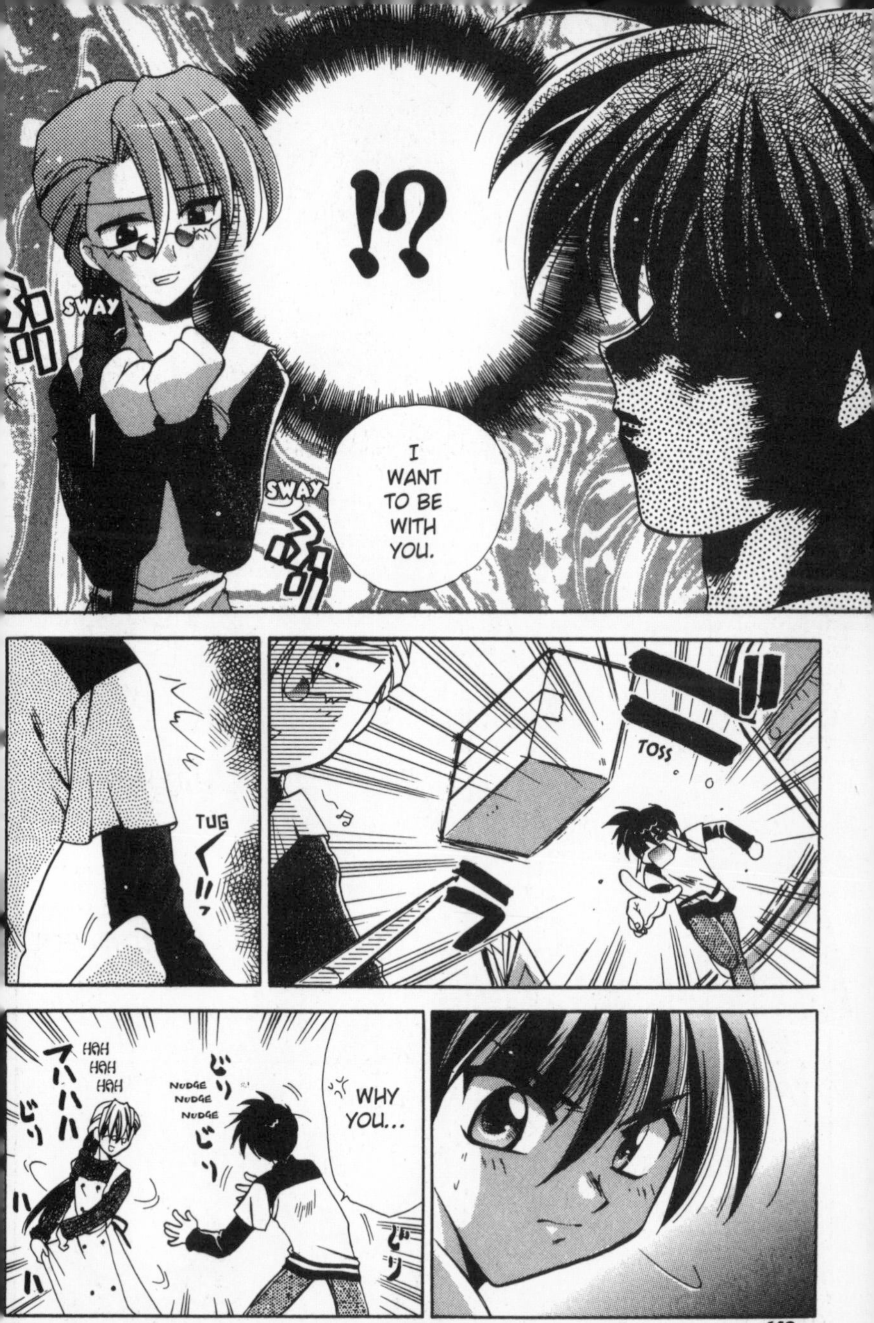
!?
I WANT TO BE WITH YOU.
SWAY
SWAY
TOSS
TUG
WHY YOU...
NUDGE NUDGE NUDGE
HAH HAH HAH

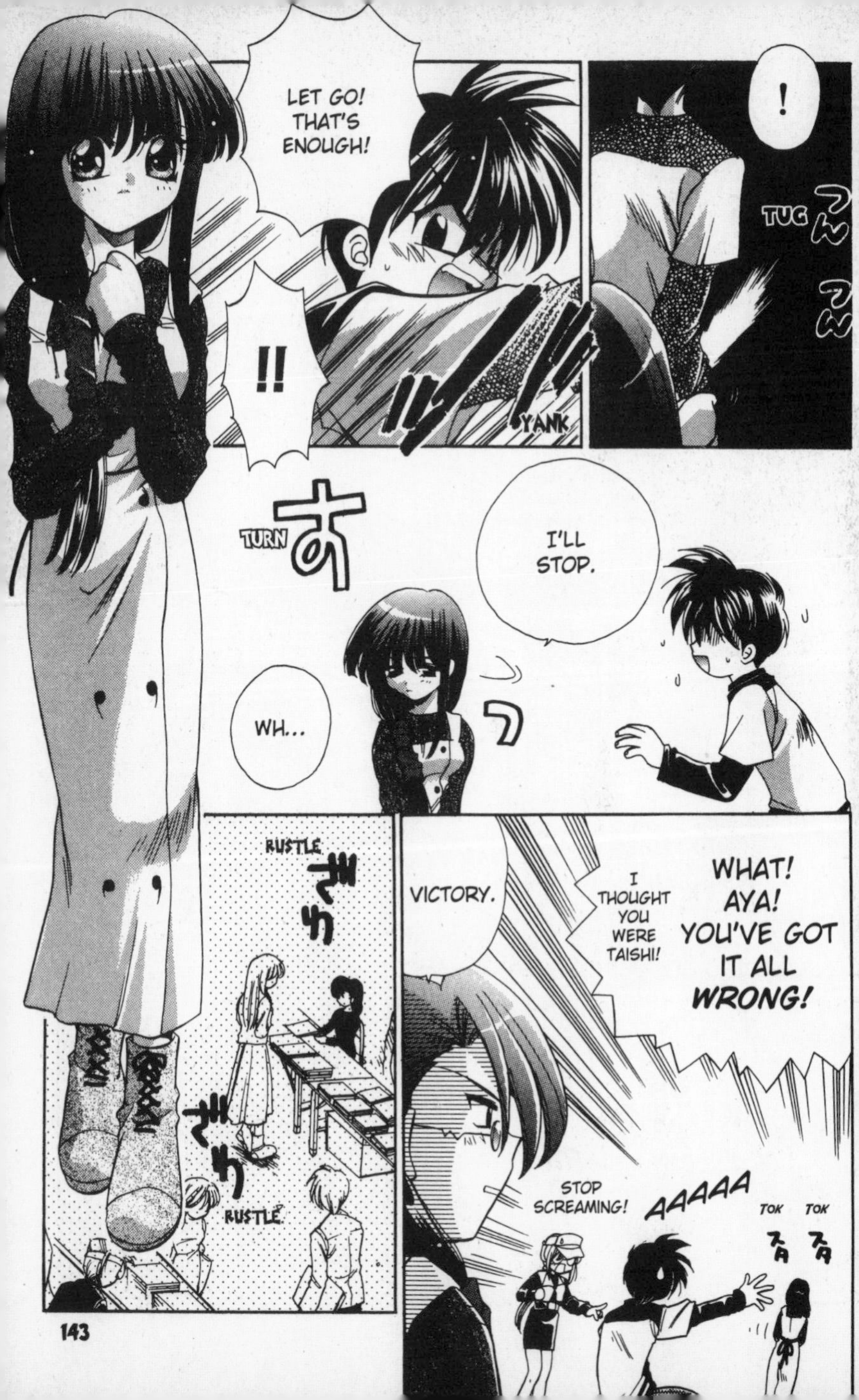
!
TUG
LET GO! THAT'S ENOUGH!
!!
YANK
TURN
I'LL STOP.
WH...
WHAT! AYA! YOU'VE GOT IT ALL WRONG!
I THOUGHT YOU WERE TAISHI!
VICTORY.
STOP SCREAMING!
AAAAA
TOK
TOK
RUSTLE
RUSTLE

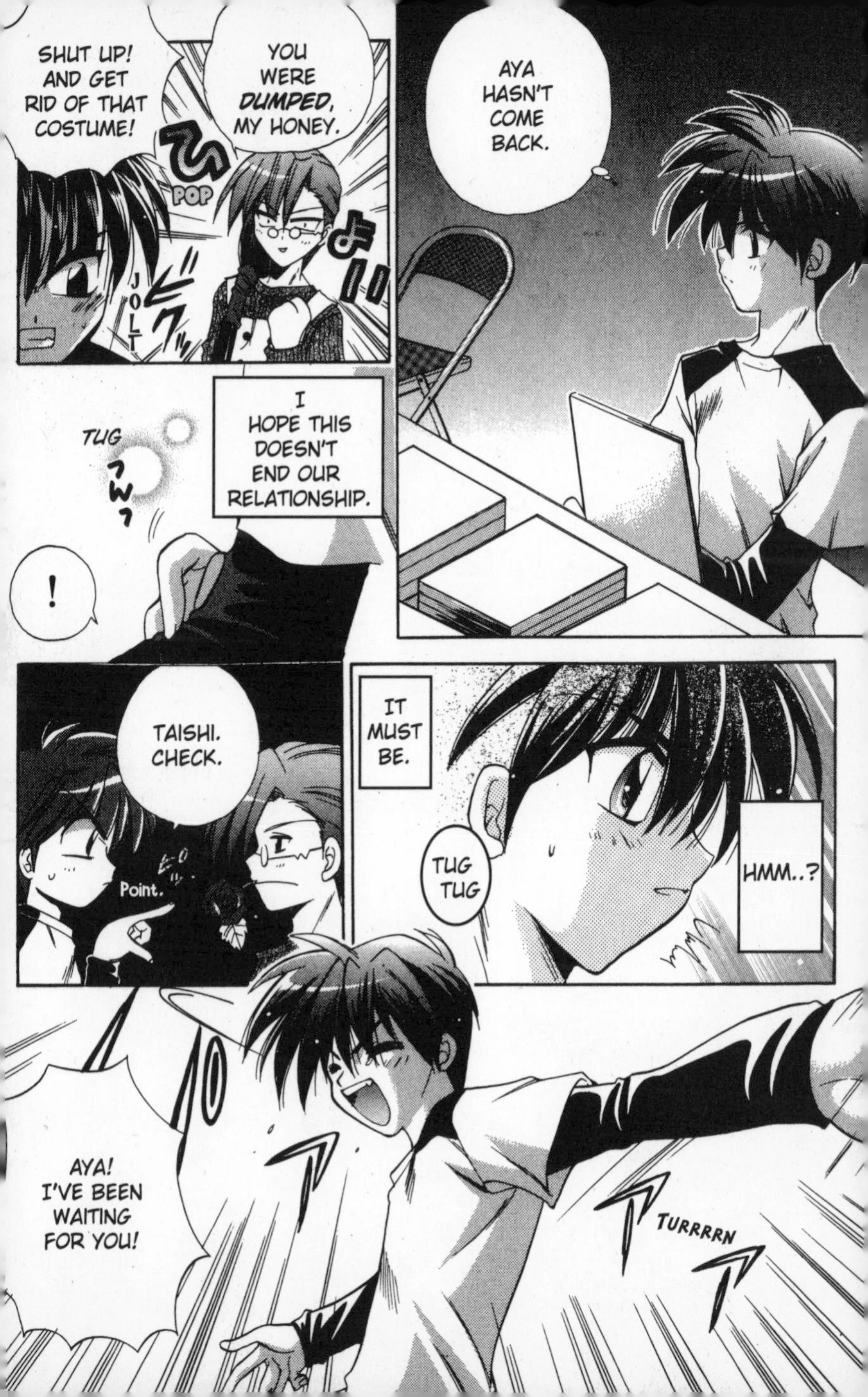
AYA HASN'T COME BACK.
YOU WERE DUMPED, MY HONEY.
SHUT UP! AND GET RID OF THAT COSTUME!
POP
JOLT
I HOPE THIS DOESN'T END OUR RELATIONSHIP.
TUG
!
IT MUST BE.
HMM..?
TUG TUG
TAISHI. CHECK.
Point.
AYA! I'VE BEEN WAITING FOR YOU!
TURRRRN

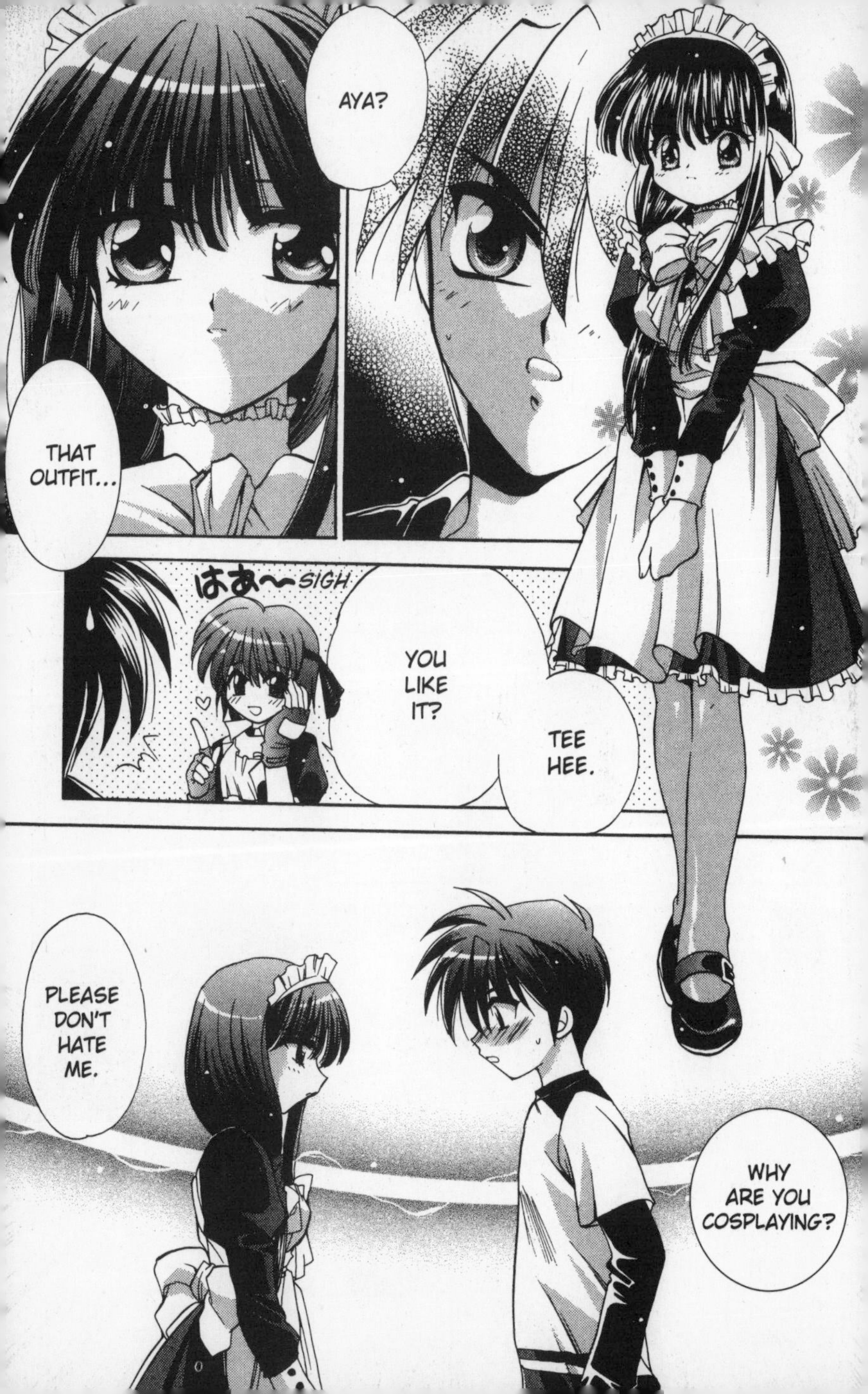
AYA?
THAT OUTFIT...
YOU LIKE IT?
TEE HEE.
はぁ～ SIGH
WHY ARE YOU COSPLAYING?
PLEASE DON'T HATE ME.

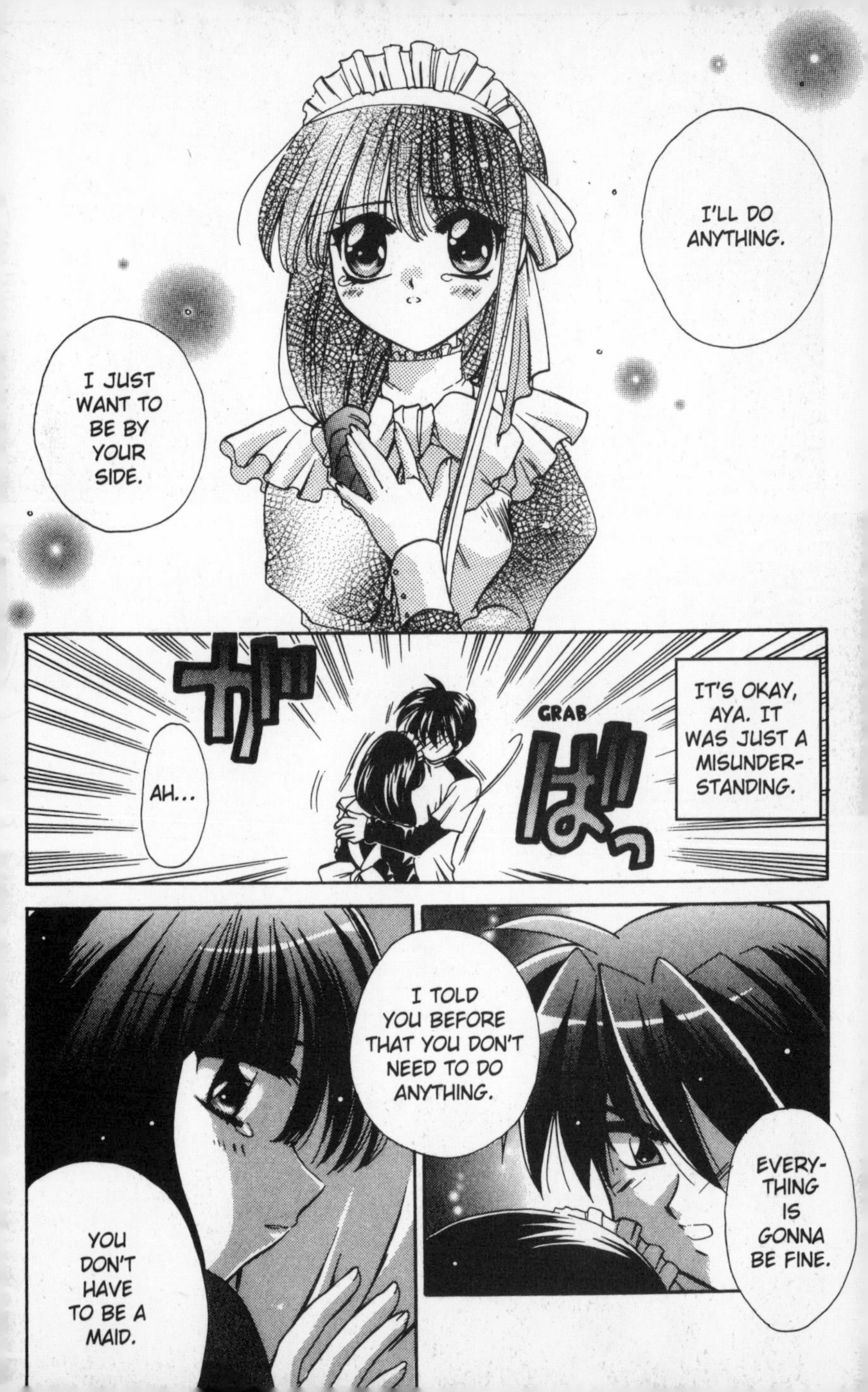
I'LL DO ANYTHING.
I JUST WANT TO BE BY YOUR SIDE.
IT'S OKAY, AYA. IT WAS JUST A MISUNDERSTANDING.
GRAB
ぱっ
AH...
が
I TOLD YOU BEFORE THAT YOU DON'T NEED TO DO ANYTHING.
EVERY-THING IS GONNA BE FINE.
YOU DON'T HAVE TO BE A MAID.

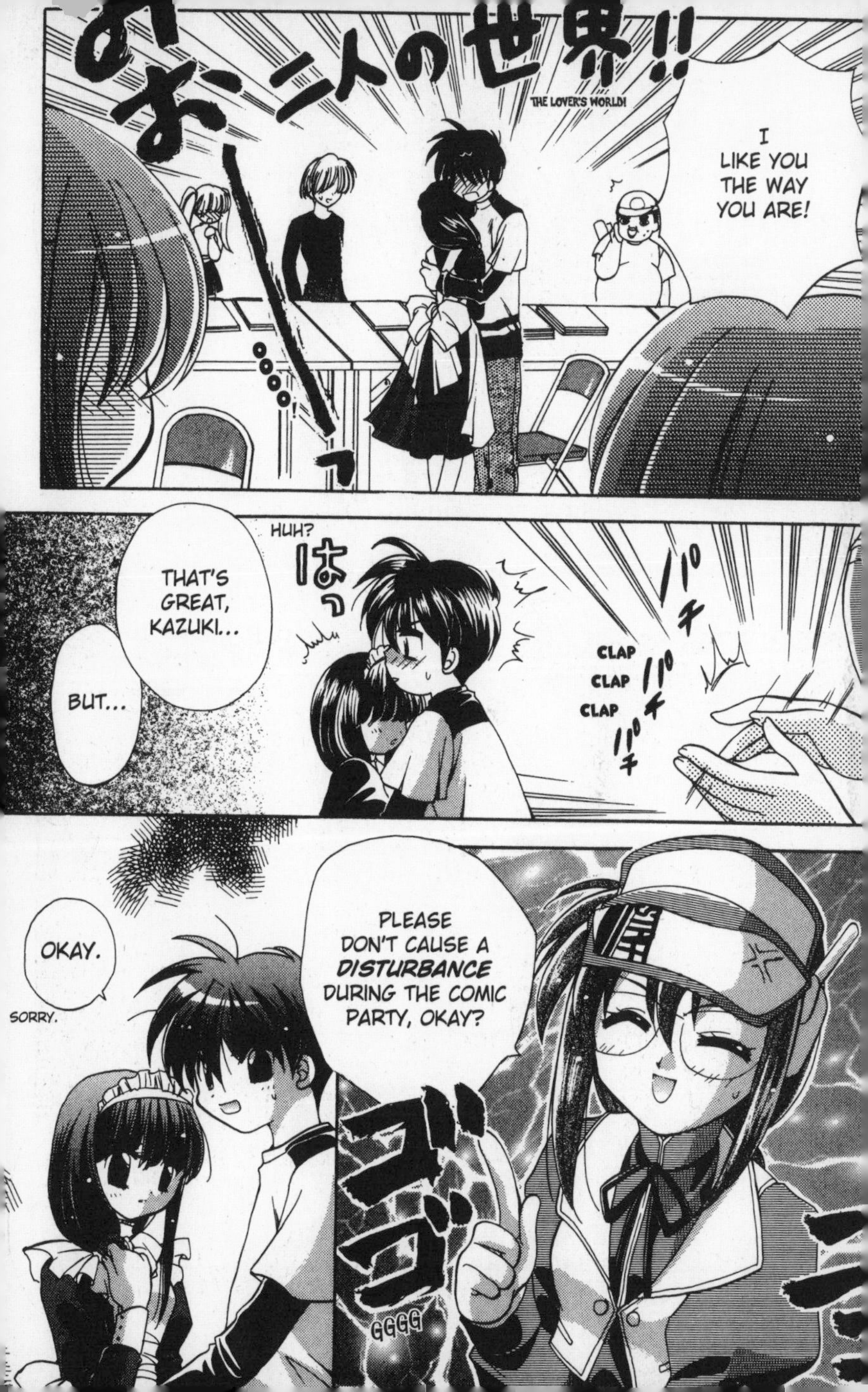
I LIKE YOU THE WAY YOU ARE!
おふたりの世界!!
THE LOVER'S WORLD!
ooooo!
CLAP CLAP CLAP
パチパチパチ
はっ
HUH?
THAT'S GREAT, KAZUKI...
BUT...
PLEASE DON'T CAUSE A DISTURBANCE DURING THE COMIC PARTY, OKAY?
ゴゴ
GGGG
OKAY.
SORRY.

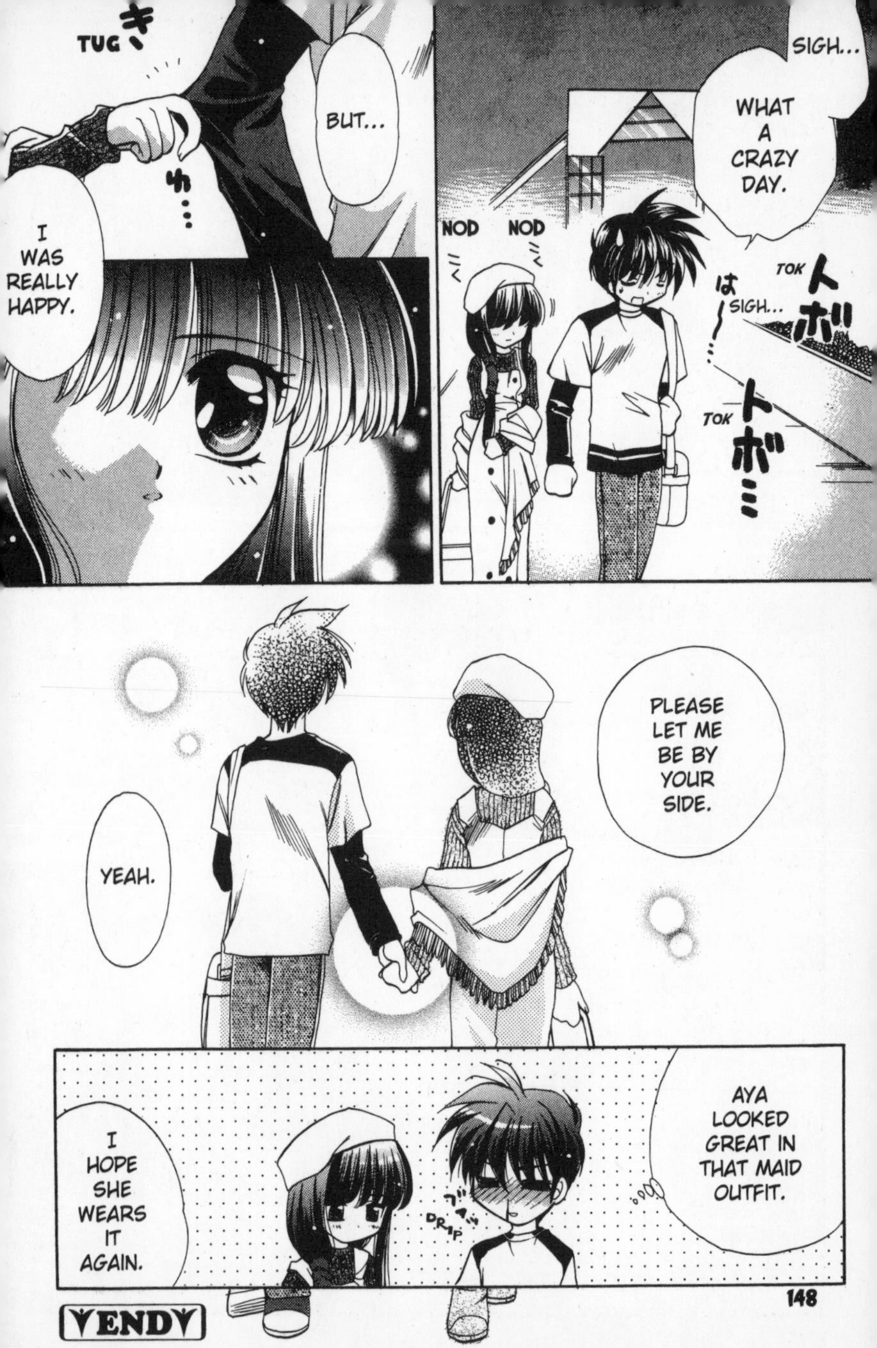

SIGH...
WHAT A CRAZY DAY.
NOD NOD
TOK
SIGH...
TOK
TUG
BUT...
I WAS REALLY HAPPY.
PLEASE LET ME BE BY YOUR SIDE.
YEAH.
AYA LOOKED GREAT IN THAT MAID OUTFIT.
DRIP
I HOPE SHE WEARS IT AGAIN.
END

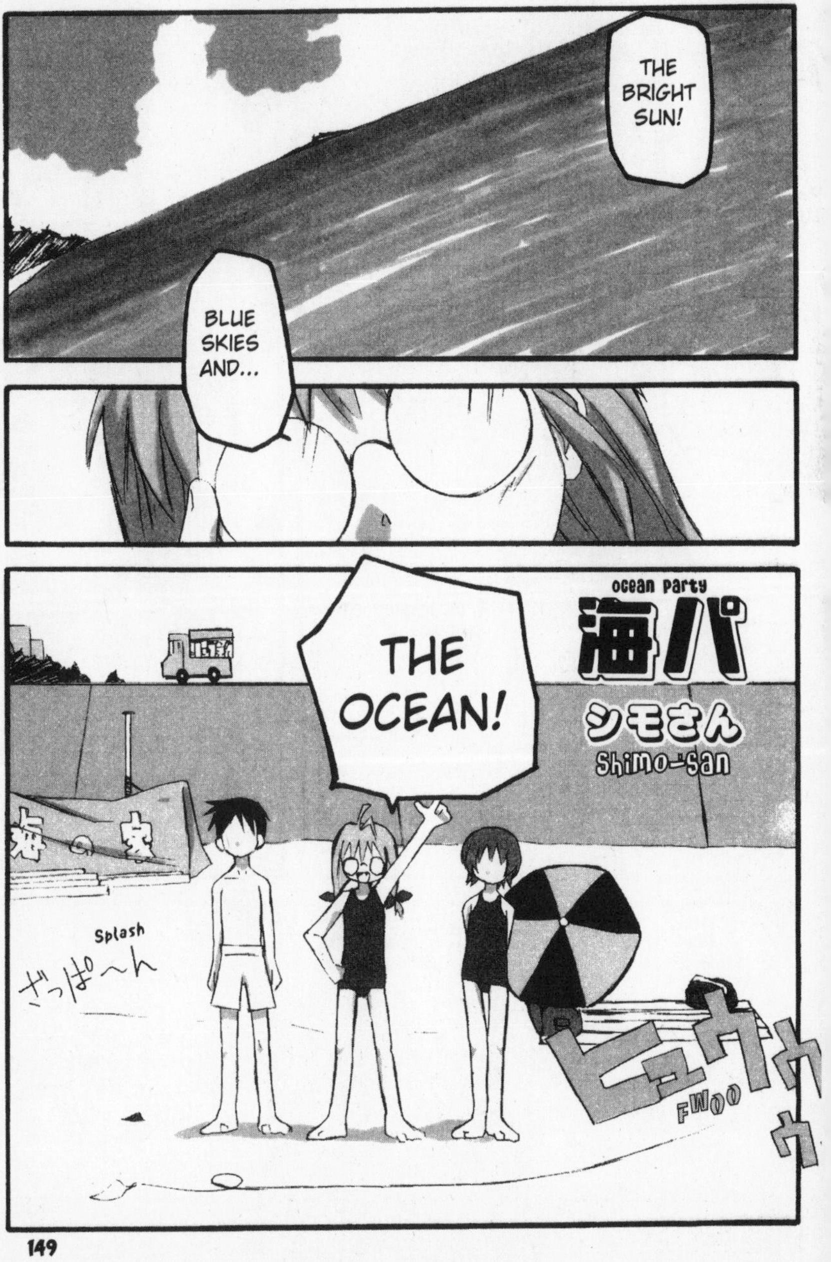
THE BRIGHT SUN!
BLUE SKIES AND...
ocean party
海パ
シモさん
Shimo-san
THE OCEAN!
FWOO
Splash
ざっぱ〜ん

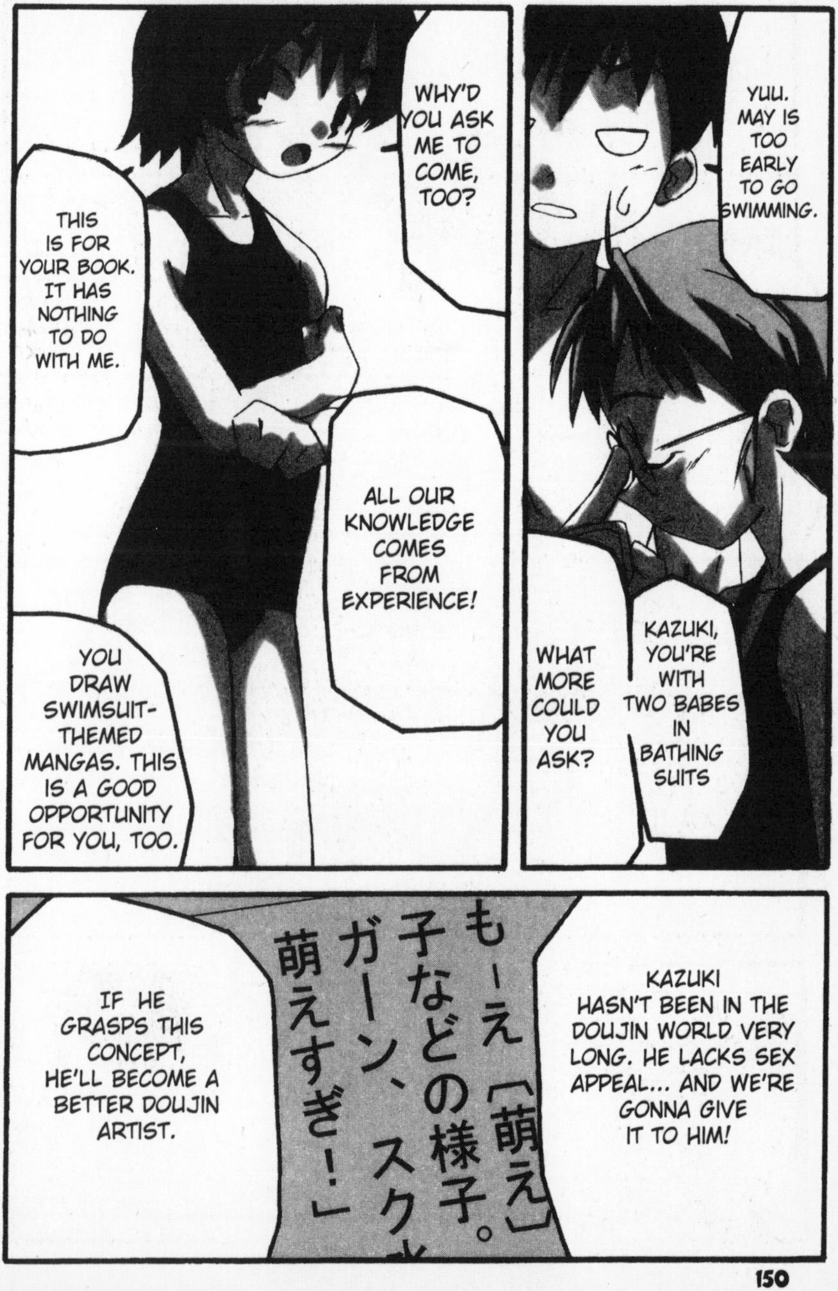
YUU. MAY IS TOO EARLY TO GO SWIMMING.
KAZUKI, YOU'RE WITH TWO BABES IN BATHING SUITS
WHAT MORE COULD YOU ASK?
WHY'D YOU ASK ME TO COME, TOO?
THIS IS FOR YOUR BOOK. IT HAS NOTHING TO DO WITH ME.
ALL OUR KNOWLEDGE COMES FROM EXPERIENCE!
YOU DRAW SWIMSUIT-THEMED MANGAS. THIS IS A GOOD OPPORTUNITY FOR YOU, TOO.
KAZUKI HASN'T BEEN IN THE DOUJIN WORLD VERY LONG. HE LACKS SEX APPEAL... AND WE'RE GONNA GIVE IT TO HIM!
もーえ〔萌え〕
子などの様子。
ガーン、スク
萌えすぎ！」
IF HE GRASPS THIS CONCEPT, HE'LL BECOME A BETTER DOUJIN ARTIST.

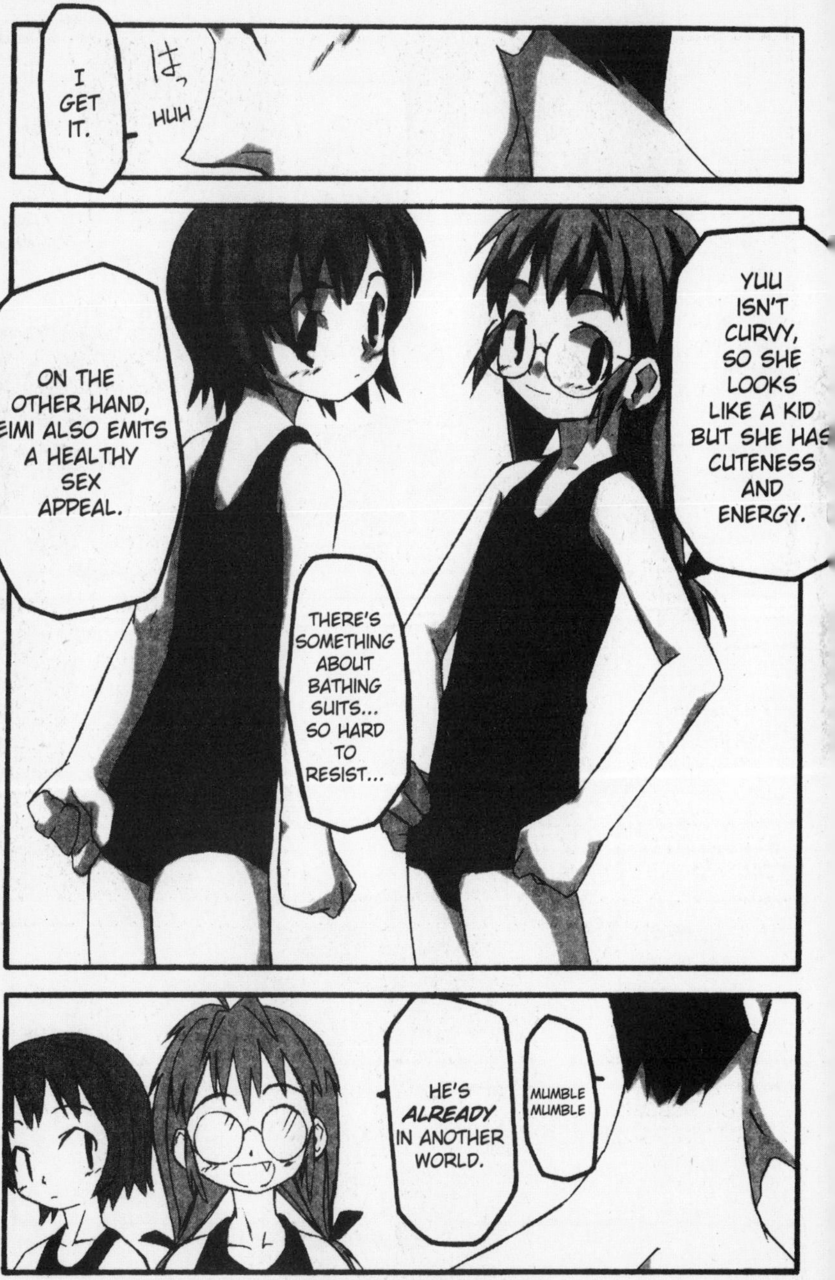
はっ
HUH
I GET IT.
YUU ISN'T CURVY, SO SHE LOOKS LIKE A KID BUT SHE HAS CUTENESS AND ENERGY.
THERE'S SOMETHING ABOUT BATHING SUITS... SO HARD TO RESIST...
ON THE OTHER HAND, EIMI ALSO EMITS A HEALTHY SEX APPEAL.
MUMBLE MUMBLE
HE'S *ALREADY* IN ANOTHER WORLD.

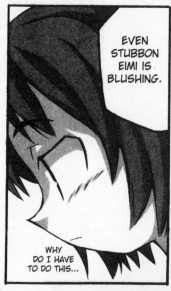

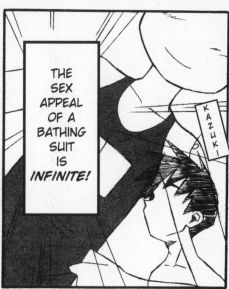

THE SEX APPEAL OF A BATHING SUIT IS *INFINITE!*
KAZUKI
EVEN STUBBON EIMI IS BLUSHING.
WHY DO I HAVE TO DO THIS...
...MY TAN LINES ARE SHOWING!
A SHORT JACKET!
S...

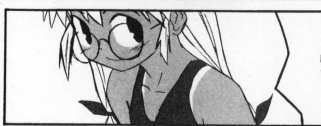

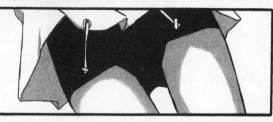

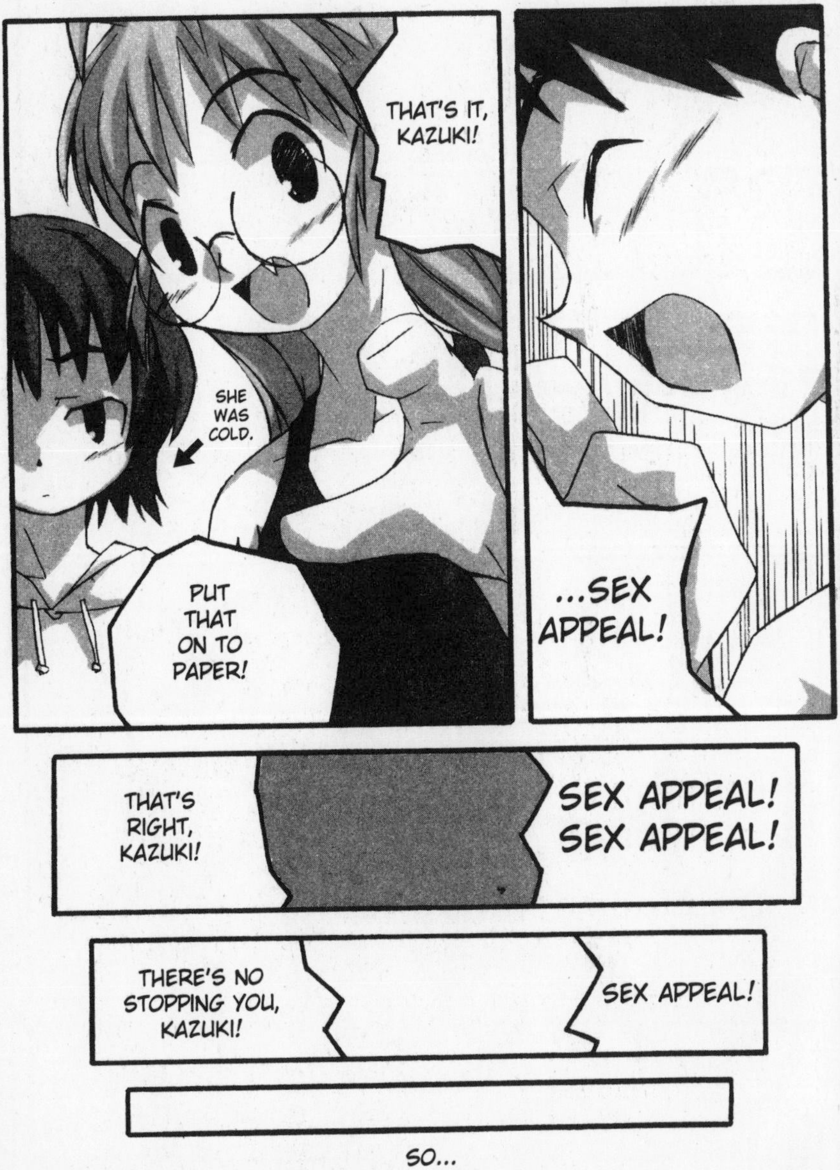
...SEX APPEAL!
THAT'S IT, KAZUKI!
SHE WAS COLD.
PUT THAT ON TO PAPER!
SEX APPEAL! SEX APPEAL!
THAT'S RIGHT, KAZUKI!
SEX APPEAL!
THERE'S NO STOPPING YOU, KAZUKI!
SO...

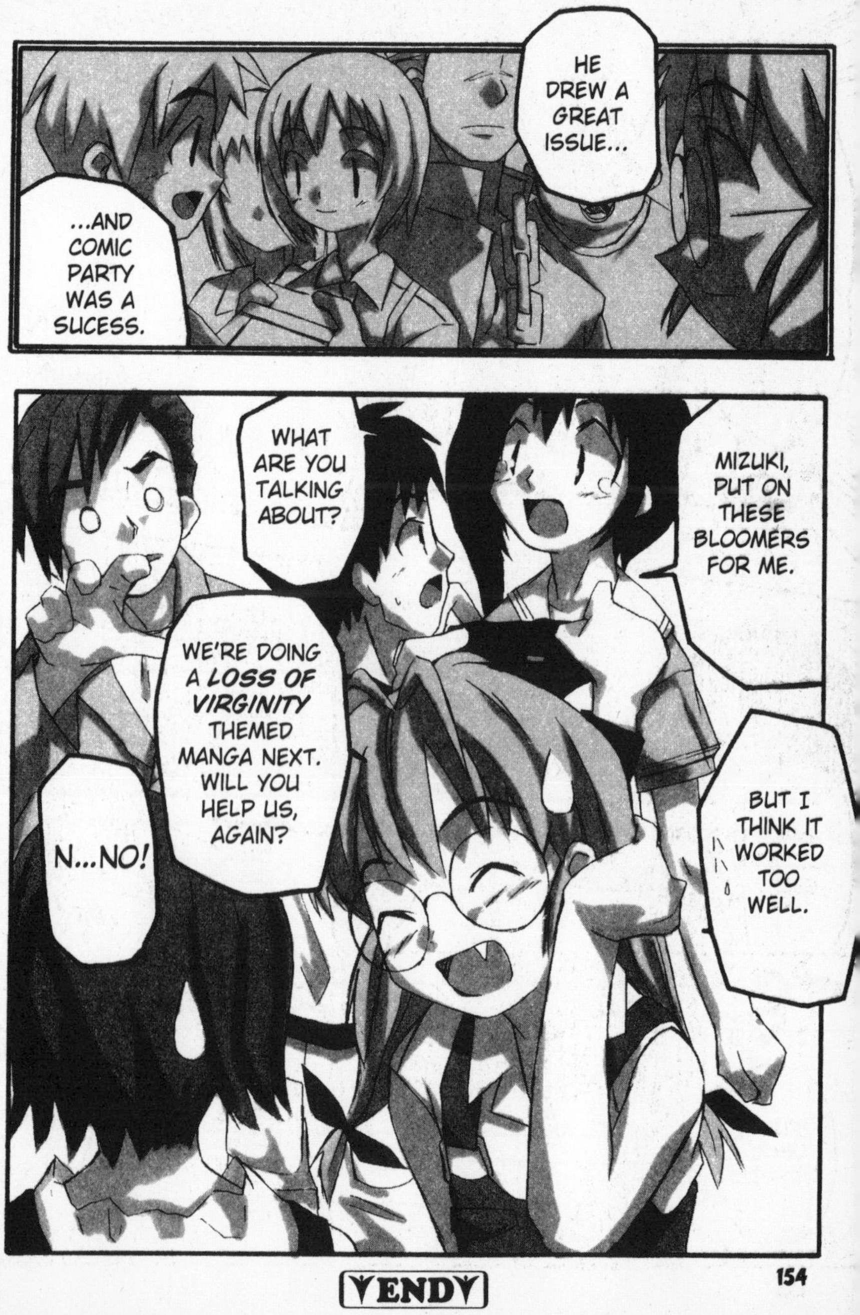
HE DREW A GREAT ISSUE...
...AND COMIC PARTY WAS A SUCESS.
MIZUKI, PUT ON THESE BLOOMERS FOR ME.
WHAT ARE YOU TALKING ABOUT?
BUT I THINK IT WORKED TOO WELL.
WE'RE DOING A *LOSS OF VIRGINITY* THEMED MANGA NEXT. WILL YOU HELP US, AGAIN?
N...NO!

END

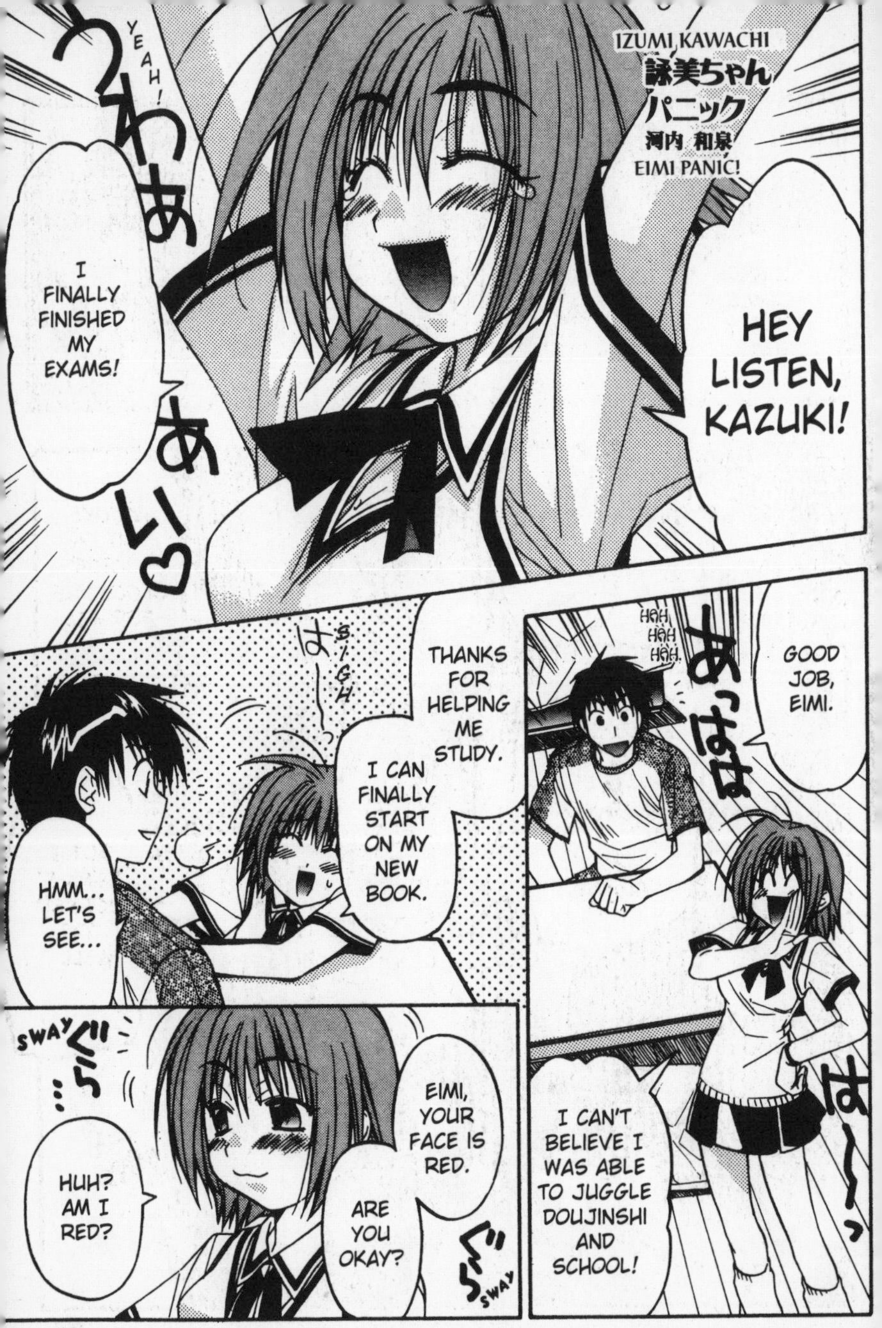
IZUMI KAWACHI
詠美ちゃん パニック
河内 和泉
EIMI PANIC!
HEY LISTEN, KAZUKI!
うわぁぁあい♡
YEAH!
I FINALLY FINISHED MY EXAMS!
GOOD JOB, EIMI.
あっはは
HAH HAH HAH
はーっ
I CAN'T BELIEVE I WAS ABLE TO JUGGLE DOUJINSHI AND SCHOOL!
THANKS FOR HELPING ME STUDY.
I CAN FINALLY START ON MY NEW BOOK.
はー
SIGH
HMM... LET'S SEE...
EIMI, YOUR FACE IS RED.
ARE YOU OKAY?
ぐら
SWAY
ぐら
SWAY
HUH? AM I RED?

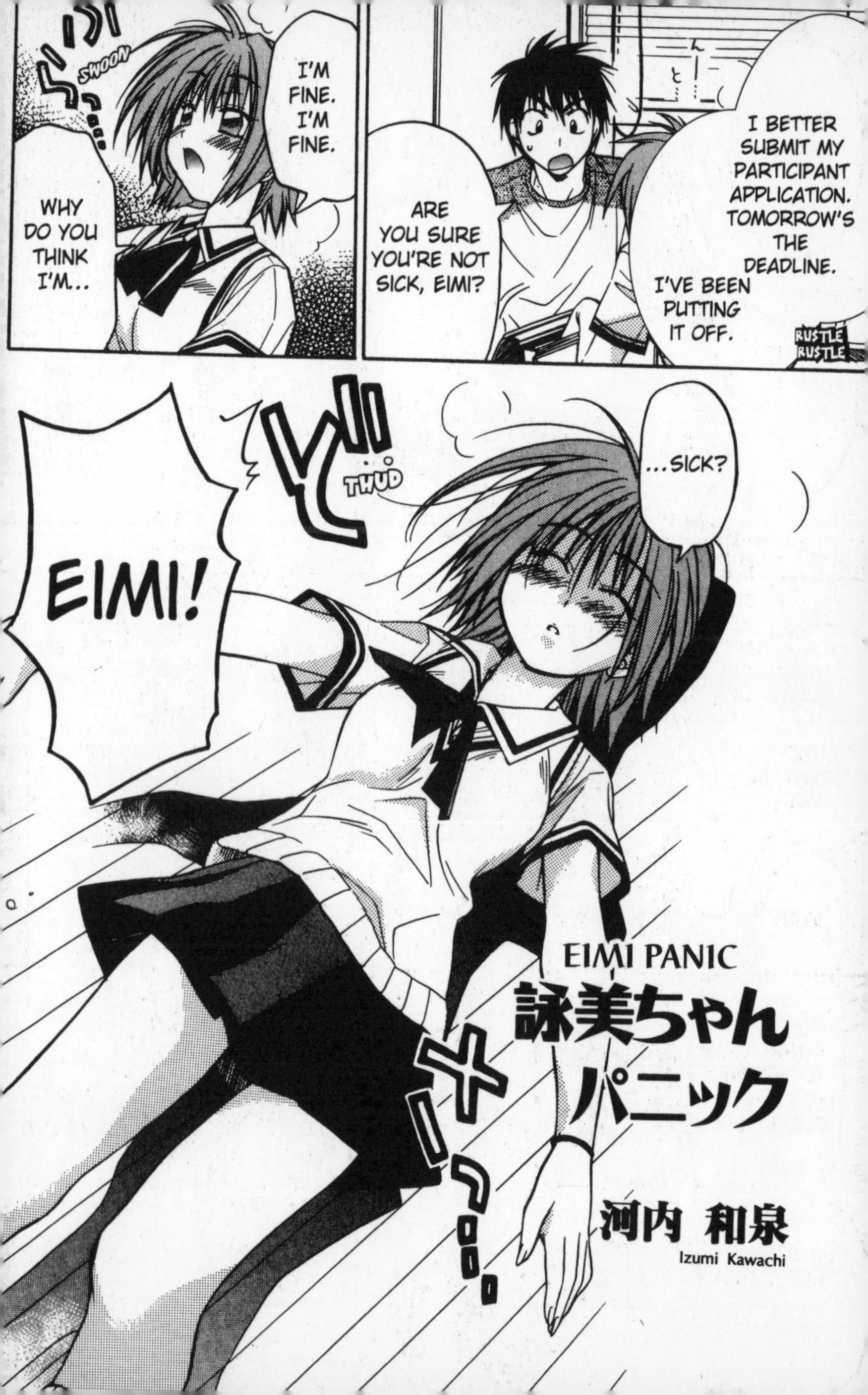
I BETTER SUBMIT MY PARTICIPANT APPLICATION. TOMORROW'S THE DEADLINE.
I'VE BEEN PUTTING IT OFF.
RUSTLE RUSTLE
ARE YOU SURE YOU'RE NOT SICK, EIMI?
I'M FINE. I'M FINE.
SWOON
WHY DO YOU THINK I'M...
...SICK?
THUD
EIMI!
EIMI PANIC
詠美ちゃんパニック
河内 和泉
Izumi Kawachi

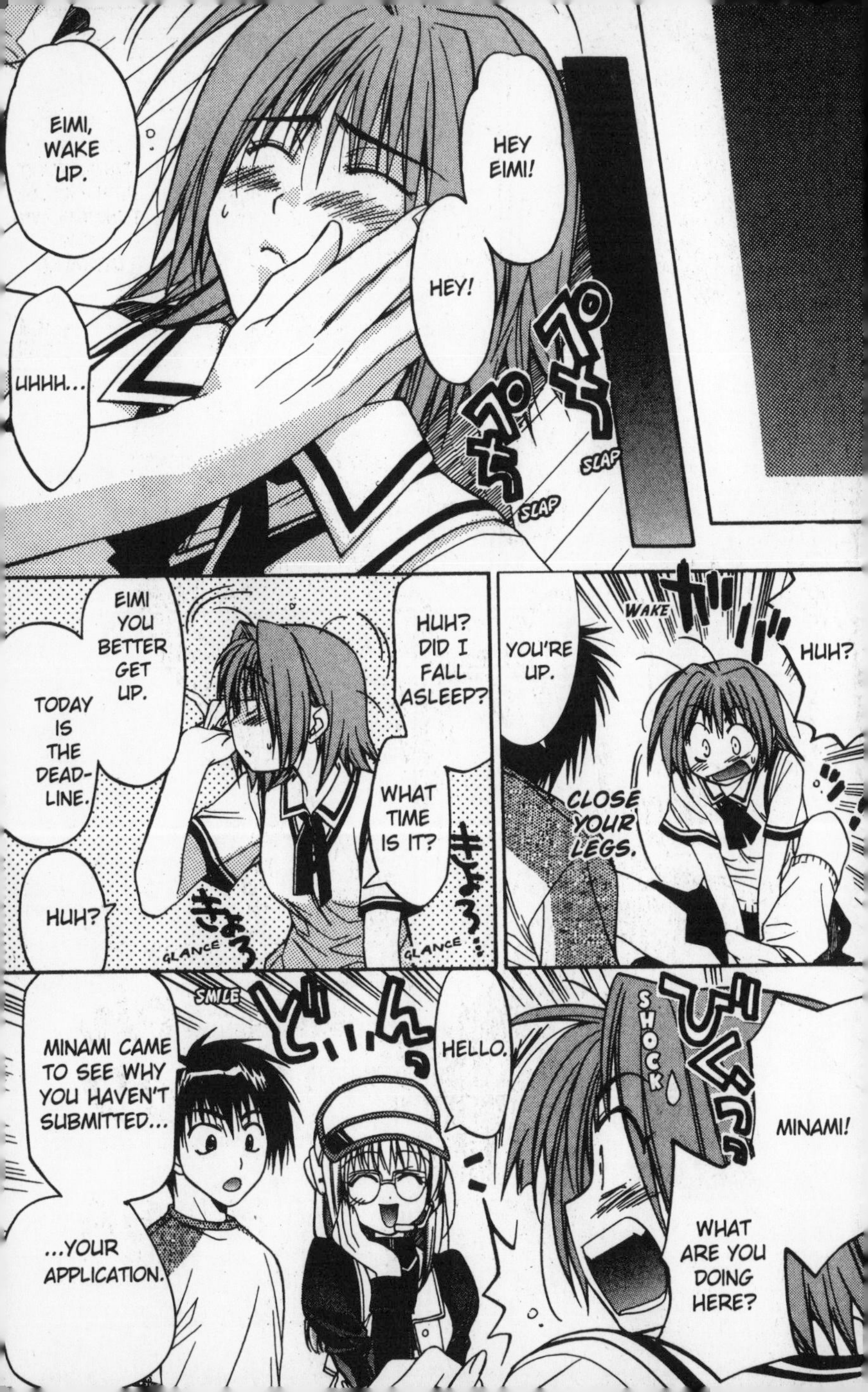
HEY EIMI!
HEY!
SLAP
SLAP
EIMI, WAKE UP.
UHHH...
WAKE
HUH?
YOU'RE UP.
CLOSE YOUR LEGS.
HUH? DID I FALL ASLEEP?
WHAT TIME IS IT?
GLANCE
EIMI YOU BETTER GET UP.
TODAY IS THE DEAD-LINE.
HUH?
GLANCE
SHOCK
MINAMI!
WHAT ARE YOU DOING HERE?
HELLO.
SMILE
MINAMI CAME TO SEE WHY YOU HAVEN'T SUBMITTED...
...YOUR APPLICATION.

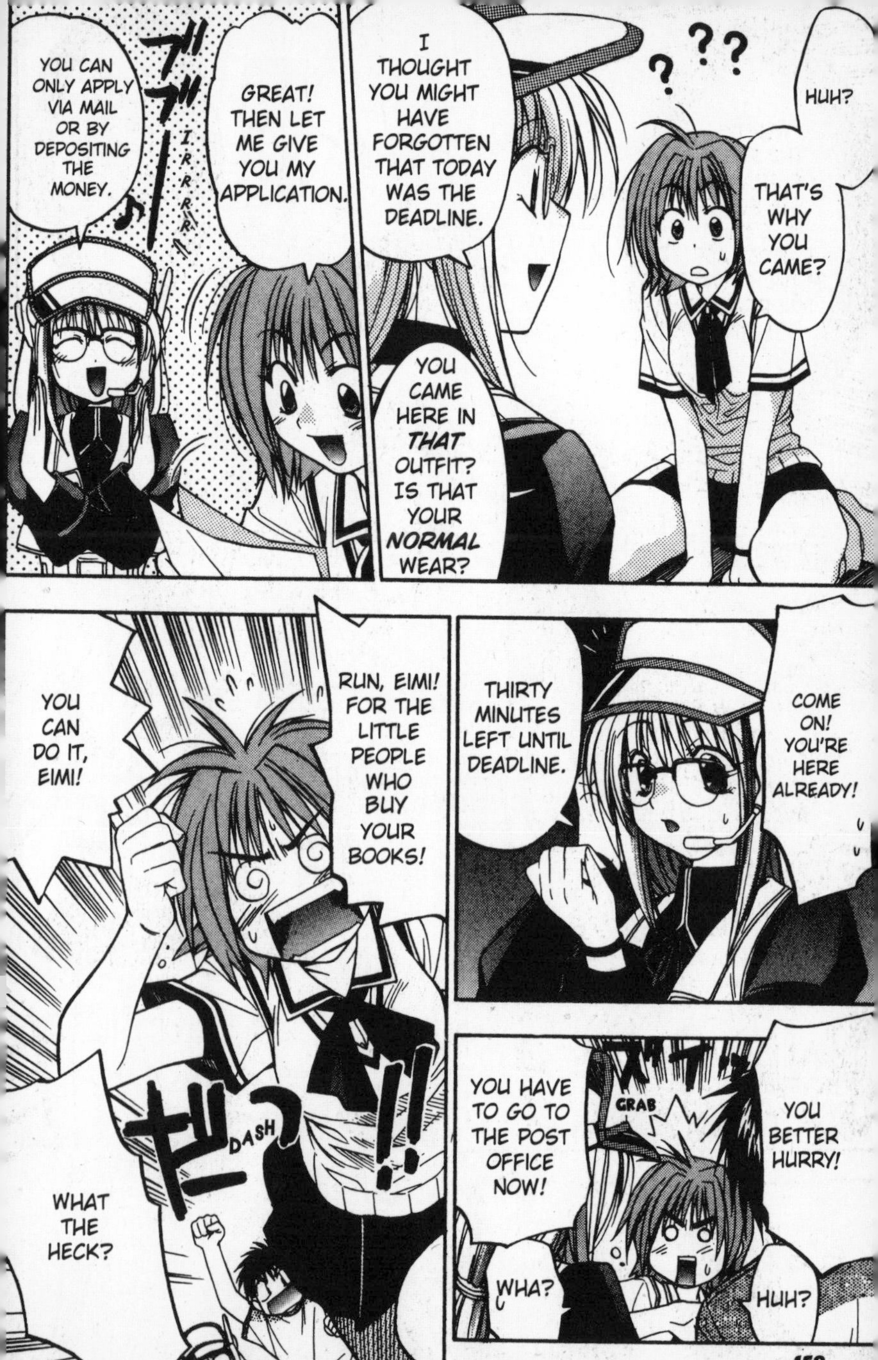
HUH?
THAT'S WHY YOU CAME?
I THOUGHT YOU MIGHT HAVE FORGOTTEN THAT TODAY WAS THE DEADLINE.
YOU CAME HERE IN *THAT* OUTFIT? IS THAT YOUR *NORMAL* WEAR?
GREAT! THEN LET ME GIVE YOU MY APPLICATION.
YOU CAN ONLY APPLY VIA MAIL OR BY DEPOSITING THE MONEY.
COME ON! YOU'RE HERE ALREADY!
THIRTY MINUTES LEFT UNTIL DEADLINE.
YOU BETTER HURRY!
GRAB
YOU HAVE TO GO TO THE POST OFFICE NOW!
HUH?
WHA?
RUN, EIMI! FOR THE LITTLE PEOPLE WHO BUY YOUR BOOKS!
YOU CAN DO IT, EIMI!
DASH
WHAT THE HECK?

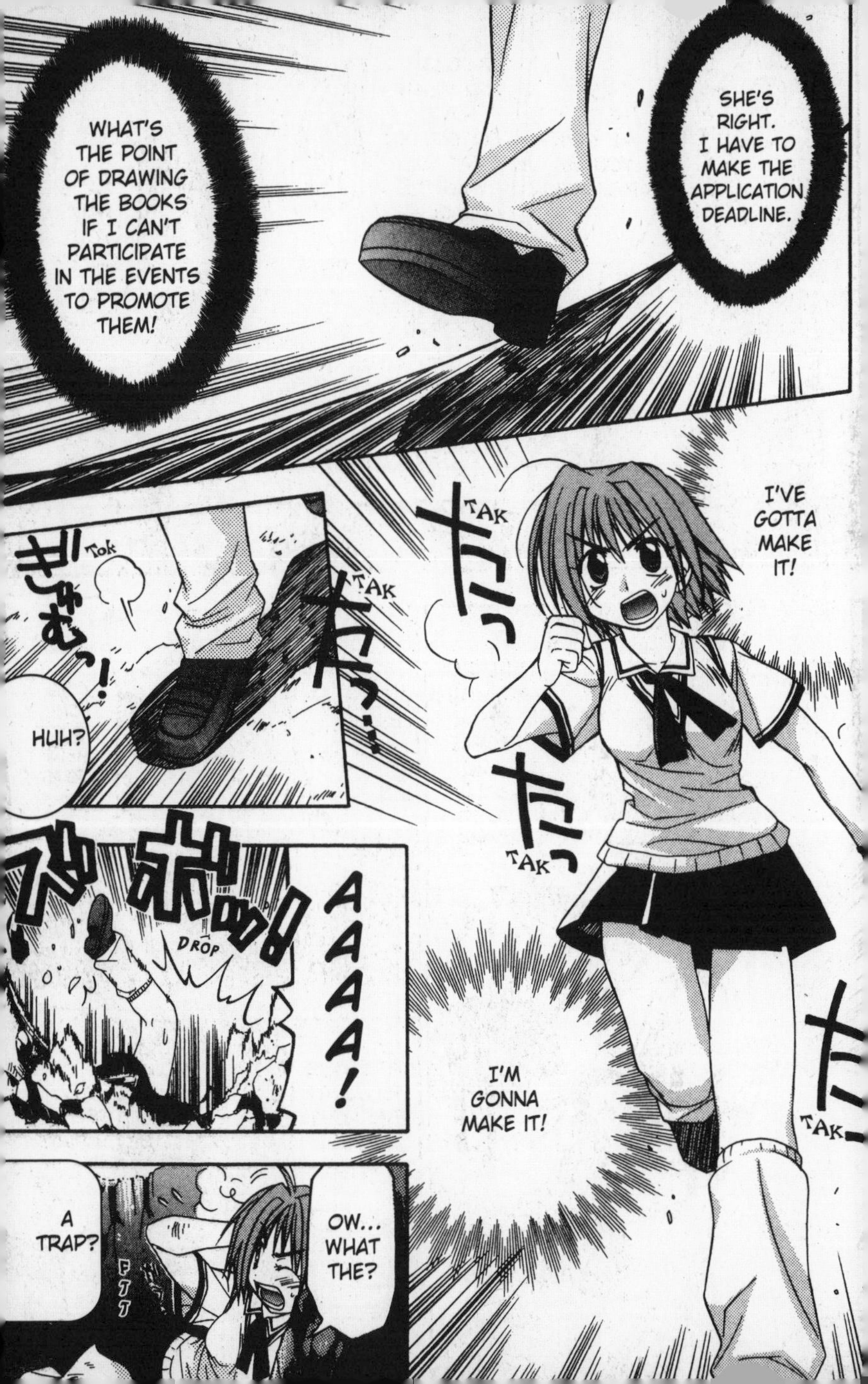
SHE'S RIGHT. I HAVE TO MAKE THE APPLICATION DEADLINE.
WHAT'S THE POINT OF DRAWING THE BOOKS IF I CAN'T PARTICIPATE IN THE EVENTS TO PROMOTE THEM!
I'VE GOTTA MAKE IT!
TAK
TAK
TAK
I'M GONNA MAKE IT!
TAK
TOK
HUH?
AAAAA!
DROP
OW... WHAT THE?
A TRAP?
FTT

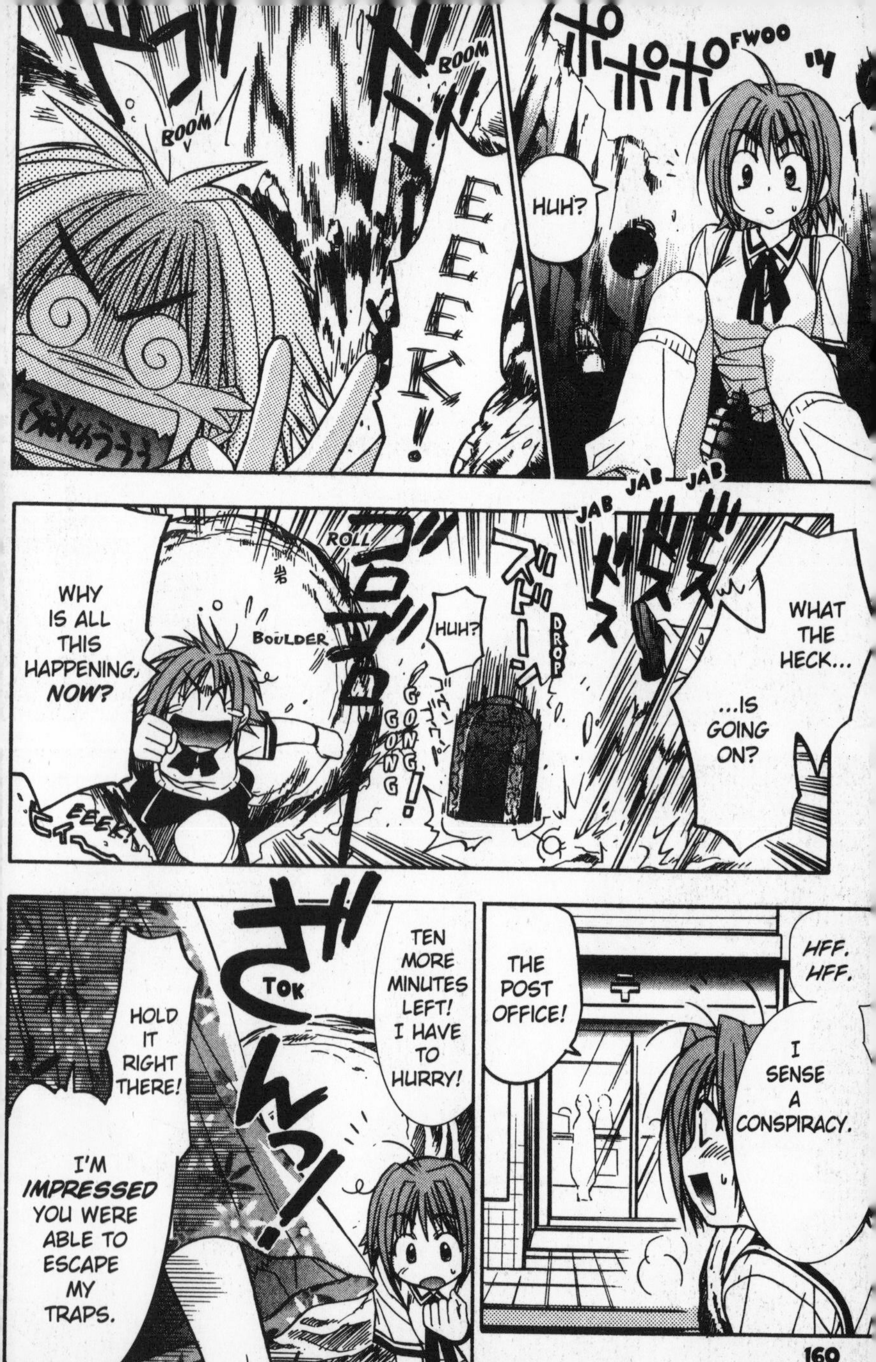
FWOO
HUH?
BOOM
BOOM
EEEEK!
JAB JAB JAB
WHAT THE HECK...
...IS GOING ON?
DROP
HUH?
GOING GONG!
GONG
ROLL
BOULDER
WHY IS ALL THIS HAPPENING, NOW?
EEEK!
HFF. HFF.
I SENSE A CONSPIRACY.
THE POST OFFICE!
TEN MORE MINUTES LEFT! I HAVE TO HURRY!
TOK
HOLD IT RIGHT THERE!
I'M IMPRESSED YOU WERE ABLE TO ESCAPE MY TRAPS.

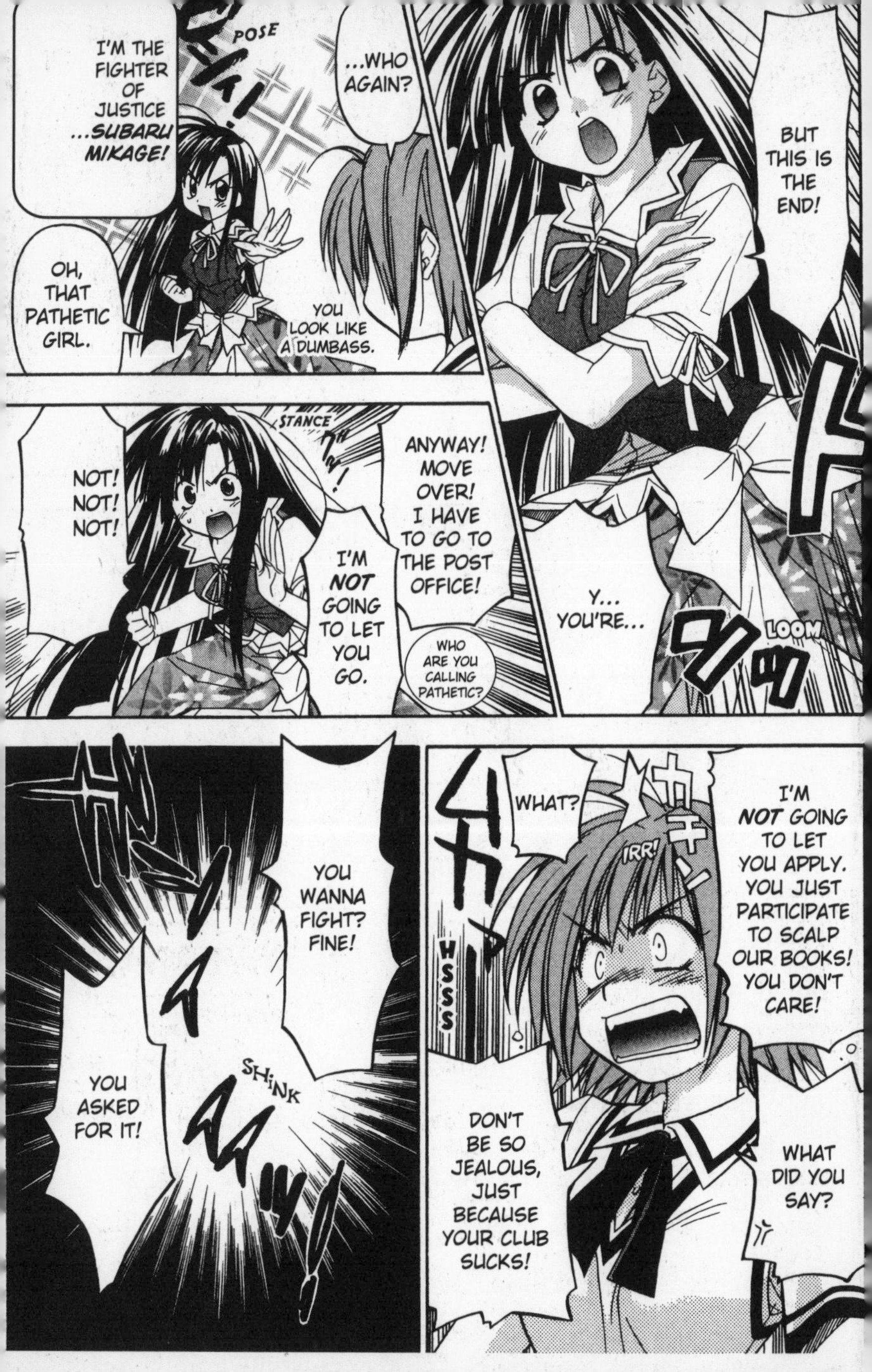
BUT THIS IS THE END!
Y... YOU'RE...
LOOM
...WHO AGAIN?
POSE
I'M THE FIGHTER OF JUSTICE ...SUBARU MIKAGE!
OH, THAT PATHETIC GIRL.
YOU LOOK LIKE A DUMBASS.
ANYWAY! MOVE OVER! I HAVE TO GO TO THE POST OFFICE!
STANCE
NOT! NOT! NOT!
I'M NOT GOING TO LET YOU GO.
WHO ARE YOU CALLING PATHETIC?
I'M NOT GOING TO LET YOU APPLY. YOU JUST PARTICIPATE TO SCALP OUR BOOKS! YOU DON'T CARE!
WHAT?
IRR!
HSSS
WHAT DID YOU SAY?
DON'T BE SO JEALOUS, JUST BECAUSE YOUR CLUB SUCKS!
YOU WANNA FIGHT? FINE!
SHINK
YOU ASKED FOR IT!

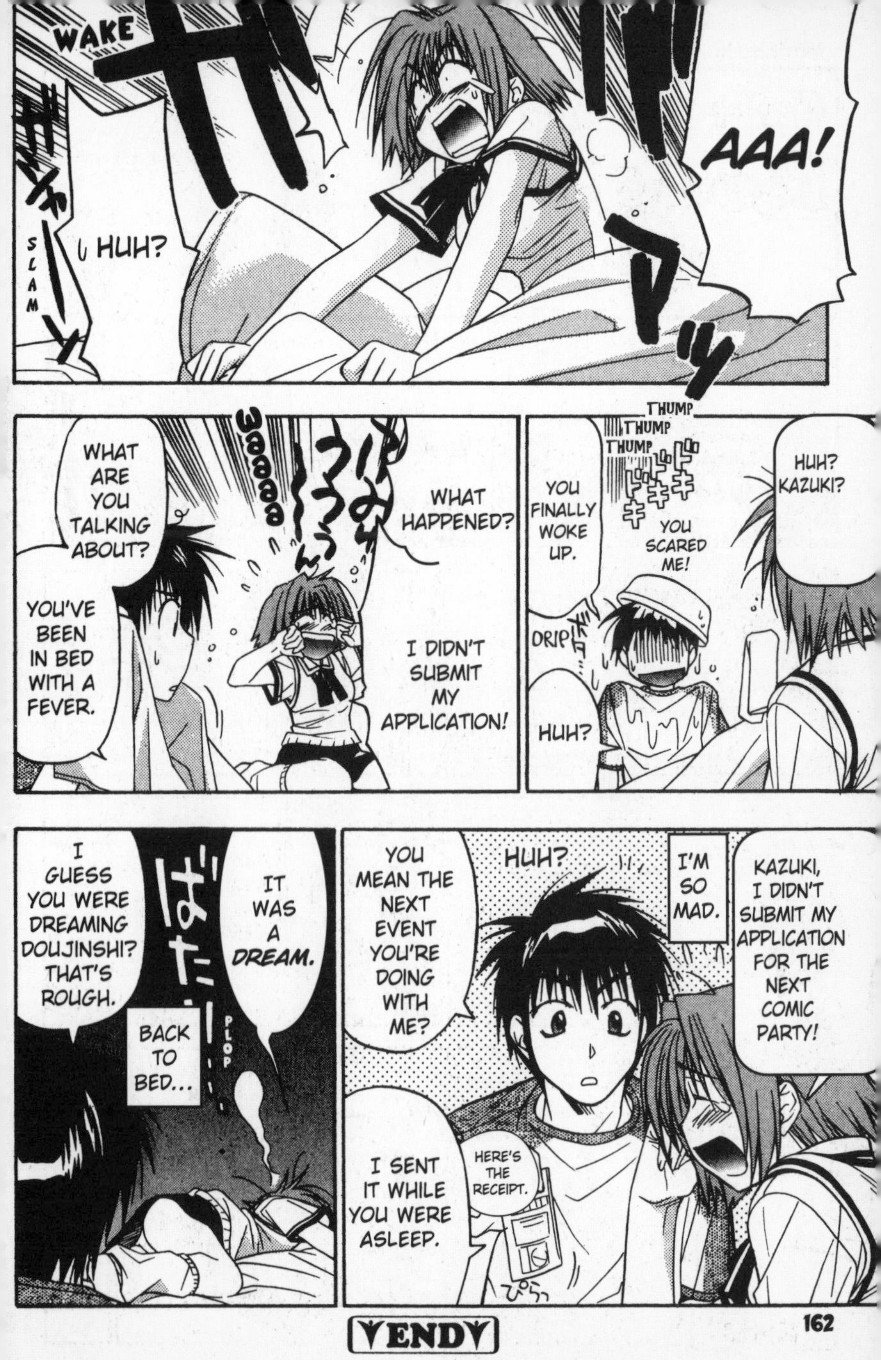
AAA!
WAKE
HUH?
SLAM
HUH? KAZUKI?
THUMP
THUMP
THUMP
YOU SCARED ME!
YOU FINALLY WOKE UP.
DRIP
HUH?
WHAT HAPPENED?
I DIDN'T SUBMIT MY APPLICATION!
WOOOOO
WHAT ARE YOU TALKING ABOUT?
YOU'VE BEEN IN BED WITH A FEVER.
KAZUKI, I DIDN'T SUBMIT MY APPLICATION FOR THE NEXT COMIC PARTY!
I'M SO MAD.
HUH?
YOU MEAN THE NEXT EVENT YOU'RE DOING WITH ME?
HERE'S THE RECEIPT.
I SENT IT WHILE YOU WERE ASLEEP.
IT WAS A DREAM.
PLOP
I GUESS YOU WERE DREAMING DOUJINSHI? THAT'S ROUGH.
BACK TO BED...

END

Morihito Kanehira

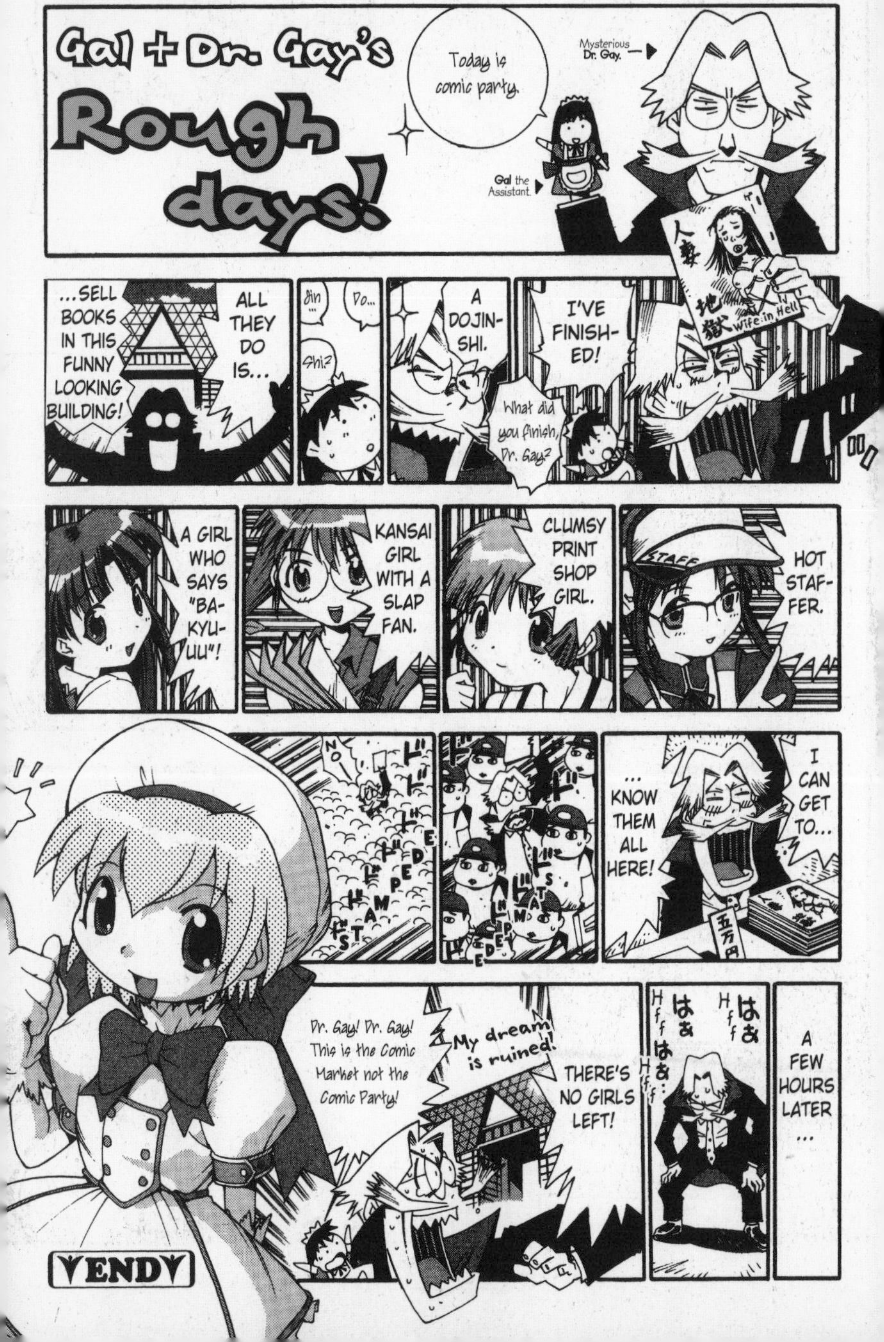
Gal + Dr. Gay's Rough days!
Mysterious Dr. Gay.
Today is comic party.
Gal the Assistant.
I'VE FINISHED!
What did you finish, Dr. Gay?
人妻地獄 Wife in Hell
A DOJINSHI.
Do...
Jin...
Shi?
ALL THEY DO IS...
...SELL BOOKS IN THIS FUNNY LOOKING BUILDING!
HOT STAFFER.
STAFF
CLUMSY PRINT SHOP GIRL.
KANSAI GIRL WITH A SLAP FAN.
A GIRL WHO SAYS "BAKYUUU"!
I CAN GET TO...
...KNOW THEM ALL HERE!
五万円
STAMPEDE
NO!
STAMPEDE
A FEW HOURS LATER...
Hff はぁ
Hff はぁ
Hff はぁ...
THERE'S NO GIRLS LEFT!
My dream is ruined!
Dr. Gay! Dr. Gay! This is the Comic Market not the Comic Party!
END

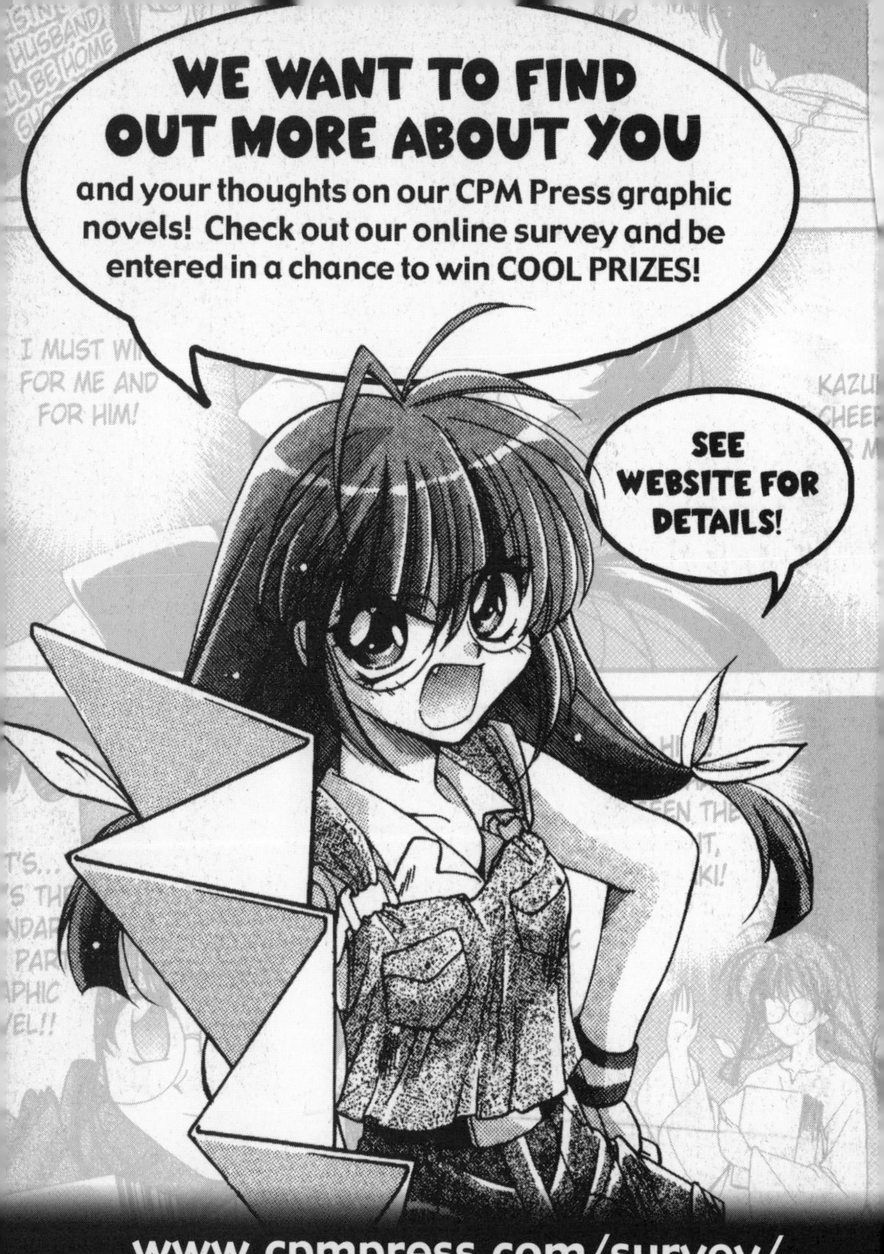
WE WANT TO FIND OUT MORE ABOUT YOU
and your thoughts on our CPM Press graphic novels! Check out our online survey and be entered in a chance to win COOL PRIZES!
SEE WEBSITE FOR DETAILS!

HEY!

YOU
YOU'RE
CALLING
ODZILLA?

This sign reads "Tomare" and it means:

STOP!

THIS IS THE LAST PAGE
OF THE BOOK! DON'T
RUIN THE ENDING
FOR YOURSELF.
This book is printed in the
original Japanese format,
which means that it reads
from right to left
(example on right).

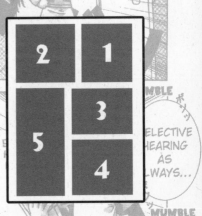

You'll find that all CPM Manga books that are part of our Original
Manga line are published in this format. The original artwork
and sound effects are presented just like they were in Japan so
you can enjoy the comic the way the creators intended.

This format was chosen by YOU, the fans. We conducted a
survey and found that the overwhelming majority of fans prefer
their manga in this format.